Extreme Value Hedging

Extreme Value Hedging

How Activist Hedge Fund Managers Are Taking on the World

Ronald D. Orol

John Wiley & Sons, Inc.

Published by John Wiley & Sons, Inc., Hoboken, New Jersey.
Published simultaneously in Canada.

For general information on our other products and services or for technical support, please contact our Customer Care Department within the United States at (800) 762-2974, outside the United States at (317) 572-3993 or fax (317) 572-4002.

Wiley also publishes its books in a variety of electronic formats. Some content that appears in print may not be available in electronic formats. For more information about Wiley products, visit our web site at www.wiley.com.

Library of Congress Cataloging-in-Publication Data

Orol, Ronald D.
Extreme value hedging : how activist hedge fund managers are taking on the world / by Ronald D. Orol.
p. cm.
Includes bibliographical references.
ISBN 978-0-470-12800-8 (cloth)
ISBN 978-0-470-45024-6 (paper)
1. Hedge funds. 2. Hedging (Finance) I. Title.
HG4530.O76 2008
332.64'524—dc22

2007019247

ISBN 978-0-470-12800-8

10 9 8 7 6 5 4 3 2 1

To my wife, Ksenia

Contents

Preface ix
Acknowledgments xvii
Introduction xxi

Part One: From Raiders to Activists and Everything in Between **1**

Chapter 1: Growth of Activism and Why Corporate Raiders Aren't Around Anymore 3
Chapter 2: Nuts and Bolts: How Activists Became Who They Are Today 25
Chapter 3: The Pack: How Activists Are Working Together (But Not Officially) 53
Chapter 4: How Activists Use Litigation to Pursue Their Agenda 75
Chapter 5: Why Activists Target Certain Corporations and Leave Others Alone 89
Chapter 6: Overperked and Overpaid: The Impact of Activists on Executive Compensation 103
Chapter 7: Hedge Specialization: Good or Bad? 117

Chapter 8: Regulation and Activists: How the Securities and Exchange Commission Helps (or Hurts) Activists 135

Part Two: Institutional Investors and Activists **155**

Chapter 9: Institutional Investors on Activist Hedge Funds: Love'em or Hate'em? 157
Chapter 10: Activists Taking on Large Corporations Must Have Institutional Support 163
Chapter 11: Institutions and Activist Hedge Funds: Breaking Up Deals Together Around the World 173
Chapter 12: Just Vote No and No and No Again 181
Chapter 13: Institutions Changing Corporate Bylaws so Activist Hedge Funds Can Get Down to Business 191
Chapter 14: Can't Be Them? Then Fund Them 201
Chapter 15: Institutions Behaving Like Activist Hedge Fund Managers 209

Part Three: Activism 2.0 **217**

Chapter 16: Technology, Communications, and Activists: Gary Lutin, Eric Jackson, and Anne Faulk 219
Chapter 17: When Is an Activist Fund Really a Private Equity Fund, and What's the Difference? 231
Chapter 18: Funds of Hedge Funds Stake Out Activists 247
Chapter 19: Distressed Investing: How Activist Managers Buy Debt and Provoke Companies 263
Chapter 20: Hedge Activists in Western Europe, Asia, and Canada 271
Chapter 21: East Meets West: Hedge Activism Goes Global to Emerging Markets 299
Chapter 22: Value Investing versus Activism: Which One Is Better? 319
Conclusion: Saturation or No Saturation? 333

Notes 339
About the Author 361
Index 363

Preface

This book tells the story of how a small but rebellious group of investors are shaking things up in the corporate world. In fact, they are prodding, pushing, and agitating to improve the share value of large, small, and midsized corporations in the United States and around the globe. CEOs are stepping down, boards are being shuffled, and the long-term governance of firms is shifting. Why? Activist investors.

Unlike most other investment professionals, activist investors believe some companies are operating either at subpar levels or in consolidating industries. They buy large minority equity stakes, often spending millions of dollars to do so, and approach executives at these businesses to find ways to improve shareholder value. If discussions don't go well, activists will step up their efforts to stimulate change at the corporation.

But their influence goes beyond each individual company they are somehow able to provoke into making changes. These investors are having a broader impact. In fact, activists are changing the investing landscape, from banking to corporate finance and management.

Many activist investors seek to press companies into being acquired. Blockbuster deals are a key way many of these insurgent shareholders can extract profit from their investment.

In researching this book, I interviewed over 50 activists between 2006 and 2007, many of whom declined to go "on the record." These interviews are still valid in the face of the worldwide financial meltdown because activists employ their tactics and press for changes at corporations in both strong and weak economies, often outperforming key market benchmarks such as the Standard & Poor's 500, even in the most troubling financial circumstances. In this book I explore why activist investors fared better than other investors during the post-Enron recession of 2001 and 2002. Their success at that time provides some guidance for how activists are performing during the latest downturn.

With the global economy in decline, struggling corporations had been hoping that a diminished mergers-and-acquisitions (M&A) marketplace would provide them some relief from the wrath of activist hedge fund managers.

Unfortunately for the legions of targeted CEOs, that hasn't happened. Although many activists themselves are coping with diminished returns and investor redemptions, they haven't gone away. In fact, they are merely adjusting their strategies to the new market realities.

A struggling stock market exposes incompetent management at particularly troubled companies. The result: more opportunities for activist investors to convince other shareholders, including pension funds, that certain companies need changes at the top. Boards and CEOs need to go now more than ever. Established insurgents who agitate for share improvement are employing a long-term governance and operational approach that involves finding highly qualified director candidates.

For the present time, activists that focus on profit and loss statements are "in," while those that spend their time looking at cash on the balance sheet are "out," at least for the short term. The activist investor strategy of pressing companies to buy back stock, provide special dividends or sell the business to the highest bidder are all off the table—at least until markets recover.

One advantage for activists is that they typically prohibit their investors from withdrawing capital from their funds for long one, two, or three-year periods while other investment managers allow monthly or quarterly redemptions. Keeping their investors "locked up" allows activisting managers to employ their long-term strategies in any economy.

Meanwhile, activists have found some M&A targets to keep them occupied during the financial crisis. Case in point: The struggling savings and loan banking market is ripe for consolidation. The U.S. government is even providing a helpful hand. A $700 billion government bank bailout program encourages quasi-healthy financial institutions receiving cash infusions from the U.S. Treasury Department to use that assistance for purchasing smaller, troubled thrifts. Other mega-financial institutions are under government pressure to sell divisions so they are no longer "too big to fail." Some activist investors, who have a specialization in smaller regional savings and loan banks, are taking advantage of these initiatives by buying stakes in banks that are soon to be acquired.

In fact activists are targeting all sorts of distressed companies, not just banks. Others are focusing their attention on embattled newspaper businesses and struggling commercial real estate companies facing consolidation.

Corporations are also embracing activist strategies more than ever before. Companies such as global beer giant InBev SA and technology giant Microsoft Corporation have used the activist toolbox to press companies into deals. InBev acted like an activist investor when it sought to replace the board of directors of Budweiser brewer Anheuser-Busch Companies as part of its attempt to take over the business. Bud eventually accepted a $60 billion offer from InBev.

This book documents the transformation of activist investors as a predominantly U.S. experience to one that is being exported to countries, companies, and CEOs around the world. Executives in the United States, Japan, and dozens of other countries are rethinking how they allocate capital and manage their business either in response to activist efforts or in anticipation of them. As the U.S. and European economies continue to decline, some activists such as Steel Partners II are focusing more of their energy on other markets such as Japan, where a wider spectrum of corporations remain undervalued.

My motivation to write this book has been to document the metamorphosis of these shareholders from either small-time, oft-ignored, gadfly outsiders or big-time raiders into governance-style activist investors.

I first became exposed to activist shareholders in 2000. I spent that year working for Dow Jones Newswires. My job was to read Securities and Exchange Commission (SEC) filings, identify key financial details, and write quick-hit articles based on those facts. While some reporters at this division, then called Federal Filings, read through annual reports and others went through electronic bankruptcy documents, I was responsible for interpreting a type of SEC filing known as the Schedule 13D. This rather staid-sounding filing is submitted by investors who own more than 5 percent of the stock of a company and have plans to communicate some strategic options for directors, shareholders, or executives to consider. It doesn't sound very interesting. At first it wasn't. But, soon enough, I began discovering an unusual collection of investors who would file 13Ds with letters to executives (later, some of these became known as poison pen letters) describing their unusual, yet colorful communications with chief executive officers (CEOs). For example, in one letter, the activist described how a CEO he had been diligently seeking out finally responded to his persistent queries: "You're a f---ing pain in the ass and we don't want to talk to you."

I began to become curious about who these investors were and I started calling them up to hear more of their stories about company mismanagement, CEO malfeasance, and what they were going to do about it. I started talking to other shareholders, company CEOs, chief financial officers (CFOs) and investor relations officials, analysts, and investment bankers—all to learn about the bigger picture of investor-company relations.

More than eight years later, now a financial reporter for Dow Jones & Company's MarketWatch, I still talk to and follow the 13D filers I met over the phone that year, and I still reach out to the oft-confused and disoriented executives of the companies they target.

Even with the financial crisis, activists are running much larger multimillion- and multibillion-dollar investment vehicles. They now have sophisticated internal and external public relations handlers and they take on much larger companies than they ever did before. Some of them are financing their own acquisition of businesses, a phenomenon that has grown as the price of corporations have diminished.

Their much larger profile and explosion in numbers has led to an outburst of financial press coverage. As the phenomenon known as activism increased in size, I began receiving phone calls from reporters working at news organizations in Montreal, Dallas, San Francisco, and many other cities, all of whom were trying to find out if I could give them some "background" on how exactly these investors did what they did. CEOs and CFOs of companies that were on the receiving end of activism for the first time would also ask me questions about the insurgent that was giving them grief. Who is this guy? What other companies has he been involved in? Why is this happening? This book is my attempt to bring together all my analysis and fact-finding on the subject.

Numerous high-profile activist investors, including Ralph Whitworth, Guy Wyser-Pratte, Jeffrey M. Solomon, Mark Schwarz, Phillip Goldstein, and Lawrence Seidman, took some time out of their busy schedules to talk about their diverse approaches to activism.

Many of these managers have been around for a while, but they really began to come into their own in the late 1990s and more recently. I've followed many more activists and watched their transformation from obscure troublemakers into well-known, established managers. They all bring unique expertise to the craft and they all actively get involved at corporations they owns stakes in with completely different strategies.

In the book, Whitworth explains how he took an unsuccessful multi-year effort by a group of labor-backed shareholders to oust Home Depot CEO Bob Nardelli and transformed it into one that succeeded in his removal. Goldstein discusses how he left a career as a New York City engineer to become an activist that launches campaigns at small capitalization businesses using every technique insurgents have at their disposal. He discusses his surprisingly successful effort at taking on a much bigger fish, the SEC. Chapman explains his completely different tack. His "social lever" activism takes a highly publicized approach that shames a target company with a poorly performing stock into removing its CEO or making some other changes such as selling the company or shaking up its board. All their strategies are different but they are unified behind a common goal: improving shareholder value.

Numerous academics also provided their take on the phenomenon. Michael Van Biema, a former Columbia Business School professor, took his contacts and experience and formed a fund of hedge funds that invests with activists. He provides details of how the fund works. Harvard Law School professor Lucian Bebchuk educates us with his explanation of how both hedge fund and institutional activists target companies with highly paid executives presiding over poorly performing companies.

The major trend of activists expanding their operations around the globe is also documented. I spent the late 1990s covering business and finance in eastern Europe for the *Prague Post* in the Czech Republic.

There, I developed a curiosity for how post-Soviet financial systems work. That interest eventually led me to seek out activist investors there and around the world. I wanted to understand why these insurgents have taken their Western-trained skills to previously untapped global locations and what impact they were having on the markets there. In researching this book, I traveled to dozens of cities, including Moscow, Toronto, and London, to meet with managers on the front lines of activist investing. Sergei Ambartsumov in Moscow enlightens us with his completely different set of problems and solutions when it comes to activism in Russia. Wyser-Pratte talks about why CEOs in continental Europe aren't worried about losing their job and how he's changing that attitude, one company at a time. Many other activists in the United States and in other countries also spoke about their experiences.

This is also a book about companies that are being pushed to the edge. I interviewed a number of executives to document how they are responding to activist efforts. James Hyman, the CEO of correctional facilities builder Cornell Companies, explains why executives must respond to effective activists quickly and early; otherwise, situations can get out of hand.

At the height of the recent economic boon, some short-term activists pressed companies to buy back stock and take on additional debt, all of which exacerbated many problems at those corporations when the market meltdown occurred. A number of corporations were forced by activists to spend cash reserves on special dividends, when they would have preferred to keep that capital in case of a market downturn. Once the downturn came, these short-term activist investors were long gone, leaving executives with the difficult task of keeping the company afloat without the reserves they had hoped would be there in just this circumstance. In some cases, corporate executives also faced insurmountable debt loads as a result of activist pressures.

However, at other corporations, activists sought to improve internal governance standards and align executive pay with performance. These companies that made difficult changes in response to a long-term activists' campaign are in a better position today to weather the financial crisis.

In October 2008, with the private equity world frozen in a deep credit crunch, a top private equity manager, Blackstone Group LP chief executive Stephen Schwarzman, said, "This kind of environment is tailor-made for making absolute fortunes in the private equity business."

But activists with capital are better positioned to take advantage of the economic downturn because they can build large minority positions while valuations are low and realize gains when the market strengthens. Activist Richard Breeden recently upped his stake in embattled jewelry company Zale Corporation to 28 percent from 18 percent. Unlike activists, private equity shops need to complete a buyout to take advantage of record low prices to buy companies. That is a much higher hurdle and one that requires difficult to attain debt financing. Activists don't have to go over the threshold of the buyout to make their returns, so this kind of situation is better suited for the activist.

Strong economy or weak, activists are here to stay. This book is in some ways a collection of stories and anecdotes, successes, and failures of various activist experiences. I felt that through vignettes, I could explain activist investor strategies more clearly and help explain how they think and operate and identify their special qualities. By collecting this patchwork of different narratives, it becomes possible to consider the bigger picture of what impact activists are having on the capital markets.

Acknowledgments

There are numerous people I would like to thank who helped make this book a reality. Lots of people took time out of their busy schedules to patiently go over key statistics, facts, and excerpts. Thank you to Scott Esser, chief operating officer at Hedge Fund Research Inc. for all your statistics and research on the activist fund industry. Thank you to Allan Kortan, David Sirignano, David Brown, Gary Lutin, Pat McGurn, Lars Förberg, Jeffrey M. Solomon, Lawrence "Larry" J. Goldstein, Barry Cronin, Paul Lapides, Ross Hendin, and Mark Schwarz for reading over my material and giving me your valuable feedback.

This book could never have been written without the support of my editor, Pamela van Giessen at John Wiley & Sons, Inc. Thanks also to Jennifer MacDonald, Stacey Fischkelta, and Susan Cooper, who aided in the production and copyediting of this book.

I would never have completed this book without the help and assistance of Ralph Whitworth, Richard Ferlauto, Charles Elson, Lucian Bebchuk, Steven Kaplan, Nell Minow, Phillip Goldstein, Robert Chapman, Seymour Holtzman, James Mitarotonda, Christopher Young,, Guy Wyser-Pratte, Stanley Gold, Manny Pearlman, Sergei Ambartsumov, Richard Lashley,

Jeffrey Ubben, Ben Bornstein, Dorian Foyil, Evan D. Flaschen, Arnaud Ajdler, Eric Rosenfeld, Peter Puccetti, James Leech, Brian Gibson, Lawrence Seidman, Herbert Denton, Bill Mackenzie, John Olson, Marc Weingarten, George Mazin, Steven Howard, Howard Godnick, Terrance O'Malley, Perrie Weiner, Christopher Bartoli, Peter Antoszyk, Peter Blume, Mitchell Nichter, Jay Barris, Tim Selby, and Justin Cable. So, thank you for taking time on several occasions to give me your priceless insights into activists, raiders, and governance.

I gratefully acknowledge all the help Alan Kahn provided in my quest to grasp activism through litigation. Frank Balotti and Geoffrey C. Jarvis, thanks to you for all your help explaining appraisal suits and deciphering Delaware law for me. For getting out your crystal ball and clarifying for me the future of technology and activism I want to thank Securities and Exchange Commission chairman Christopher Cox, Eric Jackson, and Anne Faulk.

Michael Van Biema, Sebastian Stubbe, and Dave Smith, thank you for exposing me to the world of fund of hedge fund activism.

On the international front I'd like to thank Michael Tannenbaum, William Natbony, Marc Goldstein, James Fatheree, and Aaron Boesky, who provided useful insight into hedge funds and their global ambitions, particularly in the Japanese and Chinese financial markets. I am grateful to Jason Booth for helping me parse through the first ever successful proxy contest in South Korea.

Many value investors, some of which dabble in activism, were also extremely helpful in putting together this book. Mohnish Pabrai, Zeke Ashton, Whitney Tilson, Steven Romick, Carlo Cannell—thank you for all your help.

Many current or past regulatory officials were critical to putting this book together. I would like to thank Roel Campos, Martin Dunn, and Brian Lane for their patient explanations. Thanks to Jennifer E. Bethel, Stuart L. Gillan, Christiaan Brakman, David Berger, and John Endean for their efforts to unlock the hidden world of broker non-votes.

A number of public pension fund and labor fund institutional investors contributed to this book. Thank you to John Wilcox, Mike Musuraca, Michael Garland, Daniel Pedrotty, and Brad Pacheco for your thoughts.

Special thanks to Randy Lampert and Andrew Shiftan at investment bank Morgan Joseph & Company for their time and their excellent study, "Management in an Era of Shareholder Activism." April Klein's September 2006 study, "Hedge Fund Activism," also was extremely insightful, as was "Hedge Fund Activism, Corporate Governance and Firm Performance," put together by Alon Brav, Wei Jiang, Frank Partnoy and Randall Thomas. Henry Hu unraveled the complex and shady world of "empty voting" and "hidden morphable ownership," and for that I am extremely appreciative. Tom Quinn, thank you for a peek into your SharkRepellent database. Edward Rock and Marcel Kahan both also expounded on the mysteries of investor activism in their study, "Hedge Funds in Corporate Governance and Corporate Control."

I received precious input on both the business and shareholder sides of the story from Peter J. Wallison, David Chavern, David Pasquale, James Hyman, and Charles Jones. Thank you for that.

Thanks to my great editors at *The Deal*. I received valuable insight from *The Deal*'s editor-in-chief, Robert Teitelman. Thank you for all your guidance. To Bill McConnell, Jaret Seiberg, Alain Sherter, John Morris, Chuck Wilbanks, and Ed Paisley, thank you for patience while editing all my activist hedge fund stories over the years. Also, thank you to Jane Meacham and Tony Cooke at Dow Jones & Company. If you hadn't assigned me to the Schedule 13D beat in 1999, I never would have been in the position to write this book.

None of this would have been possible without the unwavering support of my family and friends. Trevor, this work would not have been achievable without your consistent encouragement and enthusiasm. I want to make a special thanks to Lazslo Bernath in Budapest, who helped me attain a global perspective and valuable experience in the craft of journalism. To my mum and dad, thank you for inspiring me to always learn more about the world around me and supporting whatever I chose to do with my life. Dan and Julie Fesenmaier, thank you for your support and guidance. Richard Martin, your thoughtful words have not gone unnoticed—thank you. To my grandparents, thanks for inspiring me with your strong work ethic and international perspectives.

On a more practical note, thanks to my friend Robert "Tbone" Bryson. I appreciate your excellent graphic design work on the charts that brought to life many otherwise dull statistics in the book. Numerous other people helped review the book, including Sonda Gregor, Janet Bednarczyk, Caitlin Harrington, Joe Schatz, and Anna Kuznetsova. Margaret Fesenmaier, thank you for all your help with my index.

Finally, I want to thank all the activist managers, chief executives, and attorneys in the United States and in far-flung places around the globe, who patiently provided their insight to me about the world of activist investors.

Introduction

In April 2003, Robert Chapman, managing partner of hedge fund Chapman Capital LLC, ran a full-page "help wanted" advertisement in the Canadian national daily newspaper the *Globe and Mail*.

It was a color ad, and it called for the ouster of the CEO at struggling education and entertainment company Cinar Corporation. In the middle, Chapman placed a large photo of Cinar chairman Robert Després with a "Help Wanted, Replacement of Robert Després" sign in banner type directly below his face.

Després, at the time, was on vacation in Florida and appeared ill-prepared to respond to the ad. Chapman, a Cinar shareholder, wasn't surprised. A number of chief executives have felt a little confused and disoriented, perhaps even exasperated, after encountering Chapman. Others in Canada's financial community also began scratching their heads. Who is Chapman, and what exactly is he trying to accomplish with his newspaper ads and cross-border public agitation campaign?

Actually, Chapman had been urging the animation company's board for the past year to auction the business to the highest bidder—and Després was standing in his way. Després, according to Chapman, not only wasn't looking to find a buyer for the business, as many had anticipated he would, but he also appeared inept at governing it. After a series of rapid-fire questions in a phone interview, Chapman realized Després was unaware of key revenue figures. After that, Chapman moved his agitations into high gear with a public pressure campaign, which included the help-wanted ad and several other endeavors, including letters to the board and communications with potential buyers. Soon enough, long-term institutional investors, including Fidelity Investments, began showing their support to Chapman by sending Cinar their own letters supporting his campaign.

Once it was apparent that a large number of Cinar's institutional investors supported Chapman, it became clear to Després that change was in order. By October, the private-equity arm of Toronto Dominion Bank and an investor group bought the company and its popular animated children's television series *Arthur* and *Caillou* in a deal valued at $143.9 million.

Chapman, age 41, who calls himself a "bottom fisher," pocketed a profit on the sale of his Cinar shares after the deal closed (as did all other Cinar investors). Targeting small-capitalization public companies that Wall Street usually ignores with his surreptious, opportunistic style is Chapman's forte. In addition to the occasional full-page ads, Chapman inundates executives—some of whom he characterizes as "intelligence-deprived," "integrity-poor," or "confidently incompetent"—with his trademark witty letters.

These depictions have earned him the title of "rabble rouser." Chapman's letters to CEOs and boards are included in public filings with the Securities and Exchange Commission (SEC) in Washington. Unlike other investors, many of whom resent having to submit these filings, Chapman often relishes the opportunity to get his efforts at communicating to corporate executives out into the public domain. These required filings have helped him to do that, though lately he's expanded his communications effort to include press releases and e-mail blasts, all to attract maximum exposure with the investment community.

Chapman calls this multifaceted approach he uses to improve share value of targeted companies the "social lever" because it embarrasses corporate managers into stepping down or taking action to bolster the company's share price. One way of doing that is by provoking a sale of the target business. But more about that later.

While Chapman's provocative tactics may be extreme, even when compared to most of his brethren, he is very much a part of a growing trend in the investment world: hedge fund managers bucking the traditionally passive investor approach by actively engaging management and pressing for changes at corporations, in the United States and beyond.

Let's take a step back for a moment. Chapman runs a hedge fund, but the way he operates it is very different than most conventional hedge fund managers. Based on a model designed in the 1950s, a traditional hedge fund takes both long and short positions. Essentially, hedge funds make investments in a wide variety of securities, including shares, currencies, derivatives or commodities, anticipating that some will improve in value, and others expecting that they will decline in value. The key with the basic strategy of a hedge fund is to reduce commonplace investment risks and volatility and produce positive returns in both strong and weak markets. In a way, hedge fund managers hedge their bets on the stock market. Unlike mutual funds, hedge funds also can take on leverage.

Hedge fund managers have taken that basic strategy and expanded it to include hundreds of variations on the original mold. Some managers only buy and trade securities, usually equity and debt, of a few interrelated companies seeking to take advantage of pricing differences. Others invest in distressed companies that are either emerging from bankruptcy or could be facing it in the near future. Making bets on municipal bonds, emerging markets, or industry sectors are all tactics some hedge fund managers employ. Some are quants, mathematical whiz-kids that use numerical approaches and software to make investment decisions. A traditional hedge fund manager typically juggles hundreds of positions and engages in a flurry of buying and selling on any given day. It is critical to understand that hedge funds vary widely. Their performance, risk, and volatility differ greatly and depend on the strategy being considered.

Unlike these managers, Chapman and other investors in his bailiwick identify companies that they believe are operating either at subpar levels or in consolidating industries and buy large multimillion-dollar equity stakes. Afterwards, they approach executives at these businesses to discuss strategies to improve share value. There is usually no daily flurry of buying and selling as one might see with a hedge fund strategy employed by a quant, for example. A large purchase is made and held, at times for several years. Sometimes these investors go after companies that are profitable but have unusually low debt levels coupled with reserved cash that management isn't reinvesting in the business in a timely way. Or at least that's the way the investors see it. In some cases, they buy large stakes and push companies to put up a "for sale" sign. When the company is sold, its shares are purchased at a premium price. This is usually a big success for the activist. It means the investment's value has been unlocked.

These investors—usually either the largest or second largest in their target corporations—consider themselves owners, operators, and even CEOs of the businesses they buy stakes in. Managers and directors report to them, or so they would like to think.

And as diverse owners of companies, many of these shareholders take a very public, proactive approach to improving share value through a variety of mechanisms. Sometimes they nominate director candidates for corporate boards, seeking to influence management teams or at times remove ineffectual CEOs. Others take a more laid-back, collaborative approach by simply engaging management behind the scenes, making recommendations in private conversations with executives. Many of these confidential dialogues and the tangible impact these investors have made on the futures of corporations are documented in the following pages. A few activists, like Chapman, rattle their sabers and send out public messages to other shareholders, seeking to engage a critical mass of investors to back their proposals and, by doing so, convince target companies to make changes. Finally, some file lawsuits or make bids to buy companies, in their quest for stock improvement. And, of course, others dabble in all these approaches at different times.

Called special-situation, activist investors or, at times, vulture investors, this group of hedge fund managers often have investigative teams working in the back office researching alternative plans for portfolio companies to follow, often with cost-cutting measures that are eventually presented to corporate directors or recommendations that the companies they are targeting begin offering stock buybacks or shareholder dividends. If corporate directors aren't receptive to the recommendations, these activist shareholders step up their agitations by launching public campaigns that often involve efforts to put their own director candidates on corporate boards. Whether it is through lawsuits, director reshuffling, or anything else, the objective is to have the company make the changes they consider necessary to improve the value of the stock. The goal for these investors usually is not to buy the companies they are targeting, but rather have it make strategic changes on its own, such selling an asset or finding a strategic buyer. Despite being only a small part of the total hedge fund industry, activist hedge fund influence is much wider. William Natbony, partner at Katten Muchin Rosenman LLP in New York, says traditional hedge fund managers are taking notice of activist strategies, and they realize it is an approach that could work for them. At its core, activism is about the shareholders engaging in the company they own, rather than cashing out when things there go awry. "There is a more widespread belief that being involved as a shareholder can help enhance value," Natbony says.

Activists come from different backgrounds—some have worked for corporate raiders while others felt unfulfilled working for mutual funds. Some struck out on their own after working for investment banks.

Many of them are successful over the long term in that they make money for their investors. Like other hedge funds, a great deal of these managers also produce above-market returns in both strong and weak economies. But this book will look beyond their average annual percentage returns—though that part is important—and examine the impact they are having on the companies they target. Even companies that activists pass over are feeling their presence—who knows if they will be targeted next?

Despite their well-publicized status, very little is truly known about activist hedge funds. For one thing, this is a strategy that is just now beginning to be considered a separate class of investing all on its own. This book, which is divided into three parts, track their emergence, development, expansion, and exportation to markets around the world.

In a nutshell, the three sections cover: where activists came from and how they operate; how institutional investors work with or against activists; and, finally, where they go from here. Part of this book will show how activists in some instances are launching coordinated efforts in "wolf packs" to pressure companies and in other situations they go it alone, taking on corporations without the help of their ilk. One section will catalog activists and their interaction with traditional institutional investors such as mutual fund managers, public and corporate pension fund investors, and others. Another chapter documents a new activist strategy: Insurgents seeking to break up mega mergers. The heavily celebrated combination of AOL and Time Warner in 2001 and the negative consequences of that deal imbued some activist shareholders with a new sense of self-awareness and responsibility.

There is also a Washington angle. Changes to regulations adopted by the SEC over the past number of years are having their intended effect of encouraging activists to try and improve a corporation's value rather than sell their shares in frustration or attempt to take over and liquidate the business. Many activists specialize in a particular industry. This book looks at the pros and cons of activists that devote themselves to provoking changes solely in one industry, such as the small bank and thrift sector. Specialized funds are contrasted with diversified investment vehicles. Traditional, passive value investors may think their approach is better; this book uncovers some interesting relationships forming between the two groups that explain how their strategies are becoming inextricably interconnected. Finally, the Internet, YouTube, online forums, activists buying companies, distressed investing, and funds of hedge funds are all examined.

A major goal of mine is to dispel some misconceptions about activists. Many lawmakers and corporate advocates argue that as a group they are short-term, selfish individuals that hurt other shareholders, force employers and employees out and destroy companies. A prevailing argument is that they are all still 1980s-style corporate raiders making hostile bids that seek to dismantle and liquidate businesses at the expense of everyone involved except them. Or that they are "greenmail" artists that promise to stop nagging companies if only executives direct the corporation to buy their shares at a premium to what any other shareholders receive. Yes, it's true that a few insurgents still fit some of these characteristics, to an extent. Some activists pressure companies to cut costs, layoff employees, buy or sell assets, buy back stock, raise debt to dangerous levels, and force companies to be acquired or broken up for selfish, company destructive reasons.

But keep in mind that CEOs can also force companies to do bad things, including pressuring the company they are stewarding to enter into an ill-conceived merger for self-enriching reasons that hurt everyone involved except themselves. Trying to pigeonhole activists in the old corporate raider category is a mistake. In fact, the era of 1980s-style corporate raiders is over, in large part because of both the creation and dismantling of securities and banking regulations. Those changes and others have ushered in a new epoch and created a new breed of investor. Activists today have different motivations than their raider forefathers. Few of them will or have the means to make hostile bids to take over businesses for the sole purpose of liquidating them. This book will explain that while corporate raids and takeovers at one time were the only way a shareholder could demand accountability from companies, today, activists employ a wide variety of strategies and use many new tools available at their fingertips to effect change, often in collaboration with executives.

Most activists, as we will see, are long-term governance-style investors that seek first to work with CEOs to improve the operating and share performance of companies. In some circumstances, activist hedge fund managers and CEOs have worked so well together that they even become good friends. Sometimes they have joined forces to convince a skeptical board or creditor that a particular action makes sense. These interactive, enduring approaches are working to drive significant share performance that in most cases outperform the market over the long haul. But relations aren't always rosy. In many cases, activists like Chapman initiate aggressive efforts at companies with poor records. In certain situations, executive-activist relationships break down after an amicable beginning. In many of the more antagonistic cases, activists often will seek to improve a company's stock value by trying to remove executives they believe are overcompensated and underperforming. At other companies, they will press for sales or asset divestitures. In most cases, these investors say they are acting to improve the value of the stock for all investors, but they will typically put their own interests first. It's just that their interest often coincides with the interests of other investors.

When they make demands, activists are getting results. According to a study by April Klein, associate professor at the Stern School of Business at New York University, over 60 percent of the time executives acquiesce to their challengers, whether that means board representation or an asset sale or both.[1]

This group of activist investors is by far the largest assembly with the most assets under management that have ever employed such an engagement investment strategy. Their numbers have swelled, and their huge assets under management have made them a force to be reckoned with. Chief executives are finally acknowledging their influence and recognizing that they must respond to them—and quickly.

There are some data showing that when companies feel the impact of activists, their performance improves—in terms of both profit and share price. According to a 2006 study, "Hedge Fund Activism, Corporate Governance and Firm Performance," companies targeted by activists are having an impact on improving corporate operations results and, at least in the short term, share value.[2] The authors reviewed 780 instances of activism between 2001 and 2005 for the study.[3] According to their analysis, operating performance of the companies engaged by activists improved significantly in the second and third years of their insurgencies.[4] One of the authors, Alon Brav, associate professor of finance at Duke University, points out that the study doesn't consider companies or divisions that were sold during the examined time frame because they leave the sample and are impossible to follow. He adds that it's likely the average operating performance of companies reviewed would be even greater if these newly consolidated operations were taken into account.

The book also examines two key interrelated trends. One trend is that insurgent investors with billions of dollars behind them are taking on bigger enterprises. The other trend is globalization. Activists are launching campaigns around the world.

An activist that 10 years ago may have tried to push for changes at a miniscule California high-tech company, today is seeking to split up a Fortune 500 corporation and it's all taking place in Tokyo. Until recently, these gadflies were confined for the most part to the U.S. market, with a few exceptions. Now insurgents are pushing for better disclosure and board of director accountability in shareholder-unfriendly places like Japan and South Korea. Many more are reaching even further to extract shareholder value in countries such as Russia, China, Ukraine and even Azerbaijan, where concepts such as fiduciary responsibility to investors and shareholder empowerment haven't really hit home yet. In some of these countries, activists must worry less about whether domestic securities markets are secured and more about whether they themselves are safe. One investor describes how he hired a brigade of soldiers and former government security guards just to make sure an annual meeting in Ukraine would take place without any incidents. Another high-profile investor's legal battles in Siberia were squashed because judges were on the take.

These emerging market activists are the front lines battling the hidden and sometimes not-so-hidden forces that seek to make sure the markets remain opaque and unaccountable. Other economies have their own shareholder problems and solutions. This book documents the works of activists in Canada, France, Germany, Sweden, Finland, Denmark, and Norway.

As insurgents encroach into every corner of the globe, it becomes increasingly difficult to figure out who isn't affected by them in one way or another.

When a small group of shareholders that own very little of a corporation seem to single-handedly orchestrate a major combination of two companies, it begs the question: how did they do it? If you want to learn about the real behind-the-scenes story of how activists unraveled yet another mega-merger, then please read on. Whether you are a retail investor thinking about buying or selling stocks or someone that wants to get a little bit more information about how hedge funds function, then this book is for you.

Anyone that wants to learn how to profit from an alternative investment strategy and understand how activists continue to outperform the market can benefit as well. Professional investors that are curious about how these small activist shareholders can exert such power over a corporation could gain some useful insight into the mind of an insurgent shareholder with this book. If you're interested in the relationship between a company's share value and its chief executive officer's pay package, then this is recommended reading.

I've put together several panels of these portfolio managers for events organized by *The Deal.* They are always described by my colleagues and attendees as the most colorful and interesting group in a full day of panelists. Audience members are always left eager to learn more after the event is over. In fact, upon learning that I write about activist investors, people often inundate me with numerous questions. After I'm done answering, more questions remain. Hopefully this book will go a long way to answering those queries.

Whether they are located on Wall Street, Bay Street, or Main Street, activists are the marionette masters pulling the strings behind corporations around the world. This book will take you behind the curtain.

Part One

FROM RAIDERS TO ACTIVISTS AND EVERYTHING IN BETWEEN

Chapter 1

Growth of Activism and Why Corporate Raiders Aren't Around Anymore

The past few years have seen a major increase in the number of activist hedge funds in the United States and abroad. As of September 2006, Hedge Fund Research Inc. (HFR), a Chicago-based database and analysis company, estimates that roughly 150 full-time activist hedge fund managers have functioning investment vehicles—roughly double the 77 activist managers that existed in 2005. Activist funds in 2006 more than doubled to $117 billion in assets, from roughly $48.6 billion in assets in 2004, according to HFR (see Figure 1.1).

Also, activists appear to have produced strong results by outperforming the marketplace over the past number of years. In 2004, when the Standard and Poor's (S&P) 500, a noted benchmark of large-capitalization companies, returned 10.86 percent, activists produced 23.16 percent,

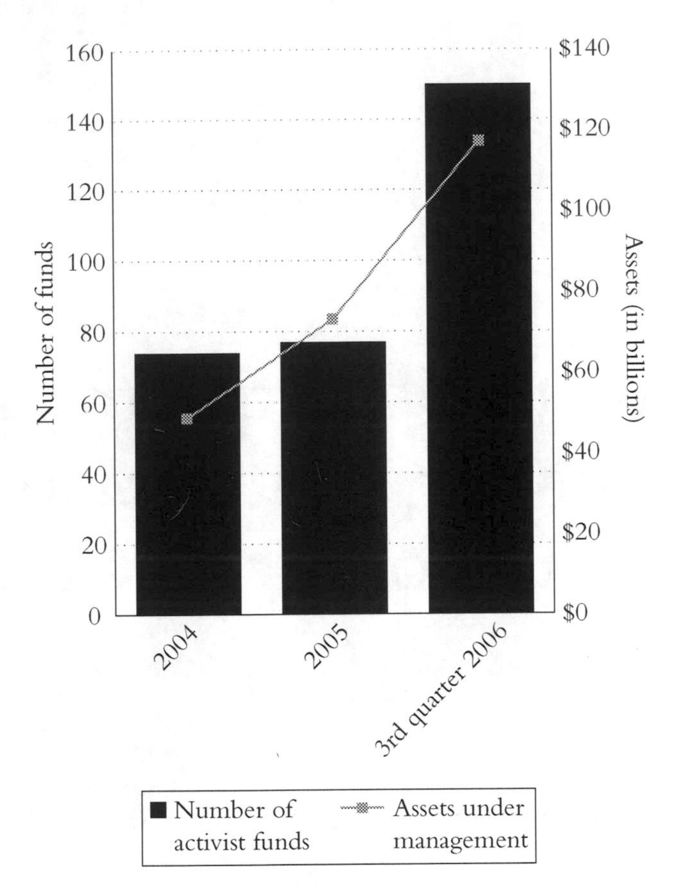

Figure 1.1 Hedge Fund Research Inc. 2006
SOURCE: Hedge Fund Research Inc.

according to HFR. In 2005, activists returned 16.43 percent while the S&P 500 reported 4.91 percent. In 2006, activists produced 16.72 percent, while the S&P 500 returned 15.78 percent. As the financial crisis expands, many new opportunities have emerged for activist hedge fund managers with the capital to invest. In an October 2008 report, Philadelphia-based consultancy Hedge Fund Solutions estimated that 1 in 10 companies in the United States were trading below their cash/share value. There are similar valuations in Europe and Japan, where activism is on the rise. In the United States, Damien Park, president of Hedge Fund Solutions, counted 54 activist campaigns in August 2008, 57 in September 2008, and 50 in October 2008.

They also are engaging and agitating for change at a wider spectrum of companies, many of which for the first time are the largest of corporations in the United States and around the world. In 2008, they prodded and engaged managers at dozens of large companies, including the Zale Corporation, Whole Foods Market Inc., CSX Corporation, Sun-Times Media Group Inc., and Longs Drug Stores Corporation. Activist Jana Partners LLC's industry-expert candidates helped facilitate a $1.8 billion sale of Cnet Networks Inc. to CBS Corporation in May 2008. Other previous targets of activism include embattled Citigroup Inc., General Electric Co., ABN Amro Holding NV, Motorola Inc., Time Warner, McDonald's, Wendy's International Inc., Heinz, Vodafone Group plc, Cadbury Schweppes plc, and Kerr-McGee Corporation. The list goes on and on. But it hasn't always been this way.

How did this once small group of insurgents explode into the massive players they are today? The answer relies on various factors that have come together to make them into full-fledged activists.

For one thing, *all* hedge funds, including activists, have become recipients of additional capital from individuals and institutions. Other major factors have contributed to the rise of the transactional-focused activist industry. For example, between 2004 and 2007, an increase in the cheap availability and variety of debt and a huge spike in deal activity, including a spike in private equity buyouts are all advancing activist goals.

The collapse of Enron, Worldcom, and other major corporations has bestowed a greater credibility on shareholders that engage corporations to improve their corporate governance.[1] All that and a transforming regulatory and legal landscape that has converted once powerful corporate raiders into activists have contributed to their evolution. Meanwhile, other previously coveted strategies, such as convertible arbitrage, are experiencing diminishing returns, leading investors to seek out new approaches, one of which is activism.[2]

Let's break down the various factors, one at a time.

Factor 1: Asset Explosion

Between 2003 and 2007 hedge fund assets under management doubled to well over $1 trillion, according to HFR. By mid 2007, hedge fund

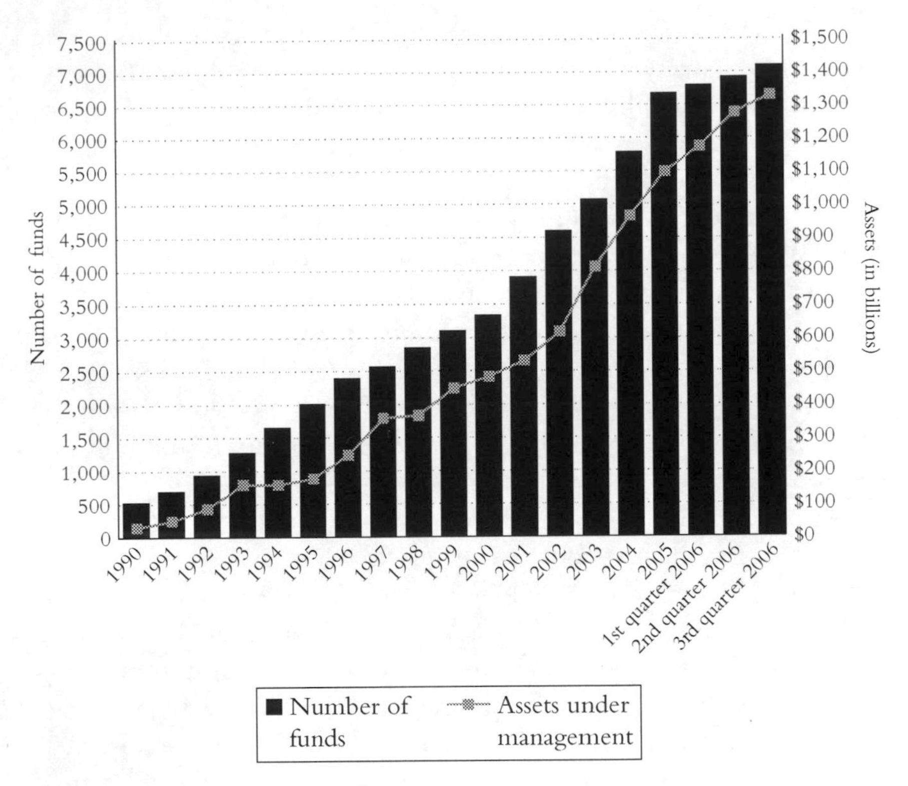

Figure 1.2 Hedge Fund Research Inc. 2006
SOURCE: Hedge Fund Research Inc.

assets were estimated to be roughly $1.6 trillion. To put things in perspective, in 1996, hedge funds managed only $256 billion. As a result of the financial crisis, hedge fund assets have dwindled as investors have pulled their money out. However, even with lower numbers, activist hedge funds and the billions they have under management represent a significantly growing piece of the total industry. Insurgent investors represent roughly 10 percent of the total hedge fund industry, HFR reports (see Figure 1.2).

Also, funds of hedge funds, which are funds that own stakes in many hedge funds, have begun investing with activists in a big way. Institutional investors such as endowments and public and corporate pension plan administrators have expanded their allocations to insurgent-type investors, particularly governance-focused managers. Consequently, activist managers are experiencing a very different investor climate than 10 years ago when their client base was more likely to be made up predominantly of a few individual high-net-worth investors. With so many assets under management, activists are under pressure to target more and bigger companies to continue producing the sweet returns their investors have grown to expect. Many traditional professional managers with expanding asset sizes are also converting into activists under the assumption that the strategy can help them maintain returns their investors have grown to expect.

Factor 2: Deal Flow

The United States and many other countries experienced a major expansion of merger-and-acquisition (M&A) activity in the early 2000s. More deals and deal makers resulted in more opportunities for activists to engage in one of their favorite share value–generating strategies: pushing companies into transactions.

In fact, a phenomenon known as *deal jumping* emerged, partially due to activist hedge fund managers pressing for more deals and better premiums on mergers. Once a company has already agreed to be acquired, another company, known as an interloper, comes in and makes its own bid for the target corporation. Activists in many cases have been driving or, at the very least, fanning the flame on the deal-jumping phenomenon. Their goal is to launch a bidding war, which will drive up the stock price.

Take Verizon's successful snag of MCI Inc. The former long-distance operator had already struck a deal to be bought by Qwest Communications International Inc. when Verizon came in with its own offer. Qwest and Verizon each made increased bids, spurred on, in part, by activist hedge fund managers pressing for higher share valuations. Shareholder Elliott Associates LP, at one point in February 2005, announced plans to vote against any MCI plan to be acquired by Verizon that was $1 billion less than a rival acquisition offer from Qwest. Elliott Associates sent that information in a letter to MCI's board. In the end, MCI's board approved Verizon's $8.1 billion bid. Even though it was 14.4 percent less than Qwest's $9.75 billion offer, it still was a significant premium to what Verizon had originally bid.[3] A few activist hedge fund managers set off a similar but much larger multibillion dollar bidding battle among banking institutions for Dutch bank ABN Amro.

Factor 3: Private Equity Funds

A tangential trend has been the recent growth of private equity (PE) companies with billions in assets. This type of investment vehicle brings together a group of investors in a fund that buys companies, typically undervalued ones, and seeks to turn them around by a variety of means such as installing new management teams that concentrate on making them more valuable. Once the portfolio business is restructured, the PE firm then either sells the business or finds another exit strategy such as a public offering. Their presence increases the potential buyer pool and likelihood that an activist's target will be acquired, particularly if activists start agitating for a merger. However, private equity firms became the first victims of the recent credit crunch. With confidence in the markets dwindling, they have temporarily disappeared as a potential buyer for a company an activist is seeking to have sold. George Mazin, a partner at Dechert LLP, notes that the increases in the number of PE funds and the assets they have under management have definitely fueled activist investing. The years 2005 and 2006 were stellar years for buyout funds.

In its 2006 report, "Management in an Era of Shareholder Activism," New York–based investment bank Morgan Joseph & Co. reports that the growth of the PE industry has created a ready market of buyers for companies that are forced into a sale by activists. "A proliferation of diverse equity funds with different mandates has broadened the array of companies that meet buyout firm requirements," Morgan Joseph reports.[4]

James Hyman, the CEO of Houston-based Cornell Companies, a builder and operator of correctional facilities, says he definitely sees a connection between activists and PE companies. Hyman was brought in as the chief executive of the Houston-based company after activists there pressured the previous CEO to step down in 2005. His stint was short. The company was sold in October 2006 to buyout shop Veritas Capital of New York.[5]

"They are co-dependent enablers," Hyman says. "The PE companies encourage the hedge fund guys to put companies in play and the activists take positions in companies and pressure for auctions enabling private equity firms to get a hold of divisions or entire companies they might otherwise not have been able to."

A connected phenomenon is that activists themselves in some cases have emulated buyout shops by making bids and buying companies

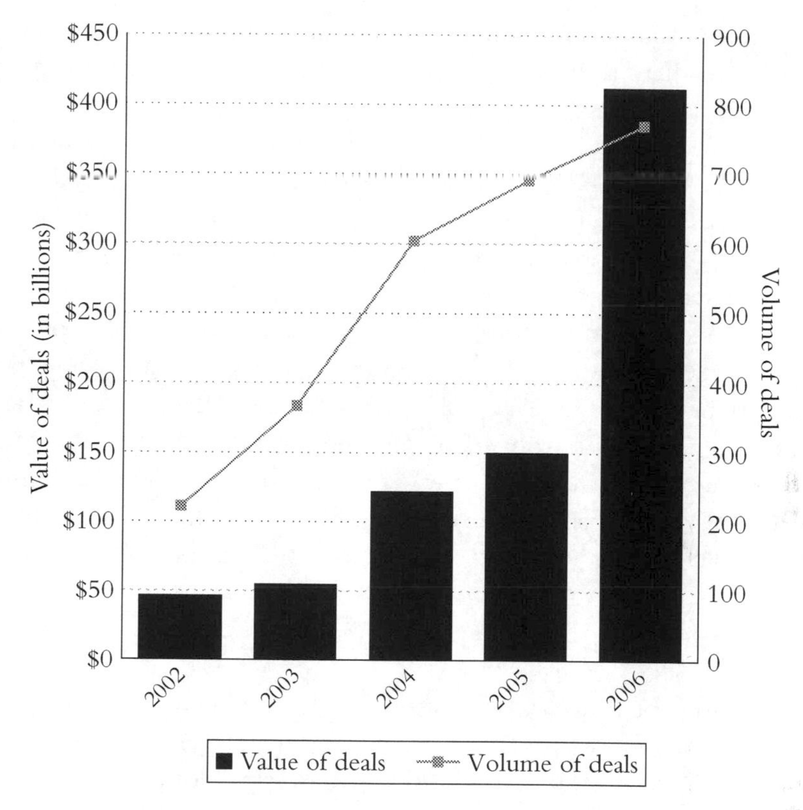

Figure 1.3 Mergermarket, an M&A intelligence and research service, 2006
SOURCE: Mergermarket, an M&A intelligence and research service, 2006.

with the intention of turning them around. Certain activists would prefer a strategic or traditional PE company to ultimately make the acquisition, but buyout shop offers and acquisitions contributed to the explosive M&A environment (see Figure 1.3).

In addition to lending for leveraged buyouts, corporations had access to much more debt financing for other purposes than ever before, and the cost of all that debt was lower than it had ever been before. This new source of cheaper debt lent itself well to the activist manager who pressed corporate executives into completing a leveraged recapitalization—in other words, raising debt levels and using the proceeds to buy back shares or issue a special shareholder dividend. Morgan Joseph's Lampert points out that company CEOs, under pressure from deal-hungry activist shareholders, had a wide variety of financing options available to them as they either contemplated taking the company private or engaging in a leveraged recapitalization.

New York-based hedge fund and buyout firm Cerberus Capital Management LP, an early adopter of the concept of hedge fund debt lending, has provided financing capital for over 10 years. In 2006, the mega fund, named for a three-headed dog that in Greek mythology guards the gates of hell, acquired General Motors Acceptance Corporation (GMAC), the financing unit of General Motors. Later in 2007, it made an even more astonishing acquisition, picking up U.S. automotive giant Chrysler Group from DaimlerChrysler AG for $7.4 billion. That deal more than any other transaction has propelled buyout shops and hedge funds out of obscurity and into the national debate. However with the markets in turmoil, both Chrysler and GMAC have fallen on difficult times. Both auto companies sought and received billions in government bailout funds in 2008 and 2009.

Factor 4: Fraud

The collapse of Enron Corporation in 2001, followed shortly by the implosion of WorldCom Inc., Global Crossing Inc. and the emergence of fraud at several other major corporations, sent a loud and clear message to the United States government. Lawmakers on Capitol Hill in Washington passed laws seeking to make sure corporations wouldn't misappropriate millions of dollars again. In 2008, a whole series of other regulatory problems, dealing with mortgages and derivatives, led to the collapse of Lehman Brothers and the government mega-bailouts of Bank of America, Citigroup, and American International Group. In response, regulators again took up legislative steps to take control of markets and to beef up enforcement of the financial sector.

The landmark Sarbanes-Oxley Act (SOX), co-authored by Senator Paul Sarbanes (D-MD) and Representative Michael Oxley (R-OH), passed in 2002 and made major stabs at reforming boards and accounting practices. Controversial corporate governance rules requiring chief executive certifications and auditor independence followed shortly afterward. Separately, The Nasdaq Stock Market Inc. (NASDAQ) and New York Stock Exchange adopted regulations that would require their member companies to have more independent directors, with little or no financial or family ties to corporate management. These regulations sought to respond to the problem of boards composed predominantly of insiders that were more interested in keeping the CEO happy rather than satisfying the company's shareholder base. Those governance rules and the financial crisis that has emerged in 2008 and 2009 created an opportunity and a ready audience for governance focused activists and their engagement style. Previously passive institutional investors have been willing to give activists a chance, especially if a central part of their campaign focuses on a lack of independent directors on a particular board. In the environment of the market meltdown, institutional investors are even more likely to support activists that have a long term governance agenda for corporations or financial institutions. When activists focus on governance issues, in recent years, they have gained credibility, which contributes to their ability to provoke change. Burned by corporations in the past, institutional investors are now more likely to support an activist that wants to put a director or two on a corporate board, as part of their effort to make corporations more accountable to shareholders. "There have always been underperforming companies and underperforming boards, but there haven't always been a significant number of funds out there that were willing to challenge them," says Morgan Joseph's Andrew Shiftan.

In the pre-Lehman era, institutional managers would either vote with their feet by selling their stakes in companies they had lost confidence in or hold on to the shares and accept management problems. As the financial crisis has emerged many previously passive institutional investors have either thrown their support to insurgents or become activists themselves.

Institutional investors such as pension funds that have invested billions in public securities markets are beginning to understand the importance of strong governance at corporations, says Corporate Library's Nell Minow. "They're recognizing that aiding an activist's efforts may be the best way to bring in the governance changes they recognize as being necessary at a corporation," she says.

Hedge Fund Solutions' Damien Park says that he agrees that activists with the right intentions can help improve the governance of corporations in a way that produces long-term share improvement. However, he argues that real governance activists are patient and understand that improvements take time. At the same time, he says, there are many fakes out there who claim to be governance experts as part of their effort to achieve a personal gain at the expense of other investors. CEOs have responded to both the fake and real governance focused activists by finding ways to leave the public markets. The hike in regulatory related costs, along with the increased difficulty many companies faced finding willing and able directors, all began to contribute to the trend of going-private transactions. In November 2006, a private-sector group headed by Glen Hubbard, dean of the Columbia School of Business, and John Thornton, chairman of the Washington think tank Brookings Institution, and former president of Goldman Sachs & Company, produced a report pointing out that regulatory requirements associated with SOX were a major contributor to why companies sought to exit the public market. The report pointed out that section 404 of the law, financial reporting of corporate internal controls, created a particularly hostile world for many public companies, particularly smaller ones.[6] According to the report, the cost for companies complying with section 404 in the first year was, on average, $4.36 million.[7]

The new price of being public, coupled with a growing weariness on the parts of many corporate CEOs to the growing challenge of meeting Wall Street's short-term earnings expectations, have all contributed to the recent trend of companies seeking a private exit. Activists have recognized these factors and, together with institutions, they have been there to give companies that final push toward leveraged buyouts.

Factor 5: Historical Context

To figure out how activists operate, it first is necessary to understand their roots. Where they came from explains a great deal about their present strategy. Corporate raiders of the 1980s, the forefathers of today's agitators, have inspired and educated many present-day activists. In fact, activists today probably would not exist without the groundbreaking insurgencies of these predecessors.

But even before the 1980s, there were shareholders agitating for change at companies, though only a handful at any one time until now. In the 1940s and 1950s, investors such as Thomas Mellon Evans, Louis

Wolfson, and Leopold Silberstein pressed undervalued companies they believed had too much cash on their balance sheets into making changes. In many ways that period represented the Wild West of activism because it took place before a regulatory regime existed that required any serious disclosures of investment information. These insurgent investors could buy huge stakes in companies, before anyone knew they were there. Diana Henriques explains in her book *White Sharks of Wall Street* how Wolfson succeeded in his goal of provoking change at Montgomery Ward, a catalog retailer based in Chicago, Illinois.[8]

In 1954, Wolfson acquired a 6.5 percent stake in Montgomery Ward and launched a campaign to oust directors from the company's board. His ultimate goal was to remove the department store chain's CEO, Sewell Avery. Only 30 percent of investors backed Wolfson's slate of board nominees, though that was enough to gain three director positions on the board and for Avery to step down. Montgomery Ward subsequently made other changes Wolfson agitated for and the company's stock improved dramatically. Other target companies for the raiders of the 1950s included Pratt & Whitney and Twentieth Century Fox.[9]

Certainly, some of the corporate raiders of the 1980s were inspired by these early agitators. But whether the larger group of activists seeking changes at companies today in the United States and around the world are just an extension of these early insurgents or a whole new phenomenon is a matter for debate. First, a definition: Corporate raiders in the 1980s traditionally would make hostile bids for corporations. In some cases, they acquired the business and liquidated it by selling off various divisions and assets of the purchased company, kind of an expansive garage sale. In essence, the corporation no longer exists as it did before the raider showed up. In other cases, to avoid being liquidated, targeted corporations or other large investors would offer insurgents a premium for their shares, known as greenmail, as an incentive to drop their aggressive campaigns and leave the company alone. Greenmail, a special payment other investors wouldn't receive for their shares, was seen as part of the "greed" environment associated with the 1980s. The strategy for many raiders was to give the company two options: sell the business to a strategic buyer or make the insurgent go away with an offer of greenmail. Either one of these approaches typically led to profits for the raider.

But unlike most present-day activists, 1980s-era raiders did not seek to improve value by engaging collaboratively with management of their targets. Nor did they seek to make corporate governance changes such as pressuring boards to alter executive compensation plans as a means of improving the share price. (In many cases, that was because raiders didn't have the tools to do so.)

These raiders have at some level motivated the group of activists pressing for changes today. For one thing, many activists leading the movement worked for raiders such as Carl Icahn, Asher Edelman, Ronald Perelman, and T. Boone Pickens. As you can read from that list, some of the raiders of the 1980s are still present and active today in a big way, and many of them operate with some of the same incentives as they did in the 1980s, though they must play by the new rules of the game.

For example, billionaire Icahn is still busy pushing companies around in many of the same ways he did 20 years ago. In 1980 and 1981 he took on Hammermill Paper Company.[10] Icahn acquired a 10 percent voting stake in the paper company and prepared plans to complete a hostile takeover. He hoped to take over the company and auction off its assets, leaving nothing behind. Instead, Icahn ended his hostile plans after the company bought back his stake at a premium over the market price.[11] In 1984, Icahn acquired American Car & Foundry Company, a consolidated railroad car manufacturer.[12] He liquidated some assets and improved the company's earnings.

In 2006, Icahn made a $10 billion unsolicited bid for South Korean cigarette manufacturer KT&G Corporation, reminiscent of his hostile bids of the 1980s. While the bid looks familiar, Icahn's target, located on the other side of the planet, shows that some things are changing. Part of what has changed is that Icahn and the remaining raiders of the 1980s are working in an environment surrounded by many of their progeny. Icahn's KT&G bid was made with the support of newcomer insurgent Warren Lichtenstein, whose team discovered the investment opportunity in the first place. Lichtenstein eventually attained a seat on KT&G's board, and now is working collaboratively with the company's management to improve share value—a very un-raider-like move. Icahn maintains his aggressive insurgent approach today, in part, because his reputation for being a corporate raider makes it difficult for him to do anything else. "It's hard for Carl Icahn to call up a company and say, 'I'd like to learn about your business,'" quips ValueAct Capital's Jeffrey Ubben.

In addition to Icahn, oilman-turned-corporate raider T. Boone Pickens is famous for his insurgencies at energy companies in the 1980s. His strategy: first buy, then split up companies and sell them in a way that improved shareholder value. The experience of a corporate raid can be particularly painful for people working for businesses targeted by raiders, particularly for the ones who were laid off in the reshuffling. Pickens is most famous for his takeover efforts at energy companies. He sought to break up Cities Services Company (now part of Citgo) in 1982. Later he went after other energy companies, including Unocal Corporation, Phillips Petroleum Company, and Gulf Oil Corporation.[13]

Another 80s raider, Irwin Jacobs of Minneapolis, known as "Irv the Liquidator," pressured many companies into making changes.[14] In 1989 he joined forces with cosmetics and beauty products direct seller Amway Corporation to buy a 10 percent stake in rival Avon Products Inc. and pressed for a sale.[15] Other objects of his attention included the Walt Disney Company and ITT Corporation.

Working for corporate raiders makes for a great education. Two investors that would eventually strike out on their own, Emanuel Pearlman and Barry Rosenstein, first worked for Asher Edelman, a raider who instigated a series of insurgencies in the 1980s on companies such as Canal-Randoph Company, Lucky Stores Inc., and Burlington Industries Inc.[16] For example, Edelman took control of the board of Canal-Randolph, the parent company of United Stockyards. Once in charge, Edelman sold the corporation's divisions.[17]

After working for Edelman, Rosenstein launched Jana Partners, an activist fund that focuses much of its insurgent efforts on energy companies. Pearlman, who went to work for Edelman for three years after completing business school, says the experience influenced him but does not necessarily represent the strategies he employs at Liberation Investment Group, the activist hedge fund he now manages. At Liberation, Pearlman takes more of a carrot-and-stick approach. "Anything we get involved in, we're looking to be an activist," Pearlman says. "We go to the management teams and talk professionally and try to convince them to do things that are good for the company, but if that doesn't work, then we engage in more public activist efforts."

Many factors contributed to the fading of the 1980s-style raider. For one thing, a number of raiders in the late 1980s lost their investors' money on the strategy. Also, numerous securities regulations changed in the early 1990s, making it easier for shareholders to hold companies accountable to investors without the need for raids.

Corporations installed brand-new anti-takeover protections such as poison pills to ward off hostile raiders, making the strategy practically impossible to pull off. Also known as a shareholder rights plan, the poison pill is an anti-takeover provision because it permits a corporation to inundate the market with shares and prevents a hostile bidder from accumulating a controlling stake in the business without the board's approval.

Delaware, where about 50 percent of all U.S. corporations are registered, passed a law, section 203, prohibiting raiders with a 15 percent stake of a target company from completing a hostile acquisition. In essence, the law sets up a three-year freeze of company assets unless the target company's board agrees to the transaction.[18] Other states, including New York and Massachusetts, adopted similar laws. The Delaware law and anti-takeover devices forced raiders to the negotiation table with boards and executives.

Mark Schwarz, president of activist fund Newcastle Capital Group LLC, points out that another major reason why the heyday of the corporate raider has passed is because insurgents today have a much more difficult time than their predecessors in the 1980s raising the debt financing they need to launch a hostile bid. During the 1980s, famous financier Michael Milken of Drexel Burnham Lambert Inc. provided junk bond–driven financing offers for hostile bids. Milken went to prison on finance-related charges and now-days that ready financing either no longer exists or is very difficult to come by. Today, Schwarz says, activists no longer can make hostile offers for large U.S. companies because major lending institutions won't or aren't permitted to provide the financing to insurgents for hostile takeovers. In fact, the Federal Reserve Board responded to the explosion of corporate raiders by establishing margin rules that prohibited shell corporations from borrowing debt to finance hostile acquisitions.[19] The rules were targeted at raiders, such as Icahn and Pickens, who typically formed shell corporations when launching hostile bids.

Instead, present-day activists must raise capital from their own investors, for the most part, to complete hostile unsolicited buyouts.

In practicality, that means hostile acquisitions are much less frequent and typically don't take place with plans to break up the company and sell it in pieces. In some cases, activists join forces to raise the capital needed to make a hostile buyout offer. A small number of high-profile insurgents have the capital and the will to launch hostile bids. But in most cases, insurgent shareholders, lacking the funds, no longer make hostile bids.

Public perception played a roll as well. Critics of corporate raiders have labeled the shareholder class as a group of disgruntled investors that never were particularly fond of the idea of improving the companies they targeted. Some activists that have popped up over the past five years may fit that mold, but it doesn't represent the majority of activists. Instead of seeking first to break up companies, many activists look to enhance value by finding ways to improve the business—intact—by collaborating with executives, often behind the scenes.

Those individuals that believe activists have emerged and stand for something vastly different than corporate raiders of the 1980s generally point to a watershed event that took place in 1986. That was the year Ralph Whitworth launched United Shareholders Association, or USA, a grassroots organization that represented small shareholders.

Whitworth, 51, today runs the extremely successful activist fund Relational Investors, which focuses on improving the governance of target companies and at the same time making money for his investors. In 2006, he was a key agitator leading to the resignation of Home Depot Chairman and CEO Robert Nardelli. Whitworth was drawn to Home Depot by what he saw as a misaligned compensation package for Nardelli, coupled with the company's unremarkable stock performance (see Chapter 6). But in 1986, Whitworth was running the USA, which received seed money from his former boss, Pickens, and other investors. Their intent was to help burgeoning, but mostly small activist, investors gain some leverage when negotiating with corporations.[20]

ISS's Pat McGurn, formerly a director of communications and research at USA, points out that the group was the first small-investor organization that focused its efforts primarily on governance and improving shareholder value. Members paid a nominal fee, roughly $50 a year, to join. At its height the organization had over 1,000 members represented by Whitworth and a team of roughly 10 people in small offices at 1667 K Street in Washington. "Fortune 500 company CEOs would come traipsing through our offices, pitching their point of view," McGurn says.

In 1989, USA launched a corporate activism program that targeted 50 companies each year that USA members identified as having some governance problem. The program, dubbed "Target 50" got off to a slow start. Only a few companies returned USA calls in the program's first year and shareholder proposals seeking to change a corporation's governance received, on average, only 17 percent support from other investors.[21] By 1993, proposals USA members introduced received, on average, 44 percent support and 22 agreements were negotiated with executives.[22] Companies agreed to remove directors with conflicts and cut out "golden parachute" severance agreements.[23] In 1992, Cooper Industries of Houston, Texas, agreed to restructure its board nominating committee to consist only of independent directors, as did Dial of Phoenix, Arizona. In 1993, Polaroid agreed to revise its poison pill bylaw to give shareholders the right to vote and remove it in the event of an all-cash tender offer for the company. Other companies that reached settlements with USA included Wendy's, Whirlpool, Time Warner, and Unisys, among many more.[24]

In addition to having a direct impact on the companies they targeted directly, the minority shareholder group also was effective in convincing regulators in Washington to give shareholders a greater voice in director elections and investor communications.

McGurn says Whitworth's recent success at Relational Investors can be traced back to his efforts at USA. Whitworth also spent some time at ISS, where he developed a better comprehension of governance style investing.[25] "At USA, Whitworth honed his skills at interacting with directors and executives," McGurn says. "He saw that he could have success in changing governance structures in a way that could spur performance."

The creation of Relational Investors in 1995 also represented a major shift from corporate raiders to governance-style activism. At the time of its launch, Relational billed itself as a unique investment fund that focused on pressing undervalued and troubled companies into improving their corporate governance practices and making other changes.

In many ways that was the first truly activist fund, breaking away from the pack of raiders. It took a much more collaborative and consensus-building approach that sought to work with executives to improve value. This was in many ways a first and is considered by governance experts as a critical moment in the transformation of raiding into activism. Relational was co-launched by David Batchelder, another investor who worked with Pickens. "He [Whitworth] changed the negative concept of corporate raider into a positive strategy of corporate governance that involved engaging management," says Liberation's Pearlman.

The emergence of Whitworth's fund also was a turning point moment for relations between institutions and activist hedge funds. Relational succeeded at gaining the support of institutions in a way that had never occurred before. Unlike corporate raiders, who typically were funded by high-net-worth individuals, Batchelder and Whitworth's fund received initial investment capital from the long-term-minded public pension fund California Public Employees' Retirement System (CalPERS). CalPERS allocated capital anticipating that Relational would engage managements and at times press undervalued and troubled companies into improving their corporate governance structures.

With CalPERS support, Relational also had an easier time attracting the backing of other public pension funds with similar mandates. All of this funding improved Relational's leverage in boardroom discussions with executives. Many activists have since followed in the Relational mold of seeking to improve a company's governance structure as a means of enhancing share value.

Activists today, generally speaking, have adopted a strategy of engaging management of the companies they target for change. The first part of most activists' strategy is to meet executives and discuss ideas for improving the company's value in a friendly, collegial manner. It's true that some activists often start their efforts by rattling their swords and making demands. But most activists try to work things out privately, and when that fails, their strategy becomes more raider-esque or insurgent-like. At that point, an activist may make an unsolicited bid to provoke some reaction. "Unlike the cold, calculating strategy of corporate raiders, activists today invest in companies they believe have potential, and they try to work with management to make the companies better," says George

Mazin, a partner at Dechert LLP in New York. "It's sort of a passive-aggressive approach."

Mazin also notes that activists have investment time considerations that bear little resemblance to that of their corporate raider forefathers. While raiders have traditionally been anxious to get in and out of an investment in a year, activists are willing to stick with their stakes and continue pressing for change for two to three years and sometimes longer (still significantly shorter than many long-term institutional holders). The activist model is closer to the strategy utilized by private equity companies, which typically have, at minimum, five-year investment holding periods. The longer holding periods employed by activists has helped the investor group continue to utilize their strategy because they aren't experiencing the same high-level of capital redemptions other investment managers with shorter lockups are experiencing as a result of the market downturn. Also, raiders would typically seek to take control of a company and immediately break it up, while activists are more likely to encourage companies to find buyers themselves.

Another difference, says Morgan Joseph's Lampert, relates to valuations. He points out that a 1980s-style corporate raider typically sought to gain a modest short term profit. Meanwhile, activist investors take a more long-term perspective with the company they are focusing their attention on and generally do a better job of unlocking the value of corporations with their engagement approach. The valuations that corporate raiders received for their efforts are typically at a discount to the maximum amount shareholders could receive from the stock and what activists often can achieve, Lampert says.

Comparing benefits achieved by activists and raiders also reveals another fundamental dissimilarity between the two groups of investors. With corporate raiders, in many cases, only the insurgent obtains the benefit. With governance focused activist investors, the benefit typically goes to the entire shareholder base, including activists, institutions, and individual investors. When an activist succeeds at installing a couple of directors who are invested heavily in the stock, an argument can be made that their interests are aligned with the rest of the shareholder base. Charles Elson, director of the Corporate Governance Center at the University of Delaware, argues that even a shareholder seeking to take control of a board to replace management does not make that investor a corporate raider. The investor needs to gain the support of a majority of other shareholders to attain that goal. The result doesn't give that dissident investor a return that is disproportionate to what other investors received.

However, executives argue that an activist effort may produce a short-term benefit at the expense of long-term value. That brings us back to the concept of greenmail. Christopher L. Young, director and head of M&A research at Institutional Shareholder Services in Rockville, Maryland, says he disagrees with any characterization that categorizes all activists as short-term, raider-like opportunists looking for greenmail. He points out that greenmail, in its traditional form, may have been prevalent in the 1980s, but for the most part that phenomenon doesn't exist anymore. "Corporations will try to paint activist motives to show that they will get some sort of advantage different from what other shareholders will gain," Young says. "But these activists stimulate benefits that all shareholders receive."

In a March 2005 *Financial Times* editorial, Jana Partners' Rosenstein expressed outrage about how he and other activists have been dubbed sharks or corporate raiders.[26] In the editorial, "Activism Is Good for All Shareholders," Rosenstein argued that activists are not short-term investors. An activist's effort at a company is good news for all investors, he argues.

Chapman Capital's Robert Chapman expressed his thoughts on the traditional concept of greenmail in a letter written in 2000 responding to American Community Properties Trust CEO Michael Wilson. In the letter, Chapman refers to the real estate investment trust's shareholder base as "public partners" to emphasize how he believes executives there are partnered with their entire shareholder base. The letter also responded to a suggestion made by Wilson indicating that Chapman may have wanted the company to buy his shares at a higher value than what other investors could receive. "I have never suggested that ACPT purchase MY shares at a premium over market," Chapman wrote in April 2000.

Morgan Joseph's Lampert points out that activists succeed when they establish credibility with the rest of the shareholder base. Accepting greenmail, even once, would damage their reputation with institutional investors in every other insurgency they would ever initiate. Activists also seek to establish credibility with surrogates for the institutions, such as Institutional Shareholder Services and Proxy Governance Inc., proxy advisory services that either vote directly for institutions or make recommendations for them. Accepting greenmail would irrevocably hurt their status with these advisory companies.

CEOs and boards are also less likely to offer greenmail, in part because securities lawyers and institutional investors lately are more prepared to respond to such a proposition with a class action lawsuit against the corporation claiming they did not receive the same price themselves. "If they [corporations] begin negotiating with insurgents for greenmail takeouts, then that will open up a whole new can of worms, with other investors claiming they did not get the same returns," Lampert says.

David Chavern, chief of staff at the U.S. Chamber of Commerce in Washington, says that not all of the corporate raider greenmail tactics have disappeared. He says that today there are various shades of gray when considering greenmail. When activists press for a special dividend or recapitalization and get it, the engagement does not comfortably fit into the traditional category of greenmail because presumably all shareholders receive the same return. But, on another level, when a company agrees to return some of its cash to shareholders as a means of satisfying pestering activist investors, that activity may offend other long-term investors who would have preferred to let the company keep that capital available within the company to grow the business. "Basically, what you're comparing is the benefit for having an activist go away versus the financial return they could have received by investing the company's cash in the business," says Chavern. "I'm not sure it makes much sense to say that shareholders at large should also be required to pay for activist campaigns because then you're making the rest of the shareholders pay to support a perspective which they may or may not agree with."

He adds that even though there are many reasons why activist hedge fund managers don't engage in most of the tactics of their raider predecessors, there are some similarities that go beyond greenmail. "Corporate raiders and activists both operate from the same theory that corporations they are engaging are fat and need to be disciplined, either in terms of cost cutting or divesting divisions," Chavern says. But he adds that unlike raiders, activists try to collaborate with management to achieve their goals and the returns they receive are distributed throughout the shareholder base.

Despite the perception by some that activists remain raider-like greenmail artists, this group of shareholders has emerged to become a unique investor class all on its own. Their growth in numbers and assets can be attributed to new funding sources. Public and corporate pension funds joining high-net-worth investors have given activists credibility and heft. Governance-style activists, in a post-Lehman Brothers environment, have unleashed a movement of institutional investors pressing boards to tie executives' compensation to performance. In fact, expect an all-encompassing reform of CEO pay package regulation to take place in Washington as lawmakers and regulators grapple with the financial crisis. Already, CEOs of mega-banks receiving government bailout dollars have strict executive compensation restrictions attached to those funds. Activist investors are not only generally supportive of the new pay regime, but they also plan to point to the regulatory changes to justify their own efforts to reform CEO compensation plans. To make sure executives are working for shareholders as much as for themselves, activists are installing independent directors on corporate boards. Armed with their governance agenda, activists are becoming a major force in the wheeling and dealing that takes place in the corporate world. Unlike many of their predecessors, who were interested in acquiring businesses only for the purpose of liquidating assets, many activists now spend much of their time working privately with executives to improve their investment's governance and share value.

The next few chapters delve deeper into what activists do to provoke changes at corporations, particularly when private, behind-the-scenes collaboration breaks down. How activists make investment decisions and what strategies they employ when agitating for change will all be discussed. With a deeper understanding of their tactics and strategies, we can get into the mind of the activist.

Chapter 2

Nuts and Bolts

How Activists Became Who They Are Today

From Value Investing to Proxy Contests and Other Activist Tactics

Before investors become activists, they have to first find the businesses they want to invest in, or as many of them like to put it, "target." That in itself is no small task considering the vast universe of public companies from which to choose.

Prior to pressing management to make changes, activists typically first buy stocks of companies they believe the stock market and Wall Street analysts have undervalued or ignored.

There are thousands of investors that make these kinds of passive investments every day. They are known as traditional *value* investors. In essence, these investors seek out stocks that are trading at a discount to the value of all their underlying assets, including debt and cash. Companies become pickings for value investors for a number of reasons. The stock market may be overreacting to bad news at the company, or perhaps a particular management team is not operating its business to optimal capacity. Most value investors today, whether they are mutual fund or hedge fund managers, are not activists.

In some circumstances, particularly with remnants of many high-flying Internet bubble companies of the late 1990s, a company has no or little debt and its cash reserves exceed its stock value. These companies, where the cash on the balance sheet is worth more than the whole company, are *really* extreme examples of value stocks and they are few and far between.

After all their research is completed value investors buy stocks that, for whatever reason, they believe are worth more than what they're paying for them. After buying the stock, value investors will sit back patiently and wait for their investment to improve in value. In many cases their stock's price improves slowly as the market adjusts to its true performance. But sometimes it takes a long time for an undervalued company's share value to improve in such a way that it reflects its real profits and revenues. In some cases, years go by and the stock still hasn't reached its "true" value. What to do then?

That's where activists take over. Most activists, in a way, are traditional value investors that have become impatient with their investment's poor stock performance and want to do something about it. Basically, they want to kick things into high gear. The activist still buys the same undervalued stock as the value investor, but instead of sitting around waiting for it to accrue in value, they are willing to push for changes and actually be a "catalyst" to unlock the stock's value in a shorter period of time. That means an activist will push the company to do something such as sell itself or buy back shares so that the stock value rises to its "natural" level. In the case of a sale, the company is purchased, hopefully, at a significantly higher share price. When a sale takes place, a premium on the trading price is offered and accepted and the value has been unlocked. That is, unless the activist thinks the stock is worth more than what is being offered for it, in which case the insurgency continues. Activists can also boost a company's share price and unlock value by facilitating a division sale or encouraging management to make certain operational changes.

Typically, activists will buy a large stake in a company, often 5 percent or more, with the intention of pressing management into making these kinds of changes. At times, traditionally passive value investors emerge from the shadows and decide that in a particularly egregious case they need to shake things up a bit at an investment they have been holding for a while. These are known as reluctant activists. Other activists will do their prodding quietly, without much fanfare, in private meetings with executives of the companies they target. Most high-profile value investors have dabbled in activism on occasion. Value investing guru Benjamin Graham engaged in activism at times, as did billionaire investor Michael Price. In 1996, Price publicly pressed Chase Manhattan Bank into merging with Chemical Bank.[1]

"The activist adds a wrinkle; they try to force an event to unlock the value in the shares," says Institutional Shareholder Services' (ISS) Christopher L. Young.

Investment bank Morgan Joseph & Company describes activists as individuals who are not prepared to hold a stock and wait for its price to rise, nor are their purchases typically intended as a first step in an ultimate acquisition of the company (though a few activists do bid and buy companies). Instead, activists seek to be the catalyst for meaningful gains at undervalued, often poorly managed, companies.

In many cases, the approach works. Phillip Goldstein, the co-founder of 14-year-old activist fund Opportunity Partners LP, has launched activist campaigns at roughly 40 companies since 1996. His fund, which was formed in 1993 with $700,000, has had positive returns in all but seven quarters since its inception to the end of 2006. (That's 49 positive quarters.) By the end of 2006, it (along with its sister funds) had more than $325 million in assets under management and averaged 16.46 percent net annual returns since its inception, while the Standard & Poor's (S&P) 500 returned an average of only 10.86 percent during the same period. That means $100,000 invested with Goldstein in 1993 would have produced $844,162 by the end of 2006, while placing the same amount with the S&P 500 would have only produced $423,000 in the same time frame.

"The only difference between value investors like Warren Buffet and activists is that the activist is willing to be a catalyst in a shorter period of time," Goldstein says.

Many activists have better returns than value investors, particularly in years when the markets are down. Activists do better than their rival hedge funds and value investor counterparts during periods of economic decline, largely because their efforts can produce critical changes at the companies they are holding in a way that is unrelated to overall market movements. But it is a lot of work that involves researching, litigating, and campaigning. The objective is to convince companies, shareholders, and their advisers that a particular change is necessary.

Most activist hedge fund managers have emerged from value investing backgrounds. But that is only a piece of what makes them tick. In addition to having a background working for corporate raiders, Carl Icahn and Asher Edelman both also have a history of risk and merger arbitrage investing.

Many successful insurgents come from a "risk arbitrage" background. In risk arbitrage, also known as merger arbitrage, a manager makes an investment in a company involved in a merger that hasn't been consummated yet. This investor takes the risk of investing in a stock at a certain price, anticipating that a proposed merger will be completed at a certain time for a certain price. The risk involves making a bet on whether the merging companies will gain the required shareholder and regulatory approval they need for the deal to be completed. Even if regulatory approval is assured, mergers arbitrageurs will make investments based on their expectation of when a transaction will close.

Merger or risk arbitrage is a subset of a broader category of investment tactics know as event-driven strategies. These investors take positions in companies involved in "special situations," such as companies emerging from bankruptcy or businesses anticipating some other major transformative event.

While waiting for that bet to come to fruition, some event-driven investors began to get irritated and a little impatient. These special-situation investors transformed themselves into activists who have started to press companies engaged in transactions or other events into making changes to prop up shareholder value. Others began to press companies to emerge from bankruptcy or other circumstances. "Event-driven managers are less likely nowadays to sit back and watch their investment's stock price get driven into the ground," says one New York investment banker.

Some activists have training in private equity investing. For example, Clifton S. Robbins left his job as a partner at private equity outfit Kohlberg Kravis Roberts & Company in 1999 and eventually founded Blue Harbour Group, a $1.2 billion hedge fund based in Greenwich, Connecticut, that engages cooperatively with directors behind the scenes.

Robbins prefers to call his strategy private equity in public capital because, unlike traditional activists who urge companies into changes they may not want, his approach is first to see whether a board or management is open to hearing his ideas. Only if executives are enthusiastic about Robbins's buying a stake and sharing his ideas will he invest in the company, usually by acquiring between 5 and 10 percent of the shares. Once he has gained the trust of executives and directors, Robbins reveals his connections in the private-equity world, including bankers, private-equity firm managers, and other advisers. Robbins and managers at the fund then work collaboratively with corporate insiders to improve value.

In many cases, that involves finding a private-equity company to acquire the business, but it can also mean stock buybacks or operational recommendations. Often, management teams in search of a private-equity partner will agree to hear what Robbins has to say. Sometimes deals are struck. Blue Harbour Group was a 10 percent shareholder of Yankee Candle when it agreed to be acquired by buyout firm Madison Dearborn LLC in October 2006 for $1.7 billion.[2] Robbins was also a large investor in *Reader's Digest,* when it was purchased by a consortium led by Ripplewood Holdings for $2.4 billion.[3]

Activist investor Warren Lichtenstein, cofounder of Steel Partners II, emerged from a background in private equity, risk arbitrage, and value investing. He began his career in 1987 as an analyst at New York–based hedge fund Para Partners, which engaged in these strategies. He then moved on to Ballantrae Partners, a value investing shop that used activist and private-equity tactics in 1989 to buy Damon Corporation a chain of laboratories for $320 million. Lichtenstein says these experiences molded him into the private-equity-like activist he is today. Steel Partners II isn't a hedge fund, nor is it a private-equity firm, even though it practices a little of both strategies. Instead, Lichtenstein prefers the moniker "Private Equity in Drag," which better describes his approach of engaging corporate executives to work on improving their businesses and the resulting improved stock valuations. "Our strategy is very similar to private equity, only we are longer-term players," Lichtenstein says.

Some activists come from both a value investing and mutual fund background. Activist Jeffrey Ubben got his start running a "deep value" fund between 1987 and 1995 for mutual fund Fidelity Investments. There he bought passive stakes in undervalued companies. But the fund grew too fast for him to handle. In a year-and-a-half period, it grew from $400 million to $5 billion, and Ubben found himself in a position where he had to buy stakes in hundreds of companies just to keep up with the inflows. "I was diluting my best positions and best ideas every day, and I was on the road to mediocrity," Ubben says. "I didn't know enough about my companies, and I began making investment decisions based on 20-minute meetings lumped on top of each other."

Ubben left Fidelity to become a managing partner at BLUM Capital Partners, where he took his value investing base of knowledge and applied it to a part-activist, part-private-equity style of investing. Instead of buying stakes in hundreds of companies, Ubben could concentrate his efforts on building relationships with management at a few companies in which Blum had large positions. At this point, Ubben expanded his repertoire of skills by learning how to become an independent director on corporate boards. "You have to hold people accountable," Ubben says. "Activism is about bringing risk capital to the boardroom."

But, ultimately, Blum Capital began to focus too much on striking deals than engaging management for Ubben's liking. He launched Stinton Capital, which took a more activist, governance-style approach. In 2000, he formed ValueAct Capital Partners LP, a private-equity-like activist hedge fund that has roughly $4.5 billion in assets. The San Francisco–based fund buys large stakes in a few companies—five new investment ideas a year—and presses managers to make changes. At ValueAct, Ubben says, he can concentrate his energy on his best investment ideas. ValueAct also bids for, and at times buys, some of the businesses it targets. Ubben took his Fidelity training of how to find a great undervalued business and married it with the activist strategy of buying a few big strategic block investments, sitting on boards and pushing to improve corporate share value.

Regardless of their background, most activists have one common trait: they are value investors, looking for cheap stocks that they believe, for whatever reason, are worth more than what they're paying for them. "We are value investors that all came from different walks of life that affect how we invest today," says Liberation's Emanuel Pearlman.

A good way to understand how these insurgent shareholders operate is to chronicle the transformation of one investor from passive value investor to activist. Lawrence J. Goldstein, managing member of hedge fund Santa Monica Partners LP in Larchmont, New York, was one such passive value investor. Until one day.

Goldstein got his value investor start researching companies for a major brokerage house in the 1960s. He describes his job at Burnham and Company as assistant to the assistant in the research department.

The investment bank in 1973 merged with another company and later became Drexel Burnham Lambert, a well-known brokerage house that rose to prominence due to its popularization of junk bonds, also known as high-yield debt. The firm later collapsed in 1990 after its high-profile star, Michael Milken, went to prison. In the 1980s, Milken, known as the "king of junk bonds," helped launch the world of the corporate raider by offering financing and the "highly confident letter," indicating that Drexel Burnham could provide financing to little-known investment managers seeking to take over businesses with hostile offers.

But before all that, Burnham and Company, it turns out, was a great place to get some basic value investment training. Goldstein's research department boss, Joe Kirschheimer, on occasion would ask him a question about a company that was too small for it to have any formal Wall Street coverage. Goldstein would get on the phone and began asking questions, creating his own research for these public companies that no one really knew much about. Goldstein was hooked. He began researching obscure companies and even specializing in small industries that interested no one else, such as the railroad freight car leasing industry, the brewing industry, and other small sectors. What he found was that many of the companies in these hidden industries actually performed quite well, but without attention from analysts on Wall Street, their stocks sagged. "I was always looking in the nooks and crannies of the market," Goldstein said. "I looked for the needles in the haystacks."

After a while, Goldstein realized that everyone knew something about all the companies trading on the New York Stock Exchange (NYSE). He estimated that 20 percent of the public companies traded on the NYSE and 80 percent of the research being produced by Wall Street research firms focused on just those businesses.

Sometime in the 1970s, a light bulb went off and Goldstein decided to start a fund looking at all those good companies that no one was looking at. He estimated that there were roughly 16,000 companies trading on the often unnoticed "pink sheets," over-the-counter securities markets in the 1960s and 1970s. Shortly after founding Santa Monica Partners, Goldstein created a slogan for his fund: "Stocks overlooked or ignored by otherwise intelligent investors."

Goldstein found many companies that were growing very rapidly, with record profits and little or no debt, but trading at incredibly low valuations. Bringing attention to these stocks would help improve their valuations, he thought. Along the way, Goldstein began noticing that some of the value companies he was invested in started to have lower earnings, but management continued to receive high salaries and unusual perks, such as country club memberships and fancy company cars.

One of Goldstein's value investments, First Years Inc., an infant products company based in Avon, Massachusetts, not only overcompensated executives, but shareholders were paying for the life insurance of the CEO and his family. At the same time, earnings were down, year after year. That got Goldstein steamed. He first approached First Years' CEO Marshall Sidman privately and pointed out that his perquisites, such as the life insurance policy, may be extreme. He was rebuffed.

It was then that Goldstein decided a proactive, public effort was in order. At that moment Goldstein changed from passive value investor to public activist. In 1988, Goldstein launched a proxy contest.

Proxy Contests: The Stick Approach to Activism (Leave Carrot at Home)

A key strategy for activists is the proxy contest. If executives are resistant to private or public pressure, an activist may want to nominate his or her own director candidates for election to the company's board.

These nominees are up against management-nominated directors. The goal for activists is typically to elect a few directors to the board, hoping that they will create enough of a dialogue with the rest of the board and management to stimulate change at the company. Or, less frequently, when permitted, activists may seek to install a full slate of directors with the goal of removing the chief executive or propelling the company to auction itself off to the highest bidder. In many cases, this approach may not be possible because companies, in a post-corporate raider environment, set up their board election rules in a way that allows only a minority of directors to be elected every year. This protects the company from the more extreme insurgents hoping to replace a full slate of management-backed directors and bring in their own candidates.

Santa Monica's Goldstein decided that he was no longer going to accept the fact that as a shareholder he was paying for First Years' CEO Seidman and his family's life insurance policy. Instead of selling his shares, as many other frustrated value investors might have done, Goldstein decided he would stick with the company and try to improve it, in part, by trying to bring in outsiders to its board through a proxy contest.

He launched two proxy contests in 1988 and 1989 to nominate directors at First Years. Both were unsuccessful in the traditional sense. Goldstein knew that they would fail even before he launched them. Sidman's family owned 54 percent of the company's shares, making it mathematically impossible for Goldstein to win the contest without Sidman's support—an unlikely prospect given the circumstances. "People said I was crazy because I could never win," Goldstein says.

But Goldstein's strategy was not to win the contest, but rather bring public pressure on the company. It was a "lose the battle, win the war" type of tactic and it worked. Each year in which Goldstein had a proxy contest, First Years management made changes making the company more accountable to shareholders. Sidman cut salaries, put in place an incentive-based bonus system, and began creating 60 to 70 new products a year with the help of newly hired product development people and marketing executives from Polaroid and Gillette, all at Goldstein's urging. Responding to Goldstein, the company also added two independent directors to the company's board, which previously had been comprised of a family of four, Sidman, his wife, son, and son-in-law. First Years' board also cut CEO salaries and set up a bonus plan. Unlike First Years, most companies have enough shares owned by outsiders (nonmanagement) that proxy contests launched by activists are mathematically winnable. A majority of participating shareholders, for example, backed activist hedge fund Pirate Capital's March 2006 proxy effort to install three directors on California-based aerospace engineering company GenCorp's 10-person board.[4] Winning seats on GenCorp's board was not an easy task, particularly since its $1.1 billion stock market capitalization meant that there were a huge number of shareholders Pirate Capital needed to win over. But the activist did get the support of numerous other insurgent types that piled into the company after them.

According to the latest Institutional Shareholder Services report, activists are turning to the proxy contest to get things done more than ever. During the first six months of 2006, there were 80 proxy fights, according to FactSet Research Systems' SharkRepellent.net. That's more than the 54 contests in all of 2005 and 40 in 2004. Investment bank Morgan Joseph & Company Inc. estimates that hedge fund managers succeeded at getting directors elected to corporate boards in more than 35 percent of the proxy fight campaigns it analyzed in 2006.[5]

But that number tells only part of the story. The majority of proxy fights don't appear in those numbers because companies either respond to the threat of a proxy contest or they settle in advance of the contest. Often, the private or public prospect of a proxy contest is enough to get the ball rolling at corporations. April Klein, associate professor at Stern School of Business at New York University, in a September 2006 study, "Hedge Fund Activism," examined the activities of a sample group of 155 activist campaigns engaged by 102 different hedge funds. She concluded that in many cases the perceived threat of a proxy fight is sufficient for the activist to gain its goal or achieve board representation.[6]

Phillip and Lawrence Goldstein (no relation) joined forces to pressure Blair Corporation, a catalog and online seller of men's and women's apparel, to sell its consumer-finance receivables division. Lawrence Goldstein recalls sitting in a room with Blair Corp.'s CEO, CFO, and VP of administration and saying, "You know, we do proxy contests." It wasn't a formal warning that they planned to launch a proxy contest, but it was a "veiled threat" of one, says Lawrence Goldstein.

But before they took steps to formally nominate a slate of directors, it became apparent that a proxy contest wasn't necessary. The company heeded the warning and announced plans to consider strategic options (code for taking actions to auction off its consumer-finance receivables division). In April 2005, the unit in question was sold for $176 million to Dallas-based payment processing services provider Alliance Data Systems Corporation.[7] The company also repurchased more than 50 percent of its shares at a substantial premium to the market price.

Other times, companies settle with activists by adding a few dissident shareholder candidates to the board after insurgents threaten a proxy contest. Relational Investors Ralph Whitworth points out that he often seeks settlements that allow him to gain at least two seats on corporate boards because the presence of a second dissident director typically gives him the two votes he needs to call for a full board vote on any of his proposals. With a board vote, dissident directors can put everyone on record about a particular strategic issue.

Many governance-style activists are happy to settle with companies if it means they can gain director positions. A seat on the board means greater say in making sure the business is run with the best interest of shareholders in mind. Other types of settlements require the company to bring in some new independent directors to the board. Activists are often satisfied with this approach because it typically means the board is replacing directors that they believe aren't accountable to shareholders. There generally are more settlements between dissident investors and company directors than one might imagine due to the extensive media coverage of higher-profile proxy battles.

A settlement typically happens when executives recognize that they have little chance of winning a proxy contest or they want to appease a vocal activist that has been pressing for changes. Settlements can often save executives the embarrassment of losing a very public proxy contest that could be damaging to their reputation. They often take place at the last minute, literally a few hours before an annual meeting. Sometimes it takes that long for executives to see the writing on the wall and realize they will likely lose the contest. ISS's Young reports that of 51 activist campaigns the proxy advisory service followed through the first eight months of 2006 that began as proxy fights, 31 were settled.

Take Third Point LLC manager Daniel Loeb's effort at Ligand Pharmaceutical. In November 2005, the New York–based activist announced his plan to nominate a slate of eight candidates to replace the entire board of the San Diego–based pharmaceutical company. That decision came after behind-the-scenes negotiations to have the company consider strategic alternatives such as a sale of assets did not prove fruitful. One month later, Ligand and Loeb settled on increasing the board from 8 to 11 directors and adding 3 new individuals chosen by Third Point. Roughly one year from when the settlement was struck, in September 2006, Ligand agreed to sell its oncology product line to one buyer and its important Avinza pain treatment rights to another buyer.[8] The company also agreed to sell the land its corporate headquarters sat on along with two undeveloped properties for $47.6 million.[9] Ligand then leased back its building, and Loeb, who named his fund after a break at Malibu Surfrider Beach, was satisfied.

In mid-2006, two activist hedge fund managers, Pembridge Capital Management LLC and Crescendo Partners II LP, launched a proxy contest to oust three directors, including the chairman and CEO of Topps Company Inc. from the board and replace them with three of their own candidates. The trading cards and strategy game maker hoped to win the contest but as the meeting approached it became increasingly clear to management that things were not going to turn out as they had hoped.

Shortly after the annual meeting began, Topps called off the contest and agreed to a partial compromise. Topps would include the three dissident directors being nominated by the activist fund managers to its board, but company CEO Arthur Shorin would remain a director. The last-minute settlement allowed Topps to keep its top executive on the board. "The Topps contest shows that sometimes companies have a misguided sense of how much support they will receive from the shareholder base," Young says.

Even though public settlements are more prevalent than completed proxy fights, there are additional behind-the-scenes agreements between executives and shareholders that most collectors of activist statistics don't even consider. In some cases, an insurgent raises the prospect of a settlement in private conversations with executives. Opportunity's Phillip Goldstein says he is very effective at building relationships with executives in private. "I always try to talk to management and tell them, 'We think you've got a problem here; let's sit down and discuss the alternatives here,'" Goldstein says.

Goldstein, whose hedge fund is based in Pleasantville, New York, privately met with management of one company he wanted to see consider selling some assets. The CEO agreed to sell a division, but not before Goldstein expressed some urgency on the matter in a confidential conversation: "You're leaving us in a position where we may have to do a proxy fight," Goldstein told the firm's CEO. "They agreed to make the changes, and it was all done behind the scenes. It would not have been possible without the behind-the-scenes negotiations."

A major incentive for both activists and companies to settle the proxy fight early is cost. According to ISS, in 2001, activists that mounted proxy contests against companies spent an average of $319,000 per battle, compared with $620,000 by corporations. In 2006, activist investor Seneca Capital began efforts to launch a traditional proxy contest to replace three directors at Reliant Energy Inc. By April, the energy company and insurgent reached a settlement. Reliant agreed to bring in a director that would be appointed by another substantial investor, and Seneca agreed to drop its contest. But before the settlement was reached, Reliant put together an estimate of what a proxy fight with Seneca would cost. In a Securities and Exchange Commission (SEC) filing, Reliant wrote its investors that it had expected to pay roughly $1.5 million, not including litigation, to carry out the contest. The hefty price included a $500,000 fee that would have gone to proxy solicitor Innisfree M&A Inc. so its employees could petition Reliant shareholders to vote for the company's slate of directors. Proxy solicitors are vote collectors that also campaign on behalf of their corporate or shareholder clients. Other costs listed in the SEC filing included payments to an outside counsel and other advisers; printing and mailing costs, as well as certain fees to banks and brokerage houses; and a fee to hire an independent inspector for the election. Even though the contest was settled on April 18, Reliant had already spent roughly $200,000 by April 13, according to the SEC filing.

Not all elections go well for activists. When a dissident insurgent does not have decent support for its nominees, it may be time to reexamine the insurgency campaign. This was the case for Opportunity Partners Goldstein at Warwick Valley Telephone Company in 2003. He argued that Warwick was, for legal purposes, an investment firm because of its passive ownership of a minority stake in a cell phone operator, which accounted for most of the incumbent telephone company's value. But when he launched a proxy contest that year to elect a director to the board, he lost 85 percent to 15 percent. "It was time to reevaluate our plan," he says.

Activism without Proxy Contests (or Even Threats of One)

In many campaigns, activists don't even raise the prospect of a proxy contest. As a matter of fact, they specifically say that they won't consider a proxy contest to elect director candidates as a strategy to make changes.

"We have no interest in being shackled by the membership rules of a Club Carreker 'insider,'" Robert Chapman wrote Carreker CEO John Carreker on June 7, 2006. "To be honest, I begin to retch at the image of my flying into Dallas to attend a board meeting as a minority director outweighed by the group-think-driven crew listed in the addressee section above. I have nightmares involving my choking down gourmet tuna sandwiches and uninformed, "long-term" business judgments, both being served in abundant quantity by you and your Texas 'pardners.'"

Activists can become frustrated with minority representation on corporate boards, particularly ones where the majority is not heeding what they or the shareholder-nominated directors are telling them. Another problem is that once on the board, activists have restrictions on how they sell their stock. This can be a frustrating situation should they find the investment sours to a point where they believe no amount of activism could improve the company. Having these kinds of prohibitions also may go against an activist's big-picture investment schemes, making it more difficult to enter into new opportunities when others stall.

But activism that doesn't include even the threat of a proxy contest raises the question of how investors can pressure companies without it. If managers know a dissident investor will not try to replace the company's board, or even a few directors, how can anything the activist does make a difference? How can one succeed at pressing for change without at least threatening a proxy contest? The answer has everything to do with embarrassing executives and mobilizing the shareholder base.

In a nutshell, this approach requires the activist to shame a target company and its board into removing its CEO or making some other changes such as selling a division or the whole business. The activist's goal is to create enough of a public outcry that a critical mass of other investors, including institutions, supports their insurgency campaign. As discussed earlier, Chapman Capital's Chapman describes this strategy as a "social lever" approach. This kind of pressure could involve publicizing an activist position and drawing attention to the company's underperformance or its executives' shortcomings, reports Morgan Joseph.

To make a public complaining campaign work effectively, activists employing the tactic also seek to expose corporate executives to embarrassment and public ridicule by outlining grievances with the company in public SEC filings. Sometimes this is done by writing letters to a target company's CEO, pointing out management problems, and including those in the filings. Other times, an insurgent's concerns are just listed in the filings. Once submitted to the SEC, the company's existing shareholder base, other activists, and a large swath of institutional investors can easily access and read the insurgent's assertions and decide whether they will back him or not. In effect, the public filings can publicize their efforts.

To get more public exposure, recently, activists are taking their public campaign efforts up a notch by supplementing these filings with press releases e-mailed directly to reporters. Activists are also hiring public relations firms to get the message out about their insurgencies. In December 2006, Chapman launched a public relations campaign to urge Cypress Semiconductor Corporation to reorganize itself and take itself private.[10] The tactic this time focused primarily on bringing attention to his concerns to existing and potential investors through a multifaceted media strategy. He sent reporters a press release that included a letter Chapman had just sent to Cypress Semiconductor's CEO.[11] The idea is to prompt financial publications to write articles about their efforts to spread the word about their campaign to other like-minded investors. Articles written in financial publications add to the public pressure activists can exert on management because their readers are typically investors that may follow the insurgent's lead. Steven Howard, partner at Thacher Proffitt & Wood LLP in New York, says the phenomenon of hedge funds hiring public relations firms and launching promotional campaigns represents a sea change in how this investor group operates. Two decades ago, hedge funds were a private discrete industry, he says, that would never talk to reporters. "Now there are hundreds seeking press coverage," Howard says.

Santa Monica Partners Lawrence Goldstein points out that his proxy contest at First Years may not have received such an outpouring of support had the local newspaper, *Quincy Patriot Ledger*, not written a series of articles in 1988 and 1989 pointing out concerns about executive compensation. Goldstein says that he believes the letters and articles were particularly effective at generating a response because First Years CEO Sidman lived in a small community, Avon, Massachusetts, where word can get around easily. Goldstein says he was able to gain the interest of a reporter at the newspaper by sending her letters he had written to First Years CEO. "It embarrassed the heck out of him [Sidman]," Goldstein says.

The "noise pollution" campaign is more effective when more activist-type investors buy the shares previously owned by the company's passive institutional and retail investor base. This transformation takes place predominantly at smaller public companies, typically those that have less than $200 million stock market capitalizations.

But even if the shareholder base doesn't change, activists are successful with a public pressure approach if they can convince a large contingent of existing shareholders to support them. The goal, of course, is the same for activists that employ this tactic or any other insurgent strategies: improved stock prices.

Once an activist has the backing of a critical mass of other investors, the next step is to make sure executives know that *fill-in-the-blank number* of shareholders are unhappy with a particular strategy. A part of that effort is to convince retail and institutional investors to send their own letters supporting activists to companies. "Inducing a 'long-term' and globally respected top owner like Fidelity to write the board a letter supporting our platform was instrumental to our campaign," Chapman says, referring to his effort to change the direction of Cinar.

Justin Cable, director of research for Global Hunter Securities, says Chapman's public exposure strategy does work. "Even though Chapman's tactic is to produce change through public embarrassment rather than board activism, his opinion does matter and it does impact the reputation of targeted CEOs," Cable says. "I wouldn't want to be a CEO on the other side of that battle."

Chapman employed a public-pressure tactic for the first time at American Community Properties Trust (ACPT) in 2000. After his activist campaign was over, Chapman claimed credit for various improvements at the St. Charles, Maryland, real estate investment and development trust company. ACPT sold numerous acres of land, cut its debt load, and created an annual dividend of 40 cents a share each year. It also sped up its rate of asset liquidation and reduced its leveraged balance sheet.

But the changes didn't happen overnight. After repeated attempts to contact ACPT chairman and CEO Michael Wilson to discuss a unit sale, Chapman took things to a brand new level by writing a letter to him on March 30, 2000, that was included with SEC filings. Here's an excerpt:

> As your largest non-Wilson family partner in ACPT, Chapman Capital's Chap-Cap Partners can definitively label your behavior as "investor-unfriendly." Our group has recorded time lapses of as long as one year of delay in return phone calls from you, even after daily follow-up messages were left with your secretary. Recently, ACPT president Edwin Kelly (who was being paid $275,000 per year) has joined the obstruction parade, returning our three-phone messages-per-day efforts only after an outrageous three-week delay.

By February 2001, Chapman made another SEC filing. This time he outlined a brief conversation he had with Wilson on the telephone. It is safe to say that Wilson probably did not expect the exchange would receive the kind of public exposure it ultimately did, Chapman says. In the filing, Chapman outlined how in February Wilson answered one of Chapman's calls and said: "You're a f---ing pain in the ass and we don't want to talk to you." Mr. Wilson then disconnected from the telephone "conversation."

According to the filing, those comments came after Chapman had asked why Wilson had been ignoring him, ACPT's largest shareholder. Activists tend to be either the largest shareholders or in the top three at most targeted small and mid-capitalization companies.

The public exposure campaign succeeded at attracting other investors to Chapman's cause and ultimately pushing the company to change its ways. And no proxy fight was necessary. "Our communications were designed to shine a klieg light on management's weaknesses, failures, and transgressions," Chapman says. "A lynch mob often results, as our courage emboldens other, previously passive owners to join the revolution."

Since Chapman's ACPT effort, many other activists have followed his lead and launched public-pressure campaigns that include detailing their grievances in letters attached to public regulatory filings. Not everyone is enthusiastic about all activists that launch public campaigns. Gary Lutin, president of investment bank Lutin & Company and a shareholder consultant, says some activists engage in these pressure tactics at the wrong companies for the wrong reasons. Lutin says he worries that activists will launch public pressure campaigns at companies, not because the management is operating poorly, but because the activist knows it can extort some response, such as a share buyback that may not be in the long-term interest of the company. "You can make a profit by shakedowns," Lutin says. "Some activists pick a company with timid management; vulnerability is one of the things they like."

SharkRepellent calculates that in 2006 there were 122 activist campaigns that did not involve proxy contests. As part of these campaigns, shareholders pestered companies to complete stock buybacks, increase dividends, sell the company or make other changes. New York University's Klein explains in her report that some public campaigns that have nothing to do with gaining board seats end up with one. However, her study also shows that activists that threaten or go through with a proxy fight generally have a better chance of attaining their goals (see Table 2.1).

Table 2.1 Relation Between Proxy Fights and Success of Activist in Achieving Their Goal and Obtaining at Least One Seat of the Target Firm's Board of Directors

		Achieve Goal?		Gain One Seat?	
	Num	**Yes**	**No**	**Yes**	**No**
Proxy fight	18	13 (72%)	5 (28%)	13 (72%)	5 (28%)
Threaten proxy fight	42	26 (62%)	16 (38%)	24 (57%)	18 (43%)
No proxy fight	95	54 (57%)	41 (43%)	31 (33%)	64 (67%)
Total	155	93 (60%)	62 (40%)	68 (44%)	87 (56%)

SOURCE: April Klein, associate professor Stern School of Business, New York University; Emanuel Zur, doctoral student, Stern School of Business, NYU, "Hedge Fund Activism," (September 2006): 43.

Liberation's Emanuel Pearlman says that even though it's difficult for an activist to sell his stake once on a corporate board, a strategy that includes either the threat of a proxy contest or an actually proxy contest seeking to elect directors to force change cannot be underestimated. "If you can get your agenda accomplished by putting people on the board, then proxy fights are a key strategy to employ," Pearlman said. "Sometimes you have to put pressure on companies, and the only way to do that is through a proxy contest."

The Expedited Proxy Contest: Written Consent Solicitations

From time to time, insurgents aren't even willing to wait until their target company's annual meeting to launch a proxy contest. In certain circumstances, when permitted, activists will ask other shareholders to oust company directors via a "written consent solicitation." This dreary-sounding but effective strategy works only at corporations that have bylaws—written rules the business must follow—that permit it. Most don't.

To employ written consent solicitations the activist distributes proxy documents to other shareholders asking them to sign a card saying they want to vote their shares to remove certain directors from the board and replace them with candidates nominated by the dissident. If investors with more than half of the total shares outstanding vote to remove the incumbent directors, the activist wins and his nominees are installed on the board.

The campaign is different from a traditional proxy contest because it does not take place on the day of the company's annual meeting. As a matter of fact, no meeting must take place for the consents to be approved and for the directors to be removed and replaced. "It's really a matter of timing," says David Drake, president of Georgeson Inc., a New York–based proxy solicitor. "The written consent solicitation process allows insurgents to act immediately rather than having them wait for the company's next annual meeting."

Shareholders participating in written consents have two options. They can return the filled in proxy card to the dissident requesting the removal of the incumbent directors or they can do nothing. If the dissident calculates that more than half of all shares have been voted in favor of removing the directors and putting in their slate, then they take the cards to the company for official verification. But, at that point, the contest isn't over yet.

Typically, in these contests, the company will send out their own letters to shareholders known as "consent revocation cards" pitching their argument why incumbent directors should remain on the board and asking shareholders to fill these documents in and send them to the company, in effect canceling their vote supporting insurgents. So when a dissident shareholder brings his cards in to the company, there is a chance that management has a sufficient number of canceled vote cards to nullify the insurgent's solicitation. "You show up at the company with your consent cards, but you don't know what the company has," says one investor.

Also, normally, there are votes that will be ineligible for a variety of reasons. If the card isn't signed correctly or it is misfiled, it's disqualified. Corporations can also argue that the card was solicited illegally. Think hanging chads, dimpled chads, and pregnant chads in Gore v. Bush in 2000. As in a traditional proxy contest, a proxy solicitor is often hired by both the dissident and the company to communicate each side's position with the rest of the investor base. Proxy advisory firms such as ISS research and make recommendations to their institutional investor clients on whether to support the insurgents candidates.

A written consent solicitation proxy contest was employed recently by Washington Redskins owner Daniel Snyder. As a dissident investor, Snyder, who manages Ashburn, Virginia–based investment vehicle Red Zone LLC, used a written consent solicitation to overthrow the board of struggling amusement park operator Six Flags Inc. and take control himself. In November 2005, Snyder announced victoriously that more than 50 percent of shareholders sent back consent solicitation proxies voting to remove the company's CEO and chief financial officer from the board and replacing them with his own candidates. It was only a matter of time before Snyder controlled the whole board and could bring in his own CEO, former ESPN executive Mark Shapiro.[12]

Snyder took advantage of his operational experience and sold investors on his promise of improving the amusement park operator's business plan and profile. To do this, Snyder assured Six Flags' institutional shareholder base that the new extreme and not-so-extreme sports, music, and television cartoon characters he could bring to the chain would attract more visitors. Whether Snyder, now in the driver's seat, can turn around Six Flags is still yet to be seen. Early indications seem to show that he's having some trouble.

Written solicitations come with pros and cons for both executives and shareholders. Corporate directors and executives have a great deal of difficulty with written consents because they do not know how long the whole process will take to be completed. They can decide to invest a great deal of time, energy, and corporate "war chest" money to promote their point of view, but the whole procedure can be over before they can get their message across to investors.

David Brown, partner at Alston & Bird LLP in Washington, draws a contrast between traditional proxy contests and political elections. "When you know the corporate election is on December 14, you do a lot of campaigning, soliciting, and planning in anticipation of that date," Brown says. "With written consent solicitations, the company and incumbent directors have no way of knowing when the process is going to end, and they have difficulty planning for it because it could be over tomorrow."

In some cases, a written consent solicitation can be over very quickly, leaving company CEOs blindsided. Activist Emanuel Pearlman once completed a whole written consent solicitation process in two days. In 1991, Pearlman was a general partner at hedge fund Gemini Partners LP, where he worked with another activist, Arthur Goldberg. He launched a traditional proxy contest to oust directors at Boston-based dental supplier Healthco International Inc., as part of his effort to pressure the company to auction itself off. But Healthco's two owners, Marvin and Michael Cyker, canceled the meeting a few hours before it was scheduled to take place, anticipating that the outcome would not be to their liking.

Pearlman, a 9.9 percent Healthco shareholder, quickly figured out that he could start a written consent solicitation and possibly remove the board with this approach. After two days of collecting consent forms from all of Healthco's major holders (who had been planning to vote for Gemini's slate in the proxy contest), Pearlman and others at Gemini walked into the office of Healthco's CEO with an official tally of more than 50 percent of all the shares outstanding represented in favor of removing the board. After Healthco decided to fight the decision in court, Gemini agreed to a settlement. Healthco agreed to drop its lawsuit, and in exchange Gemini received four director positions on the nine-member board. Shortly after that, Healthco sold itself to the buyout shop Hicks, Muse & Company Inc. for $225 million.

Pearlman says the dissident definitely has the advantage when written consents are permitted. "It's like a giant game of chicken," he says. "You don't have to have a meeting and management never knows when they are going to lose."

There are problems, however, such as figuring out exactly who holds the shares. In a classic proxy contest, the company will set a date usually at least two month in advance of the annual meeting, known as a "record" date. Only shareholders who have purchased shares either before or on that date can vote at the meeting. That means both the insurgent and directors generally know who holds what prior to the director election and can plan accordingly.

However, there is some confusion already around record dates. Corporations are required by SEC rules to send out notices of record dates to brokers, banks, and other intermediaries 20 days prior to the record date before an annual meeting. These intermediaries are not required to provide that information to shareholders and, in some circumstances, activist hedge fund managers complain that the record date hasn't been circulated in time for them to make thoughtful investment decisions.

One agitated activist explained how he acquired a stake in a corporation expecting he would have the right to vote those shares but later was informed that the record date had passed and he didn't have the voting rights for shares he had recently purchased. Meanwhile, the investor who sold it to him received a proxy statement in the mail entitling him to vote the shares. In other words, even though the seller no longer owned the stake in the company, he was eligible to vote the shares at the meeting. At the other end of the spectrum, activists can take advantage of record dates by hiking their stake from, let's say, 1 percent to 4 percent on the record date, and then turn around and sell it the same day. This allows them to "overvote" at a key meeting, whether it is a special shareholder meeting or annual meeting, without making a significant investment.

But with written consent solicitations, the mechanics are even cloudier. Usually, the date of record is the day when the company first receives a written consent. The dissidents will send the first consent (for their own shares) with a form of certified delivery that requires acknowledgment by the corporate secretary that it was received so the record date can be set. In some circumstances, the record date can be another date established by management.

There are aspects of the written approach that favor corporations over the dissidents. Shareholders launching a written consent solicitation must gain the approval of more than 50 percent of the outstanding shares—all the shares available for voting. Comparatively, it is much easier to win a traditional proxy contest where activists need just the support of a majority of *participating* share votes for the insurgency to succeed.

To illustrate this, imagine that an activist is trying to pressure for changes at a company with 100 million shares outstanding. In both a proxy contest and a written consent solicitation election, a significant number of investors just don't vote, so perhaps only 70 million shares are voted. In a traditional proxy contest, the dissident knows he needs only to attain more than 35 million of the share vote or 36 percent of the outstanding shares. In a written consent solicitation, there is still a large chunk of investors who will not vote, but the insurgent must have the votes of 50 million shares plus one additional share for his slate to win.

If a company has a broad and diverse shareholder base, a dissident may have a particularly difficult time gaining sufficient support. That's because it's hard to get smaller retail investors to respond to consent solicitations. Many retail investors say the consents look mysterious. They wonder who the insurgent is and why they keep receiving requests from somebody who is not in the company's management.

But at many small public companies with a fewer number of shares outstanding, dissidents can count on the support of other insurgent-type investors who have accumulated large stakes. Insurgents characteristically launch these kinds of written consent solicitation campaigns when they know a large chunk of the shareholder base already supports their agenda.

For example, Third Point's Dan Loeb launched a written consent solicitation in September 2006 at Nabi Biopharmaceuticals only after he had a general idea that two other major shareholders, Harvest Management LLC and Knott Partners Management LLC, supported his plan. Cumulatively, they owned roughly 30 percent of the outstanding shares of the biotech company. In this circumstance, Third Point attempted to reach common ground with Nabi by proposing to end the solicitation if the company agreed to a series of conditions, including one proposal permitting the activists to name two directors as long as they weren't employed by the hedge fund. Nabi made a counteroffer, which Loeb rejected. In November, a settlement was reached and Loeb gained two seats on the drug company's board. By February 2007, Nabi's CEO and chairman, Thomas McLain, who had been heavily criticized by Loeb for being unable to produce profits, resigned.[13]

In September 2006, Icahn took the written consent route at ImClone Systems Inc., a biotech company that was made famous for its connections to Martha Stewart. The domestic diva served a six-month jail term for purportedly lying to federal investigators about selling ImClone shares prior to news being released about a 2001 regulatory setback for its cancer drug Erbitux. Issues related to ImClone's promotion and development of Erbitux initially piqued Icahn's interest in the company and set the stage for the written consent solicitation. Investor support for Icahn was strong. On September 28, a group of institutions, including CAM North America LLC, Smith Barney Fund Management, and Salomon Brothers Asset Management, reported an 11.3 percent stake and sent a letter to ImClone explaining that they were supporting Icahn's consent solicitation. By October, ImClone had folded its cards. Its interim CEO agreed to step down, and Icahn was named by the company to its board.[14] As part of that agreement, Icahn agreed to cancel his written consent solicitation.

Despite activist efforts to utilize written consent solicitations at ImClone, Six Flags, and Healthco, the tactic is still rarely employed. Insurgents usually don't make use of this technique simply because most U.S. corporations expressly outlaw it in their company charters, a written policy, or rules of the corporation. Company laws typically say that directors can be elected only at annual meetings and in no other way. In some circumstances, according to corporate charter documents, investors need 100 percent of outstanding shares to act by written consent, a threshold that is almost mathematically impossible to achieve. In fact, it's just another way of saying to the investor that written consent solicitations are prohibited. Investors and companies often bicker about whether written consent solicitations at some companies are permitted by Delaware law.

Corporations, particularly those struggling businesses that are attractive activist targets, often permit written consent provisions in their bylaws because they want procedures in place to give investors the ability to quickly endorse debt refinancing programs in cases when shareholder approval is required for those actions. But having such a provision in place also makes the company vulnerable to dissident shareholders seeking to bring in their own director candidates.

Alston & Bird's Brown contends that, as with traditional proxy contests, in many circumstances activists will launch a written consent solicitation even if they know it has no chance of being successful. Often, corporate executives realize early on that if they do not effect the change a dissident may request, another written consent solicitation or proxy contest will likely be in the works sometime down the road—and most likely, more people will support it then. "If an insurgent loses in a close vote, he might still win his real goal, which is to force change at the company," Brown says.

Special Shareholder Meeting: Another Speedy Way to the Proxy Contest

Another tactic often employed by insurgents to expedite their quest for change is the special shareholder meeting. These are extraordinary meetings set to bring together shareholders and company officials to vote on a particular issue. Corporate directors often will call these meetings to have investors vote on a merger proposal, debt issuance, or changes to a corporate bylaw. But, in many circumstances, activist hedge fund managers will also call special shareholder meetings, typically to nominate their own director candidates, if they are permitted by company bylaws to do so.

That's why, like written consent solicitations, companies in the United States often set up their bylaws to expressly prohibit investors from calling these meetings. But if corporate charters permit the measure and provisions involved don't come with extreme conditions, dissidents are usually quick to jump on the opportunity it offers. Other countries, including Canada, the United Kingdom, Sweden, and even Ukraine, have regulations prohibiting companies from blocking significant investors from calling these meetings.

Special shareholder meetings can provide the same expedited time frame as a written consent solicitation. One major difference relates to the amount of votes insurgents need to win director election contests. In most cases, activists need to attain the support of only a majority of participating shareholders at a special shareholder meeting, rather than the majority of outstanding shares the insurgent typically requires with written consent solicitations.

Sometimes shareholders must send out a written consent solicitation asking other investors to approve their request for a special shareholder meeting. That happens at companies that have bylaws requiring a certain number of shareholders to agree to call a special shareholder meeting. Companies often seek to protect themselves by reserving the right in their bylaws to pick when that special shareholder meeting will take place.

Pearlman, now manager of New York–based Liberation Investment Group LLC, a fund with roughly $100 million in assets under management, in September launched a written consent solicitation campaign to obtain the 10 percent of outstanding shares he needed to call a special shareholder meeting at Multimedia Games Inc., an Austin, Texas–based maker of electronic bingo games, systems, and video lottery terminals.

Since Liberation already had 8.4 percent, getting the other 1.6 percent was not difficult. Pearlman planned to pit three candidates against the company's slate of directors at the special meeting, but the election was called off after the company agreed to a settlement. As part of the agreement, Pearlman was added to the board, along with one of his nominees, Neil Jenkins, a casino industry executive. Multimedia Games also agreed to have its nomination and corporate governance committees hire an executive search firm to find an independent director to put on the board, which would be expanded from five to seven as part of the deal. In return, Pearlman agreed to call off his contest.[15]

While no special shareholder meeting took place at Multimedia Games, one did occur in October 2005 at Computer Horizons Corporation. Dissident hedge fund managers at Crescendo Partners II LP called for one such meeting at the Mountain Lakes, New Jersey, information technology company. Shareholders voted to replace all five management-backed directors with a slate of candidates nominated by Crescendo, including the hedge fund's managing director, Eric Rosenfeld.[16] The new board then fired Computer Horizons CEO William Murphy and replaced him with a Crescendo recommendation, Dennis Conroy.[17] The new company proceeded over the subsequent year to do what activists were seeking all along: break up the company. Computer Horizons' three divisions were sold to three industry buyers for a cumulative $152 million. "The special shareholder meeting expedited the whole activist effort so we didn't have to wait for the annual meeting," says Arnaud Ajdler, Crescendo Partners managing director. "But since most companies in the U.S. don't allow a special shareholder meeting this was an unusual opportunity for us."

Learning about proxy contests, consent solicitations, and public-pressure tactics helps outsiders get into an activist shareholder's mind. It gives us a sense of some of the different tools they take advantage of when launching campaigns at companies. Activists come from a wide variety of backgrounds, and there are numerous considerations they must take into account before launching a campaign. Is the company undervalued? Do its bylaws permit written consent solicitations? Can I expedite change by calling for an extraordinary meeting?

Each activist employs their own specialized approach, typically based on a history of trial and error. Chapman focuses much of his energy on public-pressure campaigns, while Opportunity Partners' Goldstein launches or threatens proxy contests to gain leverage at target companies. But activists are adaptable. Since each company comes with different challenges and solutions, even tactical specialists must be ready to adeptly move quickly from one strategy to the next. Depending on the circumstances, a multiplicity of strategies may be considered to get the job done. Whether employing social lever activist campaigns or down and dirty proxy contests, each activist has the same goal in mind: share value creation.

The next few chapters take a look at some additional activist strategies and approaches. Insurgencies sometimes work best when activists engage executives in private conversations. Other times, a public campaign is necessary. The next chapter considers in more detail how public and private activist campaigns works and when is the best time to use them. It also looks at activists who work together in groups or travel together in herds to accomplish their goals. Activists are beginning to quietly understand that if they help each other out, they can accomplish their goals with greater frequency. But just because a pack of established, highly reputable insurgents all take on one company doesn't necessarily mean their collective skills will provoke the intended catalyst.

Chapter 3

The Pack

How Activists Are Working Together (But Not Officially)

Third Point's Dan Loeb wrote a letter to Star Gas Partners LP's president and CEO, Irik Sevin, making this recommendation:

> It is time for you to step down from your role as CEO and director so that you can do what you do best: retreat to your waterfront mansion in the Hamptons where you can play tennis and hobnob with your fellow socialites.

In another part of the letter, Loeb also complained that Sevin's "various acquisition and operational blunders" cost the company $570 million. Loeb also described how he tried unsuccessfully to contact Star Gas management several times through numerous phone calls. "The matter of repairing the mess you have created should be left to professional management and those that have an economic stake in the outcome," he added.

The letter, which was written in February 2005, was neatly attached to a Securities and Exchange Commission (SEC) filing known as a Schedule 13D.

Investors are required to submit Schedule 13D filings to the SEC within 10 days of owning 5 percent or more of a stock of a particular public company when they have plans to communicate some strategic options for the corporation, such as seeking to influence the control of the business, to other shareholders or company executives. At the time Loeb filed the Schedule 13D including the letter to Sevin, he owned a 6 percent stake in the energy company.

These filings are made public for anyone to read and can be found easily through various online services including the SEC's free electronic data gathering analysis and retrieval (EDGAR) database along with other corporate filings such as annual and quarterly company reports. An investor, activist or not, who owns less than a 5 percent stake in a company, is generally not required to make a public filing with the SEC.

A passive investor with 5 percent or more of a company who has no intention of agitating for change must make a less detailed Schedule 13G filing with the SEC. Unlike the 13D filing, 13G's must only be made 45 days after the end of the calendar year. So, an investor with no strategic plans for the company could technically buy a huge stake and sell it within the same year and the disclosure would not need to be made until much later. In the Schedule 13D form, activists are required to fill out various sections identifying themselves and their investment vehicles. A key section, "Item 4. Purpose of Transaction," must be completed, describing their intentions at the company. This is the section other prospective investors quickly seek out to learn about the activist's intentions. In the item 4 section of the filing, activists explain whether they want to see the company auction itself, sell a division, or anything else.

Insurgents like Loeb and Robert Chapman take advantage of the 13D form for their "social lever" public agitation campaigns at companies. After quickly describing a few goals for the company in the "Item 4" section, they will typically file so-called poison pen letters filled with pages of analysis about the company. These letters, like Loeb's missive to Star Gas CEO Sevin, are attached at the bottom of the 13D filing. As discussed earlier, this is part of their public relations campaign to gain the support of other investors they anticipate will be scrutinizing the filing for information about the company and its share improvement potential.

Any two or more investors who have communicated with each other similar intentions for the company are required to file a joint 13D filing outlining how they work together as a group to engage or possibly pressure management into making changes. Group filings are becoming a common occurrence. A September 2006 study, "Hedge Fund Activism, Corporate Governance and Firm Performance," reports that a quarter of 110 activist hedge funds its authors observed through 374 insurgent-style efforts between 2004 and 2005 were initiated by "multiple hedge funds acting as a bloc by filing a joint 13D."[1]

April Klein, associate professor, Stern School of Business, New York University, and Emanuel Zur, doctoral student, Stern School of Business, NYU, collected 13D data for 102 different activist hedge funds making 155 13D filings for their "Hedge Fund Activism" study, which was conducted in September 2006. The duo found 14 different categories of reasons why activists file 13D's (see Table 3.1).

Once the 13Ds are publicly filed, the Internet becomes a major factor in how activists today operate. As explained, the combinations of these letters and SEC filings have become a major component of an activist strategy for some insurgents. Other investors cruising around the Internet looking for financial information about companies often come across or actively seek out these activist 13D filings. After reading the letters, investors and potential investors take the new information, complete their own research, and decide whether they feel the same way.

If an investor believes that the initial 13D filer's comments make sense as a means to improve shareholder value, they may buy a large stake in the same company, file their own 13D, and write similar letters. Other, less virulent activists, preferring to engage management in a friendlier manner, stay away from these poison pen letters but may still submit their own 13Ds with shorter complaints. Finally, other even less activist-type investors who typically prefer the shadows completely buy their own stakes anticipating that the activist may trigger some share price–improving event at the company. These "piggybacking" investors expect that there is a good likelihood the stock price will improve with an activist investor there working to improve the share value. Some of these investors will stick around for the long haul, until the activist achieves its goal.

Table 3.1 Activists' Stated Reasons in Schedule 13Ds "Purpose of Transaction" and Success Rates of Achieving Their Stated Goals

Number of Reasons in 13D Filing	Hedge Fund Activists	Number of Successes
Change board of directors' compensation	41	30 (73%)
Firm should pursue strategic alternatives	29	14 (48%)
Oppose a merger	18	10 (56%)
Sell the firm or merger with another company	16	9 (56%)
Buy more stock with intention of buying the firm	12	7 (58%)
Firm should buy back its own stock	4	4 (100%)
Get list of shareholders	4	2 (50%)
Support management	4	2 (50%)
Become an active investor	4	4 (100%)
Express concerns with corporate governance	3	1 (33%)
Replace the CEO	3	3 (100%)
Cut CEO's salary	2	1 (50%)
Firm should pay a cash dividend	2	2 (100%)
Other reason	13	4 (31%)
Total number	155	93 (60%)

SOURCE: April Klein, associate professor Stern School of Business, New York University; Emanuel Zur, doctoral student, Stern School of Business, NYU, "Hedge Fund Activism," (September 2006), 43.

Others will jump on board, only to quickly turn around and sell their stake. These extremely short-term investors make these quick-hit investments because they expect a short-term spike in the stock price immediately after someone like Carl Icahn makes an investment. Their approach infuriates activists and other institutional investors.

Event-oriented piggybacking investors typically do not make any sort of activist comments and as a result do not file schedule 13Ds. But their presence does make a difference. At many companies, there may only ever be one 13D filing, but that does not mean that an activist's presence has not attracted several other quasi-activists quietly accumulating shares below the percentage required for public disclosure. Investors that may pile in after the initial 13D filing come from a wide variety of backgrounds. They may be pension fund institutions, risk arbitrage specialists or activist hedge fund managers preferring to watch one of their counterparts do all the dirty work. "This could help you if the stock goes to people who support you," Opportunity Partners' Goldstein says. "Many other investors copy our investment approach, which is fine even if they don't take an activist tack because these people owning the stock are better than those investors that vote with management."

The company may suddenly have a larger number of activists and quasi-activist investors who each own their own significant stake in the company all screaming for change. The once passive, management-friendly investor base has transformed into one that is ready and pushing for some stock price improvement. "With the flow of information over the Internet, any investor can get involved," says David Pasquale, executive vice president of investor relations consultancy The Ruth Group in New York. "The barriers to entry for an activist have gone down."

One important caveat: only small-capitalization companies can truly experience a transformed investor base after an activist launches a public effort. Activists can attract other insurgents at mid-capitalization and large public companies, but nowhere near a critical mass. At those companies, as will be discussed in Chapter 10, activists must broaden their campaign to attract a much wider swath of institutional investors for their insurgencies to be effective.

But at companies that experience this transformed investor base, it becomes increasingly difficult for management to ignore the primary activist without repercussions. This kind of situation, where there are several large 13D holders, can produce a particularly frightening situation for corporations. The unifying powerful force of several large activist investors, all owning huge blocks of a particular company's shares, cannot be underestimated.

This kind of transformed investor base and accumulation of 13D activist hedge fund filers in a particular company has been dubbed by many observers as a "pack of wolves" bent on pressing for changes. But others give the phenomenon a much more negative description, calling it a "hedge fund roach motel." This perception indicates that many long-standing passive investors, either institutional or individual, resent the accumulation of activists in the company and believe that the new investors are really interested only in a short-term result that will eat away at the future value of the company they've owned shares in for years. But in some circumstances, when the share price is particularly depressed, otherwise passive investors will throw their support behind a bloc of activists that cumulatively own a large stake in a company.

Take the events that unfolded in late 2005 and early 2006 at Knight Ridder Inc., the second largest chain of newspapers in the United States at the time. On November 1, hedge fund Private Capital Management chief executive Bruce Sherman included a letter to Knight Ridder's board with a Schedule 13D urging the mega-media company's CEO Anthony Ridder to auction the business.

In fact, Private Capital Management, which by November owned an 18.9 percent stake, had already been privately urging Ridder to sell the asset since April 2005, eight months earlier. During that period, PCM was accumulating stock and gradually increasing its stake in the newspaper company. The activist approach was not common for Sherman, who manages a more traditional value-investor shop. But at Knight Ridder, Sherman concluded that passively waiting for a return was not enough. Opportunity Partners' Goldstein describes Sherman as a "reluctant activist"—someone who will launch activist campaigns on occasion when a previously passive investment has become intractable.

The problem with Knight Ridder, from PCM's perspective, was that its stock continued to languish despite efforts by the company to prop it up. To resolve the problem, Knight Ridder implemented a whole host of share-improvement efforts such as buying back shares to boost its stock price. The general revenue growth difficulties for the newspaper industry struggling to find a model that works wasn't helping either, particularly with advertising dollars migrating away from traditional newspapers to the Internet and other media.

PCM's Sherman even threatened that he would "strongly consider" supporting efforts by other investors to install their own candidates on the board. By that time, other large Knight Ridder investors began backing Sherman's efforts. On November 3, hedge fund Southeastern Asset Management Inc. converted its passive Schedule 13G filing into an activist Schedule 13D, reporting an 8.9 percent stake. In its 13D, Southeastern said it wanted the flexibility to discuss PCM's proposal with Knight Ridder management and other shareholders. That same day, yet another activist hedge fund, Harris Associates LP, jumped into the fray reporting a 13D urging the company's management and board to find a buyer. It owned an 8.2 percent stake.

Cumulatively, the three funds held more than a third of Knight Ridder shares. They had become a formidable trading bloc, though not officially a group. Shortly after the activists began their public prodding, Ridder sought strategic advice from its financial adviser, investment bank Goldman Sachs. Recognizing trouble, Knight Ridder sought to appease the activists by cutting staff at some locations, issuing a quarterly dividend, completing another stock buyback, and in July selling its interest in the Detroit Newspaper Partnership LP, which manages the *Detroit Free Press.*[2] But Sherman and the other activists were not mollified.

By June 2006, the activists got what they really wanted when Knight Ridder completed an auction and closed a deal to sell itself to the McClatchy Company, a Sacramento, California–based newspaper publisher, for $4.5 billion.[3]

In the end, what happened at Knight Ridder? A group of investors identified that the newspaper company was not performing well, its stock was suffering, and efforts to restructure it as an independent entity were not enough, in their opinion, to fix the problem. In addition to the three large block holders, Knight Ridder probably had numerous other smaller investors supporting the public activists and expressing concern about the newspaper company remaining as an independent entity. But without the efforts of Sherman and the other activists, Knight Ridder might still be an independent company. Knight Ridder management read the writing on the wall.

A critical mass of activists cumulatively owning a significant stake in a company makes it more likely that management will take the time to listen to their advice or recommendations. And if management doesn't listen to the growing group of dissidents that own the stock, then one insurgent can make a quick tabulation of the 13D filers in the stock, add that to other smaller activists that have purchased stakes, and threaten a proxy contest to put people on the board that will make the difficult changes to improve share value. Knight Ridder management reluctantly understood what the company's investors—its owners—wanted them to do.

"CEOs believe that activist packs are wreaking havoc on the company," says Perrie Weiner, partner at DLA Piper Rudnick Gray Cary US LLP. "It's easy to say that, but those CEOs need to ask themselves, "Why are activists investing in our company?" The answer is that there is a problem that needs fixing."

Look at the hodgepodge of activists that jumped into bank consulting and payments software company Carreker Corporation. In 2005, Prescott Capital Management LLC president Jeffrey Watkins reported a 7.4 percent stake in Carreker, filed a Schedule 13D, and began expressing his desire to see the tech company auction itself. In an SEC filing, the activist noted that similar rivals to Carreker sold for high valuations. According to Prescott Capital, the company's "broad product line and extremely strong customer list well may make it worth more to a larger strategic acquirer." By March 2006, Prescott Capital's efforts were seeing results. When Watkins threatened to launch a proxy contest, the company offered to appoint him to its board. Watkins accepted.

After that, other activists entered the skirmish. Chapman Capital's Robert Chapman in June reported a 5.6 percent stake and began his own effort to nudge the company to sell itself. In a letter to Carreker, Chapman criticized the company's 2001 purchase of Check Solutions Company, a Memphis-based business that helps banks transform their systems from paper-based to electronic.

Chapman pointed out that upon making the acquisition, Carreker failed to anticipate that it would become embroiled in a time-consuming lawsuit filed by a former partner, Pegasystems Inc. A 1999 contract between Pegasystems and Check Solutions was violated once Carreker made the purchase. In the end, Pegasystems succeeded in blocking Carreker from producing software that breached that partnership.

"Given your tainted history as a 'corporate acquisitor,' we strongly advise that Carreker not utilize its $40 million in cash and marketable securities to flood its income statement, yet once again, with more intangible amortization and overall business risk," Chapman wrote on June 7. Shortly after that, Carreker said it would have its financial advisor, Bear Stearns & Company, consider strategic options such as a sale. Once Watkins and Chapman had made their presence known, another investor, Bryant R. Riley, founder of brokerage firm B. Riley & Company, reported a 10 percent stake and said he was considering a proxy contest.

The three activists together at the time owned roughly 25 percent of Carreker. By August 2006, Chapman had cut his interest in the company to a 4.8 percent stake after he reevaluated the market for technology acquisitions and determined that a Carreker sale would not return as much as he had originally expected. Chapman considered several factors before making that decision. One contributing consideration: a company in a similar industry had sold for less than he had anticipated. Upon embarking on his effort to have Carreker sold, Chapman estimated that a strategic buyer would pay roughly $12 a share for the company. By August, Chapman wrote in a third-quarter letter to his investors that he expected the company to fetch no more than $7 or $8 a share. "Seven dollars a share was not an attractive price for us to remain so large in an illiquid name," Chapman says.

But, at the time of Chapman's share sales, there was no shortage of activists and other investors seeking an auction of the company. Chapman calculated that roughly 50 percent of Carreker stakeholders were pushing for a transaction, after he cut his stake. By the time Carreker sold itself to CheckFree Corporation in January 2007 for $206 million in cash or $8.05 a share, Chapman already had liquidated his shares. Chapman says he divested the rest of his stake because he did not see much "upside" to holding it.

But the activist effort still performed well for his hedge fund, producing roughly 30 percent returns. He purchased the stake for, on average, $5.50 a share and sold it for between $6.75 and $7.75 a share. The last of his stake was sold on December 11. Chapman adds that his public efforts, combined with Prescott Capital and B. Riley, made a big difference in attracting other investors that cumulatively pressured the software company to its final outcome. "By December, I would say that 80 percent of Carreker's shareholders were pulling for a sale," Chapman says. "A cluster of block holders is not something to be taken lightly."

Activists engaging in public-pressure tactics at companies will typically own more than 5 percent of the stock of any company they want to press into changing. Owning less than that usually sends a message to management that they are not important enough to bother with (unless you spend $1 billion to buy a 1.2 percent stake in Home Depot, but we'll get to that later).

Many activists want to engage company executives in private, behind-the-scenes conversations. Shareholders seeking to keep the conversations private usually do so, in part, because they don't want to offend company executives or directors. These activists believe that change can be provoked through collaborative private discussions with executives.

In some of these cases, the activists would prefer to hold larger block stakes above 5 percent, but they won't do it because that would convert the effort from private to public with a 13D. That move could damage relations between the activist and management.

There are also several other downsides to the 13D filing system as well, from an activist's perspective. The additional investors who jump in the stock after the activist has made its case in its original 13D will typically bump up the stock price, making it difficult for the original insurgent to buy additional stock at cheap prices as their campaign proceeds.

In fact, the 2006 study, "Hedge Fund Activism, Corporate Governance and Firm Performance," reports that there is a significant positive return, on average 7 percent, during the month an activist files its original 13D.[4] The stock spike is even larger when activists engage in hostile campaigns such as seeking to have the company sold or pressuring management into spinning off noncore assets.[5] Companies encouraged by activists to find buyers had "abnormal" positive 10 percent returns during the 13D month, while insurgents seeking business strategy changes such as unit sales had 5.9 percent returns.[6] After the one-month period of abnormal returns, the companies returned to normal returns during the subsequent year.[7] Surprisingly, activism that targets governance-related insurgent efforts, such as removal of a poison pill, improved board independence or elimination of a CEO, did not produce a significant short-term abnormally high stock performance during the month a 13D was filed, according to the study. One of the report's authors, Alon Brav, associate professor of finance at Duke University, says he believes that the market may be interpreting a governance-related 13D filing as bad news rather than good news. Brav speculates that it's possible that activists seeking these kinds of changes are likely to have been pressing the company privately for a year or longer with no success. According to Brav, the activists chose to launch a public campaign with a 13D only after deciding that the company was too intractabile for collaborative private negotiations. Another possibility is that investors looking for a quick return don't believe these governance changes will produce a catalyst quickly and they avoid allocating capital to the business. Though most serious activists would agree that while their governance-related efforts may not result in a short-term hike in the stock price around the filing of the 13D, they are likely to produce a long-term improvement in share performance. In any event, the spike in stock price that occurs after deal-related 13Ds are filed is partly why many activists try to stay below a 5 percent stake, particularly in their insurgency's earlier stages. Many activists will own as much as 4.9 percent stakes in companies while they are debating tactics and strategies for taking their campaign public with a 5 percent-plus investment. Other activists will remain at 4.9 percent or below to keep their activist efforts private in an attempt to work collaboratively with management while they, perhaps, threaten to take their efforts public.

Part of the problem for Chapman is that when he files a 13D other short-term investors will quickly follow his filing by purchasing shares and quickly cashing out after the stock spikes.

He likes to call these passive investors who buy into the stock immediately after he files a 13D "free riders" or "remora," an animal that has a large sucking disk on its head for attaching to larger fish or sharks. And, of course, Chapman considers himself the shark that attacks undervalued companies with poorly performing management. The problem is that many of these remora passive investors who follow Chapman into the stock don't stick around for the long haul, Chapman says.

The long haul, for activists, is three to five years. That's how long it typically takes activists to accomplish their goals of unlocking value at their investment targets, though it can take less time or much longer. Many short-term investors will buy quickly after an activist files a Schedule 13D. But after the stock takes its typical short-term rise up, many of these investors cash out and take their winnings. That can leave the initial activist without enough investor support a few years later when it comes time for a proxy contest or serious behind-the-scenes negotiations with management. Even if investors buy the stock and stick around for however long it takes for the insurgent to succeed in its efforts, those shareholders share the benefit of the activism without spending anywhere near the time, money, and energy on the subject company as the activist does. Activists compete with these money managers or "free riders" for investment dollars.

Another problem is that different activists may have different time frames and return goals. "One manager may be working with a management team to unleash some small catalysts collaborating with executives there, when activist number two comes in and says, 'Screw this—let's get them to sell the company now,'" says Sebastian Stubbe, a partner at Landmark Investors LLC in New York. "They represent two different strategies that conflict with each other."

That's why some activists, hoping to achieve a long-term restructuring of the company they are investing in, prefer to operate in the shadows away from other activists or short-term investors. Stubbe says that many activists don't like to go where other activists are engaging management because they have distinct plans that may be different than what the other insurgents are considering.

But despite all these disclosure issues, activism within the SEC system has certain positive qualities for those filing 13Ds. Even if other activists pile on after the initial insurgent files his 13D, those other investors will not receive the same return on the activism as the initial insurgent. That's because the activist typically begins accumulating a stake of less than 5 percent, waiting for the perfect opportunity to breach that threshold and take its efforts public. During their pre-public investment period—let's call it the incubation—activists accumulating a stake below the 5 percent disclosure threshold typically are getting better prices for their investments than the secondary activists or other investors who pile in once the initial insurgent's investment becomes public with a 13D. "When they file their 13D and start pressing for change publicly, other investors who piggyback and buy stakes then will likely not get the same return on their investment as the original activist," says Morgan Joseph's Randy Lampert.

In addition, this pack or herd approach may not work well, particularly at many small-capitalization companies that may be too illiquid for a sufficiently large number of activists to pile in. "In thinly traded stocks, there may not be sufficient liquidity for more than a couple activists to get involved," Lampert says.

In some circumstances, activists or other investors will seek to gain voting rights for additional shares beyond the 4.9 percent stake in a way that they believe does not trigger the 13D disclosure rules. In one example, described in a May 2006 study produced by University of Texas professors Henry Hu and Bernard Black, an activist hedge fund with a 4.9 percent stake engaged in convertible equity swaps, a mechanism that could put it in short-term control of the equity and voting rights for large blocks of shares, without disclosing that information.[8] When these investors need the voting rights, they can simply unwind the swaps. According to the study, investors on the verge of the 13D threshold that also engage in convertible equity swaps believe they do not need to disclose their stakes because of the cash-settled nature of those transactions. In their study, Hu and Black describe the occurrence as "hidden morphable ownership."[9] Some activists use this approach to profit from the spike in price that occurs once they finally file their 13D. It can also allow them to privately communicate with corporate executives, but at the same time have hidden additional leverage that other investors may not be aware of.

In the study, Hu explains how some investors borrow shares to put them over the 5 percent threshold. These investors typically do not believe that they are required to file a 13D since they do not own equity beyond the 5 percent trigger. The key for these investors, says Hu, is to decouple economic ownership of those shares from the voting rights to those shares. The major purpose of both approaches is to increase their stockpile of votes to support their cause, whether that is installing a dissident slate of directors or approving a closely contested merger.

But most activists argue that they do not use these tactics to hide additional votes. Opportunity Partner's Phillip Goldstein says investors can try all sorts of complex strategies to gain additional votes, but without the support of the company's real investor base, they won't be successful. The key is to gain the support of a sufficiently large number of other investors, Goldstein says, which cannot be accomplished by gaining some additional hidden, decoupled voting rights. Goldstein adds that he doesn't engage in these morphable or empty voting strategies and he doesn't believe most other genuine activists use it either.

Sometimes two activists are all it takes to gain a critical mass of institutional investor support, though a campaign can take some time. Quasi-activist fund MMI Investments LP started slowly with its endeavor at Brinks Company. It acquired a 5.4 percent stake at the armored vehicle freight delivery company, filed a Schedule 13D, and indicated that management may hear from them in the not to distant future. At the same time, activist hedge fund Steel Partners II also began quietly buying shares and pressing Brinks behind-the-scenes to sell its delivery and logistics division BAX Global, a slightly profitable unit. Steel Partners' rationale for the sale? Give Brinks the ability to focus on its core armored car unit and residential/small-business security division.

The Brinks effort was all about actively engaging management in a collaborative manner and encouraging them to make changes on their own. But after the private efforts did not produce the intended response, MMI moved its efforts into high gear. By April 2005, Clay Lifflander, a member of a group with MMI Investments, wrote a letter to Brinks CEO Michael Dan that he included in an SEC filing. It recommended that the company begin looking into selling BAX Global. Other investors began piling in. By December 2005, Brinks's board agreed to sell BAX for $1.1 billion.[10] With the proceeds, Brinx paid down some debt and completed a $530 million stock repurchase program, all to the satisfaction of the activists involved.[11]

That kind of success story doesn't always take place. Sometimes a bunch of activists gang up on a target company, even win a proxy contest, but after a significant period of time, no value-generating catalyst has emerged. Four activist hedge funds separately bought large blocks of aerospace engineering systems manufacturer GenCorp Inc. stock over a period of 10 years, yet no tangible result has emerged.

First, value-investing guru Mario Gabelli of Gabelli Asset Management filed a Schedule 13D in 1995. Then Steel Partners reported a 6.2 percent stake in 2002 and made its own filing with the intention of engaging management. By November 2004, things really heated up. Steel Partners' Lichtenstein made a $708 million unsolicited offer to buy GenCorp. The offer was quickly rejected, but GenCorp's stock spiked from $14 a share to $17 a share on the news.

"Management and the board appear to have engaged in what can be best described as a game of gin rummy by buying and selling businesses with no clear corporate strategy and with very poor results, including the recent sale of the GDX Automotive business at a loss of over $300 million," Lichtenstein wrote in a letter to GenCorp's board in November 2004.

A few days after Lichtenstein's bid, activist hedge fund Pirate Capital LLC announced that it owned 2.6 percent of GenCorp and had met management and visited the company's headquarters in Rancho Cordova, California. Pirate portfolio manager David Lorber wrote a letter to GenCorp's board, outlining his own "conservative" $84 a share to $164 a share estimate of GenCorp's business, including its valuable Sacramento real estate property. Pirate blasted GenCorp for its plan to issue equity for the purpose of paying down debt because of how that kind of refinancing would dilute existing shareholder value.

Later that same month, Steel Partners withdrew its already rejected offer to buy GenCorp and tried another approach by announcing it was considering a proxy contest. That proxy contest threat was later dropped by Steel Partners after the company agreed to add a corporate governance expert to its board.

In March 2005, another activist, Sandell Asset Management Corporation, reported a 6 percent stake in GenCorp. The hedge fund outlined its own barrage of recommendations, including one asking management to "proactively" invite one or two representatives of its shareholder base to join the board. In October 2005, the New York–based hedge fund sent another letter to GenCorp, urging the company to hire an investment bank to look into strategic alternatives to "unlock" the value of the company's real estate holdings. "Failure to act by GenCorp would make it incumbent upon shareholders to initiate changes starting with the board," Sandell's letter read.

After that, in 2006, Pirate Capital made its own attempt to install a minority slate of three directors to the company's board by launching a proxy contest. It succeeded despite a legal challenge by GenCorp and a recommendation by investment advisory group Institutional Shareholder Services that shareholders should support only one of its three nominees. With three directors on the board, Pirate is still hoping its goal of urging GenCorp to sell its undeveloped Sacramento property will take place. To get things moving on such a sale, Pirate Capital specifically nominated Robert Woods, a noted real estate investment banking specialist, to the company's board.

The company has since implemented a number of governance initiatives that could help make that happen. It removed a series of antitakeover provisions and separated the role of CEO and chairman. In February 2007, an independent director became chairman.[12] The move, cheered by governance advocates, will put a razor-sharp focus on GenCorp's CEO.

Cumulatively, Sandell and the three other activists have filed over 50 Schedule 13Ds or amended 13Ds (follow-up filings to the original 13D document) since November 2006 on the aerospace engineering systems company. But despite the new governance initiatives and the separate efforts by the four different activists—Gabelli, Steel Partners, Pirate Capital, and Sandell—and possibly more behind the scenes supporters, no major "catalyst" action has emerged. To Pirate Capital's dismay, its Sacramento property sale has just not happened. The stock, while down from its high of $20 a share, has been boosted by their efforts. In 2003, it traded at as low as about $7 a share, and by mid-2007, it traded at roughly $13 a share.

Meanwhile, many of the activists involved have recently developed their own internal issues, not helping matters with their insurgency at GenCorp. In October 2006, Sandell sent its investors a letter indicating that the SEC plans to recommend that the agency take civil action against the hedge fund, according to press reports.[13] In December, the SEC formally notified Sandell that it had launched an investigation into the activist fund for its purported sale of some stock prior to a major transaction, a matter that can't help its credibility among other GenCorp investors, particularly institutions.[14]

Separately, Gabelli and other entities agreed to a $130 million settlement with the U.S. Department of Justice, reconciling charges that the activist investor and others used a number of artificial small businesses to bid for spectrum being auctioned by the Federal Communications Commission.[15]

Several employees left Pirate Capital in 2006 after the activist hedge fund reported poor performance numbers and internal problems, including its own apparent SEC investigation for not reporting some of its stock sales in a timely fashion.[16] At the same time, Pirate experienced a period of lackluster returns. Having down periods is common for activists. Usually, they do well in the long term but experience lots of volatility along the way. But Pirate's lack of returns of late and the SEC investigation into whether the hedge fund had properly disclosed changes in its stakes have made many of its investors skittish. In addition to losing some analysts and investors, Pirate was forced to divest some of its stakes earlier than it would have liked and incurred losses. Pirate in August 2006 sold a major position in OSI Restaurant Partners, owner of Outback Steakhouse and other restaurant chains, posting a loss.[17] That divestiture came too early, because by November, a group including buyout shop Bain Capital had acquired OSI for $3.2 billion, propping up its share price.[18] The fund also has been publicly pressing Walter Industries Inc. to split itself into three units since May 2005. So far that hasn't happened and the stock price has gone down significantly from the price at which Pirate purchased the majority of its shares.

And while the GenCorp effort seems to be taking a long time, keep in mind that some multiyear activist efforts can still reach fruition. Considering that its insurgency campaign really started in earnest in 2004, it appears that there still should be some time to turn things around at GenCorp. That is assuming its insurgency has staying power. Pirate Capital only has a small investment in GenCorp, though it may not be able to wait much longer for the catalyst it is hoping to unleash. But while hedge fund efforts at GenCorp still have a fighting chance, there are other times when a pack of hedge funds can cumulatively all be wrong about the value-unlocking properties of the same company.

A motley crew of activists were unable to achieve their sale objective at embattled Bally Total Fitness Holding Corporation. Activist Emanuel Pearlman of Liberation Investment Group LLC in June 2004 began instigating for change at the fitness chain. At that time, Pearlman, who had previously been a Bally consultant, introduced four governance proposals for shareholders to consider, including one instituting a mandatory retirement age of 75 for all board members. (Bally director J. Kenneth Looloian, a Bally director since 1995, was retired at 82 years old at the time.) In 2005, Bally hired investment bank Blackstone Group LP to help it consider strategic options. It subsequently sold a small health club unit, Crunch Fitness, for $45 million, but that divestiture didn't do much for Bally or Liberation.[19]

Later, other activists jumped in the fray. In November 2005, former Hollywood Entertainment Corporation CEO Mark Wattles reported a 10 percent stake and filed his own 13D at Bally. Activist Pardus Capital Management LP acquired a 14 percent stake and later launched a proxy contest that succeeded in installing three directors on Bally's nine-member board.[20]

One of the Pardus-backed directors, Don Kornstein, a restructuring specialist and investment banker at Bear, Stearns & Company, became co-chairman of the company's special committee charged with finding a buyer. Shortly after that, Bally conducted an auction with J. P. Morgan Chase & Company as its strategic adviser. To entice buyers, Bally hired

Deutsche Bank AG to provide debt financing, including $700 million in senior bank debt and subordinated debt, to any prospective buyer. Everything seemed to be moving in the right direction, from a shareholder perspective. But it was not to be. While numerous companies expressed an initial interest, in August 2006, the auction process shut down with no suitable bidder emerging. The stock traded in early 2007 at less than $1 a share, significantly less than the $3.80 to $4.60 a share Liberation's Pearlman spent acquiring his stake. Pardus bought much of its stake for less than $4 a share. Wattles later purchased many of his shares for between $4.25 and $7.28 a share. At the end of May 2007, Bally announced plans to file for Chapter 11 bankruptcy.[21]

Another group of high profile insurgents failed in their cumulative efforts to unlock value at a target business. This time activist investors went after one of their own by launching a campaign at New York–based BKF Capital Group Inc., a public investment management firm.

It all started innocently enough. In 2000, activist–value investor Gabelli filed a 13D indicating that members of his group may make reports or hold discussions with individuals, including management, about the future of the company. This, known in activist parlance as a boilerplate activist filing, did not provide much information, but other insurgent-type investors take it as a code message that this is a good value investment that could also be a good target for an insurgency.

In 2003 and 2004, Opportunity Partners' Goldstein and Steel Partners II's Lichtenstein came in with their own activist filings. Other insurgents followed shortly after that, including J. Carlo Cannell of Cannell Capital LLC in San Francisco and Jeffrey Altman of Owl Creek Asset Management.

The dissidents argued in their SEC filings that BKF management, including its CEO John Levin, mismanaged the fund and collected exorbitant executive compensation, while shareholders were left with an uninflated stock. For the nine months ending September 30, 2004, BKF lost $3.5 million. The investment fund had similar results in its previous two years: It lost $6.7 million in 2003 and $2.1 million in 2002. At roughly the same time as those losses were being recorded, BKF explained in an April 2004 SEC document that Levin's son Henry received a $260,000 salary and a $4.5 million bonus for his investment work as a portfolio manager. The activists argued that BKF was undervalued compared to its peers and it was paying its executives a level of salary and bonuses that bore no resemblance to its stagnating stock performance.

Things came to a head in June 2005 when Steel Partners, with the tacit support of the pack of dissidents, succeeded at electing a slate of three directors to BKF's nine-person board. It appeared to be a victory for dissidents. But then something happened that none of the participating activists had anticipated.

After the proxy contest, Lichtenstein offered to put the fund's founder, John Levin, who had lost his directorship, back on as a director. Levin declined and shortly afterward resigned from the company. The departure of BKF's founder was a catalyst for the investment vehicle, just not the kind the activists were looking for. In the year after the proxy contest the fund lost two-thirds of its employees, and its assets under management dropped from $13 billion in 2004 to about $2.5 billion in 2006. With Levin gone, investors pulled their money from the BKF fund. The investment firm closed some of its underlying hedge funds and stopped trading in certain popular strategies.

Shortly after that, Lichtenstein resigned from the board. Later, the company said it planned to exit from the investment management business and, eventually, completely liquidated its assets under management as of January 2007.

In the end, Levin was willing to give up most of his equity to show how indispensable he was to BKF. Opportunity's Goldstein says Levin's reaction was irrational and analogous to a financial suicide bomber.

"Our mistake was that we didn't realize Levin would destroy the company he spent so many years building rather than let shareholders have a say in running it," Goldstein says. "Levin acted out of spite and committed to a scorched earth policy."

With the benefit of looking at the BKF phenomenon as an outsider after the fact, Chapman Capital's Chapman says the insurgents violated a cardinal test of activism: If the CEO died tomorrow, would the stock trade significantly higher? Chapman says he takes on only targets where management is not "key" to the company's success or survival. BKF was a "horrible" target, he says. The ouster of Levin, the founder and key to the fund's success, was most certainly to mean that the fund's other investors would depart quickly behind him, Chapman argued.

BKF investor Carlo Cannell accepts that, in many ways, John Levin was the company. But, he adds, it doesn't mean investors and a board that is more receptive to shareholders cannot find another CEO that can do as good a job as he did. Cannell says he and other activists had some ideas about replacement candidates for Levin, but had problems bringing them in. "We were unsuccessful at injecting new talent into the company, and as a consequence it suffered from a slow death," Cannell says.

The BKF example does put a spotlight on the downside of activist investing in herds. Is it possible that activists could cause a major disruption at an operating company? Gary Lutin, an investment banker who now acts as a corporate governance adviser, believes the threat is real. His collapse scenario starts with an insurgent hedge fund manager's in-house problems. A major activist investor finds itself trying to balance a complex and expensive effort at a large public corporation and at the same time is having difficulty managing an internal scandal. The activist is hemorrhaging investors and researchers and must cash out a major block position—say a 10 percent stake—in a target company. That decision could spook other activists that have aggregated in the stock. The possibility that 10 or 15 activists and other event-oriented investors might dump their stock quickly at the same time would not only hurt other investors but could have a major negative impact at that corporation, which is already most likely struggling. "It's a race to the exits," Lutin says.

Despite that gloomy premonition and BKF's self-implosion after a pack of wolves' insurgency, the activist hedge fund gaggle approach seems to have matured into a fairly regular occurrence. Whether groups of 13D filers will experience relatively quick success, as some did at Knight-Ridder, Blair Corporation, and Carreker, remains to be seen. The destruction of BKF was a lesson for activists that may consider adding their capital and other resources to another insurgent's fight. Other lessons can be found in the long-term efforts of activists at Bally Total Fitness, which also suffered a slow collapse. So far, the catalyst events activists have been waiting for at GenCorp haven't taken place. It's also unlikely that the pack of wolves' scenarios will become pervasive at U.S. corporations targeted by activists, particularly larger ones. While activists are forming groups and filing multiple 13Ds at large-capitalization companies, their efforts require assistance. Even if 50 insurgents dropped their various campaigns and all congregated at one large-capitalization company, their presence would likely still need the support of other institutions, such as mutual fund and pension fund managers, to make a difference.

There will always be activists that seek isolation in their efforts to agitate for change. Additional insurgents with different time frames and separate objectives can hurt an initial activist's efforts, especially if a particular insurgent has a hidden agenda attached to some morphable equity stakes or empty votes. This leads many insurgents to keep their efforts separate from the pack. Certainly, as will be discussed in greater detail, many investors allocate funds with a particular activist, expecting that insurgent to make investment decisions that are different from other hedge funds. That investor may be disappointed to find his manager is allocating funds to the same company all the other insurgents are targeting. It may just be that a pack of wolves are focusing so much of their attention at one particular prey that they are missing the real score somewhere else.

Chapter 4

How Activists Use Litigation to Pursue Their Agenda

In 2002, faced with an impending proxy contest, California software producer, Liquid Audio, decided it would expand its board from five to seven seats. The intended effect: dilute or reduce the impact of two activists that each wanted a seat on the board. If successful, the insurgent shareholders would only gain two seats on a board of seven members, instead of being two directors on a board of five. Dissidents James Mitarotonda and Seymour Holtzman realized that they would need to step things up a level if they wanted their proxy contest to effect the changes they wanted to see take place.[1]

In fact, the activists wanted to see the company cancel a proposed merger that they didn't like and instead liquidate itself and distribute proceeds to shareholders. Liquid Audio was a cash-rich, yet profitless company that manufactured software enabling consumers to download and purchase music from the Internet in a proprietary digital format. Mitarotonda and Holtzman were sure that Liquid Audio's business plan was destined to fail, given all the unlicensed downloading people at the time were doing using Napster and all the other free file-sharing programs available on the Internet.

That's when they decided to employ another strategy often utilized by activists to achieve their goals: the lawsuit.

They filed a complaint with the Delaware Chancery Court, arguing that the company was violating its fiduciary duty to shareholders by expanding its board size. The court rejected their case, but Mitarotonda and Holtzman were not deterred. They appealed the decision to the Delaware Supreme Court.

While the judges were reviewing the case, Holtzman and Mitarotonda won their proxy contest and were elected to the board. In January 2003, they also won their Delaware lawsuit. The court ruled that the Redwood City, California–based company's last-minute decision to expand its board by two seats would "interfere and impede" with activist investor endeavors to exercise their voting rights in a contested election.[2]

The court decision, coupled with the successful proxy contest, set in motion the liquidation of the company, which translated into a handsome profit for the activists. In addition to distributing all its cash to shareholders, Liquid Audio also sold its technology to a music distributor for Wal-Mart Stores Inc.[3] "In some situations, litigation is absolutely necessary," Mitarotonda says. "If a company does something to thwart a legitimate shareholder initiative, a lawsuit sometimes is the only option."

Mitarotonda and Holtzman filed the suit through their investment vehicle, MM Companies, which they created after taking over Musicmaker.com, another dot-com Internet music company. The two activists sold Musicmaker.com's operating business and distributed the majority of its cash on hand to shareholders like themselves. Both investors are also activists through other investment companies. Mitarotonda is the chief executive of Barington Capital Group and Holtzman is the CEO of Jewelcor Management Inc.

Their successful lawsuit puts a spotlight on the litigation strategy as another arrow in the activist's quiver. In most cases, activists will engage in lawsuits as a strategy that complements other engagement tactics, including proxy contests, as in the Liquid Audio case. However, in some situations, as will be discussed later, litigation is the sole source of activism. The court approach isn't taken lightly because it can easily be the most expensive cost in an activist's campaign. Holtzman and Mitarotonda spent roughly $1.3 million over a period of six weeks, roughly $200,000 a week, in their litigious efforts at Liquid Audio. With costs like that, it's rare that any investors other than the highly concentrated activist investor, who has the most to gain and lose, will consider getting involved in any serious court action. Without the possibility of a huge payout if the litigation and other efforts are successful, the costs of engaging in a court case can become prohibitive. Since many court cases take a long time, activists must weigh whether it may make better sense to cut their losses and reinvest that capital into another venture.

In the Mitarotonda and Holtzman case, the Delaware Supreme Court decision set a precedent for shareholder rights. The *New York Law Journal* reported in May 2003 that the decision points to a shift by the court in favor of shareholders that was driven, in part, by the "post-Enron environment."[4] Roughly one-half of all U.S. corporations are incorporated in Delaware, making the decision all the more important.

But the court order has much broader implications beyond discouraging companies from engaging in board expansion tactics to diminish the effects of proxy contests. Jewelcor's Holtzman says it also deters executives from installing any sort of anti-takeover defenses, such as poison pills or classified boards, as a protection against an impending proxy contest.

After corporations set up these anti-takeover provisions in the 1990s to block the efforts of the previous decade's raiders, it appears now that some of the power has shifted back somewhat toward the shareholder. For Holtzman, another major effect of the court order is more subtle and typically takes place behind the scenes in discussions with executives. In meetings with CEOs at target corporations, Holtzman has referred to the case on countless occasions. "The point is to let them know that I'm a serious activist investor and they better not consider any funny business," Holtzman says. "I tell executives to talk to their lawyers about what the case means and what the implications would be for them if they installed any anti-takeover devices."

He attributes part of his success in encouraging executives to make behind-the-scenes changes at companies, such as replacing executives or selling off a division, to the weight of the decision.

The Holtzman-Mitarotonda victory was a big step for shareholder rights; though its decisive conclusion doesn't represent the typical outcome of shareholder litigation. In fact, it is very rare that an activist shareholder suit will actually result in a consummated court case. In most situations, an activist will launch a lawsuit but later will call it off after the target company takes steps to improve shareholder value. As with most proxy contests, settlements are also often reached before a court case is completed.

At Liquid Audio, shareholders and executives had already gone through a round of lawsuits earlier in 2002, prior to the Delaware Supreme Court case. Hoping to deter the dissident proxy contest, Liquid Audio CEO Gerald Kearby did what many executives in his position over the years have done. Hoping to discourage the activists, he sought to postpone the company's annual meeting indefinitely. The only way dissidents could gain seats on Liquid Audio's board, and thereby effect change, was at an annual meeting. As at many U.S. corporations, acting by written consent and calling a special shareholder meeting were both prohibited. Without an annual meeting, no change could take place.

In an attempt to expedite the proceedings, Holtzman and Mitarotonda filed a lawsuit in Delaware Chancery Court, asserting that Liquid Audio did not hold a timely annual meeting. Soon after, the two sides reached a settlement when Liquid Audio scheduled its annual meeting for July 1. Despite the settlement, the company still found a way to postpone the meeting until September 26, 2002.[5]

Other times, activist shareholders use litigation to accomplish exactly the opposite goal. Instead of pressuring a company to hold a meeting, the objective is to have that day postponed. In 2007, the Louisiana Municipal Police Employees' Retirement System pension fund asked a Delaware court to put off a shareholder vote on pharmaceutical operator CVS Corporation's proposed acquisition of pharmaceuticals benefits manager, Caremark RX Inc.[6] The activist pension fund sought a court order to postpone a vote on the deal, in part, because it needed more time to consider whether it would support that bid or not. The pension fund also alleged in its suit that Caremark directors and executives were favoring themselves over shareholders when considering the CVS offer.[7] The Delaware court, on February 13, signed an order delaying the vote on the CVS transaction to March 9 from February 20.[8] The pension fund pushed for a delay, in part, to give CVS rival Express Scripts Inc. a chance to consider raising its offer to buy the Nashville-based pharmaceutical giant. Eventually, Express Scripts and CVS became locked into a bidding war for Caremark. At one point, CVS raised its offer and agreed to pay roughly $23 billion and a $2 a share dividend that it later upped to $6 a share.[9] By March 2007, CVS had closed a deal with Caremark for $26.5 billion.[10]

Sometimes litigation is the primary form of activism an insurgent will take. Gabelli Asset Management Inc.'s Mario Gabelli is not afraid of going the litigation route to pressure companies to up their premiums on transactions. But his efforts show how sometimes litigation is an activist strategy that can take years to complete.

For one of Gabelli's recently successful legal endeavors, it is necessary to go back to a 2001 transaction. That year, consumer products and pharmaceutical company Carter-Wallace Inc. was sold in two parts for $1.2 billion.[11] Gabelli, a major shareholder, argued that the deal was completed too soon from a tax consequence point of view. Had Carter Wallace divided the company into two separate entities two years before the divisions were auctioned off, the transactions would have qualified under Internal Revenue Service rules as tax-free sales, according to Gabelli. Disappointed that Carter-Wallace didn't delay the sale for two years when he expected the market would be more favorable for an auction anyway, Gabelli voted against the deals and subsequently filed a lawsuit in Delaware Chancery Court in 2002 arguing in an "appraisal action" that the company did not complete a thorough tax and valuation analysis as part of its auction process. (Voting his shares against the deal, as Gabelli did, is required to pursue an appraisal action.)

Gabelli argued that Carter-Wallace's controlling shareholder, Henry Hoyt and his family trusts, forced a sale of the company at an inopportune time, in part, because he was about to retire, points out Geoffrey C. Jarvis, an attorney representing Gabelli and a partner at Grant & Eisenhofer PA in Wilmington, Delaware. Henry Hoyt was the CEO of the company during the auction process.[12] His great grandfather formed Carter-Wallace in 1880.[13] "Gabelli said the assets were worth a certain amount, the company said they did their best to determine the value of the company, and the judge made a determination," Jarvis says.

While this court case was going on, in May 2003, Gabelli launched a lawsuit against the Carter-Wallace founding Hoyt family and directors, this time in New York, arguing that they did not consider a tax-free plan he had proposed.

The Delaware court took its time evaluating the evidence. Oral arguments took place in 2003, and in 2004, the judge awarded Gabelli and participating shareholders a share value that was, including interest, 47 percent higher than the deal price.[14] The judge argued that the tax consequences of the untimely sale came to $4.01 a share, or roughly a 20 percent premium on the $20.44 a share price of the transaction. That meant the court ordered Carter-Wallace to provide Gabelli roughly $52 million for his 2.1 million shares, better than the $44 million he would have received had he accepted the Carter-Wallace offer. The court rendered its order roughly three years after the deals were struck, and the payment of interest for that period, as the court says, "compensates the plaintiff for the loss of the use of his money during this period."[15] A 27 percent addition to the premium was the result of interest accumulated onto the new valuation.

Carter-Wallace considered appealing the decision to the Delaware Supreme Court, but in November 2004, Gabelli settled with the corporation in both the appraisal case and the New York case for an undisclosed "lump sum" amount.[16]

Jarvis argues that appraisal action is a proven, yet underutilized, activist tactic for any shareholder willing to give it a try to improve the share value of target corporations involved in mergers or other transactions. In a May 2005 report, Jarvis points out that these kinds of appraisal cases over the past 20 years have provided average rewards to shareholders of 80 percent premiums and that, on many occasions, investors receive as much as 400 percent premiums. Jarvis says, in most cases, appraisal litigation can take as little as two years to complete, significantly less than other more complex shareholder lawsuits. Before accepting any offer price in a transaction, activist investors should consider whether companies unjustifiably pressured a deal without completing a thorough auction process. In some cases, activist shareholders can succeed just by launching an appraisal action. Simply the threat of a court case could be enough to convince managers there to sweeten the deal price. "Usually it's a positive award, but on rare occasions it has been negative," Jarvis says.

However, there are some possible drawbacks for activists considering appraisal suits. A positive result is not guaranteed, and petitioners give up the right to receive the merger price that was offered to them. In some cases, courts have concluded that the appraisal value is below the deal price. If that had happened in this case, Gabelli would have received less than the $20.44 a share price offered in the deal, in addition to his court costs. Direct costs of hiring counsel and fees associated with bringing in financial experts can sometimes reach into the millions of dollars. In many cases, those costs are nonrecoverable.

Indirect costs exist as well and need to be considered. Remember, petitioners such as Gabelli must tie up their invested capital for the duration of the case. The courts seek to remedy this situation by including accumulated interest on the appraisal award. Gabelli received significant interest intended to cover the cost of having his investment tied up during the litigation. But was the award and interest Gabelli received more than he could have earned taking the $20.44 a share in 2001 and investing it in other alternative investments instead of locking it up for three years while the court case dragged on?

In one particularly celebrated case of litigation, an activist hedge fund decided to take his skills in filing lawsuits against companies to a whole new arena: the government. Perturbed by a new Securities and Exchange Commission (SEC) rule requiring hedge fund managers to register with the SEC and open up their books to periodic examinations, activist Phillip Goldstein in 2005 decided to file a lawsuit against the agency, arguing that they did not have the legal authority to require the provision. At the time, few in the hedge fund industry or at the SEC believed Goldstein had a chance at winning his case. Many managers grumbled about the new costs associated with the rule, but few did anything to aid Goldstein in his effort. In June 2006, the D.C. appeals court handed down its ruling in favor of Goldstein, and he became an instant celebrity, appearing on CNBC and Bloomberg Television to defend his suit. Goldstein describes the effort as an extension of his activist approach to investing. Unlike other lawsuits Goldstein filed in the past, this suit did not reap any profit for his investors, though it did away with an increase in his internal operation costs. "We have stood up many times for shareholders when a company's board has violated their rights,"

Goldstein says. "We felt compelled to challenge the SEC because we were convinced it had exceeded its legal authority."

Since then, Goldstein, feeling emboldened, has filed another suit against the SEC. This time, he is targeting the agency's "13F" rule, which requires hedge fund managers with $100 million or more assets under management to disclose their portfolio investments every three months. Goldstein, who supports other SEC disclosure rules, says 13F allows other investors to copy his investment choices, which are his intellectual property. Protecting these investment choices would help improve returns for his investors, Goldstein says. His deregulatory antics have also attracted some less appealing attention. Opportunity Partners and other Goldstein funds were sued by Massachusetts Secretary of the Commonwealth William Galvin for violating the state's securities law by purportedly soliciting investors through its Web site. According to Massachusetts laws, as well as other statutes, hedge fund managers are prohibited from publicly soliciting investors through advertisements and Web sites. Opportunity Partners' Internet site, which has since been taken down, asked visitors to read a disclaimer explaining that the contents of the Web site are not to be taken as an investment offer. Despite being simultaneously on the offensive and defensive, Goldstein still continues his activist efforts and says he will continue to file suits when necessary.

Another value investor at times takes a purely litigious approach to activism. Value investor Alan Kahn, a former president at investment firm Kahn Brothers in New York, instigated litigation involving what he called a corporate child abuse story. Kahn founded the firm with his younger brother Thomas Kahn in 1978. Their father, Irving Kahn, who had previously served as a teaching aide to "father of value investing," Benjamin Graham, became chairman of the firm.

In the late 1980s, Kahn noticed that Amsterdam, Netherlands–based Royal Philips Electronics N.V.'s U.S. subsidiary, a publicly traded company named North American Philips' was being forced to buy its key components from the parent company.[17] The U.S. division manufactured Magnavox consumer electronics, including televisions and other products.

Kahn alleged that the Dutch parent company was violating its fiduciary duty to NA Philips' shareholders by prohibiting its U.S. subsidiary from buying its components from cheaper manufacturers emerging in

Asia, as many of its better-priced rivals had been doing.[18] The set-up was enriching the parent company, but depressing the competitive strength of Magnavox and hurting the NA Philips' shareholders, Kahn alleged.

The parent company, Royal Philips, effectively owned a controlling stake in the company, making a proxy contest or any change-of-control effort impossible. Kahn, an NA Philips' shareholder, filed a suit. "I sued the parent company on behalf of the child," Kahn says. "This kind of situation occurs when the parent company is taking advantage of its child, the public subsidiary."

Four days after officially receiving Kahn's lawsuit documents, Royal Philips responded by offering a small premium to buy-out the shares of NA Philips it didn't already own. A small victory, but Kahn was not finished. The premium did not incorporate the possible value of his litigation, which if taken to its logical conclusion, could have reaped NA Philips' shareholders significant capital.[19] So Kahn filed yet another suit arguing that Philips was attempting to buy off shareholders to kill the lawsuit and that the buyout price should be higher still.[20] The company and Kahn settled roughly six months later for a higher price. Kahn has since taken his lawsuit brand of activism to other companies including the Dart Group, a retail fiefdom built up by Herbert Haft, a Washington, D.C., entrepreneur.[21] Other Kahn targets included Velcro Industries, RJR Nabisco, and British Petroleum.[22]

Kahn says he believes that litigation can be an effective tool in unlocking value at certain undervalued companies where corporate abuse exists. He recommends it as a strategy to any investor or activist seeking to unlock shareholder value at a company that otherwise might never improve its stock valuation. The approach, he says, typically is one of the more aggressive forms of activism. For Kahn, engaging behind the scenes to effect change wouldn't work in many of these circumstances. "If I had approached Philips and said, 'You are treating the North American corporation unfairly; please pay back shareholders for the past 20 years of taking advantage of them,' they would have said no," Kahn says.

Whether it's used to supplement other insurgent tactics, such as proxy contests, or as an independent activist initiative, litigation is, as Mitarotonda, Holtzman, Gabelli, Goldstein, and Kahn agree, a strategy that in many cases is necessary to provoke an improvement in shareholder value. It can be used to gain a sweetened per-share transaction offer or provide leverage for other activist efforts, such as pressing a previously recalcitrant company to auction itself off.

A major deterrent to court action is the costs associated with hiring a legal team and bringing in financial experts to present a point of view on a situation. Activists are, to a certain extent, funding both sides of the battle when they choose to litigate. They invest their own funds toward the lawsuit, while the target company will use corporate funds—shareholder money—toward defending itself.

The long, drawn-out, sometimes two- or three-year process is another factor that needs to be considered. Will the court case substantially drain the cash the company has on its balance sheet—the very cash the activist would like to see returned to shareholders? Activists must consider whether litigation will advance other efforts being undertaken and whether they have the capital to stay focused in an extended lawsuit. Finally, insurgents must take into account whether their funds could be better allocated to other efforts. It's a pro-and-con comparison every activist must consider before setting down the litigation path. But one thing is for certain: Litigation is a strategy that any serious activist cannot avoid.

The Group Problem

Insurgents that shrink away from launching lawsuits as part of their activism campaigns should consider one important fact: It won't be long before one will be targeted at them. In other words, activists better learn how to litigate because litigation will eventually track them down.

One extremely common approach companies take to discourage hostile advances by activist hedge fund managers is the "acting as a group" lawsuit. Corporations often will seek to show that activists have violated securities laws by working together without disclosing that information. Wachtell, Lipton, Rosen & Katz's Martin Lipton, the creator of the poison pill corporate raider defense, argues that it's an approach that CEOs should never ignore. "Be aggressive and prepared to litigate or inform regulators immediately if there is evidence that funds have violated securities laws—including by failing to disclose the formation of a group, the identities of the group members or the group's intention...,"

Lipton wrote in a December 2005 memo to companies he coauthored, entitled "Be Prepared for Attacks by Hedge Funds."

As discussed earlier, the SEC defines a group as two or more investors acting together for the purpose of making plans or proposals at a target company.[23] Based on the Securities Exchange Act of 1934 and SEC Schedule 13D rules, certain shareholders are required to disclose their cooperative efforts by making public filings. Specifically, an insurgent planning a proxy contest who approaches another investor and strikes a verbal or written agreement to have that second investor vote his shares for the activist's slate may have formed a group. If so, the two activists must submit a Schedule 13D filing with the SEC announcing their forming of the group. Companies will employ whatever strategies they have in their arsenal to fend off an activist's attack on their tenure. Activists that file Schedule 13Ds and make it known that they are not fond of how the company they own a stake in is managed can make good targets for the group litigation approach, particularly if there are other activists that have made similar SEC filings at the same company. Charging that some activist investors are violating the SEC's group rule even if the investors have done nothing wrong is an easy way for corporate lawyers to test the will and financial wherewithal of activists. Are dissident shareholders willing to take the time and spend the capital to be engaged in a lawsuit? This can be particularly problematic when numerous activists are engaging a particular company in "wolf pack" fashion, as described in Chapter 3. Bally Total Fitness tried the group litigation strategy in late 2005 in an attempt to flick off activist hedge funds Liberation Investment Group and Pardus Capital Management. Both had been pressing for a sale of the fitness chain. Unfortunately for the fitness chain operator, a Delaware Court of Chancery judge was just not having it. The judge denied a motion from Bally that would have allowed an investigation into whether the two activists had undisclosed agreements (acting as a group) that could trigger the health club chain's poison pill, flooding the market with millions of shares and discouraging the shareholder initiative.[24]

Liberation at the time owned an 11.5 percent Bally stake, while Pardus held roughly 14.4 percent. If it were true that the two activists were acting in concert, the combined 26 percent would trigger the antitakeover defense pill at Bally and effectively end the activist campaign.

Attorneys representing activist hedge fund managers tell their clients not to e-mail or instant message with other activists in a particular fund. Howard Godnick, partner at Schulte Roth & Zabel LLP in New York, says that even an exchange of a few e-mails or instant messages (IMs) can land an activist in a world of problems. He illustrated the situation with a few fictitious e-mails:

- "I think we should get together and get a position in XYZ," writes the first activist.
- Response from the other hedge fund manager: "Buy up as much as you can."
- First activist again: "Looks like our plan is working, management will have to work with us."

That exchange constitutes the formation of a group and must be filed with the SEC, Godnick argues.

He adds that activists must be careful when talking to reporters or issuing press releases that they do not make statements indicating that they are acting as a group. These conversations can be used by the company in court to demonstrate formation of a group, all of which could hinder the activists' efforts. (All these problems put another spotlight on why many activist hedge fund managers would prefer to take on corporations in isolation without other insurgents.)

But while Godnick would like to tell his activist hedge fund manager clients not to e-mail, IM, or issue press releases, he realizes that these kinds of communications can't be stopped. "Trying to communicate their message broadly is a core part of an activist's strategy," Godnick says.

Godnick adds that companies like to file these kinds of suits, even if they are frivolous. That's because the sensitive nature of the analysis involved in this kind of court review means that a judge typically will not dismiss charges and the whole case will go to discovery. At this pretrial "discovery" stage, the company begins requesting information and documents from the activist to try and identify pertinent facts. Even if what the company finds is irrelevant to the charge, an activist would prefer to avoid having to fork over some of their proprietary information. Giving executives access to that data, while not incriminating, can provide a sneak peek into the insurgent's strategy. "No one wants someone else looking into their dirty laundry," Godnick said. "Getting access to an activist's e-mails and instant messages can put a company on the road toward making a good argument against the activist."

But activists can protect themselves. In its report, "Management in an Era of Shareholder Activism," Morgan Joseph points out that insurgents seek to escape being defined as a group by speaking together under strict agreements that they will not work together in a campaign.[25]

Opportunity's Goldstein says behind-the-scene communications with other investors helps him weigh what support he might have to launch an activist campaign. But he says many investors still won't talk to activists because they are concerned about the target corporation filing a suit against them based on the contention that they are working together with the activist in a group. "The investor knows that if I am ever sued for being in a 13D group, they are going to ask him, 'Did you ever talk to Mr. Goldstein?'" Goldstein says. "People are afraid of getting involved and talking to activists."

Goldstein added that no corporate executives would ever consider waging such a lawsuit against an activist with their own money. These lawsuits, Goldstein says, are not only frivolous but funded by shareholder capital through the corporate piggybank.

A Schulte Roth & Zabel report from 2006 titled "Beware the Counterattack Against Activist Investors: The Group Trap," recommends that activists should avoid writing up agreements with other investors concerning the purchase or voting of stocks. The terms *activist, group,* and *agreement* should be avoided at all costs.[26] Any discussions of a common goal or plan for management could be interpreted by corporations as the formation of a group, the report says.[27]

Schulte Roth & Zabel, in the report, also recommend that insurgents should make sure to hire separate counsel as an additional protection against being considered a group in the event a target company files a suit against them. Two activists that separately target a particular company but have the same counsel could be in trouble.[28] That's because a court can say that their lawyer speaks for a common group. Godnick points out that a company that has been approached by a number of activist investors may offer to have a meeting with someone that represents their common interests, perhaps as a trap. "If one lawyer were to show up for that meeting, it would feed the company's argument that the attorney is acting on behalf of all activists in the fund and they are acting as a group," Godnick says. "Even if the attorney specifically says at the outset of the meeting that he is not acting on behalf of all the activists, but will only communicate back to them what he learns, that is not good enough. It would all be fodder for a corporate lawsuit."

The group litigation tactic may be just a variation of how corporations protected themselves from corporate raiders in the 1980s. Terrance O'Malley, partner Fried Frank Harris Shriver & Jacobson LLP, says a textbook corporate defense against raiders was to argue that the insurgent did not file its Schedule 13D in a timely manner. As corporate raiders have transformed to activists and companies are finding themselves, more often than previously, coming up against a slew of insurgents, corporate lawyers are resorting to new group disclosure defense tactics. "It's an updated defense playbook," O'Malley says.

Chapter 5

Why Activists Target Certain Corporations and Leave Others Alone

Activist investors had many reasons to complain about their investment in embattled coffee roaster Farmer Brothers Company. Its lack of communications with investors was definitely one major issue.

But probably the most important thing Farmer Brothers did to raise the ire of activist shareholders was to sit on a pile of cash and passive short-term investments.

In 2003, disgruntled investors at Farmer Brothers expressed their dismay upon reading that the company reported in Securities and Exchange Commission (SEC) filings that it had almost $300 million in these lackluster short-term securities investments.[1] By the end of 2005, the investment portfolio had dwindled down to $171 million.[2]

Lutin & Company president Gary Lutin estimated at the time that the investments represented roughly 57 percent of Farmer Brothers' assets.

In fact, at one point in 2004, dissident investors even began writing letters to the SEC raising the question about whether the coffee roaster had become an unregistered investment company in violation of the Investment Company Act of 1940.[3] Companies with more than 40 percent of their total assets in cash and passive investments, such as securities, must register with the SEC as investment companies. The concern by a large group of activist investors was that Farmer Brothers was not putting its capital to good use.

Having a significant portion of a company's assets in cash and securities, with no defined plans to use that cash for operations or acquisitions, is clearly a major way of attracting the attention of insurgent shareholders. Disputes between shareholders and corporations over the proper use of cash and assets can get very emotional. Corporations that have a significant amount of cash on their balance sheets typically argue that it needs to be there for a wide variety of reasons. Perhaps a great acquisition opportunity could come along in the near future, or there may be a major economic downturn around the corner and the reserves are necessary to protect the company during that difficult time period. Companies may also argue that cash is necessary for some major anticipated expense.

But activists are usually of the mind-set that Corporate America has generally not done a good enough job of using the cash it has on hand or justifying to its investors why it needs to be there. An overinflated cash reserve also often can lead executives to avoid making critical cuts that are necessary during recessions or economic slumps. In other circumstances, they argue, corporations make poorly thought out acquisitions with too much cash on hand. In short, many activists have this argument: use it or lose it. By lose it, insurgents mean to say, give it back to shareholders. Activist investors know that a simple way to improve shareholder value is by convincing management to return that cash to shareholders in the form of a stock buyback or special dividend.

"Many companies keep too much corporate booty," says Stanley Gold, chief executive of Shamrock Holdings. "I've never met a CEO who does not want a huge war chest." According to a 2006 study produced by investment bank Morgan Joseph & Company, cash as a percentage of market value at Standard & Poor's (S&P) 500 companies is higher than it has been in more than two decades.[4] The chief operating officer of the U.S. Chamber of Commerce, David Chavern, acknowledges that corporations undoubtedly make themselves more vulnerable to activists when they accumulate large cash and passive investment positions and don't invest those funds in the business or return money to shareholders. "Most companies in the U.S. were not designed to be deposit institutions," Chavern says. "Where you are focused on growth, you're using your retained earnings to build a business and you don't sit around trying to figure out what to do with it. You make yourself a target when you become self satisfied and you sit on a bunch of money and you're not too worried about growth."

In anticipation of activist complaints, companies are beginning to review their financial policies, such as their dividend and stock buyback plans, periodically. A company that has recently implemented a significant stock buyback has more credibility with its rank-and-file institutional investors when an activist starts to take issue with its cash reserve and how the business is operated, reports Morgan Joseph.[5]

But having too much cash and securities on hand with no plans for these funds is just the tip of the iceberg. Corporations that have their bylaws—rules by which the business is run—set up without anti-takeover provisions could also become attractive activist targets. Without them in place, insurgents may start agitating to attract strategic and private equity companies to make premium-priced bids for the company.[6]

The same can be said of having an unclassified board that requires directors to be elected annually. It can make a company's management vulnerable to the kind of insurgent proxy contest that could replace the entire board and subsequently remove executives against their will. Roughly half of U.S. corporations have classified boards. Provocateurs at companies with annual elections have more leverage behind the scenes in negotiating changes, such as convincing the board to accept dissident director nominations.

The lack of other provisions could also encourage activists. For example, if shareholders have the ability to call a special shareholder meeting, they often will. Recall the case of Crescendo calling a special shareholder meeting at Computer Horizons as part of efforts to break up the company. Insurgents can use that opportunity to call a vote on matters executives may not be so keen to consider. For example, an expedited vote on whether a management-backed director should be removed and replaced is not something executives would like to see take place. Corporations protect themselves from this possibility by changing their bylaws to only allow investors to call special shareholder meetings in the most extraordinary of situations.

Some activists prefer to target companies that have no or negligible debt loads. Simple strategy: activists press the CEO to agree to some debt financing and use the capital raised to buy back shares, issue a special dividend to shareholders or invest in the business—perhaps an expansion plan. Again, this can be a problem if activists press companies to overleverage themselves into a distressed state. Alternatively, activists may be more likely to press companies with little or no debt to return existing cash on-hand to shareholders. Companies with little debt can afford some additional debt financing and at the same time return cash to shareholders, they argue.

Liberation's Pearlman has been urging Multimedia Games Inc., an Austin, Texas–based electronic game and player terminal manufacturer for the Native American gaming market, to increase it debt load and use some proceeds to either repurchase shares or invest in some other strategy that would improve the company's stock value, at least for the short term. The company reported roughly $60 million in current and long-term debt as of June 30, 2006, significantly less than many of its gaming competitors, Pearlman points out.

A stock buyback would, in the short term, help improve Multimedia Games' languishing stock valuation. It traded throughout most of 2006 in the $8 to $15 a share range; much less than the $20 to $25 a share at which it was trading three years earlier. In addition to hiking its debt load and buying back shares, Pearlman would like to see the company auction itself, which he believes will also help unlock the stock's potential. But debt was a key factor in his consideration. In October 2006, Pearlman moved closer to achieving his goal. Multimedia Games agreed to put him on the board, where presumably he will continue to press for stock buybacks, special dividends, and a sale.[7]

Unusual expenses such as related-party transactions also can help put a company in an activist's sights. These are personal loans requested by executives for purchases such as real estate, but they can also take the form of consulting contracts provided to family members of directors or executives. These fuzzy transactions entered the general public's collective consciousness after investors such as Jim Chanos and Christopher Browne exposed the provisions for what they were at Enron, Hollinger, and other major corporate collapses. "Related-party transactions typically are not in the best interest of improving the company or its share value," Randy Lampert says. "They expose the company to activists."

Companies that have an unusually large amount of assets tied up in unused real estate that can easily be sold also attract activists. For example, activists at the coffee roaster Farmer Brothers have been pressing company officials to sell the property it owns and subsequently lease back the land with its roasting, packaging, and distribution plant operations. Dissidents say Farmer Brothers could receive as much as $100 million in proceeds from a sale of the land. That capital, together with the funds from the securities investments, should be distributed to shareholders in the form of a special dividend or restructuring plan, Lutin says. However, since Farmer Brothers has not disclosed the value of the land, it's unclear just how valuable it is.

A major reason why activist hedge fund Pirate Capital began efforts in late 2004 to urge GenCorp to make changes was that it identified the company's valuable but undeveloped property outside Sacramento, California, as an asset that could be worth as much as $3.7 billion to $7 billion after some development costs. "The company has 12,700 acres or 21 square miles (Bermuda is 21 square miles and Manhattan is 23 square miles) of real estate located outside Sacramento, which the company has implied are worth significantly more than the current enterprise value," Pirate Capital wrote to GenCorp's board in November 2004.

One major factor that draws activists is the presence of disparate businesses under one roof with limited strategic connections. Complex conglomerates with too many moving parts are often the result of a poor history of mergers and acquisitions.[8] Too many different units make it difficult for outside observers to accurately value each subdivision. In such circumstances, it becomes easy for an activist to come along and value each division and decide that the company is worth more to shareholders divided and sold into separate units rather than kept together as a whole.

Case in point: Activist investor Robert Chapman's research in 2002 and 2003 at Cinar Corporation led him to conclude that the sum of the parts at this Canadian entertainment company was not greater than the whole. In fact, Chapman asserted, the business would have a greater value separated into two businesses than continuing to operate as one unit. He estimated that Cinar's education publishing business was valued at $103 million and its children's entertainment unit had a value of between $75 million and $100 million. By 2003, Toronto Dominion Bank's private-equity division and an investor group acquired the company for $144 million.[9] Not quite the valuations Chapman had been hoping for, but still good enough to make a profit from the venture.

Activists may also urge companies to divest one unrelated unit that they contend is taking management's attention away from a core business. Third Point's Loeb in 2002 was attracted to Penn Virginia Corporation of Radnor, Pennsylvania, in part, because his research indicated that the market was inaccurately valuing the company's two divisions operating under one corporate umbrella. Penn Virginia is an oil and gas exploration and production company that also partly owns a coal and timber properties unit.

Due to the amalgamated units and other issues, Penn Virginia's shares traded at a discount "to the company's intrinsic value," Loeb wrote in a February 2002 SEC filing. Rather than the $13 to $17 a share at which the company was trading at the time, Loeb reported that he believed the company was worth as much as $50 a share. "There is a gap between the company's share price and its intrinsic value," Loeb wrote.

To unlock the intrinsic value, Loeb urged Penn Virginia to auction its oil and gas unit, separating it from the coal and lumber division. Unfortunately, his efforts did not produce the desired separation. Eventually, 1980s raider Thomas Boone Pickens Jr. emerged from early retirement and took an activist interest in breaking up the company. Pickens reported a stake and made a bid to take over Penn Virginia, an offer that was eventually rejected. The company still remains independent, but its stock has skyrocketed and was trading in mid-2007 at $80 a share, well more than Loeb's earlier price prediction.

In addition to seeking out corporations that have dissimilar divisions, activists also target companies that haven't retained an investment bank to periodically examine and consider strategic alternatives such as asset sales. When activists press for a sale, they typically call on management to hire an investment bank to complete a thorough strategic review of alternatives. Management can discourage insurgent advances if they can point to an investment bank's recently completed strategic review to explain to other investors why a certain strategy opined by the activists won't work.[10] "A company that can point to a complete review of strategic alternatives makes it difficult for an activist to make the same demand," reports Morgan Joseph.

However, a CEO that is fending off a hostile activist and wants to keep the company independent may launch an artificial auction process, with no expectation of ever seriously considering the advice provided by the retained investment bank. In other circumstances, an executive may try to find an investment banker that will, in exchange for a fee, strategically value the business at a price beyond what any interested bidders offered. In other words, from an activist's point of view, provoking a company to begin a strategic review process with a retained investment bank may just be a false success, and it may take months to identify whether the company is seriously considering such an action.

Instead of hiring an investment bank, some companies may make a point of ensuring that directors at every board meeting are reviewing the CEO's performance as well as completing a marketplace analysis. James Hyman, the CEO of correctional facilities builder Cornell Companies, says companies may consider this approach rather than continuously retaining an investment bank to provide strategic advice. Directors should periodically examine the executive's plan and decide whether their approach derives more value than what others would pay to acquire the company. How the company goes about reviewing its options should be described in its annual report, Hyman says. He adds that corporations with standing strategic review board committees that contemplate transactions from time to time are more likely to convince institutional investors to reject insurgent demands. That's why he recommends making it a permanent committee, which would also reduce employee worries. Hyman points out that rank-and-file employees tend to get nervous about their job security every time an investment bank is hired to consider a sale of the business.

Activists need to decide, in these circumstances, whether calling on the company to engage an investment bank to launch a strategic review would be looked at favorably by the company's institutional investors.

Having a permanent strategic review committee could rebuff activist claims that the company is not considering a value-enhancing transaction, Hyman adds.

Small-capitalization companies, still the most likely targets of insurgent insurrections, have another problem that can't easily be remedied. One of the reasons many companies are undervalued, and therefore the target of insurgent value investors, is that they have no Wall Street sell-side analyst coverage. With independent Wall Street coverage, companies' stock prices generally navigate their way to a more accurate representation of the company's worth. Encouraging analysts to start covering the company could make the investment less attractive for activists. Even with more coverage, however, there will continue to be many undervalued small capitalization companies that slip beneath the analysts' radar and remain good pickings for activists.

Consider once again Santa Monica Partners' Lawrence Goldstein and his discovery of the undervalued and ignored railroad freight car leasing industry in the 1960s. Activists typically like to invest in companies where their own research leads them to discover that a company has a value that the market is not recognizing. That is less likely to happen at companies with several analysts researching the businesses operations and profit margins.

It may be impossible to avoid an insurgent if certain basic problems exist at the company. Corporate Library's Nell Minow says corporations can try all kinds of fancy maneuvers to avoid activists, but the most important thing they can do is provide continuing strong stock performance. "I can tell you one way of staying out of the spotlight," Minow says. "Deliver to shareholders."

Insurgents, of course, are also looking for companies with board-independence problems. Directors with financial or family ties to management exist at both companies with poorly performing stocks and companies a with strong stocks. But at the poorly performing companies, that independent directors issue will draw governance-style insurgents seeking to bring in directors without ties to the company. At distressed companies, a lack of independent directors on boards is often a symptom of a much larger problem at the company.

The post-Enron New York Stock Exchange and NASDAQ listing standard reforms are going a long way toward making sure corporations have more independent boards. But the University of Delaware's Charles Elson says companies should fulfill not only the specifics of the rules, but also the spirit of them. Struggling public companies with unsophisticated boards made up partly of family member directors that support management unconditionally can be enough to incentivize an activist to take action.

The troubles associated with a lack of independent directors on corporate boards can be compounded by a related problem. Directors without a serious stake in companies they oversee have incentives that are incompatible with those of dissident investors, who are more concerned about making sure the stock price improves. "For good corporate governance you need to have independent directors with equity in the companies they oversee," Elson says. "Companies with these kinds of boards perform well and those results reach shareholders."

Fending Off Activists: A New Corporate Agenda

The growth and spread of activist investors and the impact they are having on companies has led CEOs and their advisers to begin taking steps to prepare for an activist's advances. What does this mean for shareholders launching insurgencies? Activists planning to begin public-pressure campaigns need get their act together faster than ever. The famous Martin Lipton, founder and partner at Wachtell, Lipton, Rosen & Katz, advises corporate leaders to have a response program and people in place to react to a surprise attack.[11]

In addition to recommending that companies take all sorts of 13D group related legal action against activists, Lipton recommends that companies should consider other precautionary steps. The memo he wrote to corporate advisors in 2005 recommends that executives might want to monitor analyst reports constantly to check for "half-baked" ideas that are intended to quickly improve stock valuations.[12] "Frequently hedge funds are 'turned on' to a company by an analyst who one way or another got an idea for a way to get a quick increase in the price of the stock," Lipton wrote in the memo.

Companies can take other steps as well, such as installing sophisticated stock watch programs that immediately inform corporate executives to new large shareholders, particularly any purchases made by activists. Basically, Lipton explains, management must constantly be up to date on the company's investor base so it can respond as quickly as possible to any advances.[13] "Detection tools must be upgraded to meet the challenges posed by these purchases," Lipton writes.

Cornell Companies' James Hyman says executives must respond to activists quickly and early; otherwise the situation can get out of hand. The state of affairs at Cornell Companies did get out of hand after the company's board ignored activist investors early on, Hyman says. In 2003 and 2004, Pirate Capital and other insurgents urged the company to replace its CEO, which it finally did in January 2005 by hiring Hyman. But during the early stages of their campaign, the activists complained that Cornell's board ignored them, and when directors did finally start an executive search, it did not keep the disgruntled shareholders abreast of their progress. By the time Hyman was brought on board, several new activists had already joined the pack, and Pirate had expanded its activist campaign appreciably, by launching a proxy contest with good prospects for success. A large part of the antagonism between activists and management at Cornell could have been avoided, says Hyman, had the company kept its investors informed about the progress of the executive search.

David Pasquale, executive vice president of investor relations consultancy, The Ruth Group, in New York, says the initial response by Cornell Companies is typical of the naïve way corporations respond to activist owners of their stocks. The biggest mistake companies make is that upon receiving a call from an activist, they are either unresponsive or defensive, he says. Instead, executives and directors should immediately take some time to hear out the strategies of an activist. "They somehow think ignoring the activist is going to help the situation," Pasquale says.

In May 2005, Hyman, in damage-control mode, agreed to a major settlement with Pirate. The agreement was to put two dissident investors on the board, along with five independent directors of their choosing, leaving three former board members, including Hyman, intact. But, Hyman points out, that if Cornell's previous board had tried to reach a deal with the dissident shareholders earlier on instead of ignoring their initial advances, a complete board restructuring could have been avoided. "If the activists are out there, you [directors] are in danger of losing control of the situation. To regain control, cut a deal that is deeper than what you would prefer," Hyman says. "Had Cornell's board tried to cut a deal a few months earlier, they could have probably reached an agreement to have the old board plus one new person."

At the end of the day, Cornell was sold to a private-equity firm. Hyman says directors must actively manage their communications with major shareholders. If the CEO is a problem, the board must send a trusted director out to communicate with the company's shareholders. Without that communication, directors may not fully appreciate the level of disappointment emanating from the shareholder base.

In addition to boards and CEOs, investor relations (IR) officials are taking steps to become savvier in anticipation of an insurgent's approaches. Many IR officials are spending more time trying to get a handle on the activist investor community. In particular, they are familiarizing themselves with the activists that focus on companies in their industry. For example, some activists, as we discuss in Chapter 7, focus their agitation only on certain mid-sized banks and thrifts. IR officials for banks, which could become targets of this set of insurgents, are familiarizing themselves with possible troublemakers in anticipation of a potential campaign targeted against the institution. Some IR officials have developed a base of knowledge about whether a particular activist is prone to social embarrassment campaigns or proxy fights. With this information, these officials are beginning to provide better advice to management about how to respond. IR officials also are reaching out in greater frequency to institutional investors. Making sure a corporation's executives understand what its investor base thinks of management is important, though this new level of interaction has had the unintended effect of ticking off many passive managers that have no desire to speak with company officials. Larger companies that can afford it are hiring consultants, public relations firms and advisers, ready to take action in the event of an activist campaign.

For activists, this means that they may no longer have the element of surprise when they target a corporation. Consider what one enterprising firm has done to capitalize on the confusion companies face when targeted by insurgents. FactSet Research System developed a set of data that it sells to corporations that are either being targeted by activists or worry an insurgency could take place. The New York–based company created a database of the most prominent 50 activist hedge fund managers with details about their strategies, past successes and failures, and generally what executives can expect as they begin to tussle with a well-known insurgent. The database, appropriately named "SharkRepellent," is sold to advisers who work with corporations or corporate executives themselves that are struggling to handle an activist campaign. "This is intended to help out managers that are besieged with activists," says Tom Quinn, vice president at FactSet Research Systems in New York.

Quinn points out that once executives have these data in their hands, they can quickly find out whether a particular activist is likely to launch a proxy contest. For example, many activists may have a history of threatening to start proxy battles but never follow through. Perhaps they are not willing to take the financial risk. That kind of detail can be invaluable to an executive struggling to figure out how to respond to an insurgent.

Details about whether a particular activist has previously launched successful proxy fights are also helpful to a CEO deciding how to respond to an activist campaign in its early stages. Knowing that an activist's typical strategy is to block mergers or force a sale of its target corporations is useful, too, Quinn says, as is seeing how other companies have responded to past activist initiatives.

Quinn noted that Steel Partners, for example, has launched 84 different campaigns at 77 companies. The fund's manager, Warren Lichtenstein, launched proxy contests at 23 percent of the companies he targeted, and only in five cases, or 6 percent of the total, did he threaten a proxy contest without going through with it, according to a report. So if you are a CEO faced with a proxy threat from Steel Partners, be prepared for the contest to take place.

Executives campaigning to thwart an activist's advances will also explain to investors that all the time, energy, and capital the company spends to combat an activist's insinuations and instigations take time and money away from the orderly running of the corporation. Executives will try to make clear that an insurgent's efforts are disruptive, in part, because they upset existing and potential suppliers, customers, and employees. In many cases, activist campaigns are disruptive. Since most activists target troubled or struggling companies, the CEOs at these corporations are often focused more than ever before on making sure the company's business strategy makes sense. Pasquale says corporate executives are spending much more time dealing with the day-to-day IR issues relating to activists than they were even five years ago. "The amount of time a management team spends on investor relations is far greater now and for many companies that is because of activists," Pasquale says.

In addition to problems concentrating on day-to-day business responsibilities, an activist must consider whether, in some circumstances, executives are too busy privately doing exactly what the activist wants them to be doing.

In what may be a particularly extreme example of this, Canadian GEAC Computer Corporation's CEO Charles Jones says he had been unable to focus on an orderly but confidential auction of the business because an activist hedge fund had been pressing him to sell the company and didn't believe he was genuinely interested in selling it. The insurgent, Crescendo's Eric Rosenfeld, launched a proxy contest to install two candidates on the board. The contest was settled after GEAC agreed to bring one Crescendo director on board. GEAC eventually signed a deal to sell itself to San Francisco tech buyout shop Golden Gate for $1 billion.[14] "The only impact Crescendo had was to slow down the sale," Jones says. "I spent 100 percent of my time on the bloody proxy contest for the 60 days leading up to it."

Whether Rosenfeld had any influence on the auction—either slowing it down or speeding it up—is unclear. Rosenfeld says he had an impact on the ultimate sale of the company, acknowledging he was concerned that Jones might push GEAC to overpay for an acquisition, instead of successfully auctioning itself. "Until the deal is done, it isn't done," Rosenfeld says. "I think we were helpful in the process of bringing the deal to completion."

As activists grow in size and numbers, companies will continue taking steps to prepare for their advances. Whether faced with reluctant activists or full-out devoted insurgents, corporate executives, including IR officials, chief financial officers, and CEOs, are becoming more aware of this growing group of investors and their peers.

Executives have begun responding in a much more nuanced and prepared manner to activist insurgencies. According to one business adviser, corporate officials have begun to feel more comfortable asking hedge fund managers questions about their strategies. CEOs are reaching out faster to whatever external advisers they deem necessary to respond to activist efforts. Once confused and disoriented, unable to respond to an activist's 13D filings or their often incessant, confrontational phone calls, corporate-suite managers are learning that insurgent investors are becoming a part of life that cannot be ignored. Executives and IR officials are beginning to realize that they could be next on some activist's list.

But no amount of preparation will protect certain corporations from activist campaigns. There will always be companies that just can't help but fit the mold dissident shareholders are seeking out.

Activists will target a company that combines a number of the factors described in this chapter with a poorly performing stock. Let's face it, a company with a fast-climbing share price that also has unused real estate or a bunch of lapdog, disinterested insiders on its board may not be an activist's first choice. But a company with a stagnating stock, lots of cash on the balance sheet, no anti-takeover protections, and little debt, plus a bunch of unrelated divisions the stock market is not factoring into its share price, will more likely set off alarm bells. That company may be so attractive that friends (read: other activists) will be notified.

Of course, insurgents prefer to target corporations that have performed poorly over a number of years, with executives that continue to receive huge pay packages despite presiding over companies with deteriorating share prices. Companies with distorted compensation packages and overly generous golden parachute severances that also have executives receiving related-party transactions, such as personal loans, are likely to draw out even that category of insurgent I describe as the reluctant activist. Conrad Black at Hollinger International Inc. discovered this kind of insurgency firsthand, as have dozens of other CEOs. The battle between executives and activists over CEO pay packages is the subject of Chapter 6.

Chapter 6

Overperked and Overpaid

The Impact of Activists on Executive Compensation

In return for his duties, communications and entertainment firm Glenayre Technologies Inc.'s CEO Clarke Bailey was paid an annual salary of $1 million, including a yearly bonus.

In addition, he collected $25,000 a year in social club fees. At the same time that he was receiving all that, Glenayre Technology's stock price was sagging. For a period of roughly five years, it has traded, for the most part, between $2 and $3 a share. It started 2006 at $3.20 a share, hiked up to as much as $6 a share in May, but has since dropped to well below $3 a share.

This situation raised the ire of activist Robert Chapman, who eventually made sure all the company's shareholders knew about the wilting stock price and Bailey's social club payments. Four months after Chapman began agitating for change, Bailey resigned from his position as CEO. But even after Bailey's resignation, Chapman was not through bringing attention to the company's compensation practices.

James Caparro, the CEO of Glenayre's Entertainment Distribution Company LLC unit, was promoted to chief executive of the whole business.[1] Not satisfied, Chapman put pressure on him as well, pointing out that Caparro had no stake in the company and that his compensation package (roughly the same as Bailey's, including social club dues) did not align his interests with that of shareholders.

Caparro's plan gives him a special profit interest if Glenayre's entertainment distribution subsidiary is sold separately from the rest of the business. This is a prospect, Chapman argues, that could hurt shareholders, particularly if Caparro uses the proceeds from such a sale for a poorly thought-out future acquisition. If the whole company is sold after EDC is divested, Caparro would receive an additional change of control benefit on top of the special profit interest he received upon the sale of EDC.

"Caparro's big payday should not be tied to the sale of an asset but rather to the sale of the whole company and thus the stock price thereof," Chapman says. "Otherwise, Caparro could orchestrate a self-enriching auction of the EDC business and squander the proceeds on a poorly conceived acquisition that destroys Glenayre's public owners' investment in the shares."

Chapman's comments may be intended, in part, to embarrass management as part of his "social" lever activism approach. But they also put a spotlight on a key strategy for activist investors: identify and target a company with executives receiving unusually high pay packages and perquisites (perks) that are presiding over a company with a poorly performing stock.

Chapman and other activists seek out underperforming or distressed companies with languishing stock prices where they can bolster support for their cause among other investors by pointing out certain exorbitant compensation plans.

One area in particular is drawing a great deal of attention by activists: CEO perks. When CEOs of General Motors and Chrysler came to Washington seeking government bailout funds, the corporate jets they utilized frequently drew the ire of lawmakers who were averse to providing the financial lifeline the automakers needed. Companies that offer extreme perks, such as expensive golf club membership or company-paid family trips on the corporate jet (in Glenayre's case, $25,000 in social club membership), can become easy targets for activists. That's because perks put a spotlight on tangible excesses that activists can draw attention to as part of their campaigns to attain support for their cause. Institutional and retail investors may be more likely to oppose management if an activist can bring public attention through media reports and other means to a tangible perk that just seems extreme.

"When corporations use these kinds of extreme perks, they're saying, 'Look over here' to potential activists that could try to put the company in play," says John Olson, partner at Gibson Dunn & Crutcher LLP in Washington. "And activists just fan the flame."

The U.S. Chamber of Commerce's David Chavern says corporations are giving shareholders who want to target them a tool when they start providing unusual perks to executives. He adds that insurgents pointing out executive perks typically draw media attention, often because activist investors draw attention to the special benefits through their Schedule 13D filings, press releases, and other means.

All this creates additional problems for the company, including a greater likelihood that more activists will get involved, purchase a block of shares, and pressure to make changes. Chavern says there is one way companies can keep pestering activists at bay: moderate or eliminate the perks. "If you a pay a CEO $5 million and give him a bunch of perks, including club memberships and daily fresh flowers for his desk, you're handing weapons to people who are looking to make complaints and launch activist campaigns against you," Chavern says. "If you pay a CEO $5.1 million and no perks and he uses the extra $100,000 for club memberships, that compensation would attract no special attention."

Chavern says he believes that most activists are not usually interested in their target company CEO's compensation because the executive's salary, bonuses, and perks rarely rise to the level of "materiality" at those corporations. Activists point to the compensation, Chavern argues, because it aids them in gaining institutional and retail investor support in their other endeavors at the company, such as pressing the company to do stock buybacks or division auctions. These initiatives may not be in the best interest of long-term investors, he adds.

But Harvard Law School professor Lucian Bebchuk says he disagrees with that assessment, arguing that at these corporations, CEOs' pay arrangements are material because executives there have less incentive to improve a company's share performance if they continue to be compensated for mediocre or even worse financial results. Activists, he says, will invest in companies where they identify executives who have continued to receive significant compensation despite presiding over poorly performing companies. "The cost of a flawed pay arrangement is not limited to the excess pay; the more important costs might be the costs resulting from an executive's distorted incentives," Bebchuk says.

Paul Lapides, director of Kennesaw State University's Corporate Governance Center in Kennesaw, Georgia, says that it's true that activists try to bring attention to a CEO's compensation as part of their campaign to win over other shareholders. He adds that their arguments about executive compensation usually are genuine and something that other investors in the business should consider. Activist shareholders understand that a major reason why executive compensation matters is that employees at companies that have CEOs with poorly structured payment packages typically underperform, resulting in lower profits and revenues for shareholders. "I've seen enough companies where employees are dissatisfied with their CEO's compensation," Lapides says. "When large numbers of people are dissatisfied with their leaders, they become less engaged in their day-to-day work."

Executives with overly excessive compensation also have less motivation to improve a company's performance. Chapman points out that "absurdly high compensation" is material to a company because it lowers profits, particularly at small and midcapitalization companies. He adds that many investors in struggling companies with misaligned executive pay plans will sell their shares, further depressing the company's valuation. Poorly structured executive compensation packages also can lower the corporate governance rating a company receives from shareholder advisory groups, a result that compounds the problem of diminishing share returns. "The 'immaterial' argument is mathematically absurd," Chapman says. "Activists are truly interested in a CEO's compensation for a wide variety of reasons."

Making the company and its "overcompensated CEO" a public spectacle is a key part of the insurgent's strategy to gain the support of institutions, retail investors, and the public overall.

It especially helps if activists destroy the perception that they are looking for some "quick buck" short-term returns at the expense of institutional investors, says Terrance O'Malley, partner at Fried Frank Harris Shriver & Jacobson LLP in New York. "By targeting a CEO's executive compensation, activists are trying to explain to institutional and retail investors that they aren't the bad guys," says O'Malley. "Activists are trying to make changes that affect everyone invested in the stock, and part of that is by exposing problems with the compensation scheme at the company."

The strategy is working. Institutional investors have started backing activists' efforts to rein in executive pay packages and perks. Institutional Shareholder Services in a 2006 report, "Hot Topics for the 2006 Proxy Season and Beyond," asked investor members if they would be willing to take action against a company's compensation committee for questionable or egregious perquisites such as personal use of company aircraft, country-club memberships . . ." Of those responding, 57 percent said yes, 25 percent said no, and 18 percent said they don't know.[2]

Another warning sign, says Olson, is change-of-control severance packages that overincentivize CEOs to strike deals that are in their interest but not in the interest of shareholders. With that kind of incentives, a CEO could be more likely to sell at a less-than-fair price or a price below what the activist or other investors believe the company is worth.

Insurgents trolling through undervalued companies for possible activist candidates may make a note of any future severance payments that could be made in the form of a golden parachute to an executive in the event of a change of control. In some cases, a huge change-of-control payout plan could attract an activist based on the expectation that the CEO is incentivized to auction the business, particularly with a little nudge.

Gibson, Dunn's Olson says the trend is leaning toward executive pay and severance packages that overincentivize CEOs to sell at any price. "If you put in the kind of a severance or change-of-control package as we have seen at many companies in the last couple of years, doesn't that tell the market, including activist hedge fund managers, that this company is considering a merger or sale?" asks Olson.

Harvard University's Bebchuk says that at one time there was a concern that executives' interest in keeping their jobs overincentivized them to avoid getting involved in value-creating transactions. But now, he says, the pendulum has swung in the other direction. CEOs are negotiating additional golden parachute severance packages, consulting arrangements, or other payment plans for themselves at the same time as they are negotiating the sale of the company. "The structure of payments today might have executives getting involved in sales that should not be taking place," he says. "The ability to get a large payoff from the acquisition now may incentivize CEOs to strike a deal even though they believe the long-term value of the company is higher than what is offered."

In those circumstances, activists can move on to plan B: pressure for a higher premium once a deal is struck or seek to block the deal outright. Steven Kaplan, professor of entrepreneurship and finance at the University of Chicago's Graduate School of Business, says this activist investor response is part of an effective free-market mechanism for punishing CEOs that engage in mergers that don't benefit shareholders. Led by activist hedge fund managers, shareholders have launched public campaigns against deals, seeking to block them or pressure for additional premiums. This phenomenon is discussed further in Chapter 11.

Activists are putting a magnifying glass to this compensation and also pay packages CEOs negotiate to remain employed after they sell the company. The concern is that executives may be more willing to sell the business at a poor valuation for shareholders if they can gain some additional payment for themselves. Insurgents consider all these different forms of pay packages as part of their evaluation of whether the CEO is acting in the best interest of shareholders when selling the business.

Democratic lawmakers in the U.S. Congress are also sending a strong message that activists deserve a greater voice in executive compensation. House Financial Services Committee Chairman Barney Frank (D-MA) introduced legislation that would give shareholders an opportunity to give an advisory vote to corporate boards on their CEO payment plans. As the measure is drafted, companies are under no obligation to adhere to the vote results. But, overwhelming investor opposition to a payment plan could embarrass a corporate compensation committee enough to make changes to a CEO's pay package. A key part of the measure would require corporations to put any payment plans negotiated by the CEO, as part of a sale of the company, up for an advisory vote. After a divided House of Representatives voted to pass the legislation, the Bush administration issued a veto threat against it. The business community is opposed to the measure. However, the Obama Administration is much more receptive. If it becomes law, activist shareholders are expected to take advantage of the nonbinding votes as they lead both private and public campaigns against companies.

The issue of extreme pay and severance packages came to a head at The Home Depot, Inc. in 2006 and early 2007. Home Depot chairman and CEO Robert Nardelli resigned from the mega home hardware and improvement retailer after dissident shareholders, led by investor activist Ralph Whitworth's Relational Investors of San Diego, put him under tremendous scrutiny for continuing to receive significant pay increases despite the company's stagnating stock performance.[3]

After a chorus of institutional investors proclaimed their outrage over Nardelli's compensation plan prior to the company's 2006 annual meeting in May, Whitworth recognized an opportunity. In December, he formed plans to nominate two director candidates to The Home Depot's board at the company's 2007 annual meeting. Less than three months later, Whitworth settled with The Home Depot after the do-it-yourself hardware company agreed to put Relational cofounder David Batchelder on its board.[4] As part of the settlement, Whitworth cancelled his contest and Home Depot agreed to eventually remove four directors, who were involved in employing Nardelli.[5]

By any consideration, The Home Depot is a huge company for an activist to sink its teeth into. Relational itself did not control such a huge block of shares that Whitworth could apply significant leverage without major shareholder support. Just to give an indication, Relational invested $1 billion in The Home Depot, but all that got him was about 1.2 percent of the $84 billion stock-market capitalization company.[6] Had Whitworth chosen to find a way to invest the fund's entire $6.4 billion in assets under management that allocation would have only represented a 7.6 percent Home Depot stake. Even that would not have been nearly enough.

A significant number of shareholders put their weight behind Whitworth to generate the critical mass of investor support needed to facilitate Nardelli's departure. After facing criticism from investors over his compensation, Nardelli instituted a sort of martial law at The Home Depot's 2006 annual meeting, not helping his public perception. Nardelli was the only director present at the company's shortened 30-minute annual meeting, which took place with no investor question-and-answer period. The shareholder-unfriendly meeting and Whitworth's subsequent campaign generated more public pressure on Nardelli to resign or accept less money. Major financial publications covered the saga, putting additional strain on Nardelli and Home Depot's board to do something that would take the home repair retailer out of its negative spotlight. Once in the glare of public attention and faced with an institutional investor insurrection, Home Depot's board pressured Nardelli to reduce his compensation and severance packages.[7] Nardelli reportedly was open to cutting out personal use of the company's six corporate jets but he wasn't willing to slash his salary and bonuses.[8] The combination of Whitworth and his pressure campaign, combined with a mobilized base of institutional investors, was enough to pressure Nardelli into stepping down. "The financial media's treatment of some of these compensation issues also put a lot of pressure on Nardelli," ISS's McGurn says.

After resigning, Nardelli defended himself by pointing out that Home Depot had strong earnings during the six-year period he was in charge. But Whitworth points out that during the same time frame, the company's earnings improvement did not translate into a strong stock performance.[9] In fact, Home Depot's stock stagnated during Nardelli's tenure. Whitworth points out that Home Depot's stock performed poorly during Nardelli's tenure while the shares of the home improver's rival, Lowe's Companies Inc., tripled in value. Whitworth points out that the results weren't surprising because Nardelli's compensation was based more on Home Depot's earnings improvements than its stock performance. The compensation scheme of his successor, Frank Blake, was set up with more stock-based incentives.[10] At The Home Depot's 2007 annual meeting, Blake apologized for the company's handling of the previous meeting. Unlike his predecessor, Blake held a shareholder question-and-answer period.

Nardelli's $210 million severance package, including bonuses and pension, triggered another round of protests from Home Depot's investors. Shareholders turned to a Georgia state court seeking an injunctive order to block The Home Depot from paying Nardelli that sum of money, contending that he was an unsuccessful CEO at the helm of the company and he didn't deserve such compensation.[11] Later, in January 2007, a judge refused to block the severance pay but permitted investors additional time to research their case further. Running away from public shareholders, Nardelli took a job as head of automotive giant Chrysler, owned by the private equity company Cerberus. As the financial crisis developed, Nardelli found himself begging to lawmakers in Washington. He did receive a taxpayer-funded capital injection of billions for Chrysler, but the criticism he received at the hands of lawmakers about maintaining a corporate jet did not help matters.

The Nardelli incident points to an increasing perception among activists and other investors that many executives receive misaligned compensation and severance packages. Activists are also likely to take advantage of the SEC's recently adopted and wide-ranging set of executive compensation disclosure rules, all of which will make things even more difficult for corporate CEOs and directors. "This new disclosure will give activists more ammunition to work with," Olson says. "It's a place they can go mining for information that can help an activist's campaign or identify a potential target."

As part of the new compensation rules, companies need to provide easy-to-read descriptions of perks such as pension plans. Disclosure of detailed executive retirement benefits is a new category for corporate compensation committees to consider.

Christopher Bartoli, partner at Baker & McKenzie in Chicago, says the new disclosure rules give activists a number of options for identifying problematic executive compensation. One major asset is a new summary compensation table requiring companies to outline all the compensation paid or deferred by executives in the past year.[12] Previously, activists and other investors may have had a difficult time tallying an executive's total pay because of complicated pension schemes and stock option grants. (Compensation committees must calculate the corporation's annual option payouts based on the stock price on December 31.) Compensation committees need to include these calculations every year as they add up and report them in the summary compensation table.

For the first time, companies are also required to disclose any one-time payments to executives or other key individuals. Big severance payouts including perks received upon retirement or details of change-of-control severance payments must be disclosed as well as one-time bonus payments individuals receive for striking a mega-transaction.[13] Unusually large severance payments or one-time bonuses are exactly the kind of thing activists will latch on to. "Activists will notice the board of an underperforming company that terminates its CEO without cause and pays him all this money to go away, and they'll say, 'Something's wrong here,' " Bartoli says.

Also, with all the compensation data added up, activists can more easily compare companies within their peer group and put a spotlight on any underperforming CEO. With additional disclosure it is easier for an activist to identify if one company in a particular industry is paying its CEO as well or better than his peers. That information can subsequently be compared to the corporation's stock performance, which is matched against the industry's average share value. Of course, savvy activists can comprehend and compare company payment plans without the help of new disclosure rules. The streamlined disclosures may just make it less difficult for them to convince other investors that their assertions are credible. When insurgents start using the disclosure to point out problems with the perks or pay a particular CEO or director receives, it will be easier for a less sophisticated retail investor to comprehend as they also familiarize themselves with the new government filings. "Activists can go to other investors and say, 'This is the bottom-line number executives receive; go look for yourself in the annual report,' " Bartoli says.

The new Compensation Discussion and Analysis (CD&A) section, where management and directors need to provide additional detail, is modeled after the Management Discussion and Analysis section already required in every annual report.[14] This CD&A section requires compensation committees to explain through charts and text how they figured out how much to pay executives. Bartoli says compensation committees on the board will need to explain in greater detail how executive pay is tied to their performance. Not having that detail could put an inhospitable spotlight on the company. At the very least, activists who are skimming through financials for potential targets will take into consideration whether a particular company explains in detail in the CD&A how executive pay is tied to corporate share and earnings performance.

Corporations also must provide additional details about any related-party transactions, a major sore spot for activists as discussed previously. The bottom line is that any financial relationships between executives and their employers must be disclosed. These disclosures complement the post-Enron NASDAQ and New York Stock Exchange (NYSE) listing requirements already putting companies in a position where they must nominate more independent directors with no material financial ties to management. New disclosure rules, as SEC chairman Christopher Cox described it in July 2006, will "shed welcome new light on the degree of director independence and the quality of corporate governance at our nation's public companies."

Companies will need to disclose if a director's family member works for the company or any major supplier. Other director conflicts of interest need to be included as well. For example, activists like to put a spotlight on the cozy relationship between directors who sit on each other's boards. The most glaring example of this type of relationship, known in governance circles as interlocking directors, was Home Depot co-founder Kenneth Langone's overlapping directorship with former NYSE head Richard Grasso. Before Grasso resigned from the NYSE, he served on Home Depot's compensation committee, while the Big Board's compensation panel was headed by Langone. The rising current of institutional investor hostility at The Home Depot, in some respects, started with opposition to these two interlocking directors and later culminated in Nardelli's removal.

Anything that could be seen as a conflict between the company and its directors must be disclosed as well. Keeping a closer eye on director compensation is critical, since these individuals are the ones considered by activists to be the enablers of executive overcompensation. For example, equity grants to directors will be more closely scrutinized by activists in a new "director compensation table." The table lists each nonemployee director and provides their compensation information for the prior year. Previously, director stock grants over the prior year had been described generally in a paragraph rather than in this new, more detailed table.

An example of the prior disclosure would have looked something like this: "All nonemployee directors are granted 10,000 stock options per year for service on the board and paid an annual retainer of $10,000."

With the new rules, companies need to calculate each equity grant to every director and provide all that information together, with any cash or bonuses paid out, in a table providing the total compensation figure for each board member. Companies are already required to disclose director equity stakes in a beneficial ownership table. Board members who don't have their own invested equity in the company could also attract activists seeking to establish boards that have their interests aligned with shareholders.

Additional focus on director independence, equity grants, and change-of-control or termination payments will all add grist to the activists' efforts. Chapman Capital's Chapman says all this new disclosure makes his job a lot easier.

The agency also plans to put all this information into a new sophisticated information technology service based on a data format known as XBRL (Extensible Business Reporting Language).[15] The plan is to help investors analyze and compare financials from different companies. Unsophisticated investors are the target audience, but activists plan to use it as well, especially if they can point to results obtained by comparing statistics compiled using XBRL to convince a skeptical investor base that their approach makes sense. "It is now within our reach to get dramatically more useful information in the hands of investors," Cox said in speech introducing the plan in 2005. "Think how much better life will be when you can not only rely on the accuracy of the numbers, but you can instantly slice 'em and dice 'em exactly as you please."

Olson says he believes the agency's technology and disclosure initiative will bring out more insurgents. "I expect more companies to more frequently become targets for public criticism from the press and activists," Olson says.

The University of Delaware's Charles Elson agrees that the SEC initiatives will help activists gain support for their campaigns. Their focus on CEO pay is a good thing, he adds, and in some circumstances, it is having a moderating effect on the level of pay poorly performing executives receive. One positive thing, Elson says, is that activists elected to corporate boards bring an investor's perspective to a gathering of individuals that often lack such a viewpoint. Since most boards don't have significant equity stakes in the companies they serve, they don't have the incentive to improve shareholder value. Directors with equity ownership typically are good at keeping compensation aligned with performance, Elson says. The U.S. Chamber of Commerce's Chavern points out that activists and other investors supporting an insurgent must also be careful to consider what he calls the "contrary effect." In situations where an activist shareholder is campaigning relentlessly to change management, executives may try to revise their compensation and severance arrangements so they can receive as much as possible as quickly as possible because they are worried about being kicked out of their position. "They may want more money up front now," says Chavern. "Is that good for the corporation in the long term?"

Checking their employment agreement is the first thing executives do when faced with activists hoping to have them removed or the company sold, says Cornell Companies' CEO James Hyman. Shareholders in 2003 and 2004 pressured Cornell's board to remove Hyman's predecessor. Before reaching a settlement that put some dissident directors on the board, Hyman made sure his compensation agreement and severance package didn't make it easy for dissident shareholders and directors to remove him. "I made it clear that if shareholders wanted to remove me, they would have to take time to find someone to replace me, which could slow down their activist efforts," Hyman says.

But Corporate Library's Nell Minow says in some circumstances it may be worthwhile to pay CEOs more than they deserves to leave, just to bring in someone new. She says activists in the past rarely have had an opportunity to discuss compensation issues with corporate executives, who typically stonewall such conversations. One way to get management's attention is through the company's poison pill.

Institutions and activists, she says, don't really care that much about poison pills, but know proposals to have corporations require a shareholder vote on the measure will get a substantial support from shareholders and consequently put the company in a negative light. The prospect of losing a vote on a poison pill could capture the attention of a CEO. Once activists have access to a dialogue with the CEO, they can pull a "bait and switch" by bringing up compensation issues. Minow says activists have a limited range of tools available to them, and they will do anything as a springboard for shareholder endeavors. "Shareholders continue to use poison pills as a launching pad for shareholder initiatives because they are a reliable vote getter and sort of a foot in the door to continue a conversation with executives," Minow says. "There is always a certain amount of indirection in shareholder engagement, assuming that you've already picked a company that is in trouble, so direct conversation is difficult. What you really want is for them to stop overpaying the CEO and boost the share price."

To guarantee CEOs at Glenayre and Carreker are working to earn their compensation, Chapman Capital's Chapman says he has hired "multiple" private investigators to follow his target executives. Even if a CEO steps down, Chapman's surveillance program continues. After Glenayre's CEO Bailey resigned in November 2006, perhaps reeling from Chapman's public agitation, its new CEO, James Caparro, became the subject of scrutiny. "I want Jim Caparro to be aware that we will be transferring our surveillance efforts related to the professional deportment of Mr. Bailey over to him, now that he has taken the CEO role," Chapman told company officials, analysts and other investors on a Glenayre conference call in 2006.

As we can see with Whitworth's efforts at Home Depot and Chapman's endeavors at Glenayre and Carreker, CEO compensation is a driving point for activists seeking to pressure companies into improving their share price. Expect Christopher Cox's executive compensation disclosure and interactive financial reporting initiatives to have an impact, bringing traditionally passive institutional and retail investors into the pay package debate. Also, insurgents and smaller or less interested investors will likely begin communicating at a level never considered before. But will all this new technology have an impact on the CEO pay environment overall? That's unclear. For one thing, many executives may have distorted compensation arrangements, but instead of earning too much, they aren't receiving enough pay, in many observers' minds, to properly incentivize them to improve the business. It doesn't appear that activists are seeking to resolve this kind of performance without pay scenario. It must be noted also that activists today are putting pressure on only a small percentage of CEOs here and there. Their efforts do send a message to other executives that they should be careful—an activist may not be that far away. Harvard Law School's Bebchuk says these insurgent investors must be influencing the compensation of America's CEOs to some extent. But, he adds, it is difficult to assess the magnitude of that influence.

Chapman has an even more pessimistic perspective. "In theory, the fear of God should have been put into nontargeted CEOs as they see other members of the executive herd taken down," he says. "However, that hasn't been the case, as investors seem willing to downplay, if not ignore, executive compensation as long as the stock is rising."

Whether compensation will continue to drive insurgents in the years to come depends in large part on what kind of payment plans future CEOs receive. Corporations with executives who have compensation plans tying their performance to not only company profits but also share performance will likely be left alone. Companies that persist in awarding distorted pay packages will continue to be targeted by activists.

Chapter 7

Hedge Specialization

Good or Bad?

Richard Lashley invests in thrifts and banks and nothing else. Since 1995, he's instigated about 13 public activist campaigns, mostly to encourage banks and thrifts to merge. But that represents only a small part of the story of Lashley's activist endeavors. He has met with many more management teams behind the scenes, making recommendations and demands.

PL Capital LLC, the activist hedge fund Lashley operates, is based in Naperville, Illinois, a small, affluent town outside of Chicago with roughly 130,000 people—not exactly a major financial center. But from there Lashley and his partner John Palmer have turned a small $25 million hedge fund into a much bigger one with $150 million in assets under management in just a little over 10 years.

Unlike many other activists that throw their efforts around a number of different industries, PL Capital's strategy is to purchase only concentrated, large positions in savings and loans banking institutions. PL Capital expects to engage management and press for changes to unlock value at a select few companies. At any one time there are likely to be roughly 40 large stakes in the hedge fund's portfolio. Parts of their strategy may resemble tactics embraced by other activist hedge funds but their investment vehicle's focus on thrifts and banks sets them apart.

So far, business has been good. The fund reported average annual returns of 18 percent a year since 1996. And even though their historic returns have proven that they are effective activists, many prospective investors worry that their isolated concentration in savings and loans makes them susceptible to industry downturns.

But Palmer and Lashley disagree with that assessment. They argue that exactly the opposite is true: Their success can largely be attributed to a specialized knowledge of the industry.

That expertise, Lashley says, can be credited to the 12 years they each spent at KPMG LP honing their proficiency in the banking and thrift sector. Both Palmer and Lashley worked for 9 years in the accounting firm's bank and thrift audit practice as certified public accountants. There, the duo provided accounting and consulting services to banks. After that, they both spent 3 years in KPMG Corporate Finance, a division that specialized in providing merger and acquisition advice to banks and thrifts.

"From that experience, we understood the banking industry from the inside out," Lashley says. "We understood the analytics. We had professional backgrounds, if not formal training, in money management, and we felt we could make more money and be more enthusiastic about coming to work every day as activists in the banking and thrift industry."

The strategy of specializing in an area where one has a particular expertise and industry experience makes sense to some observers. "They develop a body of knowledge," says William Natbony, partner at Katten Muchin Rosenman LLP in New York. "An activist that specializes in the banking industry understands where potential problems originate and can see how to fix those problems."

Banking industry expertise is typically not translatable to the biotech or high-tech sector or really any other industry. Activists that understand banking can quickly read and comprehend bank balance sheets, cash flow statements, and the specific issues and benefits of the industry in a way other activists that don't focus on the sector can't, Natbony adds.

Perrie Weiner, partner and co-chairman of the securities litigation group at DLA Piper US LLP in Los Angeles, says activists that specialize in a particular area generally do better than those that spread their activism around. "There are so many activist hedge funds now that to be an activist is not enough to differentiate yourself from the rest of the hedge funds," Weiner says. "Managers are realizing that as the industry continues to grow, hedge fund managers must zero in on a particular industry and develop a track record in that industry to distinguish themselves from the others."

Weiner adds that specialization is important not just to create an identifiable brand for the manager, but also because having an industry sector focus eases the core task of researching companies for potential investments. "The industries are complex," Weiner says. "You can't possibly move from industry to industry with ease."

Managers must develop expertise and networks of contacts in a particular industry for their activist efforts to function effectively. Staffing a fund with people that are sector experts, often with additional restructuring or investment banking backgrounds, can be a good way to find the most attractive investment opportunities.

An activist that engages in proxy fights or likes to make director recommendations to companies in private communications should also have numerous board candidates waiting in the wings, ready to be nominated should the opportunity arise. To develop a network of potential director candidates with the kinds of industry expertise that other sophisticated investors and company executives will consider credible requires a strong network of key sector experts, including CEOs, retired executives, and others. But probably the most critical reason for developing an expertise in a specific field is to accurately identify undervalued companies with the potential for value extraction. Palmer and Lashley have had no problem identifying potential targets in the banking and thrift sector. Their first step was to narrow down the field to the top 1,000 U.S. banks and thrifts. Most banks in this category are mid- and small-capitalization thrifts that have little or no analyst coverage and consequently operate in an opaque world well below Wall Street's gaze. That's where Lashley steps in with his own research to identify which institutions could be convinced to either buy another bank or be bought by one.

All their research has led Palmer and Lashley to one important conclusion, which they claim has held true since PL Capital's inception: The banking industry will continue to consolidate, though sometimes it needs a little push along the way. That trend, for Lashley, means that activist investors in the industry can generate good returns, particularly if they can encourage consolidation. Lashley estimates that the thrift sector in the United States has about 250 mergers a year, down from the 500 or so deals that took place annually in the late 1990s. Even with fewer deals, Lashley estimates that consolidation and opportunities will continue. PL Capital is first a banking industry investment firm, and second, an activist, he says. Investing passively in select banks can produce good returns, Lashley says, but activist efforts are what transform PL Capital from a run-of-the-mill plain vanilla small-capitalization bank shareholder into an investor that year after year generates above average returns. "Banking is where we have our skill set, and we're comfortable with the long-term fundamentals of the industry," Lashley says. "If we went into any other industry, we would have to learn it, and I'm not convinced that any other industry has the same prospects as savings and loan banks have."

Three to five banks and thrifts typically represent 50 percent of PL Capital's total assets under management, while the rest of the portfolio is diversified across the banking sector. Palmer and Lashley will launch activist campaigns by publicly engaging executives at no more than two companies at any one time.

In April 2006, they muscled out Cranford, New Jersey–based Synergy Financial Group Inc.'s CEO and another director from the company's board and replaced them with two of their nominees, after completing a successful proxy contest.[1] It was not the first time PL Capital won a proxy contest and most likely won't be the last. But their small victory did not come quickly or easily. PL Capital filed its first Schedule 13D at Synergy in December 2004. Since then, in 2005, the hedge fund pressed management to use its excess capital on hand to repurchase roughly $20 million worth of common stock.

After that, things began getting difficult. By December 2005, with no result in sight, Palmer and Lashley met with Synergy's CEO John Fiore, chief operating officer Kevin McCloskey, and chief financial officer Rich Abrahamian, to discuss potential strategies for the company. Some key points of advice from Lashley: Synergy should reduce its noncore assets and increase its loan portfolio only if it can maintain a balance sheet funded primarily with customer deposits. In that meeting, Lashley also encouraged Synergy management to consider adding some PL Capital nominees to its board. With a 10 percent stake in the $180 million stock market capitalization company, Palmer and Lashley had some leverage. But Synergy's executives were not heeding their advice.

In February 2006, PL Capital stepped up its efforts a notch by filing a lawsuit to demand that Synergy officials hand over their list of shareholders and other information. After some prodding, the bank provided them with the list.

Executives at targeted companies are likely to withhold these lists, which activists must have if they want to identify and petition other shareholders to support their nominees in an eventual proxy contest. Filing a lawsuit to get that list is also not uncommon. Once Palmer and Lashley received it, they launched a proxy contest. By April, two dissident directors were on Synergy's board.[2] The insurgents were on their way. By May 2007, Synergy was sold to New York Community Bancorp Inc. for $168.4 million in stock or $14.18 a share.[3]

PL Capital isn't the only activist that hounds thrift CEOs. Another investor, Lawrence Seidman, age 59, also focuses much of his activist efforts only on small banks and thrifts. Seidman, like Palmer and Lashley, is driven by his desire to press for change to unlock value at banks that have poor balance sheets and overpaid CEOs that as he sees it aren't making the right decisions in a consolidating industry.

His efforts so far have produced successful results. Since 1984, his hedge fund, Seidman & Associates LLC, has launched roughly 30 activist campaigns and 28 proxy contests at 11 institutions, installing directors at six of them. Like Palmer and Lashley, Seidman also doesn't operate in a major metropolis. Most of Seidman's initiatives originate from his office in Parsippany, a small New Jersey town with roughly 50,000 people.

Unlike Palmer and Lashley, Seidman joined the ranks of activists by chance. Prior to becoming a bank and thrift shareholder, Seidman says he had little knowledge of the deposit and loan industry. But once involved, Seidman says he learned quickly what he needed to understand to make thoughtful investments. Through a confluence of events in 1984, Seidman, then an attorney, found himself on the board of Hubco Inc., a New Jersey–based bank. There, as a director, he was able to contribute to improving the bank's operations. Seidman was hooked. "We put people on the board, the bank [Hubco] became profitable, and we sold our shares in the open market," he says. "I've looked at other industries, but there are more opportunities in the banking arena."

Seidman expects the banking industry to continue consolidating at least for another 20 years, long enough for him to finish up his activist investments and retire. A major help for Seidman is that individual investors, which make up a large part of the shareholder base for small-capitalization thrifts, are becoming more involved and thoughtful about the profit and losses of the bank stocks they own. (Unlike larger banks that have many institutional investors, smaller entities are made up predominantly of individual shareholders.) This is a trend that makes Seidman optimistic about his future endeavors. A more active and thoughtful retail investor base has become more supportive of activism, he says, which gives him more leverage with bank managers.

Since 1984, Seidman has filtered through financial reports put out by hundreds of banks. He takes a multistep approach to figuring out which companies to target. The first consideration mirrors the activities of most activists: is the bank undervalued? In other words, is the bank trading at a discount when compared to its rivals? Once the value investment choices are made, Seidman's second consideration is whether the bank should consider making acquisitions or auctioning itself off to a larger entity. If the savings and loan is in a position to acquire another thrift, managers should consider what kind of institutions would make good targets and whether each possible transaction will improve the bottom line. Another consideration: What could the target bank receive if it were to put itself on the auction block?

Once Seidman decides to take his activist investment agitation efforts public, he files a 13D. But unlike other activist 13D filers, Seidman includes a laundry list of his previous activist efforts. This list, which has become quite lengthy, documents dozens of his insurgency campaigns in chronological order going back over 10 years. Seidman says he submits the list because his attorney believes that the information is material and should be incorporated. But there may be an ulterior motive: The information also can educate a possibly unsuspecting CEO about exactly who he is dealing with—someone who isn't to be taken lightly. Each paragraph describing one of Seidman's efforts begins with "in addition."

A typical excerpt: "In addition, certain of the Reporting Persons (legalese for Seidman's investment vehicle) were involved in two proxy contests involving Wayne Bancorp Inc. The first proxy contest involved the approval of certain stock plans and option plans for the directors and senior management of Wayne."

"Does it inform management about us? Yes," Seidman quips.

More recently, Seidman has focused his efforts at Yardville National Bancorp, a $424 million bank based in Hamilton, New Jersey. A proxy fight he launched in 2005 to elect three directors to the company's board was unsuccessful.[4] (Proxy advisory service companies Institutional Shareholder Services and Glass Lewis & Company both recommended that shareholders vote for the management's three-member slate). After that defeat, Seidman filed a lawsuit challenging the company's results and launched another proxy fight to put himself and two other candidates on its board. In June, roughly three years after he started agitating for change, Yardville agreed to be acquired by PNC Financial Services Group Inc. for $403 million in cash.[5] Since Seidman began his efforts Yardville's stock has surged from $25 a share to $34 a share. Yardville investors will receive $14 a share plus 0.29 of a PNC share for each of their shares. Another thrift agitator, Jeffrey Gendell, has been investing in the banking sector since 1997 when he launched Tontine Management LLC in hedge-fund hotbed Greenwich, Connecticut. For most of the hedge fund's years of operation, Gendell has focused his activism on countless thrifts and banks, but he also occasionally launches activist efforts at steel companies and other businesses. In a short period between April 2003 and October 2003, Gendell filed Schedule 13Ds and engaged management at 22 thrifts and banks, including Monarch Community Bancorp Inc., Capital Bank Corporation, and Progress Financial Corporation. Sometimes he invests in the same undervalued companies as other thrift activists. For example, in September 2003, Gendell acquired a stake in Yardville National Bancorp, the thrift Seidman had been pressing with successive proxy contests.

The U.S. energy sector is the industry activist investor Jana Partners LLC's Barry Rosenstein has his eyes set on, though he also launches activist efforts in other sectors as well. In 2005, Rosenstein pressured coal producer Massey Energy Company to buy back $500 million worth of shares with its cash on hand.[6] In 2006, he led a shareholder revolt against Houston Exploration Company, an oil and gas production company with offshore platforms in the Gulf of Mexico. Rosenstein later made an unsuccessful $62 a share offer for the oil and gas company.[7] He also joined Carl Icahn to press another energy company, Kerr-McGee Corporation, to restructure itself. Kerr-McGee sold itself to Anadarko Petroleum Corporation for $16.4 billion, netting Rosenstein a significant profit.[8]

James Mitarotonda of New York–based Barington Capital Group LP focuses much of his agitations at clothing companies and at times, he has even specialized in taking on struggling public shoe corporations. Yes, shoe companies. Steve Madden, Maxwell Shoe Company, Stride Rite Corporation, and Payless ShoeSource Inc. are all shoe chains that have at one time or another been the focus of Mitarotonda's activist attention. Once he becomes a shareholder, Mitarotonda, like other activists, engages management with his assertive approach.

But like bank and thrift agitators, Mitarotonda first narrows down the field of companies he considers for investments. Using his passive value investor skills Mitarotonda finds companies that are trading at a discount to their net asset value (total assets minus total liabilities). But what transforms Mitarotonda into an activist investor is that his final investment choices are made with companies he knows need outside input, whether they like it or not. "Every company I invest in is truly undervalued, and there is always something to do in terms of engaging management to make changes," Mitarotonda says.

Despite the concentration of shoe company investments, Mitarotonda says he doesn't specialize in any one sector. His investments regularly focus on other sectors, such as industrial manufacturers and consumer-related businesses. But Mitarotonda acknowledges that his fund, named after Bari, Italy, where he was born, does often invest in fashion and shoe companies.

A decision to concentrate on shoes and fashion companies may have something to do with Mitarotonda's background and work experience.

After finishing business school, between 1979 and 1981, Mitarotonda worked at the department store chain and fashion trend-setter Bloomingdale's in New York. From there, Mitarotonda took his burgeoning expertise in the industry and began to learn about the investment banking side of fashion by taking a job in the retail consumer banking group of Citibank. Between 1981 and 1984, at Citibank he developed a broader expertise in the retail and fashion sector.

All that fashion and banking industry experience adds up: His fund, which was launched in 2000, has annual returns ranging from 10 percent to 50 percent over that period. "I utilize my skills and various contacts in a particular industry to improve the value of businesses I invest in," Mitarotonda says. "Certainly, the more you know about one industry, the better you should do in it."

Earlier in 2004, Mitarotonda launched a proxy contest to replace three company directors at Payless ShoeSource Inc. with his own candidates. But the Topeka, Kansas–based discount shoe retailer blocked Mitarotonda's nominees, arguing that the candidates were ineligible for election because they did not comply with the company's bylaws. In filings, Mitarotonda said he had launched the proxy contest to gain a foothold on the company's board and eliminate a series of anti-takeover provisions.[9] Despite this setback, Mitarotonda was not through with the shoe business.

Mitarotonda's shoe industry connections came in handy later at Stride Rite, a children's shoe company in Lexington, Massachusetts. Barington took a 5.7 percent Stride Rite stake in January 2006 and filed a Schedule 13D, where he wrote that he might take some action such as proposing "changes to the shoemaker's capitalization, ownership structure and operations." By February, Mitarotonda wrote a letter to Stride Rite, asking the company to expand its board to nine seats from eight and install an independent director candidate with no connection to the company. Here's where Mitarotonda's fashion industry connections became useful. Stride Rite suggested adding Mark Cocozza, a shoe industry expert that Mitarotonda had known since early 2000. Mitarotonda agreed and Cocozza was brought onto Stride Rite's board as part of an agreement with Barington.[10] Cocozza previously had been chairman at another Barington investment, Maxwell Shoe, and he had worked previously for Stride Rite. By mid-2007, Mitarotonda's efforts at both Stride Rite and Payless began to pay dividends. In May of that year, Payless agreed to buy Stride Rite Corp. for $898 million, including debt. Mitarotonda declines to accept any responsibility for the transaction, though industry observers say his constant prodding at both companies factored into their negotiations.

Mitarotonda's focus on the sector has earned him accolades from some onlookers. "A few people like Mitarotonda have done lots of work in the consumer retail, shoe, and apparel space," says Morgan Joseph's Randy Lampert. "He knows it well, and that helps him with his activism."

Mitarotonda's shoe industry interventions don't end with Payless and Stride Rite. In 2004, Barington took a 6.1 percent stake and threatened a proxy contest to oust the CEO from the board at the trendy yet struggling women's shoe chain Steven Madden Ltd. Mitarotonda wanted Madden, among other things, to use its $67 million cash stockpile to pay shareholders a special dividend and buy back stock. By 2005, the besieged company, whose founder Steven Madden was sentenced to 41 months in prison for securities fraud, settled with Mitarotonda and agreed to add an independent director with retail experience.[11] The New York–based shoe manufacturer also agreed to allocate more money for stock buybacks and special dividends. "Activism is nothing more than acting as an owner," Mitarotonda says.

His efforts to promulgate change in the fashion industry go beyond shoes. In 2003, Mitarotonda started pressing clothier Nautica Enterprises Inc. of New York to auction itself off to the highest bidder. Things started moving at Nautica after Barington launched a proxy contest to nominate three candidates to the apparel company's nine-member board in June of that year. By July, Nautica sold itself to VF Corporation for $586 million in cash. The proxy contest was canceled.[12]

Later, Barington decided to follow Third Point's Daniel Loeb and take on another fashion company. Loeb had been publicly pressing Warnaco Group Inc., the designer and manufacturer of Speedo swimwear and Calvin Klein underwear and jeans, to auction itself off since August 2003. Three years later, in August 2006, Mitarotonda took up the torch, though no buyer has been found yet.[13]

Its stock is trading at around $36 as share, in part, on speculation that a deal may be in the works. That value is significantly higher than the $16 to $18 a share Barington paid for its Warnaco stake.

Several possible bidders exist, including VF Corporation, which pursued Warnaco in bankruptcy in 2003 and could still be interested in parts of the company. Another possible buyer: Phillips-Van Heusen Corporation. So far, no go.[14]

In 2004, Mitarotonda participated in a turnaround at Syms Corporation, a Secaucus, New Jersey–based discount designer apparel clothing retailer for men, women, and children. Father and daughter team Sy Syms, chairman, and Marcy Syms, CEO, own 58 percent of the company's common stock.

Many activists drift toward specializations as their expertise and contacts in a particular industry develop. But other forces may be pushing them to start spreading their investments across a wider array of companies. Morgan Joseph's Randy Lampert says that as the activist fund gets bigger with additional assets under management, it becomes much more difficult to find a sufficient number of special situations in any one industry in a way that will continue bringing in the returns the fund achieved in its earlier years. There may just not be enough opportunities left in a favorite industry category. In some ways, this trend mirrors a similar phenomenon of traditionally passive value investors growing so large that they need to become activists so they can maintain the kinds of percentage returns they were previously able to attain as much smaller entities.

Lampert points out that perhaps one reason why there are so many activists specializing in a particular industry or group of industries is that only a limited number of sectors have enough value locked up in their underperforming assets to be considered worthwhile targets for activists.

April Klein, associate professor at the Stern School of Business at New York University, studied 102 activist hedge funds between 2003 and 2005 and found that managers pressured companies in a number of different industries, but the largest concentration of insurgencies occurred at companies in business services, pharmaceutical products, retail, restaurant, hotels, motels, banking, and communications (see Table 7.1).[15]

Restaurants are a prime example of an industry just screaming for insurgents to come in and press for changes, says Morgan Joseph managing director Andrew Shiftan. "There is a lot of value locked up in the real estate restaurants sit on," Shiftan says.

Table 7.1 Industry of Target Firm (Eight or More Firms)

Number of Firms in:	Hedge Fund Activists
Business services	29
Pharmaceutical products	10
Retail	9
Restaurants, hotels, motels	8
Banking	8
Communications	5

SOURCE: April Klein, associate professor Stern School of Business, New York University; Emanuel Zur, doctoral student, Stern School of Business, NYU, "Hedge Fund Activism," (September 2006).

Some restaurant companies that activists have focused on of late: Outback Steakhouse restaurants, McDonald's, Wendy's International Inc., and Tim Hortons Inc. Dissident investor Guy Adams in 2001 succeeded at getting elected to the board of Lone Star Steakhouse & Saloon. That election was considered a breakthrough victory for investors in the restaurant industry, in part, because Adams was elected chairman, replacing the Wichita, Kansas–based restaurant chain's CEO from the board.[16] A number of activists, including Mitarotonda, later in 2006 expressed concerns about what they believed was a below-par bid a Dallas buyout shop made for the steakhouse chain.[17]

Another industry with a large contingent of activists is the software services sector. Activists say they recognize the industry is ripe for consolidation, though some companies may need a push to set those deals in motion. New York activist hedge fund Crescendo recognizes this trend. It pressed a number of software companies to auction themselves, including Toronto-based GEAC Computer Corporation. The activists pushed to have GEAC sold, and launched a proxy fight that was settled after the company's management agreed to allow one Crescendo member on the board. Later, in November 2005, Golden Gate Capital acquired GEAC for $1 billion in cash.[18]

After the deal, GEAC CEO Charles Jones acknowledges what Crescendo founder Eric Rosenfeld recognized: software companies no longer can achieve growth by adding customers or new products. The only way to keep profit margins high is by gaining customers through mergers. What is driving this consolidation? Large multinational companies that have traditionally been software company customers no longer want to deal with hundreds of information technology companies as clients. This consolidation is a reality that Jones says smaller software companies are slow to recognize and have customarily been resistant to accept. "It's a bad long-term decision for $100 million or even $400 million stock market capitalization software companies to believe that they can be well positioned in the software industry as independent entities," Jones says, "and Crescendo recognizes that."

Having both the CEO and the insurgent understand at the same time that a particular industry must consolidate is not a common occurrence. Yet with Rosenfeld and Jones that appears to be exactly what happened. Their relationship had the potential for problems early on after it got off to a rocky start. The two men first met for breakfast one Saturday at a café. Rosenfeld immediately demanded to be on GEAC's board. Not exactly the collaborative, cooperative experience Jones says he had hoped for upon meeting Rosenfeld. After the sale was completed, however, Jones and Rosenfeld discovered they lived close to each other. A friendship was quickly formed, demonstrating that not all relationships between dissidents and executives end sourly. In fact, Jones invited Rosenfeld and his wife over for dinner a number of times since the GEAC sale. Meanwhile, Rosenfeld has asked Jones to be a board nominee or to consider management jobs at other companies. "He's a personal friend of mine," says Jones. "We see the world the same way."

Instead of software industry consolidation, a group of insurgents sought software industry liquidation at a few technology companies in 2000 and 2001. These businesses had a surplus of cash on the balance sheet but not enough prospects for growth—at least that was the general perception among activist investors. At that time, the Internet dot-com boom was quickly turning into an Internet dot-com bust, leaving in its wake a hodgepodge of start-up technology companies that had raised mountains of cash from initial public offerings or overly enthusiastic venture capital donors. Many of these tech companies' stock prices fell to below the net cash they had on their books, making them especially attractive undervalued investment opportunities.

These types of investments, described by activists and value investors as "net nets," are few and far between. Net nets are stocks that trade at below the company's net working capital after liabilities are subtracted out. The combination of cash on the balance sheet, a deflated stock price, and a management team running a business with few prospects for success became hedge fund gold.

Barington's Mitarotonda invested heavily into these kinds of "broken Internet businesses" that were overloaded with cash but short on business plans. "It was like buying a dollar for 50 cents," he says.

The litigation effort by Holtzman and Mitarotonda at Liquid Audio described in Chapter 4 was part of one such insurgency. Keeping with the Internet pipe-dream trend, Mitarotonda also agitated for change at Register.com Inc., a company that sold Internet domain names. Register .com had a stock that traded at less than the amount of cash it had on hand. But while most Internet companies targeted by activists at that time were unprofitable and without a revenue source, Register.com had revenues, profits, and was debt-free.

Mitarotonda in 2004 reported a 6.6 percent stake in Register.com. By 2005, after pressure from several activists including Mitarotonda, Register.com agreed to sell itself to private-equity firm Vector Capital for $202 million.[19] Mitarotonda actually offered to buy the company in June 2005 for $172 million, but was satisfied when a strategic buyer came into the picture.[20]

Looking back fondly at that investment, Mitarotonda acknowledges that Register.com's kind of egregious situation was an example of the kind of "overly" undervalued companies that were a by-product of the times. "It was a product of the dot-com boom and bust," he says.

It was this area of technology that in 2000 and 2001 Chapman Capital's Robert Chapman also began devoting much of his attention. The strategy was simple: have dysfunctional high-tech companies stop operating and liquidate their cash before executives waste their huge cash reserves (shareholder's money) away. Like Mitarotonda, Chapman also sought out companies trading at less than the amount of cash they had on hand. "The blood of shareholders runs deep in Silicon Valley," Chapman said in 2002, after describing a particular activist endeavor.

In 2001 Chapman began buying shares in Preview Systems Inc., a Mountain View, California–based developer of technology for securing and distributing music and software on the web. A secure delivery system for music and software on the Web would be great if everyone wasn't "ripping off" that stuff through hundreds of Internet sites, he pointed out. Preview Systems in April 2001 had $90 million, or $4.50 a share of cash, yet the technology company was trading at about $2.56 a share at the time. By August, after pressure from Chapman, Preview Systems liquidated its cash and sold its technology to Aladdin Knowledge Systems Ltd. for $5 million.[21]

Chapman also took his assertive approach to Edgewater Technology. Two days after software engineer Michael McDermott killed seven coworkers at the Wakefield, Massachusetts–based Internet consulting company, Chapman stepped in with a 13D. Chapman said Edgewater was at the edge of a precipice. Taking advantage of the company when it was at its most vulnerable, Chapman urged Edgewater to return its $50 million in cash to shareholders, arguing that Edgewater could not make its strategy work.[22] Chapman pestered the company until it returned 60 percent of its cash to shareholders.

Internet boom darling, Stamps.com, which at one point in 2001 had about $188 million in cash but only a $166 million stock market capitalization, was another Chapman target. The company did not experience the liquidation catalyst event Chapman was hoping for, but he did cash out his 4.9 percent stake later that year for a profit.

Other activists piled into the California technology company liquidation game as well. Specialization in the "net net" cash-rich software and technology industry made sense then, but it's unclear whether that kind of opportunity will ever open itself up for activists again.

When insurgents focus their energies on banks, technology companies or another industry specialization, they must tread a fine line between developing the networks and knowledge base of a sector that drives their effective stock picks and the investment diversification they recognize is necessary to appease investors worried about an industry blowout. If something happens unique to that industry and the entire sector stumbles, the specialized activist could be in trouble. The burgeoning interest in activists by funds of hedge funds may be a major factor driving insurgent investors to diversify their investments. These fund of hedge fund investors, which are discussed in greater detail in Chapter 18, typically seek out activists that diversify their investments.

Also, many traditional hedge fund managers shy away from activist investing, in part, because they believe that their concentration and specialization may be dangerous in the long term. Ben Bornstein, president of Prospero Capital Management LLC in Newport Beach, California, runs a traditional hedge fund that engages in long-short hedging strategies. He believes that activists that specialize in one or two industries just aren't diversified enough. Bornstein's recommendation: run a more traditional long-short hedge fund portfolio like he does.

Bornstein warns also that owning only a few stakes at any one time will have a major impact on a manager's portfolio—it can produce massive positive returns if things go well and can cripple an investor if they don't. Traditional hedge fund managers own significantly more stakes, diminishing the impact of any one poorly performing investment. "They may have too many investments pointed in a particular direction in a particular sector," Bornstein adds. "It may also be risky to have all your money in a few stakes."

Despite the concerns expressed by nonactivist hedge fund managers and many fund of hedge fund managers, insurgents are continuing to specialize and make money doing it. One thing is clear: understanding the specifics of an industry is critical for activists, even if they only ever make one investment in that sector.

Indeed, activists with specializations in technology companies, banks, or the fashion industry are continuing to bring in strong earnings. Their steady, long-term success should make investors who allocate capital to a diverse array of companies and industries pause before discrediting the concentrated, sector-focused activist strategy outright. It's their specialization, expertise, and engagement tactics that bring in the profits. Many smaller allocations in diverse industries would dilute their expertise and hurt returns.

In the end, the devil is in the details. Specialization can mean many things to many people. Activists that invest heavily in restaurant chains that have hidden value locked up in the real estate they own represent one type of specialty. Some activists, such as Mitarotonda and Gendell, will allocate a large chunk of their fund to an industry they have an intimate familiarity with, but they also put a great deal of capital into other sectors to diversify their investments. Wary investors may believe that specialization with some diversification constitutes a sufficient compromise between the two extremes.

Some industry specialists have a history of training and a record of success in a particular industry, while others don't. Potential investors must recognize whether the activist is knowledgeable about the sector and has a network of contacts, including bankers, directors, and others, before deciding whether to allocate capital. Investors that recognize an industry is consolidating and that well-informed activists can help facilitate the trend are more likely to feel comfortable about funding an activist that specializes, especially if there is a track record of strong returns.

Certainly, investors such as Lashley, Gendell, and Seidman have made the case for savings and loan consolidation over the past decade and longer. Other insurgent investors are making thoughtful predictions about heightened dealmaking in the software and technology sector.

Someone thinking of assigning capital to these or other sector-specific activists must ask themselves if they believe there will continue to be consolidation in the chosen industry and, if that is true, whether the activist under consideration can take advantage of it. Once those questions are answered, the investment decision becomes easier to make.

Chapter 8

Regulation and Activists

How the Securities and Exchange Commission Helps (or Hurts) Activists

Another way to understand the growth of activists is through the regulations that give insurgents the tools they need to function. Activists could never have become the influential force they are today without a few key measures that the Securities and Exchange Commission (SEC) and other regulators have adopted over the past few years. And some shareholder-empowering changes are on the way.

One key provision adopted in 1992 under the helm of then-SEC chairman Richard Breeden is the so-called short slate rule. Before this rule was adopted, investors were, for the most part, unable to split their vote between management-nominated directors, the incumbents, and candidates put up by dissident activist investors. Put another way, there were significant legal obstacles to voting for a dissident candidate and also voting for an incumbent nominee.

Many dissident shareholders felt there should be a place for activists that didn't want to disrupt the company order through a change-of-control proxy contest, but wanted to inject the business with some new energy in the form of a short-slate of one or two directors representing a minority on the board.

"I'm not running a whole slate of 11 people to replace your entire board," says Nell Minow, a corporate governance expert at the Corporate Library research firm. "I think that bringing in one or two outside directors to the board is a moderate proposal you can take to shareholders who would otherwise not support a full-out insurgency."

A factor facilitating the change at the SEC was an activist campaign at Sears, Roebuck & Company in 1991. At that time, Minow comanaged an early activist hedge fund, LENS Investment Management LLC. Her partner at LENS, Robert Monks, another well-known shareholder activist, was trying to nominate himself to the board of Sears in an effort to bring some outside director influence without making any revolutionary changes. One of the three incumbent board candidates was very popular among the company's institutional investors and was likely to be reelected. According to Minow, a sufficient number of institutions had committed to vote Monks onto the board, but many of those shareholders also wanted to vote for the popular management-backed incumbent director. "There was nothing in the rules that said you could vote part of one card for one candidate and part of another card for another candidate," Minow says. "You could not mix and match between the ballots."

Ralph Whitworth, who at the time headed the United Shareholders Association in Washington, had also been pressing for the change as part of the organization's investor agenda. He pointed out repeatedly to regulators and lawmakers that without the ability to nominate a short slate, the only avenue shareholders had to make companies and boards more accountable to investors was either through what he called "jawboning," essentially public complaining, or seeking to take control of a company in a board-changing "corporate raid." In fact, Whitworth argues that many of the hostile takeovers of the 1980s took place in large part because disgruntled investors did not have a short-slate option for board representation.

Even in the 1990s when companies adopted classified boards—which means that only a minority of director nominees are up for election each year—activist investors were prohibited from targeting one particular director in the slate that they felt lacked independence or was too cozy with the CEO.

After fierce lobbying by Whitworth and others, the SEC passed the short-slate rule giving dissidents additional flexibility and in some instances transformed their game plan. Insurgents had gained an additional weapon in their arsenal of activist options: launching a proxy contest that would let investors vote for a compromise slate made up of a dissident and a management-backed incumbent. Activists could more easily attain the support for their minority director candidates from institutions that would have voted against an activist led change of control slate of nominees.

Whitworth points out that the short-slate approach has been used in a number of high-profile cases since its inception. In 1996, shareholder activist Kirk Kerkorian took advantage of it in his effort to unseat Chrysler Corporation's director Joseph Antonini. Kerkorian's campaign centered on Antonini's position at the top of Kmart during its fall from grace. In the end, after it became obvious that many institutions would support the removal, Chrysler and Kerkorian settled and Antonini stepped down.[1] "Institutions will support you because they will say having one or a couple of devil's advocates on the board can't hurt," Whitworth says.

In another, more recent high-profile use of the short-slate rule, Kerkorian succeeded at seating his nominee, Jerome B. York, on General Motors' board. Whitworth also used the approach, with success, at both Waste Management and Sovereign Bank. Activist investor Nelson Peltz took advantage of the short-slate rule to nominate director candidates for election to H. J. Heinz Company in 2006. Only 2 of the 5 candidates he nominated were elected to the 12-member board, but the approach was a victory for institutions that wanted to pick some of Peltz's candidates and some incumbent candidates. "Smart activists have cued into how this works," says Institutional Shareholder Services director Pat McGurn. "I expect it to be used more as fewer companies have classified boards."

In addition to the short-slate rule, in 1992 the SEC also adopted an important shareholder communications regulation. The rule expanded the amount of communications a possible activist could have with other shareholders when not contemplating a proxy contest. It also freed up communications between investors and reporters. Prior to the changes, an investor who wanted to talk to a reporter about whether he or she planned to vote for or against a corporate measure was required to submit a large document to the SEC for preapproval. Once it was approved, investors could talk to reporters, Whitworth says. "Now institutions post on their Web site how they plan to vote on key board issues," he says.

Brian Lane, a partner at Gibson, Dunn & Crutcher LLP in Washington and former chief of the agency's division of corporate finance under then-SEC chief Arthur Levitt, says the new communications rules meant activists could talk to or "solicit" an unlimited number of other investors to try and convince them to vote against a management proposal or director candidate, as long as they didn't plan on launching a proxy contest to install their own board members.

This in itself was a big deal for activists because they could begin soliciting other shareholders to vote against management's merger proposals, executive compensation packages and other arrangements. Investors could compare information about the companies they were invested in without fearing that they would be violating SEC rules. Activists could also lead so called "just vote no" campaigns. These are campaigns designed to convince other shareholders, in essence, to vote against an incumbent director running unopposed. They could campaign without having to make onerous, costly, time-consuming SEC filings and distributions that previously had to take place before such communications could happen. The result: More directors and executives began spending time talking to activists and listening to their concerns in behind-the-scenes conversations. Executives realized what these new shareholder communication rules could mean if the activist decided to take its efforts public. "There is an invisible hand here," Whitworth says. "Knowledge by the board that it's much easier for shareholders to target their laxities and bring it to the public's attention makes a difference."

A director targeted by shareholders would not be required to step down, but if a sufficient number of investors publicly or privately expressed their displeasure with a board member's performance, he or she may be embarrassed enough to resign. As with the short slate, Whitworth contributed heavily to the establishment of these new communication rules. As head of United Shareholders Association (USA), Whitworth energetically lobbied the SEC to free up communications among investors. He organized a letter-writing campaign on the issue. Between 1990 and 1992, thousands of USA members sent over 5,000 letters and telegrams to the SEC. It was during this period that the agency was considering its shareholder communications requirements.[2] Other groups, including the California Public Employees' Retirement System (CalPERS) and the Counsel for Institutional Investors also lobbied heavily and contributed to the passage of the communication rules. "The new rules are fostering more communications not just between shareholders, but also between shareholders and management," Whitworth said in a speech to investors in 1993.

A key recent high-profile example of what was possible after the agency freed up shareholder communications involved activist shareholders Stanley Gold and Roy Disney, the nephew of Walt Disney Company's founder. The two dissidents led a shareholder campaign in 2004 to pressure Walt Disney Company CEO Michael Eisner to resign from his position as chairman of the board. Roughly 45 percent of shareholders participating in the vote sought Eisner's removal, and the board responded by requiring that he step down from the position of board chairman.[3] Gold and Disney took advantage of the eased communication rules to communicate with other investors in a timely manner. The regulation and the communications it fomented was a key factor that made the shareholder victory possible.

Investors quickly began to communicate about mergers as well. In 1992, Centel Corporation activist shareholder Eagle Asset Management sent out a booklet in the mail to the company's 200 largest investors describing why the telecom company's merger with Sprint Corporation should be blocked.[4] Management responded, and Eagle sent out another missive in a quick and low-cost manner courtesy of the agency's regulation.[5] Ultimately, the deal was approved, but only by a small 50.5 percent margin.[6] Today, shareholder campaigns against mergers have become commonplace and their success can be traced, in part, to the new communication freedom.

But many activists still felt frustrated by prohibitions on communicating with other investors when contemplating a proxy contest. Louise Parsons, chair of the Jefferson-Pilot Shareholders Committee, expressed her support for freer communications for proxy contests in a 1992 letter to the SEC. Parsons, whose father was Jefferson-Pilot's president, waged proxy contests over three years to force changes at the company. She urged the agency to adopt the looser shareholder communication rules.[7] "Major institutional shareholders who planned to vote for us would not make their plans public for fear that the SEC might consider them to be participating in our proxy solicitation. New regulations would end such fears and enable open public comment," she wrote.[8]

Responding to Parsons and many others, in 1999, the agency adopted a rule aiding activists that were contemplating a proxy contest. The "test the waters" rule, which was adopted under SEC chairman Levitt's oversight, allowed potential dissidents to privately call up more than 10 other shareholders under certain circumstances and effectively say they were considering running themselves as a candidate for election to the board, without making an SEC filing.[9]

Prior to that, activists could talk to only 10 other investors or fewer without needing to submit documents to the SEC. The freed-up communications did improve a dissident's ability to take a poll of investors and gauge whether a proxy contest was winnable. Incidentally, it also freed up management to communicate more liberally with institutions and respond privately to activist assertions. "Activists could more easily figure out through conversations with other investors whether they had a chance of winning a proxy contest," Brian Lane says.

But activists, acting alone or in an official group, are still required to disclose to the SEC definitive plans to conduct a proxy contest or any formal agreements between an activist planning a proxy contest and another shareholder that has agreed to vote its shares for the dissident's slate.

More recently, in 2003, the SEC adopted another key measure that aids activists, this time an SEC disclosure rule. The commission, under the helm of George W. Bush appointee Harvey Pitt, approved a controversial regulation requiring mutual fund and other investment managers to disclose how they voted on key measures such as board elections.[10]

Forcing mutual fund managers to disclose how they vote had the impact of exposing their dirty little secret: in many cases, they automatically backed management's slate, even when faced with a dissident's campaign. In a world where their votes were kept secret, mutual fund managers would rather have quietly supported management's slate. "There are conflicts of interest in the way votes are exercised by mutual funds," said Pitt, who led the commission between 2001 and 2003. "Many mutual fund managers yield overwhelming voting power that they use for their own interest rather than for those shareholders for whom they are supposed to vote."

Deutsche Asset Management's decision in 2002 to change its 17 million votes at the last minute to be in favor of Hewlett Packard Company's merger with Compaq Computer Corporation, without disclosing that information to its investors, was the tipping point for Pitt. After that he moved forward quickly to require mutual fund voting disclosure, says Corporate Library's Minow. Deutsche Asset Management paid a $750,000 SEC fine for the action.[11]

Opportunity Partner's Phillip Goldstein points out that the disclosure rule has helped him evaluate a particular company's institutional and retail investor base. Knowing that certain money managers are more likely to back a proxy contest makes it easier for Goldstein to identify companies that have an investor base made up of shareholders who are supportive of his efforts. That kind of discovery, Goldstein says, has helped him identify potential investment targets.

Institutional managers have traditionally been reluctant to vote for dissidents for a number of reasons. In a nutshell, mutual fund money managers typically hold hundreds of minuscule positions. As a result, most managers have concluded that completing the research necessary to decide whether to support a dissident slate takes more time and energy than it is worth. These money managers also worry that their governance actions could alienate corporate leaders who might otherwise have allocated their 401(k) retirement pension fund assets with the fund. Some mutual fund managers argue that they had better success convincing corporations to make changes when their negotiations took place in private and that new disclosure actually discourages any meaningful negotiations between investors and corporations. Mutual fund groups argue that they now have even less reason to vote against management because any public vote against a corporate plan would hurt their ability to attract and retain 401(k) fund assets and other business.

In an attempt to resolve this issue, some mutual fund managers contract proxy advisory services such as ISS to tell them how to vote on contested elections. This way research costs are avoided and they can tell disgruntled CEOs (their clients) that the outside service told them to vote a certain way and it was not something they would have done otherwise.

Corporate Library's Minow says she understands that some investors feel that anonymity discourages reprisals and encourages frank discussions, but she believes full disclosure is necessary. Otherwise, she adds, it might be difficult to identify what truly motivates a shareholder's voting decisions. "A system where the investor does not know how votes are cast on his behalf by portfolio companies that are also possible big-ticket clients will produce the worst kind of results," Minow says.

Goldstein contends that the disclosure rule is a step in the right direction. "Mutual funds are improving, but they're generally not going to be as aggressive as hedge funds because of the litigation risks and conflicts of interest that can arise," Goldstein says.

In addition to mutual fund disclosure, the agency quietly adopted another investor disclosure and communications rule in 2003 that also helps activists. The rule requires companies to disclose whether they have systems, procedures and policies set up for communications with investors.[12] The measure requires a company's nomination committee to explain in proxy material why it rejected a director candidate recommended by an investor or group of shareholders with a 5 percent stake in the company. Companies must also explain in corporate financial documents how they identify and evaluate board nominees.

Small-cap shareholder activist Richard Lashley, cofounder of Naperville, Illinois–based hedge fund PL Capital LLC, says the disclosure rules are a step in the right direction. Directors are starting to think more carefully about whether they will reject a candidate recommended by shareholders when they know that their decisions will be made public for all investors to read, Lashley says.

In December 2006, the agency approved a rule permitting companies to post proxy material on the Internet. The "e-proxy" proposal was widely supported and pushed forward by corporations, anticipating major savings. According to the proposal, the SEC would no longer require corporations to physically deliver annual proxy material by mail unless an investor requests it. Fewer mailings equal cost savings, sometimes in the millions.[13]

But a possible unintended consequence of this new technological change is that activists launching proxy contests or "just vote no" campaigns at participating corporations will also save on the printing and mailing of their own proxy material. Instead of mailing, they can send their proxy statements electronically at a significantly lower cost. The approach could be particularly useful when activists launch proxy contests at large-capitalization companies that would otherwise require printing and delivery of proxy documents to hundreds of thousands of offices and households. Shamrock Holdings' Stanley Gold points out that just the U.S. postage cost to send out one mailing of proxy documents to Disney investors cost Roy Disney in excess of $2 million, not including printing fees. Of course, the e-proxy cost savings by activists such as Carl Icahn that take on larger companies, will represent only a small part of overall campaign expenses, which can include millions spent on investment banks and proxy solicitors.

However, many activists launch proxy contests at smaller public companies where the solicitation cost of reaching out to the smaller pool of investors is minimal. In those situations, printing and mailing are an activist's only real expenses and serious savings would take place. A proxy solicitor isn't needed because the top 20 investors in these small-cap companies represent 50 percent of their shares outstanding. Activists simply pick up the phone and contact a dozen or so investors to figure out whether a critical mass of shareholders would consider their initiative. One small-capitalization activist points out that his entire cost for a recent proxy contest was $20,000 in mailing and postage fees.

Martin Dunn, former deputy director of the SEC's Corporate Finance division, says the comments the agency received about the likely impact of electronic proxies varied so widely that he believes the truth lies somewhere in the middle. "One set of comments argue that e-proxy doesn't help reduce the costs of proxy contests at all because just putting someone's name on a web site and saying, 'Here's how you can find it,' doesn't eliminate the cost of soliciting people and getting them to vote," Dunn says. "On the other side, you have people commenting, saying this is going to create great uncertainty in the board room because it makes contests so cheap and easy."

In any case, SEC commissioner Roel Campos says he doesn't anticipate proxy contests to go completely electronic overnight. He points out that many retail investors who do not have access to the Internet will request mail delivery just to make sure they receive the proxy material. For another thing, the measure is voluntary and companies are not required to change their delivery methods—at least not yet. Corporations that initially were excited about the cost savings of e-proxy may now be weighing whether they want to create a situation that could attract activist hedge fund managers. The agency also postponed issuing rules that would make electronic proxy delivery mandatory. "It'll help initially," says Campos. "But if it's an actual contest, there is no way that electronic delivery will reach nearly the numbers that are desired. Maybe in 10 years things will be different."

An important initiative that could also give dissidents greater leverage when seeking to oust directors and in behind the scenes negotiations with corporate executives is the New York Stock Exchange's (NYSE's) proposed rule prohibiting brokers from casting director-election votes on behalf of investors who don't vote themselves.[14]

This is how it works: A large majority of retail or "street" investors do not vote in board elections. Investors that choose to participate in an election must check off the appropriate boxes on proxy material delivered to them in the mail and then send it off to an election tabulator. What typically happens is that most retail investors immediately toss the proxy statements into the wastebasket along with the other junk mail of the day. When retail shareholders chuck their proxies and don't vote in corporate director elections, brokers that hold those shares for investors almost automatically vote the uninstructed stake for the management-backed director slate. Eliminating a broker's right to vote the shares they hold for retail investors in director elections is a big deal because these artificial votes, known as "broker nonvotes" can at times tilt the election in favor of management's incumbent slate when investors launch "just vote no" campaigns. The process has been described by the Council of Institutional Investors as "ballot stuffing."[15] Corporate governance experts believe this proposal, if adopted by the SEC, will have a major impact in favor of dissidents hoping to oust incumbent directors. Disgruntled investors lead by CtW Investment Group, which manages funds for the Change to Win labor federation, launched a "just vote no" campaign seeking to remove Roger Headrick and another CVS/Caremark Corporation director at the company's annual meeting in 2007. According to the company's tally, roughly 42.7 percent of participating shareholders voted to oust Headrick. But CtW director Michael Garland points out that if the artificial broker nonvotes were removed from the calculation, the amount of investors opposing his re-election bid would be closer to 57 percent. In 2009, CtW headed up a campaign to remove Bank of America's embattled CEO, Ken Lewis, from his position as the bank's chairman. For this campaign, CtW estimated that 25% of the votes cast at the meeting are "broker non-votes," because of the bank's large retail investor base.

In 2002, Jennifer E. Bethel, an associate professor at Babson College in Wellesley, and Stuart L. Gillan, then senior research fellow at the Teachers Insurance and Annuity Association–College Retirement Equities Fund (TIAA-CREF), completed a study that reviewed 1,500 Standard & Poor's (S&P) companies listed in on the NYSE in 1998 for broker nonvotes. The study found that these rubber-stamping broker nonvotes in some elections represented a negligible amount, while in other situations the pro-management votes were quite substantial. In many cases, broker nonvotes represented 10 percent of the votes cast at annual meetings, but in others, they counted for as much as 30 percent of votes cast.[16]

"Eliminating broker nonvotes will definitely give some form of additional leverage to the activist shareholders, whether they are talking to management privately behind the scenes or engaging in a 'just vote no' campaign," Gillan says.

Companies have argued that the extra broker nonvotes are necessary for the corporation to achieve a quorum, the minimum amount of shares that must be voted for the annual meeting to be considered valid.[17] John Endean, president of American Business Conference, points out that small and mid-sized public companies typically have many more retail investors than larger corporations. He argues that eliminating the broker nonvotes would increase the costs these businesses incur to make sure enough shareholders participate, for quorum considerations, in part, because of the difficulty in obtaining a vote from retail investors. But Gillian points out that few firms, large or small, examined in his study would have had difficulty reaching broker quorum levels if broker nonvotes were excluded from the tally. Other observers point out that the quorum issue could easily be solved by permitting broker nonvotes for another tally, such as how many investors vote to retain the company's auditor.

The NYSE expects to eliminate these broker discretionary votes for NYSE-listed companies before the end of 2009.[18] That is later than many governance observers had expected after the stock exchange in April 2005 began debating the issue as part of a proxy working group it formed.[19]

The group at first produced a report recommending a ban on broker voting in director elections. Specifically, it found that election of directors could no longer be considered a routine item, and as a result brokers should no longer be permitted to automatically cast the pro-management votes for unresponsive retail investors.[20] But after lobbying by the corporate community, the NYSE decided it was not ready to move forward with this measure and instead it set up three subcommittees to continue considering it.[21] First, the subcommittees made recommendations to the NYSE board, which approved the measure. By May 2007, the NYSE finally completed its proposal and submitted it for approval to the SEC, which oversees the stock exchange's listing rules. But two years later, the proposal still languishes at the SEC, waiting to be approved.

Agency officials are debating whether as a compromise solution, companies could be required to get rid of the ballot-stuffing broker votes only if they are recipients of substantial "just vote no" campaigns. This would save the majority of corporations, which have routine director elections, the costs associated with soliciting additional voters.

But there are likely to be complications with this kind of compromise, particularly as more investors seek to launch "just vote no" campaigns. Regulators will need to consider which "just vote no" campaigns would qualify for eliminating the broker nonvotes. Certainly, extremely high-profile mega-campaigns, following the Disney example, would qualify. But what about a Yahoo! message board participant that writes a note saying he wants to see the CEO resign, would that also constitute a "just vote no" campaign suitable to eliminate the broker votes? Also, disputes about what constitutes a legitimate "just vote no" campaign raises questions about who would oversee such a system.

Leaving the decision to the NYSE could create more problems. What if a dissident shareholder of the NYSE decides to launch a campaign to oust directors at the stock exchange? Would the NYSE decide that the election was "nonroutine" and agree to remove the broker votes? Perhaps the exchange would delegate authority to its independent regulatory subsidiary to avoid that problem. Other hotly discussed compromise ideas are also being floated around. One approach known as "proportionate voting," would have brokers vote uninstructed shares in proportion to the actual votes cast. So if the actual votes break down 55 percent against the nominee to 45 percent for the candidate, a broker that holds 200,000 broker nonvotes would divide them 110,000 to 90,000, respectively. Client Directed Voting, or CDV, is another idea being debated. It would require the investor to make their decision at the time they sign brokerage agreements. Investors would be instructed at the outset to give their broker the authority to vote all their shares in a given year to support management, to oppose management, or abstain on all matters. This proposal has securities lawyers in a tizzy, and even though it is not the measure being considered by the SEC, a critical mass of support for it in comments to the agency and it may eventually become the chosen approach. In any event, the question of what to do about broker nonvotes is far from being answered.

In addition to these regulatory changes, there are a number of more indirect government measures that are aiding insurgents. As discussed in Chapter 6, the SEC in July 2006 adopted a broad series of CEO pay package disclosure requirements.[22] The new disclosure rules were adopted to help less-sophisticated investors understand how much compensation executives are receiving. The expectation is that with clearer and easier-to-comprehend compensation rules it would be more difficult for executives to give themselves pay packages that did not match up with company performance. With added disclosure, shareholders or other observers are more likely to call them out on it.

But those reaping the benefits of the disclosure go well beyond mom-and-pop individual investors. Activist hedge fund managers are likely to take advantage of the new reporting requirements, particularly the new Compensation Discussion and Analysis (CD&A) section. Company compensation committees, together with management, must use the CD&A section to opine on how they establish compensation policy. "The more details and easier-to-read details, the better," says activist hedge fund manager Arnaud Ajdler, managing director at Crescendo Partners in New York.

Despite taking pro-shareholder steps with executive compensation disclosure, communications, and short-slate rules, the SEC has been slow to move forward on one major provision many activists have been pushing to achieve. Investors have been pressuring the commission to allow them to nominate alternative director candidates, typically one or two, on the company ballot during annual corporate elections. The current system only permits activist investors to launch their own proxy contests, as discussed earlier, with their own proxy cards to elect directors onto company boards. Traditional proxy contests can be extremely expensive, as activists engaging in them may need to invest heavily in campaign costs to get their message across. A system that would permit investors to nominate a short slate of directors on the company proxy documents would significantly reduce that cost in many proxy battles, particularly at smaller companies.

For a while it looked like this alternative candidate election process, dubbed "shareholder access," was going to happen, or at least a complex version of it. In 2003, then-SEC chairman William Donaldson introduced draft rules that would in some circumstances permit shareholders to nominate a short-slate of directors on the company proxy cards.

Specifically, Donaldson's measure required that if shareholders with 35 percent or more of a company's shares withheld support for a particular director, then they may nominate one or possibly two director candidates on the company proxy card for election the following year. (Withholding support is the equivalent of voting against a director at a board election; voting materials typically don't provide an option to vote against a director.[23]) Only long-term investors with large stakes would have been permitted to introduce the initial proposal.[24] "Overwhelming investor responsiveness to proposals tied to corporate governance demonstrates the need for shareholders to have a more meaningful voice in the board election process," Donaldson told agency officials and security lawyers at the SEC on October 8. But criticism from large business groups and other commissioners at the SEC eventually led to the proposal's demise. Donaldson, at the time, had already spent a significant amount of political capital on pushing through other controversial rules and was not willing to move forward on this provision without the support of key agency officials. It disappeared from the agency's agenda as incoming SEC chairman Christopher Cox took over the watchdog agency in 2005.

But some investor groups did not give up on shareholder access and their actions forced the commission to again consider it. Richard Ferlauto, director of pension benefit policy at the American Federation of State, County, and Municipal Employees (AFSCME), has been submitting similar proposals on corporate proxy ballot on behalf of AFSCME's pension fund shares, implementing a case-by-case approach to nominating directors on corporate ballots.

The approach resembles many elements of Donaldson's now-defunct measure. Ferlauto's proposal would permit long-term shareholders of a significant size to elect one or two directors onto company boards. The institutional activist submitted the measure for consideration at American International Group Inc.'s (AIG's) annual meeting in 2005. In response, AIG petitioned the SEC to have it removed, and the agency concurred. After that, AFSCME filed a suit in the U.S. Court of Appeals for the Second Circuit, which in September 2005 ruled that the agency should have permitted the institutional investor to put the shareholder access proposal on the company's ballot.

The court decision sent the shareholder access issues back to the SEC, which in July 2007 introduced draft regulations intended to clarify its rules. In a move described by ISS's Pat McGurn as "schizophrenic," the SEC introduced two measures, one that would give investors a slightly greater voice in director elections and another that would not. The pro-shareholder measure was opposed by both activist hedge fund managers and institutional investors, who argued it was overly complex. That provision sought to give a shareholder or a group of investors that owned a 5 percent stake in a company for over a year the ability to introduce a director election bylaw proposal on a case-by-case basis. If the majority of voting shareholders back that proposal, then, the following year, shareholders can nominate a director candidate to the corporate board. However, Cox and other fellow Republicans ultimately voted against the pro-shareholder measure, once again blocking investors from nominating director candidates on corporate ballots. Nevertheless, in 2009, Obama Administration SEC chairwoman Mary Schapiro appears poised to usher in the first shareholder access measure. In May 2009, she introduced two companion shareholder proposals for consideration at the agency. Expect the U.S. Chamber to file suit, arguing it will empower special interest labor unions and environmentalists at the expense of shareholder value. Until it or some variation is adopted, activist institutions and insurgent hedge fund managers continue to submit their own simpler shareholder access proposals at various companies. New York–based activist hedge fund Seneca Capital LP submitted a director election proposal on Reliant Energy Inc.'s ballot for the 2007 election. It subsequently removed the measure around the same time that the energy company announced that its CEO was resigning, in February 2007. In addition to Seneca Capital, California Public Employees' Retirement System (CalPERS) submitted a similar director election proposal to UnitedHealth Group; and AFSCME sought a vote by Hewlett Packard Company (HP) shareholders. The HP measure received the support of roughly 39 percent of participating shareholders, not enough to pressure HP into making changes, but sufficient to give the activists some encouragement to try again. CalPERs received the support of 42 percent of shareholders for its measure. A case-by-case approach could have wide-ranging implications, though it's unclear how many activist hedge fund managers would try to use it.

Frank Balotti, a partner at Delaware law firm Richards, Finger & Layton, says activist hedge fund managers may take advantage of shareholder access by threatening to use it to gain some influence in behind-the-scenes conversations with executives. "It is something they can tell the corporation they are considering, so they can gain additional leverage in private meetings with management," Balotti says.

But many activist hedge fund managers may be discouraged from using the strategy because they would rather gain a short slate of seats in an expedited manner. Installing a director or two is usually only the first step in effecting change at a company. To the extent that activists want to effect change in a two- or three-year time frame, they may prefer to launch a proxy contest at the upcoming annual meeting or even sooner if a special shareholder meeting or written consent solicitation is possible. They also have the largest stakes in companies and as a result, a financial incentive to invest heavily in a traditional proxy contest.

Spending money on bank advisers and proxy solicitors can be justified because of the large investment activists have made in the company and the potential return that can be achieved if the corporation can be pressured to change its ways in a shorter time frame. That said, some activists may want to use shareholder access to get their nominee on the corporate ballot and still invest in proxy solicitors and other campaigning costs.

The ballot initiative, if adopted, may have the countereffect of splitting the votes of activist hedge fund managers with that of quasi-activist institutional investors. Institutions, such as mutual funds, public and corporate pension funds, and other money managers, may not be willing to invest in the costs of a full proxy contest. But with a low-cost corporate ballot approach, they may try to nominate a director or two. An activist that may have considered launching a proxy contest at a particular company would likely be discouraged from doing so if an institution has already begun a shareholder access campaign there. But, most regulatory observers argue that there is no way to really predict what director elections might look like until a shareholder access regime has been in place for a few years.

Shareholder access on the corporate ballot could also have some other unintended consequences. Some securities lawyers foresee a possible "doomsday" scenario; a number of different shareholder groups each launch their own proxy contests to nominate their own director candidate for the board of one company. One could envision several different activist investors taking advantage of a corporation's shareholder access bylaw to seize control of the company by replacing the majority of the board, each with their own separate short-slate campaign. One scenario: 5 separate shareholder groups nominate 10 candidates for election to an 8-member board. The top 8 vote getters are elected. If the top 8 candidates receiving the most votes are dissidents, the whole board could be replaced, though corporate interests argue that such a scenario is unlikely.

When shareholders succeed at setting up a shareholder access bylaw, the board could, in many cases, simply vote to remove the provision quickly before investors take advantage of it. That said, a corporation may want to think twice before axing the provision. Disgruntled investors would likely cry foul and launch a public opposition campaign painting the company in a negative light.

Relationships between activists and corporations may be influenced by a hodgepodge of yet to be thoroughly considered disclosure rules. Agency officials are brainstorming whether to adopt other measures that will affect the ability of activists to employ their strategies. Some of the ideas, if converted into rules, will help activists out, while others, not so much. One pro-shareholder initiative relates to record dates. SEC staffers are privately debating whether they want corporations to issue press releases announcing their record dates in advance. Only shareholders that have a stake on the record date can vote at the company's annual meeting, which usually takes place a month or two later. If proposed, this measure would respond to disgruntled activists that complain they aren't informed of the record date until it has already passed and consequently they, at times, buy shares expecting to have voting rights for them and later discovering that the record date has passed making them economic owners of shares with no voting rights.

Activist hedge fund managers are less enthusiastic about other voting-related changes the agency may soon consider. Some SEC officials are tossing around the idea of requiring activist investors to make additional 13D disclosures, responding to concerns that some activists and other investors have a hidden agenda that they pursue by secretly borrowing shares or employing other tactics to gain voting rights for stakes without having any economic interest in them. Should the agency discover that this is a pervasive, widespread phenomenon, a much more stringent agency response could be adopted. One possible result is that the SEC lowers the ownership threshold for requiring investors to file a 13D from 5 percent to 1 percent. Another possible regulation: 13D disclosure may need to be made in 5 days instead of 10 days after the investment is made. Hedge fund managers say they believe these conceptual changes to the 13D system would pour cold water on activist investing in the United States.

They argue that a high-profile activist investor that files a 13D five days after crossing the 1 percent stake threshold would quickly attract many "free-rider" copycat investors. That, in turn, would lead to short-term spikes in stock prices, making it more difficult for the activist to obtain a sufficiently large stake at affordable prices (while the stock is undervalued). Without a significant stake, the activist would have no leverage in negotiations with corporations. However, one possible positive result is that institutions may become more comfortable supporting an activist, especially if they know there is no hidden agenda.

Despite rumblings that the commission may make shareholders disclose more information, investor groups acknowledge that the agency has over the years made it easier for activists to have a greater influence on corporations. Greater communications freedom in itself is making it simpler and cheaper for activists to get their message out to institutions and influence corporate decision making. Additional flexibility and influence in the director election process is also making a difference regardless of whether shareholder access is accomplished or not. Insurgents are gaining institutional investor trust by nominating a short slate of a director or two and avoiding the public relations pitfalls of launching an all-or-nothing full slate contest that would not gain traction with other investors. The elimination of phantom broker-discretionary votes will also aid insurgents with their efforts to oust incumbent directors. Also, if the agency does require additional 13D disclosure, most long-term activists say they can live with it.

Understanding how the SEC has encouraged investor communications and cooperation provides a useful context for considering the phenomenon of activists gaining the trust of traditional institutions to achieve common goals at corporations. The next section examines in greater detail the relationships that are beginning to form between these two investor classes and how their collaboration is fundamentally changing the way executives around the world think about the companies they oversee.

The Martin Dunn, formerly of the SEC, acknowledges that the agency has done many things over the years to assist activists in their quest for greater leverage and influence of the corporations they own. But, he adds that some activist investors will always say the agency hasn't made significant strides in favor of shareholder rights until it moves to give shareholders access to the corporate ballot.

"I do think the commission has done a lot in terms of empowering shareholders," Dunn says. "But a lot of folks will tell you that unless the shareholder name gets on the company card, it has never gone far enough."

Part Two

INSTITUTIONAL INVESTORS AND ACTIVISTS

Chapter 9

Institutional Investors on Activist Hedge Funds

Love'em or Hate'em?

Institutional investors have had a love-hate relationship with activist hedge fund managers for many years.

At the most basic level, activist investors press for change at companies simply because they own large stakes in a few businesses that are a focus of all their value-enhancing energy and efforts. Pushing for those changes is what they do to raise the stock price and bring home the profits.

Meanwhile, most institutional investors such as public and corporate pension plan managers, investment banks, or mutual fund operators are stuck with hundreds of tiny investments. The cost-benefit analysis runs against having mutual fund managers take the time, energy, and capital to engage management at their hundreds of investments. Of course, spending time, energy, and money is exactly the sort of thing an investor needs to do to bring about change at a particular corporation.

Hence, these institutional investors are often called "plain vanilla" or "passive" investors that will be more likely to accept certain things about their investments, such as overcompensated CEOs, rather than fighting for change. The 2006 study, "Hedge Fund Activism, Corporate Governance, and Firm Performance," points out that institutions are less willing to inform themselves about "micro-level" issues that any portfolio company faces, in part, because efforts to turn around a particular corporation would at best translate into a very small improvement in the portfolio's overall performance.[1]

Institutions are also not equipped with a large enough staff to engage management at each of the hundreds of companies in which they have stakes. A related problem is that with only tiny shareholdings, institutions in many cases are not given the same kind of access to meet and discuss problems with a corporation's management team as an insurgent whose stake is usually among the largest in the corporation. Making investment decisions based on 20-minute meetings with executives was not enough, points out ValueAct's Jeffrey Ubben, about his days as a value investor for mutual fund Fidelity.

Another major difficulty blocking most institutions from actively engaging executives at the companies in which they own stakes relates to an institution's client base. Large institutions, such as investment banks, typically don't want to get their hands dirty with activist campaigns and lose potential consulting revenue sources by pressing companies in which they hold shares to make changes. Investment banks receive consulting fees for providing strategic advice to many U.S. corporations. They may be reticent to press corporations in which they own shares to make changes for fear of losing existing fees or future consulting or investment banking business.

Independent mutual fund institutions have similar problems. Managers at these funds often will avoid either launching activist campaigns or supporting an insurgent for fear of losing the retirement fund business of existing corporate clients or scaring away potential retirement fund customers.

That's why on one hand many institutional investors say they fully support management, but on the other hand they quietly egg on activist hedge fund managers to press the company to remove some board members or agitate for other changes that could improve the stock value.

In addition to internal conflicts, another bigger structural problem has also traditionally discouraged institutions from activism. As April Klein, associate professor at the Stern School of Business at New York University, points out in her September 2006 report "Hedge Fund Activism," mutual funds must be diversified, which means they cannot own more than 10 percent of the outstanding securities of any company, nor can more than 5 percent of the fund's total assets be invested in any one security.[2] However, the practical result of these diversification requirements is that most institutions will typically own much smaller stakes, typically of less than 1 percent.

While institutions are typically prohibited from buying large stakes, activist hedge fund managers often permit themselves to own much larger blocks of shares. Also, activists' incentives are typically more aligned with their investors than mutual fund managers and their investors. That's because the Investment Company Act of 1940 requires that mutual fund managers are paid a percentage of the assets of the fund. Hedge fund managers typically charge both a management fee of 1 percent to 2 percent of the invested funds and a percentage of the fund's profits, usually 20 percent. So if the fund is not profitable, activist managers get very little, but if a mutual fund does poorly, its portfolio manager doesn't necessarily suffer. Mutual fund managers do have some ability to receive a fee that relates to performance. The so-called fulcrum fee allows them to receive an additional payment when the fund's performance exceeds a certain benchmark. The fee also is reduced if the fund does poorly.

Activist hedge fund managers, with their high-performance incentives, won't passively sit and wait or dump their stocks when a company they have invested in is in trouble. Institutions with their structural conflicts and small stakes will be more apt to quietly accept problems taking place at their investments or sell their stock in outrage.

But as activist hedge funds become more prevalent and start prodding more companies into making changes, they are reaching out to other holders of stock, which more often than not are institutional investors, to support their initiatives. This trend has many institutions confused and disoriented about how to respond. One thing is for certain, insurgent efforts are making institutions take more time to think about their investments.

As discussed, an insurgent's provocations at times will involve pressuring a company to increase its debt load and use the resulting cash to complete a stock buyback or issue a special shareholder dividend. Those kinds of dissident demands place a spotlight on fundamental differences between institutions and activist hedge funds. "Activist shareholders might have different time horizons and different objectives than other investors, particularly institutional investors that often cannot buy or sell their stakes," says the U.S. Chamber of Commerce's David Chavern.

Chavern points out that observers have to be careful not to immediately draw parallels between the interests of activist hedge fund and institutions. While an activist may want to press for a short-term cash out, such as a special dividend or stock buyback, most institutions have much longer investment horizons to consider, and worry about what removal of cash and passive securities reserves will mean for the future of the corporation. Many institutions may prefer to have that cash remain on the balance sheet, ready to be reinvested in the company at an appropriate time or used to buy a critical asset that may be available only at a later date. "The quick return of a stock buyback can be fleeting and not worthwhile for many investors that have a much bigger picture, long-term outlook," Chavern says.

The University of Delaware's Charles Elson puts it even more strongly. Corporate cash on the balance sheet in many cases can be used for better things than the stock buybacks typically sought by activist hedge funds, he says. In many cases, corporations hold that cash, anticipating specific expenses that need to be paid for in the short term. "Having a stock buyback or special dividend paid to investors is probably not in the long-term interests of most institutional investors," Elson says.

But to the possible detriment of the long-term investment plans of institutions, companies have been making more stock buybacks than ever before. According to the Standard & Poor's (S&P) 500 Stock Index, a listing of large publicly held corporations, executives approved roughly $432 billion in stock buybacks in 2006, up from $349 billion in 2005 and $131 billion in 2003.[3]

Howard Silverblatt, an analyst at S&P, points out that the dramatic increase in stock buybacks and short-term returns in recent years can be attributed in part to the surge in activist hedge fund managers' pressing companies to complete recapitalizations. But, he adds, other institutions have also contributed to that phenomenon. "A lot of times companies that are under pressure for M&A by institutions and activists will agree to a stock buyback in the short term as a compromise to increase share growth instead of a merger or other transaction," Silverblatt says.

In 2004 and parts of 2005, Charles Jones, the CEO of Toronto-based enterprise software business GEAC, found himself the target of a Greenwich, Connecticut–based activist investor who was pressing for just that kind of stock buyback. The activist wanted the company to raise its debt levels and use the proceeds and its cash on hand to buy back shares.

In response, Jones immediately began his own campaign targeted at engaging the institutions that owned stakes in GEAC. He explained to them that much of the company's cash reserves were the result of its customers' paying advance payments at the beginning of the year. That cash, Jones says, was reserved to pay for customer maintenance and service. In essence, the presence of a large amount of cash on the balance sheet was an illusion, because by the end of the year it typically was gone. Getting rid of the cash would hurt the company in the long term as it struggled to find cash to fund routine maintenance and service costs. This was a situation that the insurgent either was not aware of or didn't care about because by the time the stock buyback was completed they would have been gone, leaving the company and its longer-term investors in a mess of trouble. Jones's campaign was successful. The institutions ultimately didn't support the activist's efforts. "We were not going to solve our strategic long-term value problem by buying back shares," Jones says. "It would have been great for the activist because he would have left with the additional value, but all the other institutional investors would have been left with a dark future."

But despite certain innate differences between the goals, timing, and investment horizons of activist hedge fund managers and institutions, some bonding appears to be happening. The two investor groups with characteristically opposite investment objectives are, at times, getting along and even working together, though it is often a dicey relationship.

Chapter 10

Activists Taking on Large Corporations Must Have Institutional Support

When activist hedge funds have "textbook" short-term outlooks, they will not succeed at their efforts to gain the support of institutions. This is particularly true at larger companies where activists must have the backing of many institutions for their campaigns to be triumphant.

Activist Bill Ackman of hedge fund Pershing Square Capital in January 2006 found that out the hard way. He canceled plans to push McDonald's Corporation into spinning off about two-thirds of its 8,000 company-owned restaurants after he calculated that his proposal wouldn't receive the support of a sufficient number of institutions invested in the burger chain. In a presentation to shareholders at a New York investment conference, Ackman expressed a hope that McDonald's would use the proceeds from the restaurant sales to buy back shares.[1] Generally speaking, institutions try to recognize whether an insurgent's efforts will bring long-term improvements to the company and its stock. At McDonald's, a critical mass of institutional investors didn't believe that Ackman's overall approach would aid the company in its long-term operational success.

Ackman did manage to receive the support of some institutions, but not enough. The sheer size of the company, which has a $60 billion stock market capitalization, meant that for Ackman to succeed a large number of institutions would have had to believe his strategy was good for them, too. Ackman did gain a sufficient amount of traction among institutions that McDonald's, feeling threatened, agreed to speed up its plans to convert some international outlets into franchises and increase its stock buyback plans.[2] But the totality of the changes didn't come close to meeting his expectations. Despite the initial failure, Ackman plans to buy more shares, indicating that he hasn't given up efforts to reform the large capitalization company.

Institutional owners of McDonald's weren't ready for the kind of drastic change activist hedge funds often seek out. But despite that, other insurgent investors have made inroads at large-capitalization companies. Their success must be attributed, in part, to their ability to gain the approval of a large institutional investor base.

We've already talked about Relational Investors' Ralph Whitworth's mobilization of institutions behind his successful campaign to remove Home Depot's chairman and CEO Robert Nardelli. In many ways, Whitworth's effort was the straw that broke the camel's back at The Home Depot, but his effort at such a large-capitalization company cannot be underestimated. The Home Depot has a stock market capitalization of over $80 billion, making it one of the largest companies in the world.

One of Whitworth's peers, in terms of successful activist campaigns at extremely large public companies, is activist investor Nelson Peltz. At H. J. Heinz Company, Peltz, the investor behind hedge fund Trian Partners, received the support of a great many institutions for the proxy contest he conducted in August and September 2006 at the ketchup and food giant. Shareholders, mostly institutions, elected Peltz and one of four other candidates he nominated replacing two of Heinz's management-backed slate.[3] It wasn't an easy victory for Peltz, who fought tooth and nail, spending roughly $14 million on the campaign.

In fact, since only two of his five candidates were elected, one might call it a partial victory. But Institutional Shareholder Service's (ISS's) Christopher Young sees it another way.

Trian's ability to convince a "critical mass" of plain-vanilla institutions at a corporation with a stock market capitalization of $15.5 billion to support even half of his slate represents a watershed moment in hedge fund activism. "This clearly was not a wolf pack of activists," Young says.

Indeed, unlike many small and midcap public companies where activist hedge funds have gained support for their initiatives largely because other insurgent fund managers buy up a huge chunk of the outstanding shares, Heinz shareholder base remained predominantly owned by a broad array of institutions, including mutual and public pension funds, at the time of the proxy contest. Certainly, there were some insurgents with Heinz stakes that backed Peltz's efforts and, yes, many had shorter investment horizons than the institutions. But Peltz's success means that a sufficiently large number of institutions believed that, to a degree, his influence at Heinz matched their long-term interest in improving the operations of the business.

Young argues that market capitalization is a major defense in a proxy contest. Pershing Square's Ackman did not ultimately pursue a proxy contest at McDonald's because he recognized that a sufficient number of institutions at the burger flipper were opposed to his plan. Meanwhile, Peltz succeeded. "Peltz had to convince rank-and-file shareholders who traditionally support the status quo or vote with their feet," Young says.

At a company like Heinz, it would be next to impossible for activist managers and their "wolf pack" brethren to buy up a critical mass of its shares. Peltz's ability to gain partial support from institutions surprised many observers because Heinz's performance, while sluggish, was not abysmal. It also had a decent governance record, Young adds. Another factor that made the campaign's success unusual was the fact that institutions did not come out publicly and support Peltz's insurgency. They only voted for Peltz when it counted, at the ballot box. Peltz's strong operational background was a critical factor that aided him in his victory and is something most activist hedge funds lack.

Young estimated that in May 2005, a 5 percent stake in Heinz was worth about $700 million. On April 24, 2005, Peltz reported a 5.4 percent stake in Heinz. "It shows that as an activist, if you have enough money, you can go after the larger-capitalization companies," says Marc Weingarten, a partner at Schulte Roth & Zabel LLP who represents Peltz and other high-profile activists including Carl Icahn and Jana Partners LLC's Barry Rosenstein. "But you need the support of institutions, and that includes the usually passive rubber-stamping mutual fund and pension fund money managers that automatically vote for management's slate."

Young goes on to point out that he believes Peltz's success was a milestone victory for dissidents that could potentially invigorate and inspire new insurgency campaigns at large-capitalization corporations. Activists that typically would avoid pressing for changes at larger corporations, due to the costs, time, and energy involved, not to mention the difficulty of attaining institutional support, may be having a change of heart.

But for now, most activist hedge fund managers still target smaller-sized public companies with fewer institutional investors to convince. New York University's April Klein came to that conclusion in her recent study.[4] Of the 155 activist targeted companies reviewed in the study, only 10 were included in the Standard & Poor's (S&P) 500 index, a listing of large, publicly held companies.[5] The majority of target companies traded on exchanges, such as NASDAQ or the American Stock Exchange, where typically smaller companies list (see Table 10.1).

For activist hedge funds to successfully stimulate change at larger companies they will need to close the gap between institutions and themselves. And that will not happen overnight. Not all institutions came on board for Peltz. Even California Public Employees' Retirement System (CalPERS), one of the most activist of U.S. pension fund institutional investors, did not vote for Peltz's candidates.[6] CalPERS's

Table 10.1 Exchange or Market Where Target Firm Trades at Time of Initial Investment

Number of Firms Trading On:	Hedge Fund Activists
New York Stock Exchange	47
American Stock Exchange	13
NASDAQ National Market	79
OTC Bulletin	7
Pink sheets	9

SOURCE: April Klein, associate professor Stern School of Business, New York University; Emanuel Zur, doctoral student, Stern School of Business, NYU, "Hedge Fund Activism" (September 2006): 37.

spokesman Brad Pacheco says the public pension fund negotiated with Heinz management for two months during the period Peltz waged his proxy contest. Before the election took place, CalPERS signed a corporate governance agreement with Heinz. As part of the agreement, Heinz said it would bring in two independent directors to its board, and in exchange CalPERS agreed not to vote for Peltz's slate. "In our view it looked like Heinz was taking steps to improve their governance so bringing in a dissident slate was not necessary," Pacheco says.

But despite increasing support for insurgents, the "shareholder access" proposal, if adopted, could eventually wreak havoc on institutional-activist hedge fund relations. This "shareholder access" approach, if approved by the SEC, would in some circumstances allow an investor to nominate one or two director candidates on a company's proxy card at little cost to the investor. This cheaper approach would be an alternative to the more costly, traditional proxy contests employed by activist hedge fund managers, such as Icahn and Peltz, which requires shareholders to file their own proxy materials to elect director candidates. American Federation of State, County, and Municipal Employees (AFSCME) director Richard Ferlauto is seeking support from institutions for such a measure at a few companies he is targeting.

An activist's huge investment in a proxy contest can be returned if the company is pressured to make certain changes such as sell a division. A small spike in the stock price can mean millions of dollars of profits for insurgents with their large stakes. The price tag that goes with launching an insurgency, including the printing and mailing costs, are too much for an institution and their diversified minuscule stakes. Any share-price improvement would never cover their proxy contest expenses.

The AFSCME measures have been reviled by business groups that worry it would give special interest investors, such as labor union leaders, environmentalists, and others, a disproportionately large influence over corporate decision making. Groups such as the Business Roundtable and the U.S. Chamber of Commerce, say that allowing shareholder groups to nominate directors on the corporate proxy card could put individuals on boards that would press companies into making decisions that violate their fiduciary share-improvement responsibility to all the investors. Candidates with environmental or labor union incentives may have different incentives than a mutual fund manager looking for share price improvement.

"It could lead to the election of "special interest directors" who represent the interests of the shareholders that nominated them, not the interests of all shareholders or the corporation," the Business Roundtable wrote to the Securities and Exchange Commission (SEC) on September 29, 2006.[7]

But Ferlauto argues that the CEO community should consider supporting shareholder access because it offers an alternative to the increasingly large presence of activist fund managers pressing to force much greater, sometimes short-term, changes at companies. Ferlauto points to the huge institutional investor support that Trian's Nelson Peltz received at Heinz as a harbinger of things to come unless shareholders are permitted to nominate directors on corporate ballots. A great many public and corporate pension plan and mutual fund managers believed Heinz's board was ineffective, but they also, in many cases, didn't trust Peltz's track record. "Institutional investors were stuck between a rock and a hard place," he says.

Ferlauto points out that if institutional investors could employ a mechanism to nominate their own director candidate on Heinz's proxy card then they likely would have done that rather than support any of Peltz's nominees. When faced with a change-of-control proxy contest by an activist hedge fund manager, Ferlauto says, CEOs would probably prefer to give institutions a chance to install their own director candidate on the board, rather than see otherwise passive money managers throw their support to the dissident hedge fund. "It would promote activism on the part of the institutions but in a much less aggressive manner than we are seeing with activist hedge funds," Ferlauto says. "And with it, institutions would be far less likely to turn to hedge fund managers to shake up companies. CEOs should be cheering for my proposal."

ISS's Young agrees that a hedge fund seeking a change-of-control proxy fight would have problems achieving its goal if an institutional investor launched its own less forceful shareholder access proposal at the same company. "Such a dual track process would definitely steal some of the activist's thunder," Young says.

But until the SEC moves forward to approve "shareholder access," institutions are likely to continue supporting activist hedge fund managers when faced with dysfunctional boards and stagnating stocks.

Billionaire activist Carl Icahn's efforts at Time Warner Inc. in 2005 and 2006 are a testament to the influence of bread-and-butter institutional investors. Icahn believed he could gain sufficient institutional support to pressure Time Warner chairman Richard Parsons to split up the media giant. The company's $72 billion stock market capitalization meant that Icahn needed to woo many institutions for his insurgency to take hold.

Unfortunately for Icahn, not enough institutions supported his campaign for it to be successful. He was forced to back down from his planned proxy contest. Even with the support of a group of activists, including Jana Partners, SAC Capital Advisors LLC, and Franklin Mutual Advisers LLC, Icahn did not gain the critical mass of support he had hoped to achieve. That group of activists and their huge investments would have represented a significant voting block at a small-capitalization company. At Time Warner, it represented only 3 percent of the shares outstanding.[8]

Despite the lack of institutional support, the effort wasn't a complete failure for Icahn. As part of a settlement, Time Warner agreed to increase its stock buyback program, repurchase $20 billion in shares by the end of 2007 and cut $1 billion in costs.[9] It appeared that a sufficient number of institutions were supportive of that aspect of Icahn's plan, and Time Warner, recognizing it needed to do something to make sure institutions did not join Icahn completely, agreed to the recapitalization. But a majority of shareholders did not buy Icahn's core argument that the company was worth more divided than maintained intact, and at the end of the day Parsons understood that he had leverage on that front.

"Basically, Parsons told Icahn to go jump in a lake because he understood that a majority of investors did not believe Icahn's plan to split the company up would work," says T2 Partners LLC's Whitney Tilson.

Had Icahn gone ahead with the contest, it would have been the largest activist-led proxy fight campaign ever. Even Parsons acknowledged that Icahn had a positive impact on Time Warner, noting on November 28 that the former raider helped company officials "get in touch" with its shareholder base.[10] "Icahn bit off more than he could chew," Young says. "He was not able to get a sufficient amount of the significantly large institutional vote there."

After the Time Warner effort, Icahn started off 2007 by launching a proxy contest to nominate a director candidate for the board of another extremely large corporation, $42 billion cell phone maker Motorola Inc. Icahn lost his campaign, by a couple hundred million votes. He received 717 million votes while the incumbent director attained 931 million.[11] Again, like Time Warner, this endeavor wasn't a complete loss. In what appeared to be a partial response to Icahn's campaign, Motorola later announced it would cut additional jobs, saving the company roughly $600 million.[12]

Another high-profile activist, Kirk Kerkorian, also may have bitten off more than he could chew. But instead of Motorola or Time Warner, Kerkorian set his sights on General Motors Corporation, the world's largest automaker. To what extent Kerkorian and his investment vehicle, Tracinda Corporation, was successful at provoking change at GM is unclear and still being debated. In December 2006, Kerkorian sold his 9.9 percent GM stake, ending his effort, at least for the time being, at the auto giant.[13] Certainly, Kerkorian did not accomplish his stated goal of having the Detroit-based company set up a joint venture with Renault SA and Nissan Motor Company Ltd., as a means of revitalizing itself.[14] Kerkorian's proposal also called for GM to bring on Nissan-Renault CEO Carlos Ghosn, a restructuring expert known for his successful turnaround of a once-troubled Nissan. GM agreed to consider such an alliance, based on the recommendation of Kerkorian's representative on GM's board, Jerome B. York, but ended talks after the automaker's management deemed that the partnership wouldn't improve value.

GM's CEO Rick Wagoner agreed to bring York onto the board as a means of improving relations with Kerkorian. With York on the board, Kerkorian was able to have some effect on the automotive giant. During York's stint on the board, GM agreed to cut compensation for executives and directors, reduce health care benefits for retirees, and limit pensions for some workers.[15] Many auto industry observers believe that Kerkorian and York succeeded at pressuring GM management to accelerate their turnaround plans, and a large part of that success came because the automaker knew that the activist had many institutional investors behind his strategy. But it wasn't enough. It's clear that Kerkorian did not succeed at mobilizing a critical mass of shareholders at the $17 billion stock market capitalization company. The University of Delaware's Charles Elson attributes Kerkorian's failure, in part, to his representative on GM's board. "York wasn't able to convince the board or GM's shareholders that the alliance was necessary," Elson says.

Internal relation issues between Wagoner and GM's board likely played a role in York and Kerkorian's failure to convince other directors to support the alliance. In his resignation letter, York took issue with the fact that GM's board did not do its own independent review of the Renault-Nissan-GM venture proposal, but instead accepted Wagoner's evaluation.[16] He also criticized GM management for providing key data and materials to board members without giving them sufficient time to review it.[17] (This, of course, is a tactic commonly employed by the party in power on Capitol Hill in Washington.)

ISS director Pat McGurn points out that GM's short-term stock improvement after Kerkorian proposed the three-way alliance didn't help the activist's ability to coalesce a sufficiently large group of institutional investors behind his Renault-Nissan-GM alliance plan. Many investors were satisfied with the stock's performance and didn't want to see anything rock the boat, he says. Other investors were scared away from what they perceived was going to be a serious fight between Kerkorian and Wagoner, he adds. "Institutional investors were feeling good about the stock's performance," McGurn says. "Short-term optimism cost Kirk some broader investor support."

Despite failures by Kerkorian, Ackman, and Icahn at GM, McDonald's, and Time Warner, one thing is clear: Bigger activist funds are taking on bigger companies, and they are doing it with institutional support. For one thing, the insurgents obtained some sort of positive response at all their large capitalization targets, albeit not the complete transformative concessions they had hoped to achieve.

Other activists have had an even higher measure of success at large-capitalization companies. Whitworth succeeded at ousting Home

Depot chief Nardelli. Nelson Peltz has two seats on Heinz's board. Their successes can be attributed to a new era of communications between institutions and activists. And if institutions feel their interests align with the insurgent, changes are taking place.

What about Kerkorian, Ackman, and Icahn? Suffice it to say that we haven't heard the last of them. Kerkorian may yet get involved in the operations of Chrysler, despite losing a bidding war to take over the mega-automotive company from DaimlerChrysler. Icahn, meanwhile, may follow up his failed bid to gain a seat on Motorola's board. Bruised egos or no bruised egos, these insurgents all have public plans to reinvigorate their efforts at large public companies.

Chapter 11

Institutions and Activist Hedge Funds

Breaking Up Deals Together Around the World

Faced with an unsavory blockbuster merger, institutional investors have traditionally thrown their arms up in frustration or sold their shares. This "do nothing" response fits with their institutional conflicts. Lashing out publicly against one of their investments would make it more difficult to gain a customer or financial advisory contract down the road.

In the few cases where, historically, institutions have grown dissatisfied with the price and viability of a mega-merger, any engagement with executives on the matter typically took place behind the scenes. CEOs and institutional portfolio managers discussed investor concerns quietly and in a very gentlemanly, upright, and professional manner. Corporate Library's Nell Minow relates a story of a manager at a large

U.S. mutual fund getting very angry with the CEO of one of its portfolio companies. The mutual fund manager told the CEO it was time to go, but all the communications took place in private.

Now things are changing. Institutions are beginning to put a magnifying glass onto deals struck between large corporations. Institutional investors are beginning to wake up and realize they have been on the losing end of a rash of poorly thought-out transactions. Some institutions are crawling out of the shadows and making their thoughts about deals public, particularly as they pertain to mega-mergers. Looser Securities and Exchange Commission (SEC) investor communication rules discussed in Chapter 8 are a major driving force behind this change. But eased communication regulations alone did not provide the impetus for this new institutional deal-reviewing activism.In some circumstances, institutions have started to make public comments to prop up an activist hedge fund manager that has already begun raising a stink about a particular transaction. In other cases, they are actively getting involved even when there is no activist hedge fund present.

Take Citibank Asset Management's (CAM's) January 2006 thoughts on the biotech hookup of Chiron Corporation and Novartis AG. Typically a behind-the-scenes kind of institution, CAM took a stand on the deal. It wrote Chiron's CEO and chairman, Howard Pien, a letter that was also attached to an SEC filing—making their thoughts public for everyone to hear. CAM wrote that the offer by Novartis of $45 in cash for each Chiron share was "financially inadequate." The major institutional investor, which had a 7.61 percent stake in Chiron, then threw down the gauntlet when it announced plans to vote against the deal.

CAM's public opposition demonstrates how institutions at times are beginning to publicly support activist hedge fund managers. Its opposition letter came roughly a month after activist fund ValueAct Capital Partners filed a Schedule 13D and began publicly pressing Chiron into accepting a better offer than the $45 a share bid Novartis had made. ValueAct, a 5 percent Chiron stakeholder, put itself in the position of deal breaker. With CAM's added pressure other investors began opposing the deal. In April, Novartis upped its offer to $5.4 billion.[1]

Mutual fund Putnam Investments LLC's reaction to Providian Financial Corporation's decision to sell itself to Washington Mutual Inc.

in 2005 for $6.5 billion evoked a similar response. Putnam, which owned a 7.5 percent stake in Providian, publicly declared that Washington Mutual's offer was too low, noting that the premium Washington Mutual offered paled next to the roughly 30 percent premium that rival MBNA Corporation received in its $35 billion sale to Bank of America Corporation also in 2005.[2] However, shareholders at MBNA had their own issues with that transaction. MBNA chief executive Bruce Hammonds received $23 million over two years as part of a $117 million retention and severance package that Bank of America provided to several MBNA executives, the bank divulged.[3] Despite Putnam's public campaign, shareholders approved the WaMu-Providian deal with no additional premium.[4]

Another high-profile campaign to block a transaction took place in 2004 when AXA Financial Inc. bid to buy MONY Group Inc. for $1.5 billion. Two large activist shareholders, Highfields Capital Management LP and Southeastern Asset Management Inc., joined institutions that were calling for a vote against the transaction, according to a 2006 report by Schulte Roth & Zabel.[5] The activists' public campaign appeared to be only partially successful. While the deal ultimately was consummated, the merging companies added a special dividend to shareholders, sweetening the overall transaction value. Also, MONY management agreed to smaller severance payments, which they received upon the closing of the deal.[6]

But, as a couple of academics uncovered, activist investors may have had other hidden incentives at work. In their report, "Hedge Funds in Corporate Governance and Corporate Control," New York University Law Professor Marcel Kahan and University of Pennsylvania School of Law professor Edward Rock, note that Highfields's public explanation of why they wanted to see the deal blocked did not tell the whole story.[7]

In a section of their report titled "Conflicts of Merger Votes," the professors cite a presentation that Credit Suisse First Boston gave to the MONY board, where the investment bank points out that Highfields held a large short position in a convertible debt security AXA had issued to finance its acquisition of MONY.[8] The debt security, known as ORANs, would become more valuable if the merger were consummated. But Highfields's short position in ORANs would be more valuable if the deal did not close.[9] In this situation, the activists' appeared to have additional considerations that were not disclosed. Their interests were not fully aligned with the institution's, even though, publicly it appeared that was the case.

Whether activist hedge fund managers' incentives are fully evident, particularly as it pertains to companies engaging in transactions, is a matter that many other institutions wonder and worry about. John Wilcox, senior vice president and head of corporate governance for public pension fund TIAA-CREF, says he is worried by evidence that derivative trading strategies can permit short-term investors to "game the system," even to the point of manipulating the vote for their own benefit.

One possible scenario is known as "empty voting," where the hedge fund manager acquires the voting rights for shares, either through derivative trades or borrowing, without having an economic interest in the stake. University of Texas Law School professors Henry Hu and Bernard Black first researched these kinds of situations in a study they released in 2006.

Sometimes activist investors will use this strategy to advance their interests by quietly playing on both sides of a hotly contested merger fight. In one scenario a corporation offers a huge premium to acquire a target company. The activist is an investor of the target and wants to see the transaction consummated, but shareholders of the acquirer are not so sure the target is worth what is being offered. To ensure its interests are achieved, the activist quietly borrows shares of the acquirer, for a fee, and votes the loaned stake to support the deal, thereby assuring that there are enough votes to make the transaction take place. They are, in essence, stacking the deck in their favor.

One high-profile situation related to this scenario involved hedge fund Perry Corp. and Mylan Laboratories Inc.'s $4 billion merger with King Pharmaceuticals Inc. Perry held a large stake in King and realized that Mylan shareholders appeared to be on the verge of voting against the transaction. In an effort to make sure that the transaction was consummated, Perry used a derivatives transaction to acquire the voting rights for a large block of Mylan shares so it could add to the vote seeking approval of the deal but do it in a secretive, covert way. According to professor Hu, Perry decoupled the economic interest in the stake from its voting rights. The King-Mylan transaction eventually unraveled despite Perry's covert two-sided efforts.

To reform the system, Wilcox calls on the SEC to improve disclosure about share ownership and increase the efficiency of voting and communications between shareholders and corporations so that the market knows exactly who is voting what shares. Long-term investors such as TIAA-CREF want to know the full picture when they are considering a deal, including the activities of hedge funds, he says. They are not the only ones. "Companies want to understand who their actual owners are so as to solicit appropriately," Wilcox says. "Our securities laws place a great burden on companies to extend voting rights but then they make it hard for corporations to know who their shareholders are." Whether or not these deceptive transactions are pervasive or rarely used when activists and other investors vote to block or approve deals is still unclear. But despite the possibility that some institutions may have reservations about some activists, many public and corporate pension funds and other investors are still joining forces with insurgent managers to voice their opposition to a greater number of transactions than ever before. This trend of collaborative efforts between the two investor classes has emerged on the international stage. Sometimes institutions and activist hedge fund managers are even joining force in places that have never experienced public shareholder opposition to mergers.

In February 2007, a sufficient number of institutional and individual investors backed an activist's campaign to block a major Japanese merger. The effort was the first successful derailment of a board-approved transaction ever in the country.[10] Scott Callon, the chief executive of Ichigo Asset Management Ltd., campaigned extensively to block a sale of Tokyo Kohtetsu Company, a steel company, to Osaka Steel. Merger proposals in Japan are typically special resolutions that require a two-thirds majority of votes or 66.7 percent to pass. Callon's campaign garnered more than the 33.4 percent needed to block the deal, while only 58 percent of shareholders voted to support the transaction, points out Institutional Shareholder Services' (ISS's) man in Tokyo, Marc Goldstein. "Many institutional and individual shareholders agreed with Ichigo, and together they were able to prevent the deal from being approved," Goldstein says.

Callon, whose fund manages roughly $25 million in assets, argued that the premium offered, roughly 6 percent, undervalued Tokyo Kohtetsu.[11] Instead, Callon reportedly urged Osaka Steel to pay a 30 percent premium, which he felt better represented Tokyo Kohtetsu's value. Once the acquisition was thwarted, Callon, a former Morgan Stanley director, decided to remain a Tokyo Kohtetsu shareholder.[12]

Before Callon began his efforts at Tokyo Kohtetsu, institutions and activists already had begun collaborating to thwart landmark European deals. After activist Knight Vinke Asset Management LLC of New York in early 2005 started criticizing the $6.4 billion acquisition of IMS Health Inc. by Dutch VNU N.V., some unlikely allies emerged. Both Fidelity Investments Ltd. and Templeton Global Advisors Ltd., which together owned about 25 percent of VNU's stock, said publicly that they wouldn't vote for the IMS deal. By November of that year, the companies, feeling the institutional and activist pressure, called off the transaction. Later, in May 2006, VNU was acquired by private-equity investors for roughly $10 billion, though both Fidelity and Templeton were skeptical of that deal as well.[13]

Another predominantly passive institution, UBS Global Asset Management, publicly came out in 2004 against the Mylan-King Pharmaceutical deal. UBS's public opposition, in part, contributed to the eventual unraveling of that transaction.[14] Suffice it to say that UBS was not on the same page as Perry Corp.'s two-pronged approach to getting the deal done.

Other mutual funds have morphed in some circumstances into activists. T.Rowe Price Associates Inc. opposed a management-orchestrated buyout of Laureate Education Inc., a Baltimore-based operator of online and foreign colleges.

Mutual fund OppenheimerFunds Inc. joined activist hedge funds and other investors in a public campaign to remove the management of video game maker Take-Two Interactive Software Inc. At Take-Two, OppenheimerFunds, and other dissidents held a collective stake representing roughly 46 percent of the company's shares. The mutual fund supported a proxy contest that took control of the company and ousted Take-Two CEO Paul Eibeler, replacing him with a former BMG Entertainment executive.

But while OppenheimerFunds, CAM, Putnam, and UBS have come out of the closet, so to speak, on these few instances, the vast majority of institutions are remaining passive or operating behind the scenes. Fidelity, for example, privately expressed concern about the price two buyout shops offered to buy assets from radio monolith Clear Channel Communications Inc. "These institutions that are doing it are an exception to the rule," Christopher Young says. "Just the fact that they are doing it at all is a big change."

In fact, many activist deal-breaking efforts produce no critical mass of institutional support. In 2004, children's safety products company First Years sold itself to RC2 Corporation for $136.9 million or $18.50 a share. For Lawrence Goldstein of Santa Monica Partners, that price greatly undervalued First Years and its $25.7 million in cash on hand. After spending 15 years agitating for change, Goldstein wasn't going to sit quietly and accept it. He began a campaign to block the deal, hoping a transaction could be struck for closer to $24 a share. Despite his efforts to convince the company's individual and institutional investor base to vote against the deal, it closed in with no additional premium.

Young points out that the phenomenon of activist hedge fund managers and institutions targeting merger and acquisition (M&A) transactions is a recent one. He notes that it is the activist hedge fund managers, not the institutional activists, that have been the major driving forces behind the deal-blocking trend. But Young acknowledges that the two investor groups generally need each other to get the attention of the merging companies. Typically, an activist hedge fund will launch a public campaign to obstruct a merger, but without institutional assistance its efforts will not reach fruition. "Not long ago, mergers and acquisitions advisers routinely viewed transactions as 'in the bank' immediately upon the announcement of a deal," Young wrote in a 2006 report. "While regulatory concerns could occasionally scuttle a deal, the shareholder vote was usually a foregone conclusion, but today, thanks to hedge fund activists, a shareholder vote can be very much in doubt."

He attributes the trend of activists and institutions blocking deals to a number of factors. Large mergers that just don't add shareholder value have irked the two investor classes. The combination of Time Warner Inc. and Internet service provider AOL in 2001 was a defining moment for investors, Young says. After the negative consequences of that deal and other poorly thought-out blockbuster mergers began to be known, institutions started scrutinizing transactions more carefully and, in some cases, began supporting the emergence of activists (themselves analyzing mergers in greater detail) and pressing to reject deals or at least make them more attractive from a shareholder value perspective. Government regulations allowing investors to communicate more freely have also aided in their mobilization efforts.

Shareholders faced with the collapse of Enron, WorldCom, HealthSouth, and other major corporate explosions have become more vigilant not just when looking at businesses as independent entities but also when they engage in transactions. Institutions are beginning to recognize that they need to take a proactive perspective, even if it means losing banking or retirement clients down the road, Young adds. "Today, institutional shareholders who consistently defer to management may be accused of abdicating their fiduciary duties," Young wrote.

Chapter 12

Just Vote No and No and No Again

Another instance in which institutions and activists are beginning to work together involves corporate director elections. But unlike the abrasive proxy contests insurgents' launch, pitching activist candidates against incumbents, these elections involve only management-backed directors.

The activist strategy is to convince enough shareholders to support the removal of key problematic management-backed directors. Of course, shareholders aren't allowed to simply vote against a director candidate. After receiving a proxy voting ballot, either electronically or in the mail, shareholders typically have three options: to vote "for," "abstain," or "withhold" on management-nominated directors. Checking off the box that says "withhold" represents the equivalent of a "no" vote or a vote against either the proposal or the management-nominated director.

An activist's goal with this tactic, known as a "just vote no" campaign, is to convince the rest of the company's shareholder base to check off the "withhold" box next to a proposal or the incumbent director's name on the corporate ballot card.

Shareholders cannot typically remove a director with a "just vote no" campaign even if the majority of shareholders vote to "withhold" their votes for a director. But a huge showing of shareholders voting "withhold" can send a loud, often embarrassing, message to directors and executives, enough to make them either resign on their own or with the board's help. In cases where the director or chairman also happens to be the CEO of the company, that message can be particularly embarrassing.

We've already examined the highest-profile "just vote no" campaign that was employed at Walt Disney Company. Roughly 45 percent of voting shareholders at the entertainment company in 2004 withheld their vote on a ballot for CEO Michael Eisner's reelection to the board (24 percent opposed the re-election of Disney director George Mitchell, former Senate Majority Leader in the U.S. Congress). Not a majority, but enough to send a sufficiently loud message to Disney's board that Eisner no longer should remain chairman. Shortly after the campaign, Eisner stepped down from that position, reeling from the public and investor opposition he received.[1] Shamrock Holdings Inc.'s Stanley Gold, who managed Roy Disney's campaign, points out that the vote no campaign cost Roy between $10 million and $12 million. Gold estimates that just the U.S. postage needed to mail proxy statements to Disney investors cost roughly $2 million, not including printing costs. Gold also surmises that Disney spent between $30 million and $40 million defending Eisner and George Mitchell.

Despite Roy Disney's huge costs, many observers point out that a "just vote no" campaign can also be cheaper and less time consuming than a full-out proxy contest. According to a 2006 report titled "Considerations for 'Just Vote No' Campaigns," by law firm Schulte Roth & Zabel, these types of campaigns can be considerably less expensive, particularly at smaller public companies. Activists and institutions can in many circumstances achieve their goals through this approach. As discussed in Chapter 8, "just vote no" campaigns became cheaper and more efficient after the SEC adopted key shareholder communication rules in 1992. The strategy also really began to be used effectively after the agency adopted those regulations.

Sometimes "just vote no" campaigns against directors may not initially appear to have a major effect, but they can be the beginning of something big. A "just vote no" campaign against Home Depot chairman and CEO Robert Nardelli and another director in 2006 helped propell activist fund manager Ralph Whitworth's successful effort the following year. Outraged by Nardelli's executive compensation, labor union pension fund American Federation of State, County, and Municipal Employees (AFSCME) led a "just vote no" campaign against Nardelli and Home Depot director Claudio Gonzalez. The campaign had a two-pronged message. First, Nardelli was overcompensated for an undervalued company that had a stagnating stock performance. Second, Gonzalez sat on too many boards, some of which had problematic ties to Home Depot founder Kenneth Langone. About 32 percent of participating investors voted against Nardelli, and 36 percent opposed Gonzalez.[2] A "just vote no" campaign against Nardelli in 2005 garnered only 5 percent of participating shareholders support.

The large showing of opposition in 2006 prompted Nardelli to hold a shortened 30-minute annual meeting in 2007. It also contributed to Nardelli's decision to cut the traditional question-and-answer session from the meeting's agenda. Another major departure from previous meetings: Nardelli was the only Home Depot director to attend. This prompted AFSCME's Richard Ferlauto to have someone dress up in a chicken suit and attend the meeting. "Are Home Depot directors too chicken to give shareholders a say on Nardelli's pay?" Ferlauto asked.

The opposition to Nardelli in the "just vote no" campaign, coupled with his subsequent shareholder-unfriendly annual meeting, factored heavily in shareholders feeling disenfranchised at The Home Depot. The unusual board meeting and the vote of no confidence also prompted Ralph Whitworth in the fall to acquire a large Home Depot stake and write a letter to the home improvement company's board privately explaining his plans to consider nominating a short slate of two director candidates.

Prior to launching his effort at The Home Depot, Whitworth says, he first considered the possible share-value improvement that could take place based on the changes he was considering. He also assessed how open or vulnerable the company was to change. Institutional opposition was a consideration, he says. "For us, it was assessing the likelihood for change," Whitworth says.

In response to Whitworth's efforts, Home Depot directors agreed in February to put a Whitworth candidate on the company's board. The board also put pressure on Nardelli to accept a reduced compensation package, which he didn't accept.[3] The institutional investor "just vote no" campaign began to drive a wedge between Nardelli and the board, which grew bigger after Whitworth launched his private endeavor. The board ultimately decided it was time for Nardelli to step down, Institutional Shareholder Services' (ISS's) Pat McGurn says. "Ralph's proxy contest acted as the chemical reaction at the end of a multiyear process of investor dissatisfaction," McGurn says. "The cumulative effect of all these factors, starting with the 'just vote no' campaign, caused Nardelli to resign."

AFSCME's Richard Ferlauto says the pension fund's "just vote no" campaigns "paved the road" for Whitworth. "The shareholders were already organized and prepared to confront the board when Whitworth got involved."

A less successful "just vote no" campaign took place at embattled Safeway Inc., though it was just as high profile an event, with conflict-of-interest charges being levied on both sides of the bitter battle. A number of large unions' pension and public pension funds, including New York City Employees' Retirement System, California Public Employees' Retirement System (CalPERS), the Connecticut Retirement Plans and Trust Funds, the Illinois Board of Investment, and several others, joined forces in a campaign to remove Safeway chairman and CEO Steven Burd and two directors from the company's board.[4]

The pension fund group argued to investors that among other problems he created at Safeway, Burd and some directors were not acting in the best interest of shareholders, and one major example of that was when the grocery chain agreed to acquire a business at what the investors believed to be an unreasonably high price. According to the institutional investor group, Burd had conflict-of-interest problems because of his connections to buyout shop Kohlberg Kravis Roberts & Company (KKR). KKR acquired Safeway in a leveraged buyout in 1986, later taking it public. In 1999, before KKR liquidated its Safeway stake, it sold another grocery chain it owned, Randall's Food Market Inc. of Houston, to Safeway for $1.3 billion. That acquisition soured, and Safeway was forced to record a $1.26 billion impairment charge as a result, all of which had a negative impact on Safeway's stock (which dropped from $62.50 in 2000 to $21.91 in 2003).

At the time of the Randall's transaction, a number of Safeway's directors had ties to KKR, left over from when the buyout shop had acquired the company. For example, KKR founder George Roberts, general partner James Greene Jr., and a couple of others with connections to the buyout shop held Safeway board seats.[5] Greene and Roberts also held director seats on Randall's Food Market's board.[6] The shareholder group argued that the KKR-linked directors exerted influence on the board and pressured Safeway into buying Randall's from the buyout shop at a price that benefited KKR at the expense of Safeway and its shareholders.

In response to the investor allegations, Safeway management argued that the grocery chain performed comparably to its peers over the previous five years.[7] Safeway management also pointed out that a sluggish economy combined with an encroaching Wal-Mart was affecting its share performance.[8] Safeway also contended that the amount it paid for Randall's was comparable to other similar grocery store deals that took place during the same time frame.[9]

But while the pension groups tried to maintain a focus on the perceived conflict-of-interest issue regarding KKR and Safeway, another possible conflict-of-interest issue arose that hampered their ability to gain significant support among institutions. The dissident campaign began shortly after a long, drawn-out strike of Safeway workers, initiated by the United Food and Commercial Workers (UFCW) union in California, had just come to an end. At the time of the annual meeting, in May 2004, Safeway still faced some contract negotiations with the UFCW. As part of Safeway's campaign to limit support for the group, Burd and other corporate supporters pointed out that some of the public pension funds involved in the effort had ties to organized labor and that they may have acted more due to resentment of Safeway's handling of the strike than any interest in improving shareholder value.[10]

In the end, only 17 percent of Safeway's shareholders voted no on Burd's ballot, indicating that the majority of investors didn't fully support the pension funds' efforts. Later that year, CalPERS president Sean Harrigan was removed from his position by the state of California. Harrigan, who later took a seat on the board of the Fire and Police Commissioners, claims that his Safeway endeavor and concerns about the effort by California governor Arnold Schwarzenegger played a significant role in his removal.[11]

ISS's McGurn noted that the Safeway shareholder effort became a lightning rod for controversy, bringing in groups such as the U.S. Chamber of Commerce to consider it a test case for labor-led activism. The argument presented by business groups was that Harrigan and CalPERS were acting from positions that were political in nature, rather than in the best interest of shareholders. While CalPERS is a public pension fund, many of its participants and beneficiaries are state employees that belong to unions. In addition to that, CalPERS's governance stance over the years has matched up, more often than not, with the goals of corporate labor unions.

But the campaign was not a complete loss for the institutions. The national attention certainly cost the labor funds some support, but in the end the group had a tangible impact on Safeway despite their limited showing. Safeway implemented some changes in the weeks leading up to the meeting in an attempt to diminish institutional investor support for the labor union funds' campaign. On May 3, shortly before the meeting, Safeway announced that KKR's Roberts and Greene would resign from the board within 60 days, as would another director with independence issues.[12] The supermarket chain would subsequently bring on three independent directors.

For a critical mass of institutions, Safeway's commitment to replace Greene and Roberts with independent directors was sufficient to gain their support for Burd.[13] While the labor union funds did not gain their goal of removing Burd, the new independent directors represented a measure of success for them. "Safeway has emerged from the situation with much better corporate governance practices," McGurn says. "Managers and directors there, now, more frequently reach out and have a dialogue with all institutions, including public pension funds."

In other situations, activist hedge fund managers that are typically associated with more aggressive proxy contest governance tactics, try their hand at "vote no" campaigns. In April 2006, Jana Partners LLC's activist manager Barry Rosenstein launched a "just vote no" campaign to oust directors at Houston Exploration Company. Roughly 30 percent of participating shareholders—many of which were institutions—did withhold their shares for incumbent directors of the oil and gas explorer, but not the critical mass needed to convince the board that they needed to go.[14]

Sometimes simply the threat of a "just vote no" campaign may be enough. Corporate Library's Nell Minow says she considered these kinds of campaigns while managing money for LENS, a shareholder activist fund with $100 million in assets under management. After considering the support of other institutional investors, Minow decided that in one egregious case the threat of a "just vote no" campaign might be enough to convince corporate management that they needed to change.

This particular company, Minow says, had a board made up of the chief financial officer's investment banker, the CEO's lawyer, "the guy who plays clarinet in a management-led jazz band," and an alcoholic. Minow privately told the CEO this: "Either you bring in some independent directors that are satisfactory to me or I will start to solicit what will clearly be the most successful 'no vote' campaign in history, and you will have nobody on this board."

At another company Minow succeeded at convincing executives to accept one of her six director candidate recommendations after threatening the company with a "just vote no" campaign. That effort was successful, to a large part, because the executives at the company understood that Minow had many large institutional investors backing her position. "Now it's a good time to talk about what the nominating committee does," Minow told that CEO. "I'm going to make it tough on you. The people on this board don't just have to be better than those three, which is not a high standard, but I'm going to give you the names of six people, and either you choose those six people or you pick people that are better than my recommendations."

In addition to accepting one of her recommendations, a division manager, the company eventually found other strong nominees, Minow says.

Despite all the investor support she received while at LENS, Minow is still pessimistic about traditional institutions becoming true activists. She argues that the cases of public institutional activism exhibited by CAM, Fidelity, UBS, and some others remain an exception, not the norm. She points out that most interested institutions write short letters and make SEC filings that are minimalist, "boilerplate" comments responding to hedge fund activists' efforts, rather than any insurgency they initiated on their own. At LENS, Minow spent roughly 10 years actively engaging executives and seeking the aid of institutions for her campaigns. A key part of her job was to approach institutions with research produced by LENS and ask for their support. "I would say, 'Here is all the research I've done on how to unlock value,'" Minow says. "Most of the time they [the institutions] would not help me."

The most significant institutional "just vote no" campaigns are typically led by labor union pension funds and public pension funds. But it is the activist hedge fund, Minow says, that will be the best catalyst for change. Activists complete the thorough and thoughtful research and write the detailed letters that lead to successful engagement with executives. But Minow says she expects institutions to start stepping up to the plate more often. "The fact that some institutions are beginning to publicly criticize corporations is a step in the right direction," Minow adds. "It's a shot across the bow."

Whitworth, Minow, and other activists cannot help but acknowledge that institutional investors are beginning to make a difference with "just vote no" campaigns. Whether institutions lead these efforts, as we've seen at The Home Depot and Safeway, or they follow activist hedge fund managers that launch campaigns, these investors are starting to make a difference in board governance. In other instances, "just vote no" campaigns are victorious for shareholders before they begin. As described, institutions in many cases can convince management to make board or other changes simply with the private threat of a "just vote no" campaign. In other cases, a public operation is necessary. As we've seen at The Home Depot, a "just vote no" campaign may not initially appear to make a difference, but it can set off a domino effect with a fairly successful value-enhancing outcome a couple years later. Should the SEC and NYSE move forward to eliminate the ballot-stuffing broker nonvotes, expect "just vote no" campaigns to be even more potent.

Even as institutions broaden their efforts to target specific companies with "just vote no" campaigns, they are continuing other tried-and-true insurgency tactics such as pressing companies to remove anti-takeover provisions. That is the subject of the next chapter. Those efforts usually show no immediate realizable results, but with the tangential growth of activist hedge funds, they may be indirectly producing improved shareholder value faster than ever before.

Chapter 13

Institutions Changing Corporate Bylaws so Activist Hedge Funds Can Get Down to Business

As we can see, institutions have a difficult time becoming full-fledged activists, despite their efforts to block deals or launch campaigns to force incumbent directors off boards. These kinds of activist efforts are typically done in tandem with activist hedge funds doing the heavy lifting, so to speak. But institutions have also found another way to aid activist hedge funds, though indirectly: the shareholder proposal.

Most rank-and-file institutional investors come across a wide variety of proposals at hundreds of corporations that make up their large portfolios. Every year, before an annual meeting, shareholders receive a copy of the annual report along with a booklet outlining the proposals they must vote on.

After the section on director elections and approval of the company's external auditor, investors often are exposed to a wide variety of shareholder proposals. Many of them are targeted at multinational companies, seeking reduction of greenhouse gas emissions, conserving natural resources, or establishment of global labor standards for the corporation's operations around the world. At Wal-Mart, for example, investors might see a dozen shareholder proposals, including one seeking more information about the company's political contributions.

But, unlike these measures, many corporations list other proposals calling for a shareholder vote to change the company's bylaws and charter in a way that could have a direct impact on the successes and failures of future activist hedge fund campaigns. Altering a few aspects of a company's bylaws in one year could give activists additional sway in their campaigns the following year, whether insurgents will be pressing executives behind the scenes or in full-out public proxy contests. "I would call it leverage," Nell Minow says. "The activist hedge funds can leverage the efforts of the people, in this case institutions, who are asking for less. Why not have someone else pave that road for you?"

A popular effort by institutions over the years has been to press companies to declassify or unstagger their boards. Staggered or classified boards permit only a minority of director nominees to be up for election each year. For example, at a board with nine directors, three directors are up for election each year for three-year terms.

Many companies have installed staggered boards because they prevent an insurgent from launching a proxy contest to oust all directors and replace management. Elimination of this protection makes it easier for an activist to launch a proxy fight. It also gives insurgents greater leverage in negotiating with management behind the scenes because managers know that there is a possibility that the dissident shareholder could replace the *entire* board with one less receptive to them.

Investors submitted 55 proposals to repeal classified boards in 2006, up from 48 measures in 2005, according to Institutional Shareholder Services (ISS), the Rockville, Maryland-based company that advises shareholders on how to vote for mergers, proxy fights, and bylaws.[1] Of the 55 proposals that were submitted in 2006, 65.7 percent, or 36, received majority vote support. In 2005, 63.2 percent of the 48 proposals received the approval of a majority of shareholders.[2] All this is a strong indication that shareholders continue to oppose this provision.

Typically, classified board proposals and most other investor measures are precatory or nonbinding, which means that even if more than half of the voting shareholders cast their ballot for the proposal, the corporation is not required to adopt what it says. But in an increasing number of cases, companies are taking these proposals more seriously than ever and voluntarily changing their bylaws to meet with shareholder demands.

As we've seen in other instances, the embarrassment factor takes hold. A corporation does not want to be viewed by the investor community as a company that go against shareholder wishes. As a result, companies are eliminating staggered boards in quick order. According to ISS data, only 45 percent of Standard & Poor's (S&P) 500 companies as of the end of 2006 had classified boards.[3] In 2003, 60 percent of S&P 500 companies employed classified boards.[4]

Institutions also continued to assist activists by supporting the removal of another key bylaw provision. The poison pill, also known as a shareholder rights plan, is the anti-takeover provision that permits a corporation to inundate the market with shares and as a result prevents a hostile bidder from accumulating a controlling stake in the business. This is how it works. When a hostile bidder tries to buy more than a set minority amount of a target company's stock, usually between 10 percent and 20 percent, the company allows shareholders, other than the hostile bidder, to convert a "right" they have in the company charter into a large number of common shares. This immediately dilutes the amount of shares owned by the acquirer/insurgent and makes it more expensive and typically impossible to take control of the target company.

Corporate executives love the pill, not only because it can discourage hostile bidders, but because it forces a potential hostile bidder to sit down with the company's management and board to negotiate an acquisition. Companies claim the pill defends shareholder rights, hence the "shareholder rights plan" name they have attached to it. Their belief is that the pill forces otherwise hostile bidders to the negotiation table with executives. Consequently the bidder will offer more, giving investors an additional premium value for their stock in a change-of-control situation that they may not have achieved in a hostile situation. But the pill cannot typically stop a proxy fight from taking place.

In the wake of the 1980s raiders, the vast majority of U.S. companies adopted poison pill provisions. Instead of requiring removal of a poison pill, many institutional investors are submitting proposals seeking a shareholder vote on poison pills. Introducing this measure, often also called a chewable pill, for a vote on corporate boards has long been a staple strategy of institutions hoping to gain a little more leverage in negotiations with management.

In 2006, there were only 11 investor proposals that would require a shareholder vote on poison pills, down from 24 in 2005 and 51 in 2004, according to ISS.[5] Those numbers, though, can be deceiving. The real number of pill proposals introduced over the years is likely to be much greater when considering that under pressure from activist institutions, some companies agree to eliminate or alter their poison pills before measures seeking to remove them come to an official vote. When a management team knows that the majority of investors will vote for the shareholder proposal, it may agree to make the requested changes as a means of saving face. Another factor contributing to the decline in poison pill proposals is that there simply are fewer of them than there were 10 years ago. ISS reports that in 2006, 54 percent of S&P 500 companies no longer had poison pills.[6] Tepid institutional investor interest in introducing poison pill proposals may also have less to do with fewer institutions being concerned about them, but rather the increased investor interest in other more popular proposals.

Despite that, proposals seeking shareholder votes on poison pills have been steady vote getters over the years, and that trend still continues. ISS reports that between January and June 2004, pill proposals received an average of 61.8 percent support. During the same period in 2005, the measures collected 57.8 percent approval and 55.6 percent in 2006.[7]

As with staggered boards, having a shareholder vote on a poison pill also aids activist hedge fund managers in their efforts to gain leverage with corporate boards. When poison pills are aligned with shareholders, insurgents have a key bargaining chip that they can take advantage of when engaged in behind the scenes negotiations or public proxy contests at companies. This means activists have greater influence in pressing firms to sell assets or make other changes, such as buying back shares. "Another factor that has led to more proxy fights has been the gradual erosion of poison pill plans, classified boards, and other takeover defenses," ISS reports.[8]

Unfortunately for activists, shareholder-friendly bylaw provisions don't create the catalyst for change on their own. An activist hedge fund's success still rests with its ability to garner the support of the company's other investors. When an institution votes to remove a classified board at a company, it doesn't necessarily mean an insurgent hedge fund will have their support for a dissident director candidate. Institutions that press for a shareholder vote on a company's poison pill could very easily oppose an activist's efforts to put that business in play.

But PL Capital's Richard Lashley says he finds that companies without poison pills or other anti-takeover devices are generally more accountable to shareholders. He also believes relations between institutions that support removal of these measures and activists are generally better than between insurgents and those institutions that oppose removal of the provisions.

Many institutions have corporate governance principles and guidelines that outline which specific bylaws they oppose or support. For example, the California Public Employees' Retirement System (CalPERS) offers a laundry list of governance suggestions in its "U.S. Corporate Governance Core Principles and Guidelines." Included are recommendations on poison pill approval by shareholders, annual election of directors, and giving investors the right to call special shareholder meetings or act by written consent.[9]

When a portfolio company has poison pill or classified board bylaws, many institutions will automatically vote for their removal based on internal guidelines. Some institutions also have automatic voting procedures to support these kinds of initiatives.

But one governance proposal supported by some activists that may not be on an institution's automatic voting list is the cumulative voting for election of directors measure. This once popular provision, if adopted as part of a company's bylaws, allows shareholders the option of casting all their votes for a single board nominee or a few key candidates. ISS tracked 23 proposals seeking cumulative voting at companies in the first half of 2006, up from 17 in the same period in 2005 and 23 for the first six months of 2004.[10] Even though cumulative voting proposals generally have held steady for the past number of years, ISS notes that the measure seems to be disappearing from corporate bylaws and institutional investor interest. In fact, cumulative vote proposals, on average, have not received a strong showing of support in recent years. In the first six months of 2006, cumulative voting measures received 39.8 percent support, 40.4 percent in 2005, and 34.8 percent in 2004.[11]

At least one activist hedge fund manager bemoans the slow disappearance of cumulative voting at U.S. corporations. Santa Monica's Lawrence Goldstein says these measures, which institutions in the past had vigorously supported, are important to activists. He points out that cumulative voting gives minority shareholders a voice at corporations, adding that the process is democratic in the same way the U.S. Congress gives additional consideration to voters in sparsley populated states that might otherwise not have a voice in government. Companies with cumulative voting bylaws generally take the time to listen to the grievances of smaller shareholders that might otherwise be ignored, he says. "In the last 50 years cumulative voting has gone the way of the dodo bird," Goldstein says. "It's a democratic thing because it gives some representation to a significant minority."

While cumulative voting and poison pill proposals seem to be slowly disappearing, institutions have turned their attention to a new bylaw amendment that could eventually give shareholders greater leverage in director elections. Many pension fund groups and other institutions are trying to overthrow the established "plurality voting" system, which allows corporate directors to be elected to the board even if the majority of participating shareholders withhold their vote (equivalent of voting no) or actually abstain from voting for the seat.

With the existing plurality system, a candidate can win and be elected to the board with as little as one vote in his or her favor. In practicality, institutions have traditionally voted for management-backed candidates, but their rubber stamp support may change if the process is converted to one that would allow directors to be elected to the board only if they receive a majority of the votes cast at the election. These are, of course, elections where the incumbent is running unopposed. Votes actually count in traditional proxy contests.

In effect, a majority vote system would give shareholders greater leverage when launching "just vote no" campaigns described in Chapter 12. Instead of being just symbolic expressions of concern about directors, investors can have an additional level of leverage at companies that have adopted a majority vote proposal. Activists and institutions that launch a "just vote no" campaign at a company with a majority vote bylaw could require boards to seek out replacement candidates, whether insiders want them to go or not. If the majority vote system becomes pervasive, it may one day replace the need to launch costly proxy contests to oust directors.

However, until that happens, there are many questions that still need to be answered about how exactly a majority vote system would work, not the least of which is what you would do if the entire incumbent board was voted off by disgruntled shareholders frustrated with the direction of the company. Most states have adopted a so-called holdover rule, which says a director stays in office until his successor is elected and qualified.

Intel Corporation and dozens of other companies have installed majority vote systems that reach closest to what dissident institutions want to see. However, many of these cases emerged only after corporations received pressure from institutions.[12] At Intel, a director candidate who is being nominated for the first time and does not receive the support of a majority of the participating shares would not be elected.[13] Presumably, the company could later renominate that candidate, though such a move would be seen as a foolish slap in the face to its shareholder base. Incumbent director candidates who do not receive the support of a majority of shareholders would need to submit their resignation to the Intel board, and that group of directors must decide whether they accept it or not. The provision does not put the final power in the hands of shareholders because directors can reject that candidate's resignation letter.

Dozens of companies have adopted this bylaw change, and many more have approved a quasi-majority vote policy change known as a "director resignation policy" that is similar to the bylaw provision but less onerous to remove. Corporations will try to pass off this provision, also known as the "Pfizer approach," for the company that first installed it, as a real majority vote measure. Investor groups are pushing to have companies require a shareholder vote to change a majority vote bylaw, though not even the Intel provision permits that.[14]

Labor investor American Federation of State County and Municipal Employees (AFSCME), argues that there are many options companies can consider to bring in new candidates once either an incumbent or new nominee is rejected by shareholders. One idea is to require that companies find a replacement candidate or candidates and hold another election a few months after the vote. Another approach requires the loser incumbent director remain on the board for 12 months. With this approach, the nomination committee would need to find a replacement candidate to put up for election at the following year's annual meeting. This system would prohibit the director from serving out an automatic three-year term, as is the case with many classified boards.

The SEC has gotten in the middle of this battle. AFSCME and other activist institutions have submitted advisory majority vote proposals for shareholders to consider at numerous U.S. companies. Their strategy is to try to bring a change in election procedures one company at a time, though their proposals are nonbinding, meaning the company is not required to install the measure even if the majority of shareholders support it.

In response, several of these companies submitted petitions to the SEC asking it to remove the shareholder proposals from corporate proxy documents. The agency turned down each company request. According to ISS, about 40 corporations so far have adopted full "Intel-style" majority vote for election of director provisions.[15] Most of those measures were installed in 2006, but some were adopted in 2004 and 2005. More than 140 other companies took a compromise approach by installing the less-strenuous director resignation policies.[16] More than 150 institutions submitted majority vote proposals at U.S. companies in 2006.[17] So far, 36 of these proposals have received majority support from shareholders, up from 13 in 2005.[18] These numbers indicate a significant improvement on prior years. In 2004, ISS reported that majority vote proposals received less than 12 percent support from investors.[19]

One institution came with inches of testing the majority vote proposal in a real-life scenario. According to a company tally, about 42.7 percent of shareholders voted to support a labor federation funded CtW Investment

Group proposal seeking the ouster of CVS/Caremark Corporation director Roger Headrick. Eliminating the ballot-stuffing broker nonvotes, CtW director Michael Garland says, would mean 57 percent of shareholders voted to remove Headrick. Interestingly, Garland says, had these broker discretionary votes been removed, CVS/Caremark would have been the first test case for majority vote, because the pharmaceutical drug store chain had adopted some sort of majority vote policy. "Without the broker votes, Headrick may have been required to submit his resignation to the company's nomination committee," Garland says. Even without a majority vote system in place, CtW's efforts were enough to convince CVS/Caremark it was time for Headrick to go. The pharmaceutical company's board sent Headrick packing shortly after the annual meeting.

In 2005, the Council of Institutional Investors adopted a policy endorsing majority election of directors. That same year CalPERS, which by July 2006 was managing $210 billion in assets, put together a three-point plan advocating majority vote.[20] The State Board of Administration of Florida, which manages $133 billion in assets for the Florida Retirement System, also endorsed majority vote.[21] The International Corporate Governance Network, a global organization that represents roughly $10 trillion in assets, took an informal poll of its 550 members in 2005, and 69 percent of those participating wanted a switch to majority voting in the United States.[22]

While it's certain that institutional investors are embracing majority vote provisions wholeheartedly, there is still a question about what impact their support is having on activist hedge fund managers. Corporate Library's Nell Minow points out that as majority vote becomes more prevalent, activist hedge fund managers will begin to embrace "just vote no" campaigns more thoroughly as an alternative strategy to full-out proxy contests. Majority vote bylaws would not only give institutions greater leverage in negotiations behind the scenes with corporate boards, but activist hedge fund managers would also have improved positions when pressing companies in private negotiations with executives over whether less-than-independent individuals should be removed.

It could become another modus operandi for dissidents to achieve their goals. At the very least, majority vote will be another arrow in the quill for activists seeking to enforce changes at corporations. A world without poison pills and staggered boards and where directors are elected by majority vote could give activist hedge fund managers the additional edge they desire. It could also provide enough leverage to transform once-passive institutions into a different form of activists. Would the two groups then work together or against each other?

Chapter 14

Can't Be Them? Then Fund Them

Relations between institutional investors and activist hedge fund managers are growing from another perspective as well. Public pension funds with a moderate activist streak in them, such as the California Public Employees' Retirement System (CalPERS), began funding activists in the 1990s.

These relationships were born, in part, because of most institutions' diversified portfolio of miniscule positions and their conflicting incentives. As discussed before, public pension funds have so many positions that the costs of actively focusing attention on a particular company outweighed any benefits that could be attained from a reformed corporation. Investment banks, mutual fund managers and other institutions on the one hand want to bring in more fee business from corporate clients and on the other hand seek to press many of those same corporations into making changes to improve share value.

The conundrum that these situations result in has led many more-or-less passive institutions to invest with activist hedge fund managers rather than launch insurgencies on their own. Activists do what many institutions would love to do themselves but simply can't. "Institutions use activists as stocking horses," says one investment consultant. "They become straw men for institutions."

Probably the most important connection between activist fund managers and institutions is public pension fund CalPERS's relationship with activists David Batchelder and Ralph Whitworth. We recall that in 1995, CalPERS allocated $200 million to Batchelder and Whitworth's fledgling San Diego–based activist fund, Relational Investors.[1] In return for its initial investment, CalPERS expected Relational to buy large stakes and engage managements at a small number of undervalued companies, by focusing on a corporate governance approach to share enhancement.

One of CalPERS's key principles focuses on encouraging companies to have more independent directors. Recognizing his assignment, Whitworth got right to it. He began launching governance campaigns, either behind the scenes or through public activist campaigns. On Relational's Web site, Whitworth describes the fund's mission as such: "We see ourselves as stewards of our clients' shareholdings. Proper stewardship requires active engagement of corporate leadership to spur improved performance."

With CalPERS's backing, the activist hedge fund also had on its side a major institution that could attract other institutions to contribute—either with capital allocations or by supporting a Relational campaign. Having CalPERS approval went a long way toward helping the activist fund gain the trust of other institutional investors. With additional capital and the approval of many public pension funds, Whitworth had the political capital and leverage he needed to press companies into changes, as we've seen at The Home Depot and other companies.

One of Whitworth's most recent high-profile governance campaigns to date was waged against Philadelphia-based savings and loan bank Sovereign Bancorp Inc. At Sovereign, Whitworth sought more independent directors on the company's board. He criticized Sovereign for orchestrating the sale of roughly 25 percent of the thrift to Banco Santander Central Hispano S.A. in Madrid in a way that consolidated power for management and diluted shareholder voting rights. After a drawn-out and heated battle, Whitworth agreed to cancel litigation he had pending at Sovereign, and in exchange the thrift agreed to put him and an independent director on the board. By October 2006, Sovereign Bancorp's CEO Jay Sidhu had resigned. Whitworth's proxy contest and the public exposure it brought to the Banco deal was too much for Sidhu to handle.[2]

In addition to The Home Depot and Sovereign, Whitworth has engaged the management of many other companies with his governance tack. One trucking and logistics firm, CNF Inc., was encouraged to unload an underperforming delivery and transportation business.[3] He also urged National Semiconductor Corporation to cut off product lines.[4] Waste Management Inc. installed Whitworth as chairman. He subsequently helped turn around the Houston, Texas-based company, which was bogged down in a financial scandal. Relational also engaged executives at Valeant Pharmaceuticals International Inc. and Mattel Inc., among many others.[5]

From a financial point of view, Relational's efforts have reached fruition. By 2006, the activist hedge fund had $6.4 billion in assets under management, and with an average annual return of 22 percent from its inception in 1996 through 2006, it has outperformed its benchmark, the Standard & Poor's (S&P) 500 index, which had only an average return of 8 percent during that period.[6] The investment firm typically invests with a dozen companies that each have stock market capitalizations of $2.5 billion or more.[7] This category allows Whitworth to choose companies within a network of roughly 1,100 U.S. companies.[8]

Seeing that the specialized governance-style activist strategy was working at Relational, CalPERS in 1998 allocated an additional $275 million in funds to Whitworth.[9] That allocation may seem large, but keep in mind it still was a small part of the $140 billion in assets CalPERS managed at the time.[10] Other governance-focused institutional investors, following CalPERS's investment strategy, also invested with Relational. Activist institution Hermes Pension Management Ltd., which was formed in 1995, allocated funds to Relational. The London-based fund was formed with assets supplied by its initial sponsors, British Telecom and the British Post Office. The Ontario Municipal Employees Retirement System and Virginia Retirement System also have contributed some funds to Whitworth's investment vehicle.

A similar approach to collecting institutions and launching governance-focused activist efforts is being taken by Los Angeles billionaire Ron Burkle. In 2007, Burkle, the founder of investment firm Yucaipa Companies, launched a governance-style activist hedge fund.[11] Burkle's fund, like other insurgent-style investment vehicles, will buy large stakes in companies and agitate for change with the intention of improving shareholder value through a Whitworth-style governance approach. His governance fund has a unique twist: it will be backed in large part by labor unions and their pension plan capital, giving Burkle an unusual base of investors.[12] Observers point out that he may be under pressure not to take value-enhancing actions that would go against labor union principles.[13]

But the ability of activists such as Burkle and Whitworth to gain the trust and investments of public pension and labor union pension fund managers should not be underestimated. Like other institutions, labor unions also have a love-hate relationship with activists. On the one hand, labor unions appreciate when activists like Whitworth press for the removal of CEOs that they believe are receiving exorbitant compensation. (Many labor unions supported Whitworth's efforts to remove Home Depot's Robert Nardelli.) But, on the other hand, as seen in the Safeway situation, ties to labor unions have also made activism more difficult for some institutions. While a labor union fund may want to pressure companies to tie their executive compensation to performance, it may be squeamish about investing with activist hedge funds that in their efforts to improve shareholder value will take action that could hurt unionized employees or their pensions. "Such action might be interpreted by their clientele, labor union, or public pension beneficiaries in a negative manner," says one hedge fund activist.

Mike Musuraca, trustee of the New York City Employees Retirement System (NYCERS), says activist governance-type funds such as Relational Investors fit with NYCERS's long-term investment goals. NYCERS is one of five New York public pension funds that collectively manage roughly $100 billion in assets for recipients, including a large number of labor union members. Musuraca points out that the New York funds began allocating capital to Relational in 2005. NYCERs has since invested funds with another activist fund, Shamrock Capital, the fund that managed Roy Disney's efforts to unseat Disney Chairman Michael Eisner.

Musuraca points out that cumulatively the total capital NYCERS has allocated to activists represents less than 1 percent of the funds' assets. More is planned for the future, he adds, including asset allocations to at least one European activist fund. Possible candidates include Knight Vinke Asset Management and Governance for Owners' European Focus Fund (GO), which was set up in 2005 by former directors at the U.K. institution Hermes.[14] GO has already received a huge institutional investor allocation of $640 million from the U.K. railworkers pension fund, Railpen. CalPERS allocated $200 million each to GO and Knight Vinke.[15]

Musuraca says the pension funds are careful to invest only with activists that typically have a long-term investment horizon, similar to that of NYCERS. Allocations with Relational and Shamrock fit NYCERS's two-part agenda: bringing in strong returns with limited risk and at the same time establishing long-term performance improvements at companies.

A problem public pension funds and labor funds have with many activist investors mirrors the concerns other institutions have with insurgents. Musuraca points out that many so-called activists will pressure companies to raise their debt levels and engineer stock buybacks that may not be in the best interest of long-term labor union pensions and other institutions or their portfolio corporations. That's one reason why public pension funds and labor union pension funds are still apprehensive about investing with many activists, he says. But he is careful not to associate Whitworth with these short-term insurgent investors. The type of activist Musuraca says he supports is one that will align the long-term interests of management with the long-term interests of its investors, such as the NYCERS. Musuraca says he prefers when activists can generate changes in private dialogue with managers, and he understands that's exactly what Relational typically does. Having the ability to convince boards that executives need to moderate their pay packages is a skill activists need to know well to receive allocations from the New York funds, he adds.

But it is still a long way before labor unions start allocating more capital to activists. Daniel Pedrotty, director in the office of investments at the American Federation of Labor–Congress of Industrial Organizations (AFL-CIO), points out that public pension funds and public benefit plans have $5 trillion in asset while union-sponsored funds have about $400 billion, yet very few of those funds are invested in hedge funds. "We can't do the Wall Street walk," Pedrotty says.

While other public pension funds and corporate labor unions dabble away at activism, CalPERS decided that being a leader for U.S. activism wasn't enough. It had also to become a leader globally. The fund expanded its activist investor portfolio to hedge fund managers beyond the United States to portfolio managers in Europe and Asia. By October 2006, CalPERS had $4 billion invested with activist, corporate governance funds in the United States and in other countries.

For example, in 1999, CalPERS allocated $200 million to Hermes Focus Asset Management.[16] Following somewhat in Whitworth's footsteps, some Hermes fund managers press U.K. corporations into making governance-related changes to their strategies and the composition of their boards.

In 2003, CalPERS began funding activists even further afield. First CalPERS committed $200 million to the SPARX Value Creation Fund, which buys large stakes in as many as 40 companies based in Japan and engages managements collaboratively in private meetings designed to present business-improvement ideas.[17] Unlike other activists that launch proxy contests and pressure companies to make changes, SPARX is not chartered to actually publicly press or bend the will of target company executives. Through mid-2006, SPARX Value Creation fund had 27.81 percent returns.[18]

Three years after that investment, CalPERS allocated more funds to another Japan-focused fund. It provided $200 million to the Taiyo Fund run by Taiyo Pacific Partners and billionaire steel company magnate Wilber Ross.[19] In a manner that follows the lead of SPARX, Taiyo Pacific Partners also buys large stakes in a handful of Japanese companies and collaborates with company executives, providing advice on a wide variety of subjects such as improving communications with shareholders and raising profitability. Like SPARX, Taiyo approaches companies and will invest only if directors and management are enthusiastic about collaborating with the fund. The fund had 32.48 percent returns from its inception in 2003 through mid-2006.[20]

In 2004, CalPERS, turned its focus back to the United States by committing $100 million to Roy Disney's chosen investment vehicle, Shamrock Capital, and the following year it put $125 million into Blum

Capital, a governance fund that takes a private-equity investment approach to its asset distributions. Blum's internal rate of return was 8.87 percent between its inception in July 2005 and March 31, 2007.[21]

In 2006, CalPERS also funded U.S. New Mountain Vantage with $200 million and Breeden Capital Management LLC with a $400 million injection. Breeden Capital is the activist hedge fund founded in June 2006 by ex–Securities and Exchange Commission (SEC) chairman Richard Breeden to target mid-capitalization companies with activist actions.[22] (Breeden was appointed to the SEC by President George H. W. Bush. He chaired the agency between 1989 and 1993.) The asset allocation by CalPERS represents the bulk of Breeden's assets under management so far. As of January 2007, Breeden Capital Management has roughly $500 million under management, significantly less than the $1.25 billion it sought to raise.[23]

All this has one key activist investor ready to dish out the accolades. "CalPERS laid a lot of the groundwork for governance investing so we could get to the place today where many funds now have separate asset classes for governance investors," Whitworth says. "It was something no one had done or thought of, and they pioneered it and they continue as pioneers by investing with activists in Europe and Asia."

CalPERS began the trend of public pension funds' investing with activist governance-type investors, but it now it has a long list of followers. To recap, there are two key trends under way. First, from Hermes in London to NYCERS in New York and the Ontario Municipal Employees Retirement System in Toronto, pension funds in North America and Europe are allocating funds to activists. Second, asset allocations are going to activist managers located in far-flung locations such as Japan and China. The result is that institutional investor allocations to activists are a major force driving the globalization of the strategy.

Chapter 15

Institutions Behaving Like Activist Hedge Fund Managers

Instead of allocating capital to activist hedge fund managers, some institutions simply are buying large stakes and actively pressing companies on their own. We have seen institutions become actively involved by urging companies to remove poison pills and staggered boards. Also, as we have discussed, many institutions will join forces with other institutions and activist hedge fund managers to form a group in an effort to press for changes such as breaking up deals or seeking to remove directors and CEOs. But very few traditional institutional investors will, or are permitted to, buy a large block of shares and engage management on their own in an effort to provoke some sort of serious response (i.e., proxy contest).

Some exceptions to the rule are divisions within Canada's Ontario Teachers' Pension Plan (OTPP) and Hermes Pension Management Ltd.

The State of Wisconsin Investment Board's small-capitalization portfolio buys between 5 percent and 10 percent stakes in small public companies and at times engages executives in private. In 2006, CalPERS also moved a step closer to doing its own governance-style activist investing. It allotted $600 million to invest alongside some of the activist investors it has funded. The public pension fund had been testing the approach by partnering with Relational, for example, Whitworth says.

But Canada's OTPP is unusual, in part, because of the rules, regulations, and historical development of the financial markets in Canada. The fund, which has roughly C$106 billion in assets under management, represents the pensions of Ontario's 163,000 elementary and secondary school teachers and 101,000 retired teachers. Unlike most other institutions, OTPP has become an activist manager itself on a scale not seen in the United States. Now defunct Canadian pension fund laws contributed heavily to OTPP's evolution on this front. Until recently, OTPP and other Canadian pension funds were forced to invest almost exclusively in Canada. In the early 1990s, OTPP held large 6 percent or 7 percent stakes in most Canadian companies, forcing managers to actively get to know the details of company operations.

In 1999, OTPP's Brian Gibson set up a dedicated activist division, formalizing this activist approach at OTPP. The division now has roughly C$5 billion in assets under management (a small part of OTPP's assets under management, but large when compared to the assets of other activist investors). The division, called Relationship Investing, should not be confused with Whitworth's Relational Investors, though the strategies have similarities. Gibson says his approach for picking investments mirrors that of many U.S. activist managers. The Relationship Investing group identifies undervalued mid-capitalization to large-capitalization companies, purchases large 5 percent to 30 percent stakes, and plays a hands-on role in creating value at those businesses, Gibson says. On some occasions, Relationship purchases even larger minority stakes, which gives it more leverage to provoke change. Relationship Investing focuses its activist energies exclusively on Canadian companies because of the "home court advantage" it affords OTPP investment officers, he says. The group has a strong knowledge of all the main investors and companies in the Canadian market, which is advantageous.

That hands-on role can mean anything from behind-the-scenes recommendations to replacing incumbent directors and even making bids for companies. But Gibson points out that unlike many activist hedge fund managers, OTPP's investors—the pension recipients—are not pressing the fund for immediate returns. That gives Relationship Investing the flexibility of holding on to its activist investments for a longer time, while its strategy unfolds. "Our strategy tends to be longer term," Gibson says. "We don't do hit and run investing."

Prior to 1999, OTPP was involved in some activism, but on an ad-hoc basis. Traditional investment professionals were typically taken off of their regular portfolio to focus on a particular investment that required attention. But when OTPP set up Relationship Investing, it formed a specialized activism team, pulling together people that had business and operational backgrounds in addition to investment experience. Some of the team members came from the private equity world, while others previously had merger and acquisition (M&A) experience at major corporations. "We needed people who understand how companies work," Gibson says. "It's a different skill set than a traditional pension fund manager would need."

One early high-profile OTPP activist effort took place in the mid-1990s. OTPP accumulated a 15 percent stake in Canadian textile company Dominion Textile Inc. The investment was made, Gibson says, because the shares were undervalued. There were things Dominion Textile could do to make it more competitive with its rivals, particularly new lower-price producers emerging offshore. "We didn't think they had a business model to succeed in a changing industry," Gibson says.

After the large stake was purchased, Gibson began a dialogue with the company, urging it to take steps to improve its bottom line. The conversations took place over the course of a year, with Dominion Textile taking every opportunity to ignore Gibson's advice. One of Gibson's recommendations was to focus more of Dominion Textile's capital and energy on producing denim, a textile that he believed at that time was still immune to overseas competition. While the discussions took place, the textile company's stock continued to languish.

After the year ended, Gibson says, OTPP decided to move on to plan B. Before the pension fund acquired its Dominion stake, Gibson and other OTPP managers researched the textile industry and found that there were some strategic rivals that were interested in buying Dominion. But, Gibson says, pressuring Dominion Textile to auction itself off was a last resort. Having the company improve its operations as an independent entity was the first strategy. But when it didn't look like Dominion was making any internal business improvements, Gibson says, he started talking with potential acquirers.

Gibson contacted Jerry Zucker, the chief executive of Polymer Group Inc., a North Carolina–based textile company, about possibly bidding for Dominion. Zucker bit. Polymer in 1997 made an all-cash tender offer of C$484 million for Dominion.[1] Separately, another company, Galey & Lord Inc. agreed with Polymer to buy some Dominion Textile assets once Polymer got hold of them.[2] A month later, Zucker increased his offer to C$596 million, and a deal was struck.[3] Zucker, a South Carolina resident, went on to acquire Canada's largest retailer and oldest corporation, Hudson Bay Company, in 2006 for $1.7 billion.[4]

The Dominion transaction was a profitable one for OTPP. The pension fund division purchased its stake for between $4.50 and $5 a share and sold it for roughly $13 a share. "Polymer focused on Dominion's business and fixed it up," Gibson says.

At roughly the same time, OTPP acquired a similar 15 percent stake in Canadian mining company Inmet Mining Corporation. As with Dominion, Gibson says, OTPP also believed this asset was undervalued. Inmet owned South American mining properties and Canadian exploration divisions with little in production. Inmet had been divested quickly by its German parent, which itself was struggling to stave off bankruptcy. "The company was a grab-back of miscellaneous assets," he says. "It was kind of stillborn."

Throughout 2000, Gibson engaged Inmet's management. He tried to have the company spin off some unprofitable units and acquire others. The strategy was to have Inmet focus on a few core business areas, Gibson says. Managers there were not heeding his advice, and the stock continued its downward path. At this point, Gibson says, he began communicating with Inmet's other institutional investors. Gibson met and talked on the phone with mutual fund and pension fund administrators that all owned a stake in Inmet. On some occasions, Gibson delivered PowerPoint presentations to make his point that Inmet needed new blood. It turned out that a sufficient number of institutions supported

Gibson's assertions, and he took the news to Inmet's board. In preparation for a confrontation, Gibson also found a group of people he was prepared to nominate as directors to the board in opposition to Inmet's slate. But no proxy contest was necessary as, Gibson says, Inmet's directors and management "saw the writing on the wall" and stepped down quietly. After that, Gibson brought in his new slate of directors, and they hired a new executive team.

But Gibson cautioned that approaching other institutions to urge changes at companies, particularly in Canada, is a sensitive task. A key objective is to demonstrate that as an investor you are not trying to make money at the expense of other investors. "If you come across as a short-term investor, not interested in the long-term picture of improvement at the company, then other institutions will stop talking to you," Gibson says.

Some OTPP investments have taken a long time to accrue in value. Gibson points out that in 1995 Canadian food processor Maple Leaf Foods Inc. was a case in mismanagement. Executives at the pork products company didn't invest adequately in new plant equipment, different divisions competed with each other for customers, and salespeople were, at times, vending products for below cost, he says.

Seeing an opportunity, OTPP acquired a 40 percent stake in the company and teamed up with Wallace McCain, a member of the McCain family that owns french-fry maker McCain Foods, to press for changes. The two partners later acquired control of Maple Leaf Foods and worked closely with its executives and board to improve the share value. In 2003, OTPP committed $150 million to facilitate Maple Leaf's purchase of Schneider Corporation from Smithfield Foods as part of its growth strategy. Twelve years later, Maple Leaf Foods is still a portfolio company, though its value has improved since 1995. "It was a basket case because of years of bad management," Gibson says. "It's a fixer-upper."

In 2007, OTPP followed through on its largest activist effort to date. After agitating for change at Canada's largest telecom operator, BCE Inc., the parent company of Bell Canada, the pension fund laid down the gauntlet when it led a consortium of investors to buy the asset for C$51.7 billion ($48.5 billion) in June 2007. That bid hit the record books—it was the largest private equity buyout ever. The BCE deal would not have been possible without some early activist investing action.

In April 2007, the pension fund disclosed it had a 6.3 percent stake and filed a 13D with the SEC indicating it was looking into strategic options for BCE. OTPP had been seeking partners in Canada and the U.S. to aid it in taking over the phone giant. It's possible that another consortium could swoop in and take BCE away. If that happens, OTPP will still likely earn a hefty profit from its large minority stake in the company. In that case, OTPP is an activist fund that has made a profit by agitating for change. If the pension fund closes the deal then it will have successfully acted as activist-agitator and buyout shop all rolled up in one. "Once you move from being a passive investor to one that is making all sorts of phone calls and forming alliances then you have to file a 13D," says OTPP's head of private equity, Jim Leech.

In addition to making activist investments, $1 billion of OTPP's Relationship Investing funds are allocated to other activist managers in the United States and the United Kingdom.

Like OTPP, London-based Hermes Pension Management Ltd., has some activist blood. Its U.K. Small Companies Focus Fund, which is part of Hermes Focus Asset Management, buys large stakes in undervalued small-capitalization U.K. companies that it then either collaborates with or presses into making changes. Small-capitalization U.K. companies have a few large shareholder groups that often represent the majority of their outstanding shares, making it easier for shareholders to come together and pressure a particular company in a certain direction.

In some cases, Hermes activism has helped a company defend itself against a much more hostile short-term investor. That was the case at London-based engineering company Charter plc, which makes welding equipment, automation technology and cutting systems in one unit, and industrial fans for power stations in a second division. Charter's share value suffered between 2001 and 2004 because of a series of poorly thought-out acquisitions and rising debt levels. One activist shareholder was seeking to take over Charter, but was ultimately rebuffed, in part, because of Hermes endeavors. The U.K. institutional investor acquired a significant stake and worked behind the scenes with the engineering company's management to improve their financial situation so that its investor base ultimately would oppose the hostile effort. Hermes assisted Charter in a recapitalization, which included providing assistance with its bank facility. The hostile investor ultimately sold his stake after Hermes convinced other investors to support the recapitalization.

But after fending off the hostile buyer, Hermes did urge Charter to make some changes, which included selling off two small divisions and separating the roles of chairman and CEO. (At the time, Charter's CEO, David Gawler, was also chairman of the board.) Subsequently, Charter did, in fact, bring in a new CEO, while Gawler remained as chairman. The effort fit with Hermes governance policy, which seeks to separate the position of chairman and CEO at U.K. companies.

We've discussed all the conflicts, diversification requirements and other reasons why most institutions avoid activism. Conflicting goals, incompatible investment time frames, and the possibility of scaring-off an investment company's future customer base all have contributed to keeping institutions and activists on opposite sides of the investment spectrum.

But throughout this section we've also learned about institutions stepping up and either supporting activists or even becoming activists themselves. Some will push to remove poison pills and classified boards, setting the stage for insurgents to take active roles there afterward. Other institutions take their activism up a notch by publicly announcing plans to vote against a deal or supporting an insurgent's campaign to elect dissident shareholder candidates to the board. We saw institutions support Whitworth's effort to press for changes at The Home Depot and Nelson Peltz succeed at gaining institutional votes for his election of directors at H. J. Heinz.

Institutions also gave conditional support to activist efforts by Bill Ackman at McDonald's, Kirk Kerkorian at General Motors, and Carl Icahn at Time Warner and Motorola, though they also opposed all three investors' major goals at those companies. (Maybe next time?) Institutions, labor unions, and pension funds are using the "just vote no" strategy as an activist campaign weapon in more and wide-reaching instances, seeking to mobilize and press for changes at corporations that go beyond director replacement. Without a successful "just vote no" campaign led by the American Federation of State, County, and Municipal Employees (AFSCME), institutional investors would not have been organized in opposition to the compensation scheme of Home Depot's Robert Nardelli. It is unlikely that Nardelli would have cut off communications at the home improvement retailer's annual meeting without AFSCME's campaign, and Whitworth may never have taken steps to launch his proxy contest. In other words, institutional "just vote no" campaigns are gaining ground and becoming a critical contributor to activist insurgencies, all of which are creating additional headaches for CEOs.

Expect headaches to continue as more companies set up their bylaws to require a majority vote of shareholders to elect directors. Axing the plurality vote system will put new pressure on companies to respond in some way to activist campaigns against incumbent directors. Even if 90 percent of shareholders vote to remove a company director, corporations are not required under the plurality system to have the candidate resign. That same scenario in a majority vote world would have a very different outcome. "Just vote no" campaigns would likely become much more difficult if not impossible to ignore. Also, institutions such as the California Public Employees' Retirement System (CalPERS), the New York City Employees Retirement System (NYCERS), and many other pension fund administrators, as well as some labor unions, are funding activists like never before. The groundbreaking governance success of Relational Investors and Hermes Pension Management has encouraged institutions to begin funding other activists, including Breeden Capital Management, Shamrock Capital, Knight Vinke Asset Management, and Governance for Owners' European Focus Fund, among many more in the United States and around the world. Finally, in some cases, pension funds and other institutions are emulating activist strategies themselves, as we've seen with OTPP. All this activity makes it now seem that institutions truly are taking advantage of all sorts of new gadgets and tools to engage managements with a new kind of vigor.

Clearly, activists need institutional investor support to accomplish their goals, particularly at larger companies. Putting aside all the passive institutions and millions of uninterested retail investors, there appears to be some sort of growing bond between the two categories of investors. Will that trend of cooperation continue? Only time will tell.

Part Three

ACTIVISM 2.0

Chapter 16

Technology, Communications, and Activists

Gary Lutin, Eric Jackson, and Anne Faulk

Corporations first began holding annual general meetings, in part, because physically getting together was the only way investors, the company's owners, could learn about the financial health of the business, elect directors, communicate with executives and make thoughtful investment decisions.

Today, annual meetings are no longer places where executives meet with investors to spontaneously exchange views and subsequently make voting decisions. Instead, these meetings are mere formalities where previously decided votes are tallied up for prenegotiated resolutions. Executives make short prepared remarks decided well in advance. "Nobody's going to the annual meeting to decide how they are going to vote," says Lutin & Company's Gary Lutin. "All the communications take place in ongoing dialogue with companies such as in quarterly conference calls."

Unleashing their aggravation about the current state of affairs for annual meetings, investors are turning to new technologies that allow them to come together in ways that were previously impossible. The arrival of the Internet has allowed investors to communicate more quickly and with greater frequency.

Embracing this technology and responding to investor frustrations, Lutin organizes meeting places for investors, online or in a physical location, which exist outside of the company's annual shareholder meeting. The objective is to provide a place for investors to discuss their concerns about their investments without being subjected to corporate restrictions. So far, these centers of activity have done wonders for activist hedge fund managers and other stakeholders, including institutions, seeking to understand and communicate about their investments. Lutin attributes the success of his shareholder forums, in part, to the Internet and other new technologies.

Aggravated investors can share ideas for how to improve shareholder value or do something about problem executives. In these virtual circumstances, managements don't control the process. As a result, an executive cannot influence the agenda, timing, location, or whether questions can even be asked. Chief executives have control of all these elements at most annual general shareholder meetings, conference calls, or any other conventional opportunity for investor communications. In fact, a typical tactic of besieged managements is to delay company annual meetings or prohibit investor or analyst participants from asking questions to executives. (We've seen this kind of stuff happen at The Home Depot, Liquid Audio, and Farmer Brothers Company. It happens more frequently than one might imagine.)

Lutin also has organized several meetings of shareholders in New York, though he doesn't do that much lately. Lutin says his open meetings, which were cosponsored by the New York Society of Securities Analysts, gave investors who felt ignored by corporate executives a chance to communicate freely.

But Lutin makes sure to point out that the online forums he facilitates are only a part of the new kind of shareholder communications that have been made possible by technology. Many investors are communicating on the phone, in person, or through e-mails or Internet message boards.

Unlike Yahoo! Inc. message boards, where investors discuss everything under the sun, Lutin's meetings are moderated by him, whether they are located in a physical location or online. Part of the reason Lutin says he conducts the meetings is so discussion focuses on the company and its issues without getting sidetracked. As overseer of the process, Lutin does not own any shares of the company the forum is discussing so that communications between him and participating shareholders will not trigger the Securities and Exchange Commission's (SEC's) investor communication Schedule 13D rules. Lutin typically encourages sponsorship contributions from large shareholders, who benefit from the forum process. "A big part of the forum communications transpire behind the scenes," Lutin says.

One successful forum, which involved both online and physical meetings, targeted online book seller Amazon.com Inc. Investors gathered at a number of investor meetings organized, in part, by Lutin to discuss concerns about the validity and quality of financial information being provided by the Seattle, Washington–based company during its early years at the height of the dot-com boom in 2000 to 2001. The problem, Lutin says, was that Amazon.com, like many other Internet companies at the time, was reporting "pro-forma" financial statements, which have assumptions or hypothetical conditions build into their data. Lutin adds that Amazon also wasn't disclosing how the pro-forma numbers related to real financial figures.

Through the online forum and New York meetings, which involved a number of SEC officials, investors succeeded at pressing Amazon.com to reconcile its pro-forma financials to Generally Accepted Accounting Principles (GAAP), the Western standard for accounting. While the Amazon effort took place, the SEC began drafting new rules that would eventually require companies using pro-forma financials in reports or in press releases to explain how they are different from GAAP.

The forums were established as a venue for investment professionals to ask and seek answers to questions at companies with unresponsive investor relations officials. But as they expanded, Lutin noticed that many small investors who felt disconnected from the companies in which they invested began to participate.

Also, large investors sought to take advantage of the forum by asking anonymous questions to management. The strategy, Lutin says, was to ask the difficult questions they sought answers for, but do it in an anonymous way that maintains their collegial relations with management. At the same time, Lutin's forums became a safe place for management to provide information or exchange views with shareholders without violating the SEC disclosure rules.

In 2001, Lutin set up a shareholder forum for investors of Willamette, the U.S. forest products company targeted at the time by rival Weyerhaeuser. Communications among investors took place at physical meetings, by e-mail, and by phone. Later, a Web site was formed.

The forum was set up so that investors could share information and their views with each other and Willamette's directors and executives. At the time, Willamette had been blocking Weyerhauser's approaches, but ultimately, after Weyerhaeuser upped its bid in 2002, Willamette agreed to be acquired.[1] "That forum provided information independent of a proxy contest to make it clear that a majority of Willamette's shareholders were supporting management's orderly and open exploration of a combination with Weyerhaeuser," Lutin says.

In 2001, Lutin sponsored a shareholder forum for a dissident investor at Lone Star Steakhouse & Saloon Inc. Guy Adams, an analyst turned activist, launched and ultimately won a proxy contest to install himself on the Wichita, Kansas-based restaurant company's board, replacing its CEO, Jamie B. Coulter, from his chairmanship position.[2]

Lutin acknowledges that a large number of shareholders had already expressed dissatisfaction about the way Coulter had been running the operation. But it wasn't until investors could communicate their point of view about Lone Star on the shareholder forum that support for Adams coalesced.

But even a mobilized group of disgruntled investors can't always achieve its stated reform goals. Coffee roaster Farmer Brothers' management has tested the patience of a hodgepodge of activist and value investors who own shares in the company. In 2002, Lutin launched a shareholder forum to begin bringing together investors at the Torrance, California–based company to debate a number of common concerns. (www.shareholderforum.com/FARM).

That year, Farmer Brothers held its annual meeting on the day after Christmas, no doubt to make it as difficult as possible for disgruntled shareholders to show up and vent their concerns.[3] The timing of the meeting was intended to discourage activist investors. Instead, the decision just emboldened investors who, it turned out, weren't prepared to vote with their feet and sell their stock.

Initially, activist Franklin Mutual Advisers LLC, a large Farmer Brothers investor, sponsored the forum. It subsequently became a virtual place where investors could read about recent changes at the company—developments such as court decisions, management statements, hires, and periodic reports, as well as analyst research reports and investment banking valuations. Lutin says investors expressed to him that they felt the forum was particularly useful at Farmer Brothers, a company whose management did not communicate much with investors.

In fact, until shareholders began to really start complaining, the company did not mail annual reports for investors seeking information or issue periodic earnings updates. Activists, led by Franklin, began pressing Farmer Brothers to make a number of changes, the largest of which was to have the company auction itself off. Five years later, the largely family-controlled company has yet to budge.

Standard Investment Chartered Inc.'s chairman and CEO Jack Norberg, who describes himself as a trader in "thinly traded" undervalued securities, is a participant in the forum and a Farmer Brothers stakeholder. He says the online meeting place is unique because Lutin is an independent operator. "The forum provides a venue for minority stockholders to let their views be heard," says Norberg. "The key is that it is not being driven by one large party."

At CA Inc., the company formerly known as Computer Associates International Inc., Lutin in 2004 set up an online discussion group to bring shareholders together behind a proposal to oust two directors. The goal was, in part, to remove Alfonse M. D'Amato, a former senator from New York who was on CA's board during a period when it was subsumed with accounting scandals. Many shareholders also put pressure on CA chairman Lewis S. Ranieri, a former vice chairman of Salomon Brothers, to resign from the board as well. Many shareholders believed that Ranieri failed to investigate accounting issues raised in 2001. The initiative failed after the SEC approved a petition by CA to remove the proposal.[4] But in June 2007, shareholders had a measure of victory on that front. Bruised from the investor revolt, Ranieri stepped down from his position as chairman, but remained on as a director.

Looking ahead, Lutin plans to try some new strategies to bring together investors. One approach, he says, would be to pick a hot topic among activist investors and craft a proposal focusing on it that could be applied to several companies with similar deficiencies. Accounting for stock option pricing may be the first subject matter the forum considers, Lutin says. He has already scheduled two meetings to discuss the effort.

Even with a new strategy, Lutin believes the traditional company-focused forums will continue to remain vital to many investors, including smaller shareholders. As part of the forums, corporate executives and directors are in a position to listen and respond openly to shareholders, Lutin says, without the costs and risks of separate private meetings with selected investors who claim to represent all shareholder interests. "It's a great leveler for the interests of all shareholders, including small ones," Lutin says. "Just like an old-fashioned shareholders' meeting, the forum gives everyone fair access to ask questions and express views."

But there are problems. Lutin points out that the forums are not profitable for him and he rarely even breaks even. However, he adds that he doesn't plan to stop hosting them. They are set up as a public service activity, he says, without any intent to make a profit. Ideally, Lutin says, the forum would be set up as an independent nonprofit organization. "These programs need to be communally controlled by the marketplace, and with academic ties to assure integrity," Lutin says. "The programs need stability, beyond what an individual volunteer can offer."

Another activist investor has taken a different approach to online forums, this time by mobilizing investors in the blogosphere into voting blocs. Eric Jackson, a retail investor of Yahoo! Inc. stock, recently set up a video of himself that he uploaded to the high-traffic Web site, YouTube. "Yahoo! is drifting," Jackson says to the camera." We shareholders have an opportunity to come together to effect change."

The video is part of a broader Internet strategy Jackson is employing to effect change at Yahoo! It brings together the tactics of activist hedge fund managers and the communications revolution of the Internet to draw out Yahoo!'s disgruntled retail investor base. Jackson says his approach is novel and is motivated by his admiration for big-time activist hedge fund managers, such as Carl Icahn and Nelson Peltz, coupled with his respect for the way Connecticut Democrat Senatorial candidate Ned Lamont exploited Internet blogs and online social networking sites such as MySpace.com to mobilize support for his election campaign. Lamont won the Democratic primary but ultimately lost to Senator Joe Lieberman, who ran as an independent. Despite his loss, Lamont's Internet strategy of bringing together potential voters and online campaign donations struck a chord with Jackson. "We've gotten some interest with this approach," Jackson says. "It's a way of using the Internet to find people who are motivated."

Distraught with the Internet portal's sagging stock price, Jackson first began providing details of his concerns with Yahoo! on his blog, Breakout Performance, under the heading "Yahoo!: Plan B." On it, Jackson compares Yahoo! with the much stronger performance of its archrival, Google. One key statistic Jackson points out: Google Inc. has performed 21 times as well as Yahoo! Inc. since its August 2004 initial public offering.[5]

In addition to his YouTube debut, Jackson expanded his campaign for change at Yahoo! by adding polling data, more videos, and links to Internet business networking sites such as LinkedIn. He also set up a Wikipedia-type site where users can add their own thoughts on Yahoo!

Jackson's demands reflect the concerns about CEO performance typically voiced by high-profile activist investors. He launched a campaign to have Yahoo! replace its CEO Terry Semel with Susan Decker, an executive at the firm. His campaign also sought to replace long-term company directors (two board members have served for 10 years) with industry experts who have purchased significant stakes in the company with their own money. Jackson wants Yahoo! to form a special strategic option committee to develop a vision for how Yahoo! can compete with its rivals. Overlapping Yahoo! divisions, such as MyPhotos and Flickr, must be consolidated, he adds, while cash reserves could be given back to shareholders in the form of a $3 billion stock repurchase. Many of Jackson's supporters have their own demands for Yahoo!. Some would rather see the Internet company's board complete its own executive search and possibly bring in an outsider for the role of CEO. Jackson says he's open to suggestions.

Following in the footsteps of some traditional activists, Jackson launched a "just vote no" campaign to pressure the company to oust 7 of its 12 directors. Jackson says he set up his campaign with a very low budget, despite observations by governance experts that a successful campaign would cost at least $200,000—money he doesn't have. As part of his campaign, Jackson sought support from a normally passive retail investor base. Institutional investors, including mutual funds and endowments, also were contacted, but Jackson admits he needs to do a better job courting this large investor base.

The goal was to gather together a group of investors who cumulatively owned a 10 percent stake in Yahoo!. Jackson points out that Yahoo! has 250 million registered users. If 10 percent of those each bought 50 shares and participated as a member of his group, the collective assembly would easily meet his goal.

But on the day of the annual meeting, Jackson and his supporters were far from reaching that goal. That day he had the public backing of 100 other investors representing about two million Yahoo! shares, roughly $61 million, in support of his plan. That's far less than 1 percent of Yahoo!'s shares outstanding, about 0.16 percent. It also was well short of the 136 million shares he needed to reach his 10 percent goal. In the end Jackson did not generate a critical mass of opposition, yet Semel stepped down anyways. Jackson's YouTube video-blogging approach is being hailed by activist investors, institutions, and executives as a preview of what we can expect from investor revolts in the years to come.

Also, Jackson says he may be back next year. He makes sure to point out that if Yahoo! doesn't make any substantive changes in the coming months, he will not be shy about re-invigorating his activist campaign. Until then, Jackson is keeping busy with a Web campaign to force change at Motorola Inc. Presumably, Carl Icahn's troubles there have not phased Jackson.

Institutional Shareholder Services director Pat McGurn says that he expects many activist investors to follow in Jackson's footsteps. McGurn points out that the SEC's new so called "e-proxy" rule, which took effect July 1, 2007, is slowly making it cheaper and easier for activists to launch campaigns to oust directors. That's because at participating companies it permits investors to post proxy material online rather than incur the huge costs associated with printing and mailing their materials to shareholders. Those cost-savings could encourage otherwise passive retail investors into emulating Jackson's video endeavors to launch activist campaigns, says McGurn. "The SEC hopes that all investors will get everything online," McGurn says. "We will see lots more activist investor activity on the Internet."

Anne Faulk, chief executive officer of Swingvote LLC in Atlanta, says Jackson may be the vanguard of how shareholders and corporations communicate with each other in the future. Her company, Swingvote, facilitates communications between shareholders and executives using the Internet as a forum. With new technology, Faulk says, both groups can interact with each other in a compelling way that was not possible before. Investors can maintain their privacy, if they so choose, through Swingvote's system, she adds, or they can find other innovative and effective means of expressing themselves. Executives will also need to embrace technology for investor communications to make their messages compelling to shareholders, Faulk says. "It's a YouTube world," she says. "You want to take a video of a CEO explaining to the company's shareholder why executives want to re-price their options or why a particular group of directors have been selected and the communication to investors happens at the moment they are going to make their voting decision."

At the same time, Faulk says, technology can make it easier for shareholders and CEOs to communicate in an ongoing manner throughout the year, rather than only a few times a year. She envisions a future world where shareholders can go to corporate Web sites and have a look at director candidates the company's nomination committee and its executive search firm are considering. If investors take issue with the management-backed slate, they can make their own recommendations, perhaps uploading the resume of someone they believe would make a good nominee. "This way communications can be a collaborative tool," Faulk says. "That communication can continue away from the ballot."

But, Faulk adds, Swingvote can also help activist hedge fund managers and institutional investors use technology to communicate with other investors as part of their proxy fights or "just vote no" campaigns. "We're simply the conduit and technology for that communications, so if an investor wants to run a slate of director candidates and they are authorized by the SEC, we're happy to take it," says Faulk.

SEC Chairman Christopher Cox says he is prepared for a world where investors and executives communicate using streaming videos.

He predicts a time in the not-too-distant future when electronic communications between agency officials and the outside world may also take place incorporating YouTube-like videos.

Whether shareholders are meeting in virtual online forums or physical locations, one thing is apparent: technology has transformed the way securities-holders communicate with each other and with companies. Previously isolated and ignored, big and small shareholders are finding each other and communicating their frustrations. The result: Their collective voice is becoming stronger.

Not all Internet communications among investors benefit all shareholders. Ironically, Yahoo!'s Internet message boards allow millions of investors to exchange information about thousands of stocks anonymously, every day, hidden behind "handles," fake names people give themselves in the Web world. Google Finance and other online stock sites carry their own anonymous investor message boards as well. Unlike Lutin's forums, which draw mainly professional investors, Yahoo! and Google message boards attract predominantly retail investors, with divergent incentives and limited business training and expertise.

Some message board participants want to see the stock price improve, while others are sending phony negative messages because they will profit only if the share value plummets. Small investors will take advantage of a micro-capitalization company's message boards to perpetrate the kinds of shareholder scams an experienced investor would avoid in a heartbeat.

Despite all the negatives, there is a rationale not to ignore Yahoo! and Google message boards outright. Disgruntled employees will often post insightful complaints. In other cases, speculators may provide useful information about the future business prospects of the company in question. Recognizing that there may be nuggets of useful information hidden among all the garbage, some activists take time to monitor the message boards. Chapman Capital's Robert Chapman is not so sure. He says they are worth monitoring if you have time to search for "needles in haystacks." Its unclear whether message board traders, ensconced in their chaotic investor communications world, will embrace video or audio technology for dialogue. It's likely many will want to remain hidden behind their handles. But others will emerge from the noise and static to create a new form of investor communications. Whether in

Lutin's moderated, issues-oriented meetings or Jackson's blogs, complete with YouTube videos, investors are beginning to see and understand each other in a way they have never experienced before. This is an empowering tool. Previously passive, disconnected investors are transforming into active shareholders, ready to prod companies into making changes. Another result is that executives facing a disgruntled investor base are having a harder time limiting shareholder communications. Home Depot CEO Robert Nardelli's decision to eliminate the question-and-answer period at the home improvement retail chain's 2006 annual meeting did not sit well with the company's investor base. In the end, his effort backfired. He may have been better advised to take his message to investors via a YouTube-like video campaign. Expect more CEOs to embrace Internet video and audio communications with shareholders, in a quest to gain their support as more activist and "just vote no" campaigns emerge.

The universe of activists is expanding in large part because investors are taking control of their communications with each other and with executives. And it's just the beginning. Expect more shareholder forums—online, streaming, and physical—down the road.

Chapter 17

When Is an Activist Fund Really a Private Equity Fund, and What's the Difference?

In February 2006, activist hedge fund, Dallas-based Newcastle Capital Group Inc. joined forces with Steel Partners to buy restaurant chain Fox & Hound Restaurant Group for $168 million.[1] What made that deal so special was not only that it was completed by a couple of activist hedge fund managers, but that they succeeded at wrestling the company away from a traditional private-equity company. Buyout shop Levine Leichtman Capital Partners Inc. had already inked a deal to purchase Fox & Hound for about $160 million.[2]

Newcastle president Mark E. Schwarz says he originally sought to launch a hostile offer for Fox & Hound but was unable to raise financing from traditional sources, many of which were prohibited from sponsoring hostile-like, unsolicited bids from insurgent investors. That's when he found Warren Lichtenstein's Steel Partner II LP, another insurgent with a specialization in activism and private equity. The two managers raised capital for the bid on their own. "We couldn't get financing for it," Schwarz says. "We had to write 100 percent of the offer ourselves."

The acquisition represents a shift among some activists. At one time Lichtenstein focused most of his energies on the insurgent strategy of buying large minority stakes in undervalued companies and pressing management to make changes through proxy fights or boardroom negotiations. But lately, he has supplemented that approach with a new strategy: buying companies outright in the way a traditional private-equity company would. Eight months after the Fox & Hound acquisition, Steel Partners and buyout shop American Industrial Partners joined forces to buy Hutchinson, Kansas–based ambulance maker Collins Industries Inc. for $110 million.[3]

How did these activists become buyout players? A history of involvement in private equity makes a difference. Schwarz says he and Lichtenstein developed in similar ways. They both launched their funds roughly 15 years ago. Schwarz set up Newcastle on January 1, 1993, with less than $1 million in assets. By the end of 2006 it had $750 million in assets under management. Coming from activist and buyout shop Ballantrae Partners, Lichtenstein was involved in the company's 1989 acquisition of laboratory chain Damon Corporation for $320 million. That experience may have left an indelible impression on Lichtenstein. Schwarz got his own buyout shop experience in the 1990s providing financial advice to the Lamar Hunt family, which did its own private-equity deals at the time.

Both activists have worked at activist endeavors together over the years. They acquired companies periodically, but buyouts only became a serious component to their repertoire later on as each hedge fund's asset size increased. Schwarz says many hedge fund managers evolve following a common path: "You start as a value investor, then move on to becoming an activist and then expand that to include private equity."

The call of improved returns generated by private equity was too strong for Schwarz to ignore. Today he owns several businesses that collectively have roughly 8,000 employees. Newcastle Capital has reported an average annual return of 23.3 percent over the 14 years since the fund's inception. Despite all of Schwartz's buyout activity, his activist minority stake investor side hasn't disappeared. Schwarz owns large minority stakes at several companies he has actively been pressing. For example, in 2006, Schwarz began urging one of his minority investments, Memphis, Tennessee–based ServiceMaster Company, to auction itself off. In private conversations with ServiceMaster's CEO, Schwarz says he pointed out ways the company could improve its value through a sale or other changes. ServiceMaster is well known for a number of its consumer products including TruGreen LawnCare and Rescue Rooter. By November 2006, Schwarz's effort appeared to have borne some fruit. The company that month announced at an investors' conference in New York that it had hired two investment banks and a legal adviser to consider a sale of the company.[4] By March 2007, ServiceMaster was sold to buyout company Clayton, Dubilier & Rice Inc. for $5.5 billion.

In recent years, Schwarz has also bought large minority stakes and pressed for changes at other companies. In 2004, he managed to secure four seats on the board of Pizza Inn, a chain of pizza restaurants modeled after Pizza Hut. Later, seeking to deliver outside expertise to the restaurant chain, Schwarz brought on two Fox & Hound officials to sit on the Pizza Inn board. Schwartz and Lichtenstein later used capital from the Fox buyout to pick up another restaurant chain,Champps Entertainment Inc for $75 million. He also owns Hallmark Financial Services, a Fort Worth, Texas–based insurance company.

Another factor leading activists into the world of private equity: more assets under management. Economies of scale matter when it comes to buying businesses. Over the years, Steel Partners II LP became flush with capital. It launched in 1993 with $3.5 million in assets under management and now has roughly $6 billion.[5]

Banking regulations adopted in the late 1980s to block corporate raid also prohibited most traditional financial institutions from sponsoring hostile bids by investment companies. Without access to traditional sources of capital, activist investors typically must rely on their own fund raising for hostile bids. "The rules have changed," Schwarz says. "We're not playing rugby anymore—now it's football."

However, Peter Blume, partner at Thorp, Reed & Armstrong LLP in Pittsburgh, says that an activist's ability to finance its own buyouts gives them an advantage. "These activists can afford lengthy fights with management and executives have to take their buyout threats more seriously," Blume says.

As assets under management increase, activists have a greater flexibility to both take control of some companies and launch activist efforts at others. With additional capital, the activist can remain quite diversified in its investments even with private-equity type acquisitions. Perhaps five years ago, taking control of a company would have eaten up 25 percent of total assets, but now that activists are more flush with capital than ever before, that kind of acquisition may only represent 5 percent of a particular investment vehicle's total funds.

Acquiring a few small-capitalization companies here and there will not necessarily prohibit many of these bulked-up investors from continuing to pursue their bread-and-butter activist strategies at other companies.

There are several similarities between buyout shops and activists. An activist fund's investment objectives and time frame often mirror that of a private-equity company. Traditional hedge fund managers have short-term investment outlooks of less than a year, while activists have longer-term investment horizons of three to five years. Therefore, it appears that activist investors are closer relatives to buyout shops, which also have long-term investment horizons, than most hedge fund managers. Schwarz argues that activists are much closer relatives of private-equity companies than they are with the rest of the hedge fund industry because they have a mindset that is comparable to buyout shop managers. The decision to buy a large minority stake requires an understanding of the private market value of a public company. This requires a special set of skills that most traditional hedge fund managers don't have. In fact, the large minority stakes activists take are often considered "controlling interests" because of the influence they wield at these companies. Their activist investment strategy has trained many insurgents to think like operators of the businesses in which they own minority stakes.

"What a knowledgeable buyer would pay for 100 percent of a company is a very different analysis than anticipating what the market might value a company's stock next week," Schwarz says. "The rest of the hedge funds are more oriented to public market values and how they can generate returns at a higher price."

In addition to Steel Partners and Newcastle Partners, there are many other activist-type investors that have become hybrids—half buyout shop, half activist investor. Insurgent extraordinaire Kirk Kerkorian launched activist governance-style efforts to prod General Motors into making share-enhancing changes, but he also launched successive bids to buy Chrysler. First, Kerkorian formed a partnership with former Chrysler CEO Lee Iacocca in 1995 to make a $20 billion offer for that automobile company and then in April 2007 he launched an independent $4.5 billion acquisition offer to buy the company, which by then was a division of DaimlerChrysler.[6] Kerkorian lost that bid to hybrid hedge fund private equity shop Cerberus Capital Management LP, which offered $7.4 billion for the automotive giant.

Carl Icahn fits into the mold as well. ESL Investments Inc., controlled by activist-turned-distressed-debt-investor Eddie Lampert, is also in this category, as is ValueAct Capital Partners LP of San Francisco. ValueAct, for example, in 2007 completed a $780 billion leveraged buyout of Houston-based oil and gas services industry provider Seitel Inc.[7] According to Dealogic, hedge funds were involved in approximately 50 private-equity deals in 2006, some of which were completed by activist managers.

In fact, Steven Howard, partner at Thacher, Profitt & Wood LLP in New York, says activist hedge fund managers have grown to the size that they can commit tremendous amounts of capital to a buyout situation quickly even without seeking out bank or other third-party financing. Activists' can capture significant shareholder value overnight using this buyout strategy, he adds.

The phenomenon of activist managers with more assets than ever before is largely a result of their changing investor base. Institutional investors such as corporate and public pension funds, along with university endowments and the emergence of funds of hedge funds, are all major new contributors to activist hedge funds. These capital allocations are supplementing traditional allocations made by high-net-worth investors. This metamorphosis is discussed in further detail in Chapter 18. "More assets under management certainly means an activist can make more bids, which can put additional pressure on management," says Opportunity Partners Phillip Goldstein.

Mitchell Nichter, partner in the Investment Management Group at Paul, Hastings, Janofsky & Walker LLP in San Francisco, says he sees convergence in the industry. Activist hedge fund managers that may have once bought large minority stakes in public companies and agitated for change have evolved to the point where they are making buyout offers. On the other end of the spectrum, some private-equity managers are concurrently converting themselves into quasi-activists, buying large minority stakes and assisting executives in their hunt for buyout partners. Buyout shop managers turned activists, says Nichter, can be more nurturing that traditional activists. Buyout-type activists are taking their skills and contacts in the private equity world and offering them in a friendly but active investor manner. Former buyout shop Kohlberg Kravis Roberts & Co. partner Clifton Robbins's Blue Harbor Group is a great example. Robbins's Blue Harbor Group buys large minority stakes and works collaboratively behind the scenes to assist companies to improve their share performance.

Why are all these transformations going on? Nichter says the trend is the result of managers seeking new profit avenues. For many traditional and activist hedge fund managers, returns have been slightly down. The result is that investors are seeking out new, innovative strategies that they hope will significantly improve their positions. For some, this means taking a stab at activism. For many activists, success means dabbling in the illiquid world of private equity. For private-equity companies moving toward activism, it's a way of creating greater liquidity but still actively being involved in cultivating companies behind the scenes. Distressed activist–style vulture funds are starting to buy large stakes in company debt, as part of their 'loan to own' effort. "They're all trying to figure out new ways of getting returns," says Nichter.

To Bid but Not to Buy

A tangential activist strategy is to make bids to buy companies hoping that a strategic or private equity buyer comes along to pick up the asset. The approach is to metaphorically kick up a dust storm around a business in an attempt to attract other bidders, perhaps a "white knight" strategic buyer that would strike a more hospitable deal with present management than that proposed by the insurgent activist.

The trick to differentiate the false bidder from the genuinely interested acquirer, says Newcastle's Schwarz, is to establish which activists have actually bought a company before. "The key is to find out if the guy owns any companies today," Schwarz says. "If he doesn't, that tells you something."

It's true that some insurgents don't believe the target company will take their hostile offers seriously, but despite their false pretenses, these activists wouldn't be disappointed if their bids are accepted. That's because activists with this strategy in mind usually make lowball bids they expect to be rejected by a company's management and board. Their hope is that the board puts the company in play. This approach was embraced by many corporate raiders in the 1980s, but they did it with a different playing field. "Many activists eschew buying companies outright," says Morgan Joseph's Randy Lampert. "They would rather push the company to be acquired by someone else."

Opportunity Partners' Goldstein and his investment group bid $115 million to buy rural Hector, Minnesota–based telecommunications company Hector Communications Inc. in September 2005.[8] His offer was taken off the table 10 months later after a consortium of Minnesota telephone companies agreed to buy Hector for $147 million.[9] Goldstein says his investment partnership earned Opportunity Partners $6 million, or a 65 percent return, on its $9 million investment.

Goldstein, who had been pestering Hector to auction itself since August 2004, says his September acquisition offer was a key turning point that led to the eventual Hector sale. Hector had already engaged investment bank Stifel, Nicolaus & Company to assist it in looking at strategic options such as a sale of the business, before Goldstein's bid. But Goldstein says the company was taking too long to make a decision and the offer put pressure on executives to accelerate the auction process. "We usually make a bid in order to prod management to seek out other buyers," Goldstein says. "When we do make a bid, while it is "real," we are pretty confident the company could be sold for more via a competitive sales process."

Goldstein acknowledges that he isn't an operator of businesses, even though he makes bids to buy companies on occasion. He's made unsolicited bids to take over Gyrodyne Company of America Inc. and Wells Financial Corporation, but neither of those companies accepted the offers. There isn't an expectation that companies receiving the bids will approve them, he adds. "If you look at the history of unsolicited "hostile" bids, it is hard to find even one that was accepted, so we are not going to worry about the extremely unlikely event of management accepting the offer," Goldstein says.

Carl Icahn, who has a long history of making unsolicited bids for companies, will happily draw out strategic bidders in some cases and seek to buy companies in other instances. In January 2006, Icahn bid $1.2 billion for control of Fairmont Hotels & Resorts Inc. of Toronto, but his offer was trumped by Saudi Prince Alwaleed bin Talal and another buyer for $3.9 billion.[10] That transaction netted Icahn a strong profit, though he likely would have been comfortable owning the hotel chain at the price he had offered. Icahn paid an average of $27.63 a share for his Fairmont stake, much less than the Saudi prince's estimated $45 a share bid.[11]

In February 2007, Icahn offered $2.75 billion to buy struggling auto parts interior and seat maker Lear Corporation.[12] Many speculated that Icahn's goal at Lear was to entice strategic buyers to make bids for the company. Icahn's offer also often produces the unintended consequence of activist pitted against activist. Pzena Investment Management LLC, a large Lear investor, immediately responded by publicly calling on the company to reject the bid as being too low for the assets. Other investors subsequently made similar public pronouncements. One activist filed a suit to block the consummation of the deal based on the argument that Lear's CEO may have had personal motivations to strike a deal that violated his fiduciary responsibility to shareholders. In July, Lear accepted a raised offer by Icahn of $2.9 billion, but shareholders subsequently voted to block that deal. The Lear transaction shows how Icahn is perfectly willing to acquire the companies for which he makes offers. In fact, the vehicle Icahn set up to buy Lear, American Real Estate Partners LP in Mt. Kisco, New York, is a real estate company he acquired in 1990 from real estate syndicator Integrated Resources.[13] That vehicle holds condominiums, hotels, energy assets, golf courses, and casinos, including the Las Vegas–based Stratosphere casino, hotel, and tower, and other assets he owns.[14] Overall, the companies Icahn controls have roughly 22,000 employees and run the gamut from telecommunications company XO Communications to Houston, Texas–based PSC Industrial Services Inc., an environmental and industrial cleaning company.[15]

Activist ValueAct Capital Partners LP made two genuine offers to buy Internet information provider OneSource Information Services Inc. in 2003 and 2004 for $110 million and later for $95 million. ValueAct's second offer was actually approved by OneSource's board when InfoUSA Inc. arrived on the scene. InfoUSA sealed a deal to a buy OneSource for $103 million, a transaction that rendered the definitive agreement it had with ValueAct moot.[16] What separates ValueAct's bid from many other activist offers is that the fund was serious and capable of buying the company outright.

Santa Monica Partners LP's Lawrence Goldstein was able to ferret out a strategic buyer with his $125 million offer to buy infant products maker First Years Inc., but it wasn't to his liking. After Goldstein launched a proxy contest, the company reluctantly began an auction process and sold itself in June 2004 to RC2 Corporation for $136.8 million, a price he campaigned against unsuccessfully.[17]

The trend of activists making strawman bids for companies is going global as well. In October 2006, Steel Partners's made an unsolicited bid to buy Japanese noodle maker Myojo Foods Company. But soon afterward, strategic buyer Nissin Food Products Company, the largest instant noodle company in Japan, made a friendly bid to take over Myojo.[18] Steel Partners offered a 14.9 percent premium on the price of Myojo Foods shares, significantly less than what many observers believed was necessary to really take over the business.[19] Consequently, observers indicate that by making the low bid, Steel Partners was really trying to put the company "in play" by attracting strategic buyers to the table. That is exactly what ultimately happened.

Nichter says he worries that some activists making fake bids to buy companies may end up finding themselves in a situation where they have to operate a business. "A successful hedge fund manager has a skill set that may not translate into the skills needed to operate a business," he adds. "Hedge fund managers trade securities; they don't have the same skills and focus that a traditional private-equity firm does."

Acquisition offers can also put pressure on companies to make other changes such as stock buybacks or special dividends—anything to gain institutional investor confidence and stop the activist's advances. Opportunity Partners' Goldstein points out that an unsolicited takeover bid may be a useful technique to pressure companies to make changes, such as installing dissident director candidates to the board or increasing a company's stock buyback program.

Steel Partners' unsolicited $250 million bid to buy Yushiro Chemical Industries Company Ltd. and $190 million offer to take over wool dye and processor Sotoh Company Ltd., both of Japan, were rejected. In their efforts to discourage investor support for the activists, both Yushiro and Sotoh offered significantly increased dividends, a result that Steel Partners and other shareholders profited from. Sotoh promised to increase its annual dividend to 200 yen, a 15-fold increase.[20]

In October 2005, ValueAct retained UBS Securities Inc. and made a $2 billion hostile takeover offer for data and software firm Acxiom Corporation, a bid that eventually aided the activist in gaining a seat on the company's board. The activists planned to finance the acquisition through equity and debt financing, but the offer was rejected by Acxiom in December.[21] In April 2006, ValueAct launched a proxy fight to elect three directors on the company's board. By August—roughly a year after the initial acquisition offer—a settlement was reached, with ValueAct agreeing to call off its contest and Acxiom agreeing to accept one of the dissident candidates onto its board.[22]

Blume says that an unsolicited bid like ValueAct's offer to buy Acxiom puts pressure on the target company's management to respond because it is a credible offer that shareholders would be likely to approve. In Acxiom's case, the bid contributed to ValueAct's ability to ultimately install a director on the board, the first step to improving the company's share value, says Blume. With a director on the board, ValueAct was finally able to convince the company to agree to a buyout. In May 2007 Acxiom agreed to be taken private by both ValueAct and buyout shop Silver Lake Partners for $2.24 billion plus the assumption of $756 million in debt.[23]

The ValueAct effort demonstrates that activists must be capable of following through on their proposals if they expect a response. A smallish activist that cannot raise funds for a bid would never be taken seriously by its target company or shareholders there. Consequently, company boards are unlikely to respond to bids from these kinds of activists.

ValueAct had a similarly successful result, albeit on a smaller scale, in 2004. That year it made a bid to takeover MSC Software Corporation for $357 million. But the private-equity-like activist rescinded its offer after MSC Software agreed to expand its board from five to seven directors and install ValueAct partner Gregory Spivy to the board. The settlement demonstrated that MSC Software recognized that ValueAct had made a credible offer and some sort of response was necessary to appease investors. "Credible unsolicited bids are often used to precipitate some kind of change at the company, and they are often successful," says Nichter.

Hedgies Set Up Funds to Buy Companies

Many activist hedge fund managers are changing the structure of their investment vehicles to account for acquisitions of companies. Even if managers have never bought a business, they are setting up their hedge funds to prepare for the possibility.

One thing activist managers are doing to make acquisitions of public companies more feasible is prohibiting their investors from redeeming or pulling out their capital for longer periods of time. Typically, hedge fund managers permit their investors to redeem capital four or more times a year. But more activist hedge fund managers are requiring that their investors keep funds "locked up" in the fund for two years or more. That approach can allow activists to buy companies and know that a critical mass of investors will remain there for the duration of the portfolio company's life in the fund. Another reason why managers are lengthening their lockups is because their activist strategies require a few years to complete. More frequent redemptions by investors could make that goal more difficult to achieve.

This approach to making buyouts could backfire for some managers. New activists may have a difficult time attracting investors that will agree to long lockups. Alternatively, established and coveted hedge fund managers will have an easier time attracting investors willing to agree to such lockups.

Even though both activists and buyout shops hold their investments for longer periods of time, each entity's structure varies greatly. A buyout shop can utilize its investor capital typically for a set lifetime or lockup of between 5 and 13 years, with no requirement to return its investor allocations until the portfolio company is sold or the life of the fund expires. That time frame differs greatly even when compared to an activist with 2-year lockups. Even if its investors capital is locked up for 5 years or more, there is a requirement to permit more frequent redemptions even if the portfolio company isn't sold.

That's why instead of lockups, most activists are setting up other arrangements in their hedge funds in anticipation that they may one day buy a company or real estate property.

This arrangement bifurcates a hedge fund's assets into two divisions: a highly liquid fund and a much less liquid long-term investment account known in industry parlance as a side pocket. The side pocket is set up so that the activist can buy a company or make an investment in another illiquid asset, without upsetting the activist strategy employed by the rest of the fund. In essence, any private-equity-type investment that falls outside their traditional activist strategy fits into these special so called side vehicles.

When a hedge fund manager decides to set up a side pocket, its investors are asked whether they want to participate. At that time they can opt out of the side pocket and keep all their funds in the more liquid portion of the investment vehicle. At the most, only a small portion of an investor's investment will ever be appropriated in the side pocket, but investors need to consider whether they can afford to make such a long-term commitment with their funds. Typically, investors that allocate funds to a side pocket arrangement are committing that capital for an indefinite period of time, basically until the hedge fund is able to sell or take the acquired company public. Some side pockets are set up with a maximum time limit on how long an asset can remain in the special structure before a manager is required to step up efforts to sell it. But basically, the side pocket is set up following the model of private equity companies.

The side pocket arrangement emerged after hedge fund investors complained they were stuck with too many illiquid positions in Russian securities after the former Soviet-bloc country's economic meltdown in 1998. At the time, many hedge fund investors struggled to redeem their investments in collapsing Russian securities. Early investors that were quick to cash out their stakes were paid off by the fund selling down its liquid holdings. Those investors who were late to withdraw their investments found the portfolio of investments left to be particularly illiquid and difficult to cash out. Setting up investment vehicles that separated liquid from illiquid investments helped bring timid investors back into emerging markets, such as Russia, says William Natbony, partner at Katten Muchin Rosenman LLP in New York.

But even today, activists typically do not devote a large part of their funds to these structures. Natbony says he urges his hedge fund manager clients not to allocate more than 25 percent of their total assets into side pockets. An activist that puts any more capital than that in a side pocket really needs to explain to its investors that its primary strategy involves illiquid investments and their time horizon for realizing profit has changed. As discussed previously, an activist typically tries to achieve a profit within roughly three years with each of its investments. As private-equity companies realize, buying companies and producing profits through those investments takes significantly longer and hedge fund investors must be aware of that time consideration before participating in a side pocket.

But Nichter points out that the percentage of a fund's total assets that are allocated to a side pocket depends on the strategy the hedge fund manager employs. If investors are supportive of an activist's allocating 75 percent of the fund's total assets into an illiquid side pocket, then a hedge fund manager should not be discouraged from setting up that structure, he says.

ValueAct Capital Partners in 2003 revised its charter to allocate 25 percent of its assets into side pocket illiquid investments. Prior to that, ValueAct was set up to appropriate only 15 percent of its funds into these kinds of investments. ValueAct founder Jeffrey Ubben notes that the change in the investment company's structure was made at that time to take advantage of an increase in opportunities in the market to take companies private.

In April 2005, ValueAct had $1.7 billion in assets, of which $425 million were allocated to the side pocket.[24] By December 2006, ValueAct had grown to $4.5 billion and its side pocket arrangement held $1.125 billion in assets. Ubben says ValueAct may consider expanding the fund's side pocket again. "I can see this percentage increasing," Ubben says.

Newcastle's Schwarz says his fund's investors are given the option to provide new capital to invest in a special-purpose buyout fund that is set up to make acquisitions. These asset allocations are separate from money invested in the hedge fund. But once capital is invested in the special entity, it is locked up there until a liquidity event takes place (i.e., sale of the acquired company).

Jay Barris, partner at Cramer, Levin Naftalis & Frankel LLP in New York, points out that activists may want to set up a side pocket before buying a private company or an illiquid stake in a private company that they anticipate could have a lucrative public offering in a few years. "It could be a phenomenal opportunity, perhaps to buy the next Google, but the investment requires patient investors that are willing to keep their money in the investment for longer periods of time, sometimes 10 years or longer," Barris says.

Other types of hedge fund managers are utilizing side pockets to make illiquid investments in alternative sectors such as municipal bonds. The phenomenon of these quasi private-equity-like activist hedge funds is creating a lot of problems for fund of hedge fund managers.

Funds of hedge funds complete a certain level of due diligence on their portfolio hedge funds. They consider the periodic share value of an activist hedge fund's equity investments. But illiquid investments, along with liquid stakes, can complicate their evaluation of the value of the hedge fund.

Mitchell Nichter points out that fund of hedge funds may be disinclined to invest with activists that have illiquid investments, such as portfolio companies, because of the difficulty associated with valuing the fund's underlying assets. Acquisitions that go into side pockets typically are valued at cost, but as time passes, it is harder to concretely value the investment, which can increase the risks for a fund of hedge funds, Nichter says. "The more illiquid investments a hedge fund has, the more difficult it is for a fund of hedge fund to value," he says.

ESL Investments chairman and chief executive Edward Lampert may be the latest high-profile activist to turn into a hybrid private-equity investor. He took control of Kmart in 2003 by buying bonds and distressed debt. Through his efforts, he brought the company out of bankruptcy. Most observers did not anticipate what he would do next. Lampert orchestrated Kmart's takeover of Sears, Roebuck and Company. After he devised that takeover, Lampert became chairman of the combined company and began actively operating the business. *Institutional*

Investor magazine reports that Lampert made $1 billion in 2004 and $425 million in 2005.

But before the Kmart-Sears acquisition, Lampert spent much of the 1990s as a traditional activist buying large minority stakes in a few companies and pressing executives to make changes. Between 1997 and 2001, Lampert pressured AutoZone Inc., a car parts retailer in which he owned a large stake to make changes.[25] In 1999, Lampert, a 15 percent AutoZone shareholder, met with the company's founder Joseph Hyde III to talk about the business. Later, Lampert gained a seat on AutoZone's board, furthering his efforts to influence the company. AutoZone tried to bring in a poison pill, but after Lampert expressed his concerns the company decided against installing it. Later, after AutoZone CEO John Adams stepped down, Lampert led AutoZone's special committee to seek out a replacement. In 2001, Lampert brought in Steve Odland, an executive from Ahold USA Inc.[26] Lampert also has a large minority stake and is a director of AutoNation Inc. There, Lampert also pressed for changes. In March 2006, AutoNation increased its debt load by roughly $1 billion and use its cash on hand to buy back shares.[27]

What happened to turn Lampert from an activist to a buyer? The combination of increased assets under management coupled with a growing expertise in operating businesses attained through his in-depth activism days all contributed to his evolution, says Steven Howard.

Several factors are converging to make the phenomenon of activist hedge fund managers buying companies a more common event. More capital allocations to activists, the standardization of side-pocket and similar arrangements, and the broader trend of capital allocations going toward buyout opportunities are all combining to make the strategy a key part of some insurgents' repertoires. More side pocket arrangements are giving managers the flexibility to buy companies, should an attractive opportunity arise. In the quasi-activist buyout shop realm, old hands such as Carl Icahn and Kirk Kerkorian are meeting a new generation of activist private equity shops led by Lampert, Ubben, Mark Schwarz, and Warren Lichtenstein.

The buyout option is also part of a broader trend of hedge fund managers seeking out new and innovative approaches to increasing profits in a way that differentiates them from other activists and hedge fund managers. "Activists already are investing in less liquid securities, so it's not a stretch that they may want to take a company private in the way a private-equity company would," Natbony says.

But at least one investor in activist hedge funds warns that buyouts may not be the best strategy for activist hedge fund managers. Sebastian Stubbe, a partner at Landmark Investors LLC in New York, says activists should stick to their knitting and focus on what they do best. He believes buyout shops are reaching saturation levels as opportunities dry up. Activists, he points out, are successful because they can achieve value-enhancing changes without the investment of time and energy that taking over companies requires. "When people look back at the period of private equity's decline, they will also notice that another group of investors—activists—made money while buyout shops suffered," Stubbe says. "The shareholder activists that got in nine months earlier and made their money by pressing businesses into buyout situations will be the ones that produce results."

Chapter 18

Funds of Hedge Funds Stake Out Activists

In 2003, Sebastian Stubbe launched Landmark Investors LLC, a $66 million activist fund of hedge funds.

Every year he accepts visits from 15 to 20 activist hedge fund operators. Each manager is hoping Stubbe will include his or her funds in the pooled portfolio of activist hedge funds he operates. He carefully picks Landmark's underlying activist hedge funds based on each manager's ability to understand their own investments. Stubbe says he wants to feel that activist managers understand their investments as well as or better than the CEOs operating the corporations in their portfolio. Not an easy task, to say the least.

Many don't pass the test. Of the 15 to 20 activists Landmark meets with every year, the fund will invest with only one.

His investment approach is part of a growing trend in activism: Funds of hedge funds, pools of assets allocated to hedge funds, are devoting a growing amount of their capital to activist managers. The strategy is transforming the investment landscape. Hundreds of millions of dollars are going to insurgents, beefing up their assets under management, and making it easier for them to engage a greater number of companies, many of which are larger than ever before.

For many individuals with fewer assets to invest, funds of hedge funds may be the only way they can allocate capital to a private, professionally managed activist investment vehicle. Government regulators prohibit investors with lesser means from investing in hedge funds based on the argument that these investment vehicles are more risky than traditional mutual funds and that people with lesser means have more to lose. Many activists set up their internal bylaws to accept capital only from the wealthiest investors, accepting no less than $1 million to participate. That kind of capital leaves even many high-net-worth investors with no other option than funds of hedge funds to gain exposure to activists. (The trend of hedge funds floating their investment vehicles in the public markets may soon give retail investors other opportunities to invest with activists.)

Some investors prefer funds of hedge funds over investing directly with hedge funds because they have lower investment thresholds and provide access to otherwise inaccessible talented hedge fund managers. Many investors also believe that the diversification a fund of hedge funds provides can lower risks. However, multiple layers of fees that come with investing in a fund of hedge funds can also diminish the reward that comes with eliminating the risk of investing with a particular dud manager.

Landmark's fund of funds portfolio represents a new source of capital for activist managers. Even five years ago, the average activist, like most hedge fund managers, would have relied predominantly on high-net-worth investors and some mutual and pension fund money to keep them in business. Funds of hedge funds have been around in one form or another since the 1970s, but they have only recently begun investing with activist hedge fund managers.

The phenomenon of fund of hedge funds investing with activists is part of a broader trend. Once satisfied with investments in hedge funds employing traditional market neutral or long-short strategies, this group of portfolio managers is seeking out more esoteric hedge fund managers that are demonstrating strong returns through different and new strategies. One of those strategies is activism.

Stubbe's decision to launch an activist fund of hedge funds didn't happen overnight. In 1999, Stubbe and his partners launched Landmark Value Strategies fund, which focused predominantly on value investments. By 2001, the fund's partners included some activist managers and some value investors that occasionally engaged in activism, so called part time activists, to the fund. The activists and part-time activists did so well that Landmark decided to launch the Landmark Activist Strategies (LAS) fund in 2003, a devoted activist fund of hedge funds. LAS holds stakes in roughly 8 to 10 insurgent-style managers at any one time. The underlying managers themselves typically hold only a handful of large concentrated positions. As of 2006, Landmark Value Strategies fund had $450 million in assets under management, about 20 percent of which is made up of activist investors. The partners also set up Landmark Value Strategies Global fund, which also allocates to activists and value investors and has $105 million in assets. "Our decision to start an activist fund was driven by demand from our clients and the fact that these managers were performing so well," Stubbe says.

The managers that make up Stubbe's activist fund typically are on the constructive or friendly end of the activist spectrum. These managers will first try to work with management in a behind-the-scenes collaborative manner to effect some positive change. Stubbe says he steers clear of the activists that are hostile instigators, though he concedes that many of the activists that make up the Value Activist Fund have on occasion stepped up their efforts a notch by engaging in public campaigns to press unresponsive companies into action. "An activist that develops a reputation of routinely threatening and cajoling will have a difficult time performing a meaningful due diligence, particularly if people at the company don't return your calls," Stubbe says.

The partners at Landmark—Stubbe, Ahmed Fattouh, and John Salib—all emerged from careers in merger and acquisition (M&A) advising at investment banks—a background not too different from that of many activist hedge fund managers. Stubbe says he and the others gained experiences in valuing companies while working for investment banks. That experience, Stubbe says, helps him evaluate whether activist managers really comprehend the critical income statement and balance sheet details of the companies that make up their portfolios.

Like Stubbe and Landmark, another fund of hedge funds manager, Barry Cronin, slowly worked his way into setting up a dedicated activist fund of hedge funds. In 2003, Cronin launched his firm's first fund of hedge funds, an investment vehicle that allocated capital to a broad spectrum of managers including value-oriented managers that on occasion would engage management in a collaborative behind-the-scenes kind of activism.

In 2006, Cronin took his faith in the effectiveness of the activist investment strategy to a new level with the launch of the Taylor Waypoint Fund LP, a fund of hedge funds that seeks to invest with concentrated value managers that at times will become activists. However, Cronin says, to be clear, his focus is on long-term governance-oriented activists that will take their efforts public only as a tool of last resort if they believe action is warranted. Cronin, like Stubbe, says he does not advise investing with the activist manager that buys large stakes with the intention of picking a fight. Likewise, Cronin says he avoids managers that have a short-term goal of pressuring the company into a leveraged recapitalization at the expense of the long-term interests of the rest of the shareholders.

Cronin says he invests with activist managers because they have the talent to identify hidden value and then act as a catalyst to unlock that value. "A number of these managers are exceptional stock pickers first and activists second, only when appropriate," he says.

But despite the early success of activist funds of hedge funds, many fund managers are still reticent about investing with some activists that would appear to fit the required characteristics. PL Capital's Richard Lashley says fund of hedge fund managers are turned off by his fund, despite its low volatility and high returns over its 10-year existence. The problem? Fund of fund managers are discouraged by PL Capital's concentrated stock positions and lack of industry diversification, he says. The activist fund invests only in banks and thrifts, yet has continued to produce above-market returns year after year. As discussed, many insurgents have a unique expertise in an industry, such as banking, fashion, or restaurants. These specializations make fund of hedge fund managers nervous, in part, because of the possibility that a particular sector could have a bad year due to external uncontrollable factors.

In addition to concerns about too much of a focus on one industry, the general perception by traditional funds of hedge funds is that activist fund managers don't fit the profile they are looking for because they typically invest in equities that are correlated to the stock market as a whole. One fund of hedge fund manager points out that investors are very skilled at assessing the risks associated with their investments in stocks and bonds, but they come to a fund of funds because it has an expertise in investing in strategies that are uncorrelated to the stock market. In other words, investors expect them to allocate funds to hedge fund managers that produce returns which are not connected to whether the stock market is performing well or not. Activists typically buy securities "long" for capital appreciation, unlike most hedge funds that hedge the markets by making calculated bets that some securities will improve in value while others will diminish in value.

But activist fund managers and some fund of hedge funds managers disagree with the evaluation that their strategy is overly concentrated, undiversified, and follows the trends of the stock market too closely.

Landmark's Stubbe says that since activists for the most part don't sell short, or bet against the stock market, they appear to have some correlation to equity indexes such as the Standard & Poor's (S&P) 500. But he considers that perception deceptive. An activist hedge fund's concentrated position is uncorrelated to the market because it has the ability to agitate and unlock value, he says. While it may seem that an activist's stock pick is following the general market fluctuations, sometimes for months or years, that relationship will ultimately come to an end when a catalyst is unleashed, Stubbe says. "It could be flat-lining for six months and then there is a pop," Stubbe says. "And that pop is not correlated to the market." Stubbe adds that activists are specialists in finding "diamonds in the rough," or hidden undervalued, misunderstood companies that generally will outperform the market even without a catalyst. Their ability to find these deeply undervalued companies is a hedge against the market, he adds. Activist managers also typically hold cash on hand ready to deploy should the opportunity arise, another hedge against the market.

The bottom line for fund of hedge fund managers who believe in the strategy is that activists as a group have outperformed the markets consistently over the past several years. The most striking example of their outperformance comes when one compares activists to the S&P 500 in down years for the stock market. One example of that was in 2002. That year, the equities market as a whole did poorly, while most activists had stellar years. Another example was in September 2001. After the terrorist attacks in New York and Washington, D.C., the markets took a while to recover but activist hedge fund managers continued to perform well, Stubbe says. "In many cases when the market has a big selloff, activists do well," Stubbe adds.

Opportunity Partners' Phillip Goldstein corroborates that statistic. In 2002, the S&P 500 index was down 23 percent, while his activist hedge fund was up 5 percent from its position the year before. Activist PL Capital returned 16 percent in 2002, significantly better than the S&P 500 that year. Goldstein points out that his hedge fund's best results have come in years that the stock market performs poorly. But he concedes that Opportunity Partners generally performs in a way that is more correlated to the stock market than a market-neutral hedge fund. "My fund is somewhere between a market-neutral hedge fund and a fund that only invests in the equity market overall," Goldstein says.

Some fund of funds managers are ready for a little activism, but they will devote only a portion of their funds to the strategy. Dave Smith, CEO of Coast Asset Management, a $6 billion fund of hedge funds based in Santa Monica, California, says he invests with a wide variety of managers, some of whom are part-time activists that buy concentrated positions. Activist investors that buy only large concentrated positions are too volatile for his fund. Smith's Coast Diversified Fund has three part-time activists, and his Coast Sigma fund has two. The three activists make up only a small percentage of Coast Diversified Fund's 50 hedge funds, which include managers that specialize in market-neutral and merger arbitrage strategies. Smith says these reluctant activists are included in the pool because they are talented managers that can provoke value-enhancing change at badly run companies with overcompensated executives. "They are not strictly activists," says Smith. "The kind of executives these activists go after are the type that need to be reminded that they work for shareholders."

Concentration: Good or Bad?

Barry Cronin takes issue with the idea that activists are unnecessarily more risky than traditional hedge funds because they have concentrated large stakes in a limited number of companies, typically less than a dozen.

In fact, he's encouraged by that approach compared to a traditional hedge fund's investment style. "When you're concentrated, you do a lot more work focusing on those investments than hedge fund managers who own hundreds of positions," he says. "These guys buy well-researched, thought-out stocks, and they've identified value and ways to unlock additional value for all shareholders."

Landmark's Stubbe says that not only does he prefer managers that own only a few concentrated positions, he questions whether any individual can understand more than 25 companies really well. Stubbe says he believes managers with hundreds of positions in a portfolio don't truly understand the fundamentals of each position. Landmark's activist fund of hedge funds isn't so much a fund of managers, but rather a fund of positions, he says. "Any manager that runs 100 positions is diluting their best ideas," Stubbe says. "You can't research and understand 40 different investment ideas."

Cronin points out that activist hedge fund managers with 10 concentrated positions are likely to be less correlated to the equities market than a traditional hedge fund manager that has hundreds of positions. "Having fewer stocks means you have a lower correlation to the stock market," Cronin adds.

But some onlookers warn of problems that can arise. Fund of hedge fund managers must be careful to diversify their activist managers, says Lutin & Company's Gary Lutin. He points out that fund of hedge fund managers concentrating on activists should make sure the underlying hedge funds are not all investing in the same few companies. The "wolf pack" approach of activists all buying stakes in the same company and pressing management to sell the company may have the effect of creating enough leverage to trigger the catalyst that produces above-market returns. But if the situation fails and a fund of hedge funds has stakes in all the managers that failed to profit from the venture, it could mean trouble for the fund of funds' overall performance. The collapse of BKF Capital may have been a difficult lesson for any fund of hedge funds that invested heavily in the hodgepodge of activists that participated in that fiasco, Lutin says. A large number of activists all bought large stakes in BKF, hoping to press the company to rein in its key executives' compensation. But after dissidents won a proxy contest at the company, the fund promptly imploded. Its founder and key reason for existing,

CEO John Levin, left the fund, taking many of its investors with him.[1] "When you try to diversify with 10 different activist hedge funds and they all invest in the same 10 companies, then you have no diversification," Lutin says.

Taylor Companies' Cronin says most fund of funds managers make sure they invest with hedge funds that aren't overlapping each other from an investment standpoint. One way to do that, he says, is to diversify from a geographic point of view. Stubbe points out that the phenomenon of investors piggybacking on an initial shareholder's idea is not isolated to activist managers and activist strategies. Other investment styles, including event-driven or merger arbitrage strategies, also experience a large number of managers jumping on the bandwagon by following the investment approach of one initial investor that does a lot of research. In other words, investing in managers that employ other strategies may not solve that pack-investment problem. "I compare it to an MBA class of 70 that has 10 students doing all the homework and passing it around to everyone else," Stubbe says.

So far, Stubbe doesn't consider the wolf pack approach such a pervasive phenomenon that it is a problem for his activist managers. The activists in Landmark's fund employ a variety of strategies and engage companies in different industries and geographic regions—all of which makes it unlikely that any of the portfolio managers will invest in the same company, Stubbe says.

Geographic diversification is also another key way to lower risk. UBS AG's activist fund of hedge funds invests with insurgent-style managers in different countries around the world. As of the end of 2006, the fund has roughly 50 percent of its portfolio in the United States and the remaining assets allocated to managers in Europe and Asia.

A fund of hedge funds with managers on different continents accounts for various kinds of ups and downs. For example, one country's economy may be performing well one year, while another nation is having an economic downturn. Funds of funds operated by both Deutsche Asset Management and Shimoda Resources Holdings allocate capital to Kiev, Ukraine-based Foyil Eastern Europe & Russia Focused Fund as part of their efforts to diversify their portfolios into emerging markets, according to Dorian Foyil, the fund's manager.

Tim Selby, partner at Alston & Bird LLP in New York, says investors and fund of fund portfolio managers must be careful not to automatically assume funds in different geographic areas around the world are automatically uncorrelated to each other. Funds that combine U.S. activists and emerging-market activists that all invest only in technology companies obtaining the same critical components from China could collectively suffer the same negative returns should Asia have an economic meltdown or that particular industry sector experience a difficult period for one reason or another.

But even with geographic, industry, or other concentration concerns, there are many advantages associated with investing in a fund of activists as opposed to just one insurgent. Cronin pitches prospective investors by pointing out to them that money allocated with a single activist manager can be risky. Investors that allocate their capital to an activist fund of funds are investing with as many as 20 activist managers. The impact of a struggling manager in an activist fund of funds to the vehicle's overall performance is not as great as if the investor had gone and invested directly with that poorly-performing manager, Cronin adds. Investing in 10 managers each with 10 positions increases the number of positions to 100, reducing the risk associated with any one manager's having a bad year, assuming there is no overlap of positions. That portfolio, he says, would still be made up of large, concentrated positions in each manager's best stock picks. "You're placing a tremendous amount of importance on getting the manager selection right when you invest with a single manager," Cronin says.

Another form of diversification that funds of activists can provide relates to the size of companies managers engage. Some activists focus their energies on small-capitalization companies, while others take on mid- and large-cap corporations. A fund of hedge funds that invests in activists that buy stakes in different-sized public companies is more likely to avoid the problem of being invested with too many managers crowding into the same positions. If in one particular year, small-market-capitalization companies do well while large-cap companies do poorly, the fund is diversified to balance that risk. "You aren't likely to perform well if you're invested in activists that only invest in small-cap companies in a year where large caps outperform small caps by 100 percent," Cronin says.

Investors allocating funds to a single manager activist fund better be ready to close their eyes for five years because the fund is likely to be very volatile, experiencing some highs and lows before a positive return is realized. Stubbe compares direct activist investing to private equity investing. Both approaches require long waiting periods before returns are realized. "If you're thinking about investing and exiting in six months, then you shouldn't be in activism," Stubbe says.

Canadian activist hedge fund manager Peter Puccetti, chairman of Goodwood Inc., acknowledges that the Toronto-based fund will have its ups and downs because that is the nature of activist investing. Goodwood seeks to have roughly 20 percent returns, on average, every year. That may mean a 40 percent year and a zero percent year, he adds. So far the fund has averaged 21.3 percent annual returns since its inception in 1996. "We're not a market-neutral fund," Puccetti says. "The first thing we tell potential investors is that we're going to be lumpy; there are going to be negative periods."

Opportunity Partners' Phillip Goldstein points out that focusing on a few isolated quarterly reports could be deceptive. As an example, Goldstein says he had been pressing a local telecommunications company, Hector Communications Corporation, to auction itself since April 2005. In June 2006, a deal was struck and the stock "popped" to $35 a share around that time, from the $29.50 it had been stagnating at previously. Opportunity's second-quarter results would have been down about 0.5 percent if the announcement had come a few days later, he says. "Activists will have down periods, just like other strategies, but overall they will do well," he says.

Having 50 to 100 activist positions, each with managers pressing for catalysts, is also more likely to produce more consistent returns. Not only will a fund of activist funds help investors avoid the risk of allocating all their money with a self-imploding insurgent, but it will also make sure that returns continue to come in even as some managers have "lean" or poorly producing years. "Not all activists produce strong returns every year; sometimes catalysts take time to be realized," Cronin says. "Investing in a pool of activists reduces the likelihood that an investor will have to suffer through a difficult period."

Michael Van Biema, 50, has taken yet another approach. In 2004, the former Columbia Business School professor formed Van Biema Value Partners, which now operates two funds of funds that invest with value and activist value managers who have emerged in part from his classes at Columbia and in part from the group of contacts he has made from his affiliation with the institution.

The Columbia Business School environment is a great place for developing contacts in the value and activist space. Van Biema Value Partners has several high-profile former Columbia Business School grads, many of whom also happen to be activist value investors, on its board. Value activist "godfather" Gabelli Asset Management's Mario Gabelli and value investor extraordinaire Chuck Royce are directors and provide advice to the investment vehicle. In addition to Royce and Gabelli, several other famous value investors, including Warren Buffett, Glenn Greenberg, Walter Schloss, and John Shapiro, have emerged from Columbia Business School. The concept of value investing was pioneered in the 1920s at Columbia by finance professors Benjamin Graham and David Dodd. Graham and Dodd believed that the true value of a stock could be identified through research. Even back then, Graham engaged in activism, at times.

Van Biema Value Partners' 20-plus underlying hedge funds run the gamut when it comes to activism. Some will only engage management behind the scenes, while others are devoted full-time activists that are not afraid to take their insurgencies public. Others fall into the reluctant activist category. "We have one manager that shies away from activism but he has become more active at one company because he believes a particular corporate action was so egregious that it no longer could be ignored," Van Biema says.

The fund has roughly $180 million in assets under management and invests with managers that have between $10 million and $500 million in assets. Van Biema's domestic fund had compounded average annual returns of 13.3 percent since its inception in 2004, achieving an internally set performance goal.

The strategy is to invest with start-up, small, talented managers that fly below Wall Street's radar. That means most of the managers in the fund are not well known in the hedge fund industry. They are usually smallish funds that will invest in ideas and companies that are not normally considered by hedge fund managers, Van Biema says. "We have a wide diversity of styles," he says. "Some of our guys are opportunistic feeders in micro-cap pink sheet stocks while others put capital toward unusual ideas in larger companies."

Roughly 10 participating managers have less than seven years' experience managing their own funds, Van Biema says. These managers, he adds, have worked previously at larger, more established funds operated by trusted individuals. "They didn't just come off the street," he says. The other 10 managers have longer track records and older shops, he says. One manager has a 22-year record of 19 percent average annual returns.

Activist value investor Alan Kahn says he was initially concerned about whether Van Biema's approach could work. Kahn says he was worried that the fund's double layer of fees, as is typical with any fund of funds, would depress the positive results the underlying managers produced.

But then after several meetings with Van Biema, Kahn signed on to participate on the fund of hedge fund's board, which is responsible for identifying and screening possible investment choices. Kahn, who also agreed to invest with the fund, says he had a change of heart because he realized Van Biema had a unique skill in identifying and investing with expert "diamonds in the rough," managers that produce significant returns with their activist and value investments. "Mike has the ability to bring to the table access to talented value managers before anyone else can find them," Kahn says.

Van Biema says he is sensitive to the concern people have about the double fee structure of a fund of funds. But he points out that the fees are justified because of the hard work involved in identifying the best managers. "These guys are difficult if not impossible to find," Van Biema says. "We get paid our fees because we do that work, plus I have a world-class network of contacts in an industry that I've known for years."

After setting up and monitoring the operation of the domestic fund, which invests in the United States and Canada, Van Biema launched a similar fund that invests with managers allocating capital to companies outside of North America. He created the second fund, in part, so his investors could diversify their investments between U.S. and global allocations. Van Biema now has plans to split his global fund into two divisions—Europe and Asia—after receiving requests from investors who want to focus their allocations more specifically. "Once we figured out the strategy could work domestically, we expanded globally," Van Biema says.

Due Diligence

Many activist managers, hoping to gain fund of hedge fund capital, typically travel to meet with Stubbe to present their strategies and portfolio.

Most managers present a collection of their previous investments, case studies of possible future investments, and a PowerPoint presentation explaining why appropriating capital to their funds makes sense.

The vast majority of managers, Stubbe says, show him their three top ideas, but after that, their presentation usually peters out. Managers who can show they understand concrete operational details and can explain a coherent motivation and analysis for investing in their 13th, 14th, and 15th choices are the ones that complete enough of a due diligence to deserve allocations, Stubbe says. The best managers will typically have spent at least 10 to 12 weeks researching a position before jumping in, Stubbe says, and they will understand their target investments enough to realize when value can be unlocked. "You would be surprised how many activists overhear some rumor and follow other investors into a particular position without doing their own research," he says.

Understanding and completing a thorough review of underlying companies is critical. That means getting to know executives and meeting vendors, suppliers, and industry experts before identifying ways to improve a company's stock performance, Stubbe says. How long activists are willing to stick with a company they are engaging is another important factor to consider. Activists who look only for quick returns are not considered for the Landmark portfolio. Stubbe adds that he makes sure to avoid investing with managers that engage in style drift. In other words, managers who indicate to their investors that they will be using one particular strategy and then switch to another one without disclosing that information to their limited partners will not be tolerated.

Activists who are good stock pickers and have a demonstrated record of creating value at past investments usually top Cronin's investment list. Talking to institutional investors to gauge how the activist is considered by the broader institutional investor community is another key consideration. Negative responses don't bode well. As discussed in Chapter 10, an activist that is supported by the institutional investor community has greater leverage in negotiating changes with executives in either a friendly behind-the-scenes manner or a public effort. Some institutions will not side with certain activists in most situations.

Making an effort to talk to executives at companies that have had encounters with the activist being considered for the portfolio is another due diligence consideration. These conversations are useful to gauge whether the manager and CEO can to work collaboratively on improving value. Finally, the public perception of the activist is also important. If managers have a negative image among all stakeholders, they aren't going to become part of the fund, Cronin says. "An activist's ability to gain the trust of the rest of the investor base or the CEO of the target company factors into their success," Cronin says. "The reputation of an activist among other shareholders is truly critical."

How long will funds of hedge funds continue to pour money into activists? Peter Blume, a partner at Thorp, Reed & Armstrong LLP in Pittsburgh, expects institutional investors and fund of hedge fund managers to keep throwing more money in the general direction of activist hedge fund managers, at least for the short term. Whether the trend will continue in the long term depends in large part on activists' abilities to continue bringing in sturdy profits. "Because of their successes, I think the trend of fund of hedge fund managers investing in activists will continue," Blume says. "In the long term, continued asset allocation will depend on the ability of activists to maintain a high level of profitability."

But there are some problems facing an activist's ability to continue attracting this new investor group. Mitchell E. Nichter, a partner with Paul, Hastings, Janofsky & Walker in San Francisco, points out that the trend of activists investing in illiquid assets, by buying companies or real estate, may have negative implications from a fund of hedge fund perspective. Companies that activists buy and put into side pockets typically are valued at cost, but as time passes, it is harder to concretely value the investment. Some funds of funds avoid investing with activists that make illiquid investments because of this valuation problem. The fund of hedge funds manager must be able to provide periodic valuations to its own investors and illiquid investments make that difficult if not impossible. In the end, a fund of funds manager that can't put a concrete dollar value on a hedge fund, in many cases, will not allocate capital to it, no matter how successful their track record. Consequently, activists who have drifted from liquid to illiquid positions, either because they are now buying companies or they have acquired positions as directors on corporate boards, may be cut off from a fund of funds. "The more illiquid investments a hedge fund has, the more difficult it is for a fund of fund to value," Nichter says.

Landmark's Stubbe says he avoids investing with managers that have significant illiquid positions because it would make it more difficult for underlying investors to redeem their capital. Landmark has a two-year lock up, which matches the lockups of the managers that make up its portfolio.

Legislation being considered on Capitol Hill in Washington would increase taxes on hedge funds and many funds of funds. If passed, a new tax burden could discourage entrepreneurs from either continuing or launching activist funds.

Despite liquidity and tax issues, fund of hedge funds will continue to allocate funds to activists. In fact, activists are diversifying their underlying strategies to meet the demands of fund of fund managers looking for homes for their capital allocations. For example, as fund of fund managers seek to expand their portfolio to include activists on different continents, activists are meeting those demands by setting up operations in countries around the world.

In addition to contributing to the globalization of activists, these funds of funds are also pushing managers to produce new innovative activist strategies, whether that means focusing on mid-capitalization companies or producing a fund that is part value investor and part activist. Activists seeking out fund of hedge fund monies are putting even more of a laser-sharp focus on their investment choices. Understanding the fundamentals of 3 out of 12 investments just isn't going to cut it if a fund wants capital from a fund of funds.

The emergence of true activist funds of hedge funds has cemented activism as a bona fide strategy that can compete effectively with hedge fund mainstays. Their "activist" approach has been added into the lexicon of investment approaches, along with long-short, bond, and macro fund strategies. The continued allocation by funds of hedge funds to activists is all but assured. Only one question remains: how much capital will be dedicated to activists as they mature and become enshrined in the world of hedge fund investing? Only activist hedge fund returns can determine the answer to that question.

Chapter 19

Distressed Investing

How Activist Managers Buy Debt and Provoke Companies

A company that may be on the verge of bankruptcy or one that has already collapsed into chapter 11 doesn't sound like the kind of business any investor would want to go near with a 10-foot pole.

But all sorts of investment professionals buy securities—bonds or stock—at these kinds of distressed companies every day. Some corporations are either about to enter or exit bankruptcy, while others are in financial distress and are willing to complete a debt restructuring to avoid bankruptcy. In a restructuring, the company, which can no longer make all its debt payments, must negotiate with banks, creditors, and suppliers, often by altering the debt-to-equity ratio on the balance sheet.

Often, creditors of a company that has become distressed are apprehensive about the securities they own. They are willing to sell rather than hold on and wait to see what kind of value their deflated stake may ultimately produce as the distressed company struggles to improve its bottom line and bring itself back to profitability. Many institutional investors of bonds in companies that have become distressed are required by the risk parameters of their internal bylaws and charters to sell their investments when things start looking bad. Institutions, such as insurance companies and mutual funds, that find they own a hefty amount of low-level D-rated bonds, may need to divest; otherwise, their total debt rating may drop to below a permissible level. "The selloffs are for technical and psychological reasons," says Matt Wirz, editor of Debtwire, a data and news organization for the distressed-debt and leveraged finance markets.

That's when distressed-debt activist investors, also known as "vulture funds," pounce. After completing their own in-depth due diligence on the target company, these insurgents are willing to buy securities from their original holders, typically at a deep discount. Many times, activist investors believe that despite the company's immediate woes, the future looks bright. Activist investors engaging in the distressed strategy often pay only pennies on the dollar for stocks or debt of distressed or bankrupt companies.

These vulture funds and others anticipate that the distressed company will recover and ultimately emerge from its failures—either that or the company at some point in the not-too-distant future will be acquired for a premium. While mutual funds or insurance companies may have bylaws prohibiting them from investing or remaining in these types of distressed investments, vulture funds have no such prohibitions. In fact, vulture fund managers are willing to take a risk, betting that the investment will bring strong returns down the road. They are willing to actively get involved to make that value-enhancing scenario take place. As in the equities world, many speculative distressed-debt investors that have done little to no valuation research will pile in as well.

Activists and other distressed-debt investors ultimately can profit from their investment in a variety of ways. The most frequent approach is through a debt-for-equity swap, which could take place when the company emerges from bankruptcy. The activists, also known as creditors or debt holders, agree to cancel some or all of the debt they hold in exchange for equity in the restructured business. Now the activist controls shares of a public company. But debt-for-equity swaps are not the only way vulture funds can profit from a restructuring or bankruptcy. In many cases, activist distressed investors can buy and sell debt securities and turn a profit while the company is still in bankruptcy restructuring. Some of the secured debt, which may have been acquired by activist debt holders, can likely get refinanced during bankruptcy. "You can get taken out while the company is in bankruptcy," says one distressed debt specialist.

Famed value investor Martin Whitman, manager of investment firm Third Avenue Management LLC, has had a great deal of success focusing much of his energies on a specialization in distressed investing. In the post-Enron period of bankruptcies, Whitman skillfully acquired bonds in distressed entities such as Kmart Corporation. Many of the bonds acquired by Third Avenue Management in this period eventually converted to significant equity positions when these companies emerged from bankruptcy protection.

Debtwire's Wirz argues that equity activists and debt insurgents are very similar. He points out that many equity-style activists have the skill set to become distressed-debt investors. In fact, many traditional activists actually have dabbled on the debt side, and vice versa.

Like equity activists, distressed-debt activists acquire large positions in the companies they target. The only difference is that distressed activists acquire securities in distressed companies or businesses restructuring in bankruptcy. A distressed-debt activist fund is more likely to buy company bonds to initiate their efforts. Also, like equity activists, distressed insurgents typically complete an in-depth review and analysis of the company to determine what they believe to be its true value before buying a block of securities. Also, like their traditional activist counterparts, distressed investors will use their large stake to clamor for change at the company. They will often negotiate with executives, just like their equity activist investor brothers. Unlike traditional activists, however, many of these negotiations will take place in out-of-court proceedings involving other creditors.

Distressed-debt insurgents typically will want to buy a large enough stake of a company's debt, such as a 30 percent stake, so that company management there will listen to their demands. Owning one-third of the debt gives the investor a "blocking position," which is a significant enough stake that company executives must consider their claims. The approach is very similar to the behavior of equity activist shareholders who buy a large block of shares in a company to gain sufficient leverage in their efforts to press for changes. "An activist fund that specializes in distressed debt will seek to acquire a large enough debt stake so that they can go to management and say, 'We have enough of your debt that you can't ignore us,' " says Evan D. Flaschen, a partner at Bracewell & Giuliani LLP in Hartford, Connecticut. "This way, they become a key constituent in restructuring negotiations with the company."

The similarity between the two strategies has led many activists to launch both equity and distressed-debt insurgent-style investment campaigns at different target companies. Harbinger Capital Partners of Birmingham, Alabama, has moved from being predominantly a distressed-debt house into one that focuses on debt-and-equity activism, says Wirz. Many other activist funds, such as Silver Point Capital and Elliott Associates LP, among others, partake in both distressed and traditional activist investing strategies.

The relationship between activists and distressed investors may be coming together in another way as well. As we have seen with a few earlier examples, some activists in the equities market are driving the trend of more overleveraged companies, by nudging firms to increase their debt load to provide capital for stock buybacks. One securities lawyer says he wonders how many of those activists pressuring for higher and possibly dangerous debt levels at target companies are also "swooping in" on the other end, ready to offer debt financing once the company falls into distress, which occurred in large part due to the insurgent's pressure on the front end. "They're attacking the company from both sides," he says.

An activist that owns a significant portion of a company's debt in a restructuring or bankruptcy will have greater influence in a wide variety of areas once the company emerges from its troubles. Peter Antoszyk, partner at Proskauer Rose LLP in Boston, says these major debt holders could demand board observation rights or director positions. Large-debt holders often seek and succeed at influencing the company's business plan. "Owning a significant amount of the debt can have a big impact on the restructuring," Antoszyk says.

Loan to Own

Sometimes activists take their efforts to influence management of distressed companies to a whole other level. In 2003, billionaire Carl Icahn took control of telecommunications and broadband services company XO Communications Inc. of Reston, Virginia.

He didn't do it by purchasing the stock of the business, as is typically how most companies are bought. He did it by buying up XO Communications debt while the company was teetering on the edge of bankruptcy. In fact, Carl Icahn purchased almost all of XO Communications' senior bank debt and eventually traded it for a controlling equity stake in the company when it emerged from its restructuring. In the end, Icahn gained more than 80 percent of the equity of the reorganized company by exchanging his interest in the bank loan.[1]

What Icahn succeeded in accomplishing at XO Communications is often described as the "loan to own" strategy. With this approach, an activist fund makes a major loan or investment in a distressed or underperforming business prior to its bankruptcy. Distressed debt activists take on the loan with the knowledge that there is a reasonable probability that the borrower will default on the debt and seek chapter 11 bankruptcy protection. (Companies seek chapter 11 protection for many reasons, such as failure to make a scheduled payment on a loan.) In some cases, the activist can pressure the company into chapter 11. In many cases, once in bankruptcy, Icahn and other "loan to own"–type investors seek to convert that debt into a majority or controlling equity stake in the reorganized company. The investment fund can also receive a cash distribution in exchange for the cancellation of some or all of the debt it owns. Loan to own is part of a larger phenomenon of insurgent hedge funds providing financing to corporate entities, an activity that was once the traditional territory of banks.

More activist distressed investors are employing the loan-to-own strategy as a means of differentiating themselves from the increasingly saturated sector of investing. Put another way, managers are looking to "loan to own" as a means of finding better returns. "This is a legitimate business tactic for gaining control of the company," Flaschen says. "Once a fund acquires a significant equity stake in a reorganized business, it has the opportunity to influence its business goals and maximize value and a return on equity."

Flaschen adds that in many cases activist investors seeking to take control of companies prefer to go the debt route when the company is distressed, for economic reasons. "Buying distressed debt can be a more economical approach than a hostile takeover because the activist fund has the ability of purchasing the debt at a discount," Flaschen says.

In another situation, an activist hedge fund worked the bankruptcy process to take control of not one but two companies. Harbinger Capital, previously known as Harbert Distressed Investment Master Fund Ltd., took control of distressed jewelry chain Friedman's Inc. of Savanna, Georgia, with a package in December 2005. Harbinger subsequently accumulated the unsecured debt of Oakland, California–based ailing fine jewelry chain Crescent Jewelers as part of a plan to consolidate it with Freidman's Inc.[2] Harbinger's acquisition of Crescent Jewelers' unsecured debt is an example of how a distressed-debt investor with a sufficiently large debt position can block the company's restructuring plan and instead propose its own plan for the company, says Bracewell Giuliani's Flaschen.

Despite being opposed to Harbinger's efforts, Crescent management eventually figured out it had to accept their plan. The jewelry company's emergence from bankruptcy will take place with Harbinger in control. We've already discussed how, on a much larger scale, ESL Investment's Eddie Lampert used a similar activist debt-and-equity approach to consolidate Kmart and Sears.

Proskauer Rose's Antoszyk points out that the rise of activist distressed investors has put pressure on executives of troubled companies. The chapter 11 process was designed, he said, to protect management from creditors and allow executives to drive the process of restructuring. But combative activist vulture hedge fund managers have, in many cases, taken control of the restructuring process away from the executives. "Activist distressed managers can be very aggressive," Antoszyk says.

Distressed-debt investors also, at times, form their own groups of creditors seeking to pressure a company into making changes. The approach can resemble the "wolf packs" activist hedge fund managers at times form in the stock of public companies, as a means of mobilizing opposition to a corporate strategy. Flaschen points out that at times vulture funds will want to acquire a significant debt position and engage management in negotiations on their own. Other times, one fund will become the main creditor, while other, smaller debt holders will invest and follow their lead.

Investors that understand and focus their investment energy on distressed-debt investing have actually done quite well over the past number of years. While many other hedge fund strategies produce volatile returns, distressed investing has been a strong performer.

This, of course, has led other activist hedge fund managers to pile into the strategy. According to Hedge Fund Research Inc.'s distressed securities index, distressed-debt investors averaged 15.8 percent in 2006, 8.27 percent in 2005 and 18.89 percent in 2004. A study by New York University professor Edward Altman reports that roughly 160 investment funds specialize in distressed company investments, a number that has gone up significantly over the past few years. Distressed investors did particularly well investing in discounted debt in 2003. After Enron Corporation, WorldCom Inc., and other major corporations collapsed in 2001 and 2002, distressed investors such as Martin Whitman made money, in part, by trading in the debt of these mega corporate bankruptcies. As a group, these investors returned on average 30 percent in 2003, according to Hedge Fund Research Inc. (See Figure 19.1.)

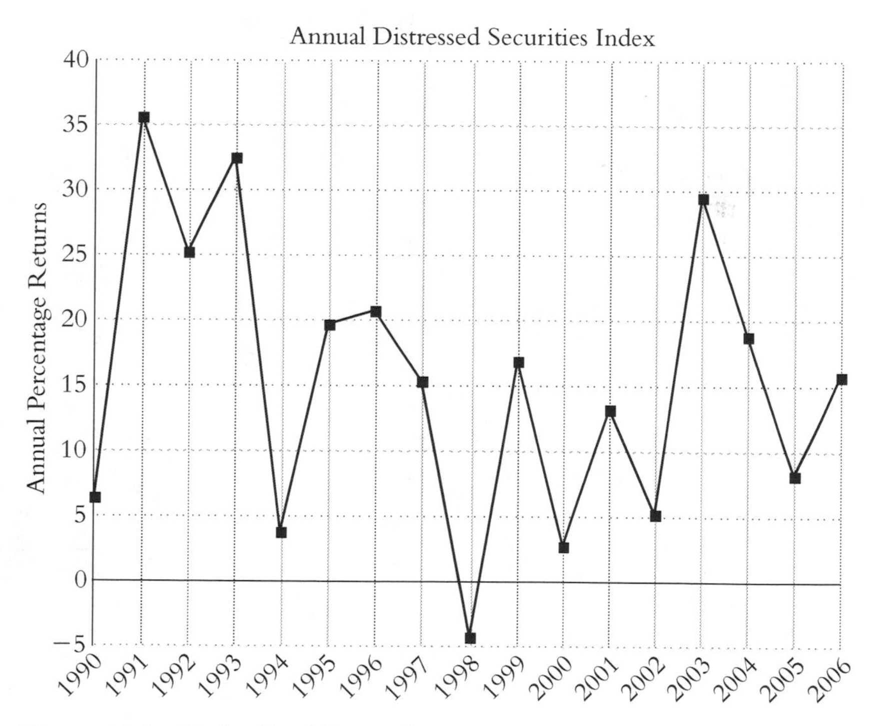

Figure 19.1 Hedge Fund Research Inc., 1990–2006
SOURCE: Hedge Fund Research Inc.

Distressed investing is a model that will continue to thrive, in part due to the trend of more companies embracing more leverage. Companies in a supercharged merger-and-acquisition environment as we have today are loading more debt on their balance sheet to finance their businesses with the capital they believe is necessary to compete effectively with their rivals. Without this additional financing, executives worry that they may not have the investment capital needed to gain an edge against their rivals in the United States and around the world. The only problem is that with more debt on the balance sheet (driven at times by activist hedge fund managers) it becomes harder for companies to succeed as they spend more capital servicing all that debt. All of these factors are leading to more distressed companies and more profitable distressed investors. "The result is more companies with unhealthy balance sheets," Wirz says. "This, in turn, leads to more distressed investors supplying the debt."

Chapter 20

Hedge Activists in Western Europe, Asia, and Canada

Guy Wyser-Pratte, who considers himself a "corporate vigilante," has little respect for a growing number of European CEOs.

Lack of proper corporate governance codes and a very limited market for corporate control—fewer mergers and acquisitions compared to the United States—have made many European CEOs, in his opinion, complacent. Many European institutions and government regulators have sought to prohibit any serious shareholder activist efforts. The result: corporate boards in Europe continue to be made up of "old boy" clubby networks that aren't keeping management teams accountable to shareholders.

Referring to Greek mythology, Wyser-Pratte says European executives are missing the "Sword of Damocles" hanging over their heads. In other words, despite being in a position of power, executives in countries such as Germany and France aren't worried about losing their jobs. In Wyser-Pratte's view, they should have that concern. At least, they should consider themselves more responsible to shareholders. Only the occasional activist that comes to "try and upset the apple cart" keeps European executives in line, Wyser-Pratte says. "There are lots of obstacles to the free market in Europe," he says. In Wyser-Pratte's analysis, these corporate realities have diminished the share value of many European companies and given the United States and other markets a competitive edge in the global marketplace. This situation, Wyser-Pratte says, means most of Europe is prime pickings for activists looking to unlock undervalued companies. For many years, Wyser-Pratte may have been a lone soldier upsetting the European apple cart, but lately, others have joined the fray. In fact, insurgent shareholders in Germany and other European countries have transformed the investment environment from the passive, even tranquil place it was just a few years ago to a place where executives must completely re-evaluate how they structure deals. Some activists have reached even further to antagonize unsuspecting CEOs in Japan, South Korea and other previously untouched markets.

In 2005, activist hedge funds, including U.S activists Atticus Capital LLC, Jana Partners LLC, and London-based Children's Investment Fund, thwarted what they believed to be a poorly thought-out acquisition offer by Frankfurt Stock Exchange operator Deutsche Börse for the London Stock Exchange.[1] The activists' success at blocking that deal left many German regulators scratching their heads. It prompted then-chairman of Germany's ruling Social Democratic Party, Franz Müntefering, to call hedge funds a "swarm of locusts," that were devastating German companies.[2] Those comments set off a trans-Atlantic dispute about whether hedge funds have a positive or negative impact on economies. Responding to the buggy allegations, U.S. Treasury Secretary Henry Paulson rose to the defense of hedge funds, arguing that they diffuse risks and help eradicate inefficiencies. But many in Europe weren't heading the advice. A number of high-profile Europeans continued to describe activist hedge funds as investment vehicles that force mergers, which in turn create job losses and economic instability. Activist hedge funds are also often associated with another perceived devil: the growth of buyout shops taking over European companies. The transatlantic squabble about the positive or negative implications to global markets of activist hedge funds and private equity companies became even more complex in 2007 when a number of U.S. Democratic lawmakers began expressing concern about the impact of the industry on employment, unions, and job security. A key U.S. congressman, Barney Frank (D-Mass), called on President Bush to discuss the issues related to the investment groups at the June 2007 G8 summit in Heilligendamm, Germany. Specifically, Frank wanted summit participants to discuss how these financial pools impact jobs and the long-term viability of corporations. Other European leaders joined with Frank to express similar concern about the two industries in messages to German Chancellor Angela Merkel, but the G8 leaders appeared to have other more pressing issues to debate. Good or bad for the economy and jobs, activists appear to be in Europe for the long-haul, and their targets are becoming larger. Insurgent hedge fund Knight Vinke Asset Management LLC pushed to end a deal between two major French utilities, Suez and Gaz de France, in part by running advertisements in several French newspapers outlining the fund's justification for wanting to see the transaction axed.[3]

Other countries and continents have also seen a rise of activism, with activists, often from the United States, finding similar dysfunctional companies and unresponsive managers. Pirate Capital of Norwalk, Connecticut, and other insurgents prodded Canadian resort owner Intrawest Corporation to hire Goldman Sachs & Company and auction itself off. Soon after Pirate Capital launched its campaign, Intrawest was sold to American buyout shop Fortress Investment Group.[4] Powerful pro-shareholder regulations taking hold in Scandinavia and the United Kingdom are enabling fledgling activist investors in those countries to gain seats and influence corporate boards. The regulatory situation is just the opposite for shareholders in many Asian countries such as Japan and South Korea, but Western activists, such as Steel Partners' Warren Lichtenstein, are making inroads anyway.

With all this activism going on it's hard to imagine that not too long ago, in the mid-1990s, there were only rumblings of public investor insurgent activities in many of these countries, if any noises at all. At that time Wyser-Pratte was already stirring the pot at many European companies. His first foray into European activism took place in 1995 at

U.K.-based utility Northern Electric plc., a company he pressured into restructuring even though he owned only a 1 percent stake.[5] Shortly after that, Wyser-Pratte moved his efforts to France, where he was born (Vichy, France). In 1996, he used an activist investor approach to press for changes at Institut de Participations de l'Ouest, a French venture capital company. Since then, Wyser Pratte has launched efforts to improve shareholder value at many other French companies including investment firm Siparex, supermarket franchise operator Guyenne et Gascogne SA, and chemical and power transmission company Dynaction SA.[6]

Wyser-Pratte says his French passport and combined U.S. and French background made the transformation from U.S. activism to European activism an easy transition. In fact, the roots to Wyser-Pratte's activism can be traced back to his father, who started an international arbitrage investment firm, Wyser-Pratte & Co. Inc., in 1929. Born in Vichy, France, Guy and his family emigrated to the United States in 1947. In 1948, Wyser-Pratte's dad reopened his firm in New York. In 1966, after four years on active duty as an officer in the U.S. Marine Corps, Wyser-Pratte joined his dad there.

The investment company eventually was acquired by Bache & Company in 1967. By 1982, Bache & Company was acquired by Prudential Insurance Company. Throughout this period, between 1971 and 1991, Wyser-Pratte oversaw the firm's risk and merger arbitrage desk. Like many other insurgents, that risk arbitrage experience set the stage for his later activism. In 1991, he relaunched Wyser-Pratte & Company and began engaging and pressing U.S. companies to make changes. That worked well until some European friends asked him to get involved in a corporate control situation in France. After that experience Wyser-Pratte quickly realized that as a value investor, he needed to start focusing attention on the other side of the Atlantic. He made a key discovery: Many European companies trade at significant discounts to their U.S. counterparts. Wyser-Pratte was hooked on Europe. "It's not unusual for someone to go back to his country of origin to straighten things out," Wyser-Pratte quips.

Today, Wyser-Pratte's fund owns large activist stakes in roughly 10 to 15 mid-capitalization-sized companies. His staff of 16, including 7 professional managers, actively interacts with executives at these corporations. Unlike other activists that may try to talk to management behind the scenes to see if some sort of adjustments can be negotiated privately, Wyser-Pratte does all his activism out in the open. The fund, which often contracts European investment bankers to aid it in researching target companies, has had average annual returns of about 25 percent. "We publicly declare our holdings and concerns and then go out and state our case to management," Wyser-Pratte says.

One focus of Wyser-Pratte's attention over the past few years has been German Industrial machine maker IWKA AG. In 2003, Wyser-Pratte began urging the company to sell units that make packaging and processing equipment and focus all its attention on an extremely profitable industrial robots division. The company's most recent CEO, Gerhard Wiedemann, who took over in January 2007, engaged an investment bank and sold the company's packaging division a few months later for $340 million.[7] But the result Wyser-Pratte had been looking for was a long time in the making. It involved constant attention and the ouster of not one but two CEOs before it became a reality.

Wyser-Pratte and a group of investors including British activist institutional investor Hermes Focus Asset Management Ltd. and institutional firm Threadneedle Asset Management sought unsuccessfully in 2004 to remove then-IWKA CEO Hans Fahr, after divisions they had hoped would have been divested still remained intact.[8] But Fahr's victory was short lived. Wyser-Pratte won a proxy contest at IWKA in 2005 and effectively succeeded in ousting Fahr a year later.

Fahr's replacement, Wolfgang- Dietrich Hein, committed to sell all divisions that did not meet profit projections. In fall 2006, Hein engaged Deutsche Bank to review a sale of the packaging division, but decided to keep it intact.[9] He resigned shortly after the announcement.[10] Wiedemann, the CEO that finally sold the packaging division, was brought on soon after Hein's resignation. "It was a long effort," Wyser-Pratte says.

At other target companies, Wyser-Pratte pursues different strategies to unlock shareholder value. Prosodie SA, a French provider of technical services to Internet and telecommunications companies, was recently the target of a Wyser-Pratte lawsuit.[11] In this case, Wyser-Pratte, a Prosodie director, claimed the company's board was not informed of its founder and CEO Alain Bernard's plans to sell the company to U.S. buyout shop Apax Partners Inc. Wyser-Pratte's suit, which is being reviewed by the commercial court of Nanterre, alleges that management violated its fiduciary duty to shareholders by ignoring a superior bid of euro 27 a share for Prosodie made by BT Group plc, formerly known as British Telecom.[12]

In October 2006, Apax Partners agreed to buy Bernard's 46 percent of the company for euro 20 (US$25.70) a share on the condition that the buyout shop would also make an offer for the rest of the business by year-end. The private-equity firm subsequently offered euro 23.40 a share for the rest of the firm. Wyser-Pratte contends Bernard agreed to a deal that enriches himself and his "collaborators" at the expense of shareholders. Later in February 2007 Apax hiked its offer to euro 25.25 a share. The lawsuit, Wyser-Pratte argues, and general public outrage over the incident is the primary reason why Apax hiked its offer for the rest of the company. "Until we raised a real uproar about it, it looked like this sweet deal was going to take place," Wyser-Pratte says. His decades of strong performance through activist investing earned Wyser-Pratte a lifetime achievement award in 2007 from *Alternative Investment News,* a publication of Institutional Investor News.

Activism in Europe can also be homegrown. A duo of Swedish-born and bred activists are throwing a wrench in the works at one of their country's great manufacturers, Volvo AB. The former maker of super-safe automobiles has in recent years reshaped itself into the second largest global maker of trucks and buses. But that reorganization isn't good enough for Lars Förberg and Christer Gardell.

The two Swedish activist managers have been acquiring large stakes in undervalued Swedish companies and agitating for change since 1997. In 2002, the duo formed Cevian Capital LP, a Stockholm, Sweden–based activist fund that focuses on the Nordic public markets. They've developed a specialty targeting companies based in Sweden, Finland, Denmark and Norway. Cevian's Web site describes the strategy as a private-equity approach to public companies.

Why do Förberg and Gardell focus on Scandinavia? The combination of their expertise in local companies, director and management candidates, and customs, taken together with a surprisingly investor-friendly regulatory landscape has made the market an activist investor's goldmine for them. Most Scandinavian boards are made up predominantly of independent directors. Each company has a separate director nomination committee, which typically consists of four or five of its largest shareholders. Unlike roughly half of U.S. corporations, all Swedish corporate directors are up for election annually. Investors holding 10 percent stakes can call extraordinary general shareholder meetings—no questions asked. That's a far cry from a shareholders ability to call EGMs at U.S. corporations.

There are some corporate protections. As in Canada and the United States, a number of Swedish companies have two classes of shares, giving certain investors or insiders the ability to maintain control of the company, possibly at the expense of shareholders in the other class of stock. But despite that, Förberg says, overall, Sweden's corporations are more accountable to shareholders. "The division of responsibility between shareholders, boards, and management is more equitable," says Förberg. "Shareholders have a stronger position than in the United States or many other countries."

The pro-shareholder environment compelled billionaire activist Carl Icahn to describe Sweden as an investor and governance "paradise," Förberg says. Upon hearing about the lay of the land, Icahn promptly decided to become a Cevian investor, Förberg adds.

The Cevian team has generated roughly 50 percent annual returns net of fees for the past ten years. Since Cevian was founded, the investors have returned even more annually, Förberg says. Their fund has $2.5 billion in assets under management. Similar to most hedge funds, Cevian takes a management fee and a share of profits, although in an effort to align their interests with their investors, the latter is postponed until the end of each investor's lockup, which in most cases is several years.

The Swedish governance structure has made it much easier for a shareholder to attain a director position, especially compared to the costly proxy contest–driven Western corporate environment. The ease with which shareholders can gain seats on corporate boards in Sweden has also, to a large extent, shaped Cevian's activist strategies. Instead of working from the outside to press companies into making changes, Förberg and Gardell typically seek to gain board seats as a key part of their efforts to effect long-term change and improve shareholder value. In roughly 80 percent of its endeavors, Cevian nominates one of its own for corporate board seats. At other companies, Cevian finds outside candidates for board seats. "Gaining a board seat is critical to effecting change at Swedish companies," he says. "Only directors can have access to the kind of strategic information that is necessary to determine, from an operational perspective, how to improve the company."

In 2006, through board representation, Cevian was a key driver in changing the entire business direction of TeliaSonera AB, a $35 billion stock market capitalization Stockholm-based mobile and fixed telecommunications company. First, Cevian's Gardell acquired a significant stake and attained a seat on TeliaSonera's election (nomination) committee. The committee, which was made up of other large shareholders and TeliaSonera's chairman Tom von Weymarn, expanded its size from five to six to include Gardell.

From his board position, Gardell called for a special shareholder meeting, something that was well within his rights as a 10 percent shareholder. At the meeting, with the support of others on the nomination committee, Gardell and Cevian restructured TeliaSonera's board by removing five directors and replacing them with four new officials. The board's total size went down from eight to seven. The whole effort took less than a year. The new board, Förberg says, took the company in a different direction.

Förberg acknowledges that despite all the Swedish pro-shareholder rules he believes that many of the Scandinavian country's corporate directors are still members of an insider's club that protects executives from outside pressure. Part of the problem, he says, is that even though investors have many rights, there are still very few shareholder activists in Sweden. He adds that these clubby board insiders often genuinely seek to improve shareholder value, but they are unable to turn the corner and bring in a new approach. In those cases, fresh blood is needed. "Sometimes a board has embraced a strategy that may have made sense at the time but no longer works," Förberg says. "For those directors, it is difficult to reverse the strategy and new people need to be brought in to strike out in a new direction."

In addition to TeliaSonera and Volvo, Cevian has taken activist actions at life insurer Skandia AB and debt collector Intrum Justitia AB.

Their long-term activist approach runs counter to the perception of hedge funds by many in the Swedish corporate world. Cevian, Förberg says, is perceived by some as an investment firm that focuses all of its energy on draining corporate cash reserves and hurting business prospects. Pressuring companies to return unused cash to shareholders through stock buybacks is only a small part of the overall strategy,

Förberg says. The plan, he adds, is to double the value of any target company—an effort that cannot be achieved simply through an invigorated share buyback program.

That said, part of Cevian's efforts at Volvo has been to pressure the company into using its cash reserves to finance a share buyback or special dividend.[13] That endeavor is only part of their considerations at Volvo. Förberg would also like to see Volvo divest certain noncore divisions.[14] To achieve their goals, the group formed Violet Partners and acquired a 5.2 percent stake in the truck and bus maker. Through the investment vehicle, Förberg and Gardell succeeded at gaining a seat on Volvo's six-member election committee.

Volvo officials defend the company's cash reserves. They argue that Cevian's goals are short term and don't represent the interests of a majority of shareholders. John Hartwell, investor relations director at Volvo, says the truck company considers various uses for its cash, including dividends and share buybacks. But he also points out that Volvo needs to consider costs associated with more stringent European truck and bus emission standards that are being implemented over the next few years, when contemplating various uses for its cash reserves. "With cash on the balance sheet, we've been able to invest in new products that meet new emission standards," Hartwell says.

Hartwell adds that its cash reserve also gives the company the flexibility to make acquisitions at appropriate times. In fact, Volvo rejected Cevian's calls for returning cash to shareholders and instead made a series of major acquisitions, expanding its equipment business.[15] Volvo officials meet with investors on a regular basis to learn about their demands, Hartwell adds. "You have some hedge funds that are looking at the returns one quarter or two quarters away," Hartwell says. "Our board has a much more long-term outlook."

Förberg concedes that identifying the best use for Volvo's cash reserves can be an emotional issue. Many Swedish companies, he says, have bloated balance sheets, a problem that creates a high cost of capital. The key, he says, is to get past that and have a practical debate about the future of Volvo's capital strategy. He worries that Volvo and many Swedish corporate elite make overly conservative judgments about how much cash reserves they need to have in the event of an economic downturn. "These managers are still living in the past, when the country's capital markets were malfunctioning. It's time to move on," Förberg says.

But he reiterates that Volvo's financial structure is only one part of the puzzle. "Companies need to make other strategic and operational changes and that's what is more difficult," Förberg says.

Japan

In addition to Europe, other countries exhibit similar clubby insider-controlled characteristics. Japan's corporate culture still makes it difficult for activist investors to provoke executives to work in the interests of shareholders. Until the 1990s, executives and directors at Japanese corporations were largely shielded from outside shareholder pressure by the *keiretsu* system of domestic companies and banks with interlocking business relationships and cross-holdings (the system was actually looser than the prewar *zaibatsu* system of interconnected Japanese businesses). While still intact to a certain extent, the collection of interconnected companies has started to break down while Japanese corporations outside the system have begun to emerge as significant competitors. At the same time, a few foreign activists and institutions have pounced at new opportunities.

Tokyo's SPARX Asset Management Company Ltd., backed by the California Public Employees' Retirement System (CalPERS), was an early activists seeking to engage Japanese corporate executives. Launched in 2003, SPARX's Japan Value Creation Investments fund takes a behind-the-scenes approach to activism in Japan, working collaboratively with all its portfolio companies. Like U.S. activist funds, it buys large stakes in underperforming companies and privately makes recommendations for executives to consider. But don't expect SPARX management to take its efforts public if the companies in which it owns stakes do not take their advice. Other Japanese activists, including Asuka Asset Management Ltd. and Taiyo Pacific Partners LP, take a similar behind-the-scenes approach.[16]

Their strategy contrasts significantly, at times, with Steel Partners' public agitation tactics in Japan. Warren Lichtenstein dreamed up Steel Partners' Japan Strategic Fund LP in 2001 as an investment vehicle that would take his private-equity style of U.S. activism to the uncharted territory of Japan. The Japan fund is a joint venture with Boston-based hedge fund Liberty Square Asset Management LP.[17] As discussed briefly in Chapter 17,

Lichtenstein launched unsolicited takeover bids for two Japanese companies in 2003, in part, to extract special dividends and stock buybacks. Though his efforts were only partially successful, they were groundbreaking for a country not known for unsolicited takeover attempts.

Lichtenstein bid $250 million to buy Yushiro Chemical Industries Company Ltd. and $190 million to take over wool dye and processor Sotoh Company Ltd. Both bids were rejected. In their efforts to discourage investor support for the activist's takeover offers, both Yushiro and Sotoh offered significantly increased dividends. Sotoh promised to increase its annual dividend to 200 yen, a 15-fold increase.[18]

More recently, in October 2006, Myojo Foods Company, the maker of instant ramen noodles, agreed to be acquired by Nissin Food Products Company after Steel Partners' Japan Strategic Fund made a hostile takeover bid to buy Myojo.[19] Steel Partners offered 700 yen per share to buy Myojo, but Nissin outbid the activist with an offer of 870 yen per share. Before Steel Partners launched its takeover attempt in October, Myojo shares traded at roughly 609 yen each.[20] Lichtenstein may not have acquired the noodle maker, but he certainly extracted some serious value from it.[21]

In addition to Steel Partners, another high-profile activist investor has been publicly prodding companies in the Japanese market. Until recently, Yoshiaki Murakami, age 46, a former Japanese government bureaucrat, operated the Murakami fund. After being indicted for insider trading in 2006, Murakami began the dissolution of his fund, which at one point held roughly $3.4 billion in assets.[22]

During its height, the Murakami Fund bought large stakes in undervalued companies and urged numerous Japanese corporate executives to consider his suggestions for improving shareholder value. In 1999, long before Steel Partners began its takeover bids, Murakami went against long-held Japanese protocol by making a hostile offer, the first ever against a Japanese company, to take control of real estate and electronic parts maker Shoei Company.[23]

He also bought a large stake in Japanese department store chain Matsuzakaya and approached executives there with a plan for it to review its strategic options, including consideration of a management-led buyout. Murakami opposed a proposal by Matsuzakaya management to change its ownership structure into a holding company and demanded that it buy back shares he owned.[24]

Murakami also invested in Hanshin Electric Railway Company, which owns real estate and the popular Japanese baseball team, the Hanshin Tigers. Murakami acquired a 45.73 percent stake in Hanshin and pressed the company to consider constructing apartments and shopping centers on real estate it owns. After Murakami exerted pressure, the company agreed to reform the way it uses its real estate assets, which have a $2 billion value.[25] But Hanshin rejected Murakami's other demands, including his insistence that the Hanshin Tigers baseball team be spun off via an initial public offering.[26]

Murakami also pressed other companies, including the Osaka Securities Exchange, Tokyo Style, and Tokyo Broadcasting Systems Inc., into making changes, before he closed the fund.

James Fatheree, president of the U.S.-Japan Business Council Inc. in Washington, points out that in addition to being a Japanese government bureaucrat for the Japanese Ministry of International Trade and Industry, Murakami spent some time in the West as an investment banker. That experience and his Japanese cultural and government background left an indelible impression on the activist. "He has the mindset of a Western investment banker," Fatheree says. "He has brought to Japan the Western idea of investing in an undervalued asset and enhancing its value."

Fatheree adds that he believes that the hostile offers for companies by Murakami and Steel Partners are a novelty in Japan. Both insurgents have succeeded at achieving their goals of improving shareholder value in a country that often ignores its investors. Fatheree points out that shareholder incentives such as the stock buy-backs or special dividends Murakami and Steel Partners have attained, are extremely unusual and less frequently provided in Japan.

But despite the measure of success these investors have had in Japan, Fatheree says he doesn't anticipate a major increase in Western-style insurgents bringing their brand of capitalism to Tokyo and Osaka, at least not in the short term. For one thing, he says, Murakami's indictment has tarnished the image of activist shareholders in Japan. "Conservative business types, politicians, and bureaucrats can hold Murakami up as case number 1 for why this is bad stuff—never mind the distinction between perpetrating illegal trading activities and legitimate activities," Fatheree says.

There is another reason why Fatheree doesn't expect an immediate uptick in the number of activist's launching hostile takeovers or initiating proxy fights. Activism, he says, is still a foreign concept in Japanese culture. In Japan, not only are there virtually no proxy fights, but annual meetings at Japanese corporations take place like clockwork every June, with little variation. These events are generally very structured, without any surprises or deviations from the script, he says.

Despite Fatheree's pronouncements, some things are changing. The number of Western institutional investors in Japan has increased significantly in the past three years. Roughly 25 percent to 30 percent of the daily volume of trades on the Tokyo Stock Exchange is now made by non-Japanese investors. Most of that flow has been allocated to more stable, large-capitalization Japanese companies, such as Orix Corporation and Toyota Motor Corporation, which are generally not the target of activist investors. But a portion of the new western investment allocations have reached smaller public companies, some of which could eventually be susceptible to activists.

Other major public Japanese corporations are still owned by "old school" *keiretsu* Japanese investors who were raised in the insulated Japanese system and don't want to relinquish control. These investors were educated to believe that they are only one of a group of larger stakeholders, including management, suppliers, and employees, and there is a symbiotic relationship that exists among all these parts. Through their investments, traditional Japanese shareholders believe they have a broader social purpose to provide stable employment and economic output that will drive the economy. The executives at Japanese companies rise through the ranks and can become CEOs only when they are past the age of 60. These "aging men" are in control of the Japanese companies, Fatheree says, and they want to keep the isolated Japanese system intact, if at all possible. "Japan is a very stratified, hierarchical society," he says. "There is a premium placed on seniority, and shifting to a merit-based, competitive system takes time."

In the long term, Fatheree predicts that activist shareholders may have a place in Japan's future, though no change will happen overnight. A new generation of younger Japanese taking control of corporations may be more receptive to activist efforts. But for now, it just isn't happening. "They don't want some 35-year-old kid to come in and take over the company," Fatheree says. "But globalization is pushing them into a system that might make that happen."

South Korea

South Korea, like Japan, has its own *keiretsu*-type system, known as a *chaebol*. This conglomerate-like interlocking structure is made up of several dozen large, family-controlled Korean corporate groups that play a major role in the country's economy, assisted by government financing.[27] This centralized ownership in which families and a few other groups own controlling blocks of most companies leaves little room for outside activist shareholders.

But there are a few exceptions, leading at least one activist to pounce on an opportunity. Steel Partners discovered that not only was South Korean-based ginseng and tobacco company, KT&G Corporation not a traditional *chaebol* corporation, but roughly 75 percent of its shares were freely traded. In addition, about 50 percent of those "free float" shares were owned by foreign investors, making the former state-operated tobacco company about as attractive a target as possible in a country where outside investor influence is lacking.

After meeting with company executives on several occasions, Lichtenstein felt his suggestions were not being seriously considered. KT&G CEO Kwak Young Kyoon told Lichtenstein in a meeting that if Steel Partners didn't like the company's strategy, he could sell his stake. Unfortunately, Kwak Young Kyoon didn't anticipate his adversary's reaction. Instead of cashing out, Kyoon's comments made Lichtenstein even more determined to stick around and effect change.

Lichtenstein had advised the company to spin off its ginseng unit, divest some real estate holdings into a separate entity, and increase its dividend, among other proposals. Several months into the effort, Lichtenstein asked Carl Icahn to join forces with him to pressure KT&G into making improvements. Icahn agreed, and they formed KT&G Full Value Committee, an investment vehicle created to hold their collective 7.68 percent stake in the ginseng and tobacco company.

After that, Icahn and Lichtenstein launched a proxy contest, a strategy for change that both investors have employed with much success many times in the United States, but one that had never been successfully employed in shareholder-unfriendly Korea. Before deciding to engage in such a campaign, Lichtenstein researched Korea's regulations and discovered that the Korean securities agency had rules on the books to permit a proxy contest. "You can see that they were feeling their way in the dark," pointed out one observer to the proxy contest. "All the sides were looking in the rulebooks and saying things like, 'Really, you can do this?'"

Lichtenstein nominated three candidates, including himself, a lawyer, and a tobacco industry expert from the United States, for election to KT&G's 12-person board. Six seats were up for election, including four positions on KT&G's audit committee. Lichtenstein's plan was to win at least one seat on the company's audit committee, really a critical place to learn the inside workings of KT&G, but things didn't work out as he had hoped. In an attempt to limit Lichtenstein's efforts, KT&G management said Steel Partners would be prohibited from nominating candidates for the tobacco company's audit committee because that specific request was not made at the outset of the proxy contest.[28]

As a result, Lichtenstein's three candidates became eligible to compete only with the company's two nonaudit positions on KT&G's 12 seat board.[29] Frustrated, but undeterred, Lichtenstein began a letter-writing campaign presenting his point of view to shareholders. The letters were submitted to KT&G management and then made public to reporters covering the proxy fight, as part of Steel Partners' public pressure campaign.

International proxy advisory firm Glass, Lewis & Company recommended in a report that shareholders vote for Lichtenstein's slate of candidates.[30] As the election grew closer, the division grew greater. KT&G CEO Kyoon traveled to Europe, the United States, and parts of Asia to vie for the support of international shareholders, which by then controlled over 60 percent of the company's stock.[31]

Included among Lichtenstein's many demands was for KT&G to cancel its trove of Treasury shares. Lichtenstein worried that the Treasury shares could be sold to a sympathetic domestic buyer and that transaction could dilute minority shareholders, which included Steel Partners and other foreign investors. There was some speculation that a group of domestic Korean investors, including Woori Financial Group and Industrial Bank of Korea, were considering plans to buy the Treasury stock with the intention of using it to vote for management's slate.[32] The group, which created the KT&G Growth Committee, already held stakes in KT&G and had announced plans to support KT&G's management backed slate. About 57.7 percent of Industrial Bank of Korea is owned by the Korean government.

On February 24, Lichtenstein and Icahn stepped up their activist efforts by making an unsolicited bid to buy KT&G for roughly $10 billion. A few days later, that bid was rejected.[33] Shortly after that, Lichtenstein indicated that he may launch a hostile tender offer, taking his bid directly to shareholders. Making their bid hostile would put Icahn and Lichtenstein in rare company. Like in Japan, hostile offers in Korea are rare, and successful hostile bids are even rarer.

At the same time, Lichtenstein's proxy contest continued on a number of fronts. Less than a week before the election, Lichtenstein argued before the District Court of Daejeon, where KT&G is based, that the tobacco company was violating Korean laws by prohibiting him from nominating three candidates to the board. The effort failed.[34] The activist also experienced another setback. Korea's investment regulator, the Korea Securities Depository, had abruptly stopped accepting electronic votes from investors on March 9, a day before many investors had expected to be the deadline.[35]

In the end, shareholders voted to elect Lichtenstein to KT&G's board. While the two other Steel Partners candidates were not voted in, the result is still an impressive victory and the first time a dissident investor group succeeded in electing one of its nominees to the board of a Korean company. Lichtenstein can thank the multitudes of foreign KT&G investors for his seat, though some domestic investors also supported his effort. Even though many institutional investors saw KT&G as a good company with a decent corporate governance record, many foreign institutions had become fed up with its maneuvering on a variety of factors such as its reevaluation of who could sit on the audit committee.

A key turning point came on March 8, when Franklin Mutual Advisors LLC, a Short Hills, New Jersey–based quasi-activist investment firm that owned an 8 percent KT&G stake, announced that it was supporting Lichtenstein's effort. Lichtenstein's allies contend that Franklin's public statement of support went a long way toward securing Lichtenstein's position on the board. There was some confusion about Franklin Mutual's position earlier on. After KT&G's Kyoon met with Franklin Mutual officials, a South Korean paper, *Maeil Business*

Newspaper, reported that the New Jersey investment company had agreed to support management's slate of directors. The report cited an unidentified government official. After that, on February 22, Franklin said in an e-mail to a Bloomberg reporter that it denied agreeing to support KT&G's slate.[36] During the campaign, the activists received a substantial amount of bad press. Icahn routinely was called a pirate or a shark by South Korean papers.

The proxy contest and hostile bid generated significant debate among Koreans about the role of foreign investors and the nature of their markets. Lichtenstein and Icahn's efforts at KT&G forced Koreans to consider whether they felt it was time for the country to move toward Western-style capitalism or stay the same. During the period immediately preceding the proxy contest, many Korean investors and the general public became very nationalistic about the cigarette asset. Their position reflected a general nationalism for all major domestic companies. The prevailing perception within the Korean investor community was that Steel Partners was only a short-term raider interested only in breaking up KT&G and liquidating it. As a result, the vast majority of Korean shareholders voted for KT&G's management slate. It appears that any movement toward a Western shareholder-friendly system of capitalism is still far off. "It was a litmus test of the openness of financial markets in Korea," says a source familiar with the Steel Partners campaign. "If you want to be part of the international market, you have to play by international rules."

Despite winning only one board seat, Lichtenstein did eventually provoke some change. In August 2006, responding to Lichtenstein and Icahn's pressure, KT&G agreed to return $2.9 billion to shareholders in dividends, a major investor victory in a country that is not known for providing these incentives to investors.[37]

Once on the board, Lichtenstein provoked the company to sell its 43.7 percent stake in local Korean retailer, By The Way.[38] Lichtenstein is also encouraging KT&G to find other means to improve shareholder value. Despite Lichtenstein's early efforts to incite the company into selling its ginseng and real estate division, those assets remain intact. But lately, Lichtenstein is more comfortable with keeping the ginseng division together with the rest of the company, at least for the time being. The plan is to improve the division's operations so KT&G could consider selling it for a higher valuation at some future date.

Meanwhile, in December 2006, Icahn cashed out his stake, bringing in a $111 million profit and ending speculation about a possible hostile bid for KT&G.[39] The asset sale also brought with it some grumbling by Western observers that Icahn's move fulfills the stereotype of the short-term Western investor that is being given such a bad name in Korea. From beginning to end, Icahn held his stake for roughly a year, still much longer than many quick-hit Korean traders. And Lichtenstein is still a large shareholder. Only time will tell if he decides to launch another proxy contest to gain greater control of KT&G's board.

One final note on proxy contests in Korea. While the KT&G effort was the first successful proxy contest in Korea, it wasn't the first ever attempted. In 2005, a Dubai-based investment company, Sovereign Global Investment fund, tried to remove the chairman of SK Corporation, a Korean oil refiner. The effort failed, despite the fact that SK Corporation's chairman had been convicted of accounting fraud.[40] Many Western observers might call that result surprising, but in reality it was a simple demonstration of the determination of South Korean investors to fend off outsiders.

As the Steel Partners–Carl Icahn effort was unfolding, another group of investors began ramping up an insurgency at a Korean company. Ramius Capital Group of New York has roughly $8 billion in assets under management, half of which is in a fund of hedge funds. It also has an activist hedge fund, the Starboard Value and Opportunity Fund, which invests about $400 million predominantly in U.S. companies where managers believe there is value to be unlocked.

Another Ramius division, Safe Harbor Master Fund LP, is an event-driven investment vehicle that owns a stake in Gravity Company Ltd., a South Korean Internet game developer that trades on the National Association of Securities Dealers Automated Quotation system (NASDAQ). After completing a thorough due diligence of the game maker's financials, Ramius officials discovered that deals with conflicts of interest were taking place between Gravity management and directors. The conflicts were hurting minority shareholders. After evaluating the situation and meeting with Gravity's management to discuss the issue, Ramius officials decided that they needed to take action. Together with another New York investor Moon Capital Management LP, Ramius accumulated a significant stake and filed a 13D on Gravity in March 2006. Later, they set up the "Gravity Committee for Fair Treatment of Minority Shareholders," as part of a campaign to convince other investors to support their efforts.

Effecting change at the gaming company would not be easy. Gravity's CEO Il Young Ryu, one of the targets of Ramius's efforts, controlled 52 percent of the outstanding shares, reducing the likelihood that a shareholder revolt would be effective. The activists implored Gravity's independent directors to watch out for the minority shareholders, but those efforts fell on deaf ears. Ramius insisted that Gravity should auction off its Japanese license for a popular online video game it produced, or it should spin off a division to handle that business. The company ignored its demands. Both sides met to discuss the situation. Gravity executives flew to the United States to meet with Ramius, and Ramius officials later went to Korea to meet with Gravity officials, but discussions did not generate any tangible results.

After being rebuffed, the two activists began an effort that involved litigation and public pressure. The investors demanded that Gravity hold an "extraordinary general meeting of shareholders" in December. Moon and Ramius, which by November held 17.6 percent of Gravity stock, began a campaign to send a message to Ryu and the company's investors that insider dealings would not be accepted by minority shareholders.[41] The group launched an effort to remove two of Gravity's top management executives, including Ryu. Ramius knew its attempt would fail, due to Ryu's controlling stake. But if the dissident investor could convince a majority of the minority shareholders to support their endeavor, then perhaps Gravity's management would stop ignoring minority shareholders.

The contest was successful, or as successful as Ramius could hope for. Roughly 87 percent of minority shareholders, including their large block, supported the dissident effort.[42] When considering that some South Korean minority Gravity shareholders didn't vote at all, the numbers are even more one sided. Of the minority shares that showed up, 97.4 percent voted for Ramius's proposal. Put another way, 2.9 million shares voted for the Ramius measure, while only 4,600 voted against it and the rest abstained. Those tallies, of course, do not include Ryu's controlling stake. On December 26, Gravity announced that its investors supported keeping management in place.[43] "Rarely do you get that kind of turnout from minority shareholders," says Ramius managing member Jeffrey M. Solomon. "It validates our actions, and now we have to translate that into internal pressure on the company to unlock value for all of the shareholders."

Solomon points out that the Gravity situation is the exception to the norm for Ramius investments in Asia. "This is a situation where the majority shareholder is abusing the minority investors," he says. "The bulk of situations are not like this."

In addition to Gravity, Ramius does engage executives at other Asian companies. But for the most part, these efforts take place in private, says Solomon. One strategy, he adds, is to stimulate a brainstorming session with executives. "We engage directly with management and express our views with the hope that management will come back with better suggestions," Solomon says.

Interlocking businesses and board insiders, whether in Japan's *keiretsu* or South Korea's *chaebol* system, have all played a role in the less-than-attractive valuations of hundreds of companies in various locations around the world. William Natbony points out that these kinds of interconnected businesses aren't isolated to Asia. In many ways, the Far East's clubby atmosphere reflects the environment in Europe and somewhat in the United States as well. The only difference is that lately CEOs and boards in these countries have become susceptible to activist investors seeking to unlock value.

Canada and Its Bailiwick

Arnaud Ajdler, managing director of New York–based Crescendo Partners, says he loves being an activist in Canada.

Many U.S. activists share his views and are eager to cross the border to intimidate their neighbors to the north. As in Sweden and the United Kingdom, shareholder rights in many circumstances are stronger in Canada than in the United States, Ajdler says, and that in itself is incentive enough to seek out undervalued companies north of the 49th parallel.

For example, Ajdler says, he likes that shareholders owning a 5 percent or 10 percent stake at most Canadian companies are entitled to call a special shareholder meeting—no questions asked. As discussed earlier, only a small number of U.S. companies permit shareholders to call extraordinary meetings, and even many of those put up hurdles making it very difficult. Another factor encouraging shareholder initiatives, he adds, is that most Canadian companies have boards that are elected annually, while still roughly half of U.S. companies discourage investor efforts by continuing to employ staggered or classified boards. William Mackenzie, a director at the Canadian Coalition for Good Governance in Toronto, says these factors and some others give activist investors and other shareholders more leverage, particularly behind the scenes, with Canadian companies. "When comparing boards, executives, and investors between the U.S. and Canada, you will find there is a significant difference in the power balance," Mackenzie says.

However, there are also cases of entrenched management teams in Canada. Roughly 20 percent of the largest 200 Canadian companies have dual-class capital structures. Voting control at many of these companies has become disconnected from ownership, he says. In some companies, family-controlled management teams own multiple voting shares, such as 500 votes per share, leaving minority shareholders with almost no influence. Many U.S. corporations employ the same executive entrenching tactics, though these corporations represent a much smaller percentage of the U.S economy. As we've discussed, dual-class stocks also exist in a number of European countries.

In Toronto, activist fund Goodwood Inc. has been embracing behind-the-scenes activism. The fund, operated by its chairman Peter Puccetti and CEO J. Cameron MacDonald, launched with $3 million in 1996 and by 2007 had more than $600 million in assets under management. So far, Goodwood has reported returns of 21.3 percent, net of fees, a year, since its inception.

Puccetti says about half of the fund at any one time is invested in activist positions—the top five or six investments typically represent 40 percent to 50 percent of total assets. He and MacDonald chose not to launch a dedicated activist fund because they wanted to avoid having to constantly find insurgency-oriented positions and ideas to keep the fund's performance up. "We're much more comfortable running a value fund that can short and can also take on an activist agenda," Puccetti says. "If we had to do it all the time, we would be under such great pressure to send letters to companies even if there was no underlying value."

One behind-the-scenes effort took place at Great Atlantic & Pacific Tea Company. A relationship between Goodwood and the CEO of the Montvaile, New Jersey–based grocery store company emerged over a three year time frame. Originally, Puccetti and MacDonald purchased the stock because they considered it to be "statistically cheap." After holding a stake for a couple years, the activist hedge fund duo realized that the market wasn't fully valuing A&P Ontario, a smallish Canadian grocery chain that Great Atlantic owned. Engaging management on the issue wasn't easy, Puccetti says, as the company was experiencing its own problems in the United States. Great Atlantic did everything in its power to avoid contact with shareholders, including holding its annual meetings in out-of-the-way locations such as Nantucket, Massaschusetts, and Sudbury, Ontario.

Puccetti began writing letters and meeting with Great Atlantic management, pointing out that even though A&P Ontario had only a 15 percent market share in Canada, that small stake would be attractive to midsized Canadian grocery groups, including Sobeys Inc. of Nova Scotia and Metro Inc. of Montreal. Both these Canadian chains were trying to increase their size so they could compete more effectively with national chain Loblaw Companies Inc. of Brampton, Ontario. To prod Great Atlantic to consider selling the chain, Puccetti says he made the argument that A&P would have a difficult time competing in the Canadian market with Wal-Mart Stores Inc. and their mega grocery stores' encroachment on the horizon. Finally, in July 2005, Great Atlantic sold its 236 stores in Ontario to Metro for $1.5 billion.[44] The price tag on the asset was significantly beyond the $600 million to $1 billion estimates U.S. analysts had predicted Great Atlantic could get for the unit, Puccetti says. "There was no proxy contest or even public pressure—this was all done in private," Puccetti says. "It was all about arguing intelligently that this was the best time to do the sale."

Goodwood's efforts at Great Atlantic didn't end there. After that sale was complete, Puccetti sought to convince Great Atlantic's board that the whole grocery store chain should be merging with grocer Pathmark Stores Inc. In March 2007, Pathmark and Great Atlantic struck a $1.3 billion deal after being rumored to have been in talks for several months. Before the deal was struck, Puccetti says that Great Atlantic's CEO Eric Claus asked him to write a letter to the company's board outlining the benefits of a possible merger with Pathmark. "We've developed a good working relationship with senior management and the board," Puccetti says. "The fact that he [Claus] asked me to do that is a testament to our strong relationship."

Goodwood's Great Atlantic endeavor demonstrates that, in some cases, activists and executives can collaborate to accomplish something that may not have appeared possible otherwise. Executives often are trying to convince boards to take a particular action, but directors and other stakeholders are not engaged. A large investor who agrees with management's goals can bolster a CEO's campaign. Goodwood purchased the stock at prices averaging out to roughly $8 a share in 2003. Great Atlantic's stock subsequently rose to as high as $37 a share on news of the possible combination. Prior to the Pathmark transaction, Great Atlantic also provided a substantial dividend to shareholders, adding to the total value of Goodwood's investment.

On some other occasions, Goodwood managers have found no other option than to take their concerns out of the shadows and into the public domain. But to do that has required a delicate touch and some credible allies from the United States. At one point in its history, Creo Inc., a digital equipment supplier for the printing industry, controlled 100 percent of the market share of its specialized industry. That put it in the "competitive barriers to entry" category listed by Goodwood as one of the criteria it considers when making an investment. Goodwood picked up the stake, with no expectation that a public activist effort would be necessary to realize value. But Creo began to lose its market share. Hoping to improve its profits, Creo began to consider a capital-intensive expansion strategy that involved producing plates for the printing industry. The Burnaby, British Columbia–based company hoped to sell its digital printing equipment bundled with its new plate product. But Puccetti says he believed it would be very difficult for Creo to compete with the three companies, Fuji, Eastman Kodak, and Agfa, which controlled 92 percent of the plate-making industry. "We became very concerned about whether the new strategy would improve the situation," Puccetti says.

That's when they began to plan a public pressure and proxy campaign to nudge Creo into auctioning itself to a larger entity. But Goodwood needed a credible ally, someone that had the experience to get the job done. It needed to be someone that could mobilize the shareholder base behind a public pressure campaign. An ally was necessary, says Puccetti, because the Goodwood team, up to that point, was inexperienced when it came to these kinds of public activist efforts. But finding a credible associate took time. Puccetti and MacDonald spent roughly a year approaching a number of activists that had records of successful pressure and proxy campaigns under their belt. Goodwood hoped one of these insurgents would take the lead in an activist campaign against Creo. New York activist Eric Rosenfeld of Crescendo flew to Toronto to meet with Puccetti, but was either too busy or not interested in leading a campaign against Creo.

Through a mutual contact, Puccetti and MacDonald were introduced to Robert G. Burton Jr., a U.S. activist investor with a series of successful turnaround projects under his belt. Between 2000 and 2002, Burton resolved a series of issues at troubled Canadian printing company Moore Corporation. Between 1991 and 1999, Burton operated World Color Press Inc., a portfolio company for New York buyout firm Kohlberg Kravis Roberts & Company.[45] Puccetti found Burton in semi-retirement, operating Burton Capital Management LLC investment firm in hedge fund hotbed Greenwich, Connecticut. Within a week of their initial contact, Burton was on board. Crescendo, with Burton, moved into full-gear public-engagement mode. They filed a joint 13D filing in October 2004 and began moves to oust the board in a proxy contest. By October 2005, feeling the pressure, Creo sold itself to Eastman Kodak Company for $980 million, or $16.50 a share.[46] The sale price was roughly twice the amount Goodwood paid for a huge block of shares shortly before launching the contest.

Puccetti attributes the successful turn of events at Creo to Burton and his ability to gain the confidence of existing shareholders and other activist-type investors that acquired the company's stock after the public campaign was launched. Roughly 70 percent of Creo's shares turned over within a month of the 13D filing, Puccetti says. "When you file one of these things [13D] and you have credibility, it makes a huge difference in mobilizing a shareholder base interested in a sale," Puccetti says. "Burton has a huge following among U.S. hedge funds."

Without a serious chance of winning such a contest, the risks can be extreme, Puccetti says. The effort's legal costs were huge, running to roughly $700,000, which Goodwood and Burton split.

After the Creo success, Burton asked Goodwood to participate with him on another printing industry effort. The two groups joined forces once again in 2005 to provoke change at Englewood, Colorado–based commercial printer Cenveo Inc. Burton and Goodwood acquired a 9.6 percent stake and filed a 13D in April 2005. Along with the securities filing, Burton sent a letter to Cenveo's board demanding to be installed as chairman and CEO. By September, Cenveo relented and agreed to let Burton reconstitute the board and become CEO.[47] A large reason for the success of this effort can be attributed to Burton's ability to gain the confidence of an investor base that is comfortable with the idea of him running the business, Puccetti says.

Other activist shareholder campaigns in Canada have also been successful, but as in the cases with Creo, many of them typically require the support of U.S. insurgents as well. Canadian and U.S. activists, including Enterprise Capital Management Inc. of Toronto and New York-based Crescendo, joined forces to push for a sale of Spar Aerospace Ltd. to L-3 Communications Holdings Inc. U.S. Highfields Capital Management LP joined other investors seeking to block the combination of Canadian Molson Inc. and U.S. Adolph Coors Company (that effort failed).[48] In 2006, Highfields Capital protested Great Canadian Gaming Company's sale of shares to its CEO, Ross McLeon.[49]

A high-profile campaign against Manitoba Telecom Services Inc., a provincial phone company, took place in 2004. Enterprise Capital led a shareholder effort that included U.S. investors, such as Highfields Capital of Boston. The shareholder campaign focused on pressing Manitoba Telecom to convert itself into a Canadian income trust, a mechanism that would allow the company to take advantage of tax breaks that could boost the stock value. The company indicated that it was going to complete that transaction, but later changed track and chose instead to buy Toronto-based business broadband and telecom company Allstream Inc.[50]

Whether it is Warren Lichtenstein tackling Japanese and Korean companies or Eric Rosenfeld seeking changes at Canadian companies, one thing is clear: U.S. activists have expanded their efforts outside the United States to parts of Asia, Europe, or Canada. That's not to say other countries don't have their own domestic activists. Cevian's Förberg in Sweden and Goodwood's Puccetti in Canada are examples of homegrown insurgents. U.S. activists venturing outside of their home turf are finding that they need local expertise for their efforts to work, and vice versa. Goodwood's activist efforts combined with Burton of Connecticut made for a successful shareholder outcome. New York's Lichtenstein had an expert on the ground in Korea that helped coordinate his activist strategy at KT&G, the ginseng and tobacco company.

In all cases, a certain amount of knowledge of local customs, culture, and regulations is necessary for the foreigner activist to succeed, or at least understand what went wrong. But cross-border collaborations point to growing transglobal partnerships that are making activism work in new ways all over the world.

In some cases, activists justify their expansion to other countries, in part, by citing those nations' shareholder-friendly regulatory climates. As in Canada and Sweden, significant investors in the United Kingdom can call special shareholder meetings to push their agenda. U.K. investors are also permitted to have "advisory" votes on all CEO pay packages. According to Stephen Davis, a fellow at Yale University School of Management, British companies are so worried about the reputational damage that comes with such a vote that they are willing to work privately to collaborate with shareholders on pay packages and other matters. Shareholder-rights groups and some United States lawmakers are trying to bring a similar pay package advisory vote to America arguing that if it works in London it should work at home as well. However, business groups portend that it is impossible to compare the U.K. and U.S. systems because each country has many unique factors contributing to its corporate governance approach. For one thing, U.S. investors have greater flexibility than their U.K. counterparts when it comes to filing class action shareholder litigation against corporations.

But the additional leverage shareholders in these countries have in private as a result of advisory votes and other shareholder friendly regulations cannot be underestimated. A great deal of activism in Canada and Sweden takes place behind the scenes in corporate boardrooms and on the phone as a result. Just knowing that a particular investor can automatically call an extraordinary shareholder meeting can be enough in these countries to compel CEOs to listen.

Other activists, such as Wyser-Pratte, argue that less shareholder-friendly countries such as Germany and France are full of eligible targets. Wyser-Pratte notes that these countries have poor governance codes that create undervalued companies, and only activists can unlock their true value. That said, Swedish activist Förberg points out that despite the investor-friendly regulatory framework in Scandinavian countries, he believes that the region's traditionally passive investor base means many companies remain severely undervalued, just like their continental European counterparts. So any activist in Scandinavia has many opportunities to unlock value, just as in Wyser-Pratte's continental European environment. A history of poor governance and bad management is just as pervasive in Scandinavia as in the rest of Europe, Förberg says. "Although the tools are available for an active shareholder to influence companies, this opportunity has in most cases not been seized, as few, if any, investors have both the skill set, financial resources, and mandate to do so," Förberg says.

Ramius's Solomon believes that governance is a key factor for activists to consider when hunting for investments outside of the United States. He thanks new post-Enron corporate governance rules for helping activist investors gain credibility abroad in places like Korea and Japan when pushing form board reform. Once other cultures see board independence work in the United States, they will come around to the idea in their countries, Solomon suggests. "The world is becoming smaller," Solomon says. "When one country improves its governance rating, investors will flock there."

International institutional investors are likely to begin investing in Indian debt after Standard & Poor's in 2007 improved the country's debt rating to BBB minus, the lowest investment grade rating.[51] Improved markets in India may convince investors to move their asset allocations out of other markets, Solomon argues. Before pulling their capital out, investors will consider board independence, among other factors. "The markets are all interconnected now," he says. "Our job is to talk to executives and directors and make clear that we represent the views of a large part of the shareholder base."

Included in all this new interconnectivity are emerging markets—the last great investment adventure for battle-hungry insurgents. The next chapter will discuss activists that are reaching out to the most inhospitable, investor-unfriendly countries, such as China and Russia, to provoke companies into improving the value of their shares. In many cases they are coming up against a brick wall.

Chapter 21

East Meets West: Hedge Activism Goes Global to Emerging Markets

Jin Jiang International hotels, a Chinese chain comparable to Marriott Courtyard or Red Roof Inn in the United States, recently got into the fried chicken business.

Managers at the hotel chain decided to set up Kentucky Fried Chicken franchises in the Peoples Republic of China. Business is good, fried chicken is selling well, and Jin Jiang now owns about 150 to 200 Kentucky Fried Chicken franchises across the country.

Enter Aaron Boesky, director of activist hedge fund Marco Polo Pure China Fund. Boesky, based in Hong Kong, invests in stocks listed on the Shenzhen and Shanghai stock exchanges in China. After carefully evaluating Jin Jiang and the Chinese market, Boesky and his team quietly began encouraging the company to devote more finances to its KFC business, based on its profitability projections, and allocate less capital to the hotel division. "We saw that the profit margins in the KFC chain are so much better than with the hotel business," Boesky says. "We've been pressing them to invest more heavily in the KFC business."

The advice Boesky offered up to Jin Jiang is typical of the kind of business analysis and guidance Marco Polo Pure China Fund managers give dozens of its portfolio companies. Boesky, a graduate of Beijing Foreign Affairs College for studies in language and economics, is fluent in Mandarin and since 2001 has concentrated his efforts on understanding the transforming Chinese market.

The fund manages roughly $50 million in assets and has produced strong returns. Boesky attributes his success in part to "kicking the tires" at little-known Chinese companies and providing them with international business connections and Western strategies for success. He takes time to emphasize that the Marco Polo approach has no connection to his infamous cousin, Ivan Boesky. Ivan Boesky, who was sentenced to 10 years for insider trading, represents to many the extremes of 1980s-style capitalism.[1]

The Marco Polo fund represents a different strategy: collaborating with Chinese companies and opening them up to the possibilities of global trade and communications. So far it has few similar rivals. Only about 1 percent of the Shanghai market is foreign owned, due to foreign ownership restrictions. Marco Polo is often the first foreign stakeholder of the companies it invests in, which may make it a harbinger of things to come, or at least the proverbial "canary in the coal mine" testing out the waters before other Western investors are willing, interested, and able to plunge in. For many activists this strategy is too risky because it's unclear how the volatile China business market will evolve.

But, despite the risks, other investors may be coming. Boesky predicts internal foreign ownership prohibitions will be loosened, permitting more Western investors to enter the market. That, in turn, will lead to a flood of foreign capital, all of which he expects will bring record gains in line with the dramatic 300 percent and greater rise in the Taiwan stock market between 1986 and 1990. Boesky compares China's Shanghai stock exchange listed companies to the types of misunderstood small-capitalization U.S. corporations many of his rivals seek out. "There is a tremendous amount of inefficient pricing that can be exploited by people who will go in on the ground level and meet with management," Boesky says.

Aaron Boesky's Marco Polo fund is part of a growing trend—activists going global to markets with often incomprehensible and opaque economic systems. Most activist investors have traditionally stuck to the U.S. market, focusing their efforts on companies in a regulatory and business cultural environment they understand. But lately, as international travel and communications have become more economically feasible, U.S. activists are venturing further afield. We've seen them take on European and some Asian companies. Others like Boesky are trying to identify completely new opportunities. Some members of this generation of U.S. activists are moving their operations to countries such as China, Russia, and beyond to find out if they can produce "alpha," industry lingo for super-sized returns that beat market performances. Prior to launching Marco Polo, Boesky managed a family investment fund in Michigan. But the call of new prospects abroad set him on a new course. "Activist funds are looking outside the U.S. to find new opportunities and increased returns," says Michael Tannenbaum, partner at Tannenbaum Helpern Syracuse & Hirschtritt LLP in New York. "They are finding those opportunities in inefficient oversea markets."

The phenomenon of U.S. activists utilizing their skills in other countries is provoking investors from those countries to try their hand at activism as well. The once unique U.S. and U.K. phenomenon that is activism is no longer isolated to those countries. "The principle of activism originated in the U.S. and is spreading to markets that are appreciably less familiar with it," says William Natbony, partner at Katten Muchin Rosenman LLP in New York.

But not everybody is ready to be an activist in places like the People's Republic of China. It takes an uncommon individual with the appropriate background, education, and energy to be a successful emerging market activist. Required characteristics include firsthand, unique knowledge about the emerging country and its regulations and investment environment, as well as important contacts and relationships there. But that investor typically must also have a background and financial education in the West. Such "East meets West" activists are usually the most successful. "Emerging markets are generally not understood by the investing community," says Tim Selby, a partner in Alston & Bird LLP's New York office. "There are not that many people knowledgeable enough to make thoughtful investments in many of these markets."

Finding special situations in countries that aren't typically targets of activism can give an investor the chance to produce returns that are uncorrelated, or unrelated, to the returns their U.S. rivals experience. The ability to perform well in a way that is different from other funds is, in part, driving this global activist trend. Looking for profits through activism in former Soviet-bloc countries, for example, not only helps attract fund of hedge fund capital that is looking for an edge, but it can also aid a manager in drawing a direct investor base hoping to avoid an oversaturated U.S. market. The other side of this coin is that investors may shy away from the possible risks and rewards of investing with an emerging markets activist simply because they themselves are not familiar with how it operates. "Not as many investors are interested in buying into emerging market activist funds as there are investors willing to buy U.S. activist funds," Selby says.

However, investors willing to trust these activists with their money recognize that confusion about emerging markets can be a plus. Many emerging markets, such as Russia, China, and other countries, are naturally inefficient because of their opaque or dysfunctional regulatory systems and lack of coverage by international research and analysis companies. These kinds of countries breed the types of undervalued, misunderstood companies activists seek out but can't find at home in the United States. Smart investors who can dig down and really understand a company in an emerging market are the ones that will uncover the next Microsoft in Russia, Selby says.

Becoming actively involved in trying to improve companies and unlocking their true value in these markets may be difficult and, at times, dangerous work. In some markets, only the most courageous activists are up to the task, because the chore of improving company valuations may mean pecking away at a system that is often based on corruption and theft. Activist strategies depend on legal and regulatory structures to be effective. In developing countries, those structures are not in place, creating greater risk that the activist effort will fail. In some markets, there is a possibility that the entire economy could collapse.

In Russia, for example, activist hedge fund Hermitage Capital Management Ltd. is pressing a small number of energy companies in which it invests to clean up their internal self-dealing and act more in the interests of all their shareholders. The $4 billion, 11-year-old fund describes itself as the "leading advocate of good corporate governance practices" in Russia. Managers there have taken a two-pronged approach to activism, employing both litigation and Western-style proxy contests to effect change. Their efforts have unleashed some strong adversaries. Hermitage Capital's founder, William Browder of the United Kingdom, was prohibited from returning to Russia based on an assessment that he poses a threat to national security. Many observers believe Browder's efforts to expose corruption and corporate governance problems at the companies his fund invests in led to his rejected visa.[2]

Browder is still running Hermitage behind the scenes from London, though his exile prompted a group of high-profile U.S. senators, including Senator John McCain (R-AZ) and then Senate Majority Leader Bill Frist (R-TN), to write a letter to President Bush contending that the Russian government should provide a "credible explanation as to why it is denying entry to its largest foreign portfolio investor."[3] The letter was sent to Bush prior to his participation in the July 2006, G8 Summit in St. Petersburg. That month, Russian President Vladimir Putin said he did not know why Browder was barred from entry into Russia, adding that he imagines that "he broke the laws of our country."[4]

Meanwhile, in Moscow, Hermitage Capital activists are busy at work. Sergei Ambartsumov, a fund manager, is working with other managers at the fund to identify problems and effect change at Russian energy giant OAO Gazprom. Ambartsumov, like many Russian activist investors, has a background in both Russia and the West. He studied accounting and finance at the London School of Economics and later took successive jobs in Moscow at Bank of Investment & Novations and Alfa-Bank. All this has combined to mold him into the activist investor he is today. Ambartsumov, who joined Hermitage in 2001, says corruption in Russia can be routed out if an international spotlight is put on it.

Ross Hendin of Hendin Consultants, a political communications consulting firm, points out that Hermitage isn't alone in seeking to mitigate the impact of corruption by drawing media attention to the problem. Hendin argues that former Yukos Oil CEO Mikhail Khodorkovsky tried to put a spotlight on corruption from within Russia by offering an example of how a transparent company can be successful despite Russia's corrupt business culture. When he was the CEO of Yukos Oil, Khodorkovsky subjected the energy giant to stringent, Western-style accounting standards and transparency requirements, Hendin points out. The energy company has since filed for bankruptcy and Khodorkovsky is serving an eight-year prison term in Siberia for tax evasion. Yukos shareholders believe his sentence was punishment for having political ambitions. The assets of bankrupt Yukos have since been appropriated and sold to different buyers.[5]

At Gazprom, Hermitage has tried unsuccessfully over several years to elect a director to the company's board. The corporate governance strategy involves electing a candidate to Gazprom's board that will be a strong advocate for minority shareholder interests. In Russia, a shareholder must own at least 2 percent of the voting stock of a company to nominate his candidate to the board. At Gazprom, a candidate requires the backing of roughly 7.7 percent of the outstanding votes to win the election and gain a director position. In 2006, Hermitage received a little more than 5 percent of the outstanding votes, only slightly below the margin needed to gain a seat.

To attract investor support for their director candidate, Hermitage managers each year prepare a research presentation on Gazprom that they show institutional investors. Hermitage officials believe that even a failed proxy contest attempt can produce positive returns. That's because the contest brings public attention and scrutiny to Gazprom's inefficiencies and puts pressure on its management to work in the best interest of all its shareholders, including minority investors such as Hermitage. Doing that also educates the government owners of Gazprom on what is taking place inside the company. The government directors on the board exert some oversight, but generally don't have the resources or ability to complete a thorough enough analysis and due diligence of all the company's business plans, Ambartsumov says.

For example, in 2005, Gazprom announced plans to build a new pipeline. As Gazprom started working on the project, analysts at Hermitage realized that Gazprom planned to spend significantly more capital on the pipeline than they believed it should cost. Hermitage expressed concern about the issue and made reference to it as part of their director election campaign that year. Responding to the public pressure, Gazprom reevaluated its expenditure estimates and produced more reasonable estimates, Ambartsumov says. The effort was part of Hermitage's strategy to put outside pressure on companies, executives, and directors through a public media campaign. At the time of the Gazprom director election in 2006, only 15 to 20 percent of Gazprom's shares were available for purchase by minority investors. But that may be changing in a way that could give foreign investors a greater voice. The gas giant is liberalizing its ownership structure to allow for more foreign shareholder participation. Ambartsumov says he had hoped Hermitage would launch another proxy contest for a seat in 2007, in part because Gazprom's liberalized ownership structure would likely provide additional foreign investor votes. But a Russian government list of approved nominees that was produced in February did not include Hermitage's nominee.[6] It did include a who's-who list of Kremlin-backed candidates.[7]

At another investment, Siberian-based oil and gas company OAO Surgutneftegas, Hermitage has taken another tack. The hedge fund decided early on that a proxy contest approach wouldn't work. Surgutneftegas management would surely vote against any outside influence. Its executives owned between 60 percent and 70 percent of the voting stock, making it impossible for any outside director candidate to win election to the board. Instead, Hermitage chose litigation as its modus operandi for provoking change at the company, which they considered undervalued.

In a PowerPoint presentation the investment company prepared for institutional investors, Hermitage pointed out that Surgutneftegas has underperformed when compared to its Russian peers, including Gazprom and Lukoil, between 2003 and 2005. The presentation goes on to explain that the poor share performance of the energy company can be attributed, in part, to its CEO, Vladimir Bogdanov, who has run the company as "one of the most investor-unfriendly" companies in Russia.[8] The presentation points out that in 2002 Surgutneftegas ceased publishing financial reports in Generally Accepted Accounting Principles (GAAP), the Western accounting system employed by many companies in Russia as a means to convince foreign investors that its financial accounting records meet international standards.[9] Surgutneftegas also stopped using an internationally known auditor in 2002. Meanwhile, it began accumulating a huge cash reserve.[10] In 2005, Surgutneftegas had $13.8 billion in cash on hand, up from $11 billion in 2004.[11] All these factors have discouraged most international investors, but Hermitage's managers believe that their campaign can provoke an improvement in Surgutneftegas's low stock valuation.

Surgutneftegas management owns a controlling stake in the company through Treasury shares.[12] Hermitage contends that Russian corporate law requires Treasury shares controlled by a company's management to be canceled within one year. Surgutneftegas, Ambartsumov says, continues owning the Treasury shares through a web of subsidiaries and convoluted cross-ownership structures. He adds that there is an ambiguity in Russian law about whether such an ownership structure is permitted.

Seeing that legal action could be the only way to give minority shareholders a voice in company affairs, Hermitage filed a lawsuit in March 2004. According to Russian law, a lawsuit must take place in the home jurisdiction of the company in question. So Hermitage filed its suit against Surgutneftegas with Khanty-Mansiysk arbitration court in the company's home district of Siberia.

Ambartsumov points out that shareholder cases against Russian corporations are typically lost in their home districts, but investors must go through the motions and first file a lawsuit there so they can eventually appeal the decision to a higher court. Why are shareholders not likely to win a court case against companies in their local jurisdiction? As Ambartsumov puts it, large companies, particularly in smaller Russian cities, have a tremendous influence on local political and economic life and the local population in general. The goal of Hermitage's court strategy was to bring the suit to Constitutional Court in Moscow, the closest equivalent to the Supreme Court in the United States. This court is the most transparent and least likely to be influenced by "regional meddling," Ambartsumov says.

But the road to Moscow takes time. After losing the case in Khanty-Mansiysk, Hermitage in July 2004 appealed to Federal Arbitration Court in Tyumen, Siberia. After receiving a rejection there, Hermitage filed its case with Supreme Arbitration Court in Moscow. By May 2005, Hermitage filed with Constitutional Court in Moscow, where the case is still pending.

Attempting to improve value and create greater transparency at Surgutneftegas takes an excruciating amount of time, money, patience, and will—a lot of which takes place privately even before the papers for the first lawsuit are drafted. Citizens of small towns and villages where large energy corporations such as Surgutneftegas are based generally will unconditionally support the companies that provide the jobs and are the "lifeblood" of the region. And while the cost of filing a suit itself is minimal, the research that goes into uncovering the Byzantine internal corporate structure of companies like Surgutneftegas is no small feat.

Hendin explains that Hermitage is engaged in a process at Surgutneftegas known in international legal circles as "exhaustion of local remedies." In many cases, these types of investors, Hendin says, will go through the motions of formally appealing to all local Russian courts so that they can say they made a "good faith" effort to use the domestic judicial system. This is a requirement for them to later take their case to international courts or tribunal on the grounds that they have done everything they can in the country and can't find justice or rule of law there. That said, it's unclear what Hermitage would do should its Surgutneftegas effort ultimately fail.

Ambartsumov says researchers on the Hermitage team spend hundreds of hours traveling to remote parts of Russia and investigating complex bureaucratic companies like Surgutneftegas. Vadim Kleiner, director of Hermitage's research department, is often on the road seeking out some new bits of information that can aid the investment firm's case. "Kleiner and other Hermitage officials go to Siberia and dig into local registries, collecting all these various sources bit by bit and then composing the research documents," Ambartsumov says.

A key indicator and also a source of credibility for a particular market is Morgan Stanley's Capital International Inc.'s Emerging Markets (MSCI Emerging Markets) index. The index is a benchmark for allocating capital with managers investing in eastern Europe, Asia, and other emerging markets. Fund of hedge fund managers and other institutional investors recognize that countries making up a large part of the index have sufficient liquidity and make good investment destinations. Only countries where investors can easily buy or sell stakes reasonably quickly and in large volumes without dramatically changing the stock price are included in the index. "Countries that are investable can get on the index," Ambartsumov says.

Emerging markets such as Russia, Hungary, and China still lack sufficient liquidity in the minds of many investors and therefore are too risky. As described earlier, numerous shareholders had a difficult time cashing out their Russian hedge fund investments after the 1998 ruble collapse. Early investors seeking to cash out their stakes were paid off by the fund selling down its liquid holdings, leaving other investors with illiquid stakes that could not be sold. The whole experience acted as a warning to investors and initially discouraged capital allocation to Russia and other Eastern European countries that were also hurt by the economic situation. Many hedge funds investing in Russia collapsed, including Rurik Investment, Russia Value Fund, and Signet New Capital, while others like Hermitage experienced an extremely difficult period. Hermitage had –88.63 percent return in 1998.[13]

Investing in a market that could experience an economic collapse is just one of the liquidity risks that activists and their investors must consider. A market's currency could be unstable or a lack of financial transparency may make it difficult to really gauge whether a company is performing well or not.

Hermitage's endeavor to have Surgutneftegas convert its financials to GAAP is an example of the kind of thing activists in emerging markets employ to effect change. Activists can improve their comfort level for an investment by prodding their target corporations into westernizing their accounting mechanisms and hiring credible outside auditing firms to approve financial statements. On the other hand, activists that can understand the non-GAAP financials produced by companies in emerging markets have an advantage over other investors less willing to take the time and energy to understand a particular company. "The activist can take the position that they understand the financial reports here even though they are not consistent with GAAP, but the company is a great performer that will only improve," Selby says.

Even more so than other types of hedge funds, activists in emerging markets must reflect on their ability to find a buyer for their stakes should their investment sour. More traditional hedge fund managers can buy large numbers of tiny stakes in a variety of companies in emerging markets. That enables them to move more nimbly in and out of markets. Activists, however, must buy large stakes that are much more difficult to sell under duress or even in the best circumstances. Emerging market investing can come with many complications. The market could collapse, a legal challenge may fail, or it becomes apparent that a particular effort to unlock value will not succeed. Activists that own large stakes in illiquid stocks will likely move the market when they buy or sell. Buying a stake will increase the stock price, making it more expensive to buy more. Selling a huge block bit by bit will have the effect of lowering the price of an illiquid stock, also an unwelcome prospect.

That's why activists seeking to sell a block of shares will want that trade to take place immediately. However, buying or selling large blocks of shares in illiquid markets may take time. An activist may place an order to sell a block of a particular stock at $10 a share at one moment, but because of a lack of interested buyers, those securities may be picked up at lower prices, over a longer period of time. The activist may get $10 a share for some of the block, but only $9.50 and $8 a share for the rest of it over several months.

All this is discouraging news for activists in emerging markets. Managers don't want to feel like they are locked into a particular investment. In one respect, activists that cannot sell a stake may lose their leverage with the company they are targeting. An activist investor that has a large position, say 5 or 10 percent, but is unable to garner much support from the rest of the investor base, typically will have an even more difficult time effecting change if the managers at the company realize that divesting the stake will be difficult. "A target company that realizes that the activist is stuck in the investment can call the shots," says Tannenbaum.

The other possibility is that emerging market companies with extremely illiquid shares run the risk that an activist with a meaningfully large stake could consider acquiring the company and turning it around. "If the activist can't vote with his feet at a company going into the ground, he may consider buying the business as a solution," Selby says. "It could cut both ways."

Settlement procedures in emerging illiquid markets are often cumbersome and problematic. In the high-volume U.S. markets an investor seeking to buy 1,000 shares of IBM will receive those shares almost instantaneously after submitting the order. But in emerging illiquid markets, that trade may take longer because of the more bureaucratic systems in place. "It's not like eBay, where the payment is transferred immediately electronically to your PayPal account," Tannenbaum says.

Natbony points out that the combination of liquidity problems and the greater difficulty activists have in emerging markets because of regulatory, corruption, or legal issues compounds the risks investors take when they chose to become insurgents under these circumstances. "There is a real liquidity difference between western European companies and eastern European companies," Natbony says.

But many emerging countries are experiencing greater liquidity and increased foreign investor presence—all good news for activists that like to operate in these markets. Countries that are included on the MSCI Emerging Markets index generally have more foreign investments and higher liquidity and could be more accessible to activists. Russian energy giants, such as Gazprom, are slowly becoming more liquid, a positive trend for activists that invest in oil and gas companies based in former soviet bloc countries.

Gazprom was almost not represented in the index, but recent liberalization plans by Russian President Vladimir Putin have changed all that. A few years ago, Gazprom represented only 3 percent of MSCI Russia, which was only a small component of the overall MSCI Emerging Markets index. In May 2006, the first stage of opening up Gazprom to foreign investors took place and Russia increased to roughly 8.7 percent of the index. In August 2006, the second stage took place, and Russia rose to 11 percent of the index.

Some emerging markets, such as Ukraine, don't have sufficient liquidity to be included in the influential index. In fact, only $7 million to $10 million is traded daily on the Kiev International Stock Exchange. That's a pittance compared with what one large-capitalization stock trades on a major U.S. exchange in a day—or even the $300 million daily turnover of shares on Russian exchanges. The result: investing in Ukraine is even more risky for activists than some other emerging countries, though the returns can also be better if managers can effect change. "There are more possibilities for greater rewards, yet the ability to achieve better rewards carries greater risks," Natbony says. "If you buy a huge stake in a troubled company in a country with an opaque regulatory system and are successful at unleashing a catalyst to improve value, then that return will likely be much better because so many others are discounting the value of the stock."

In other words, the spread between the buy and the sell in opaque, illiquid, and often corrupt markets is much greater. Dorian Foyil, president of Foyil Asset Management, has embraced the risks of investing in emerging countries and for him the rewards have been great, lately. Foyil's Eastern Europe and Russia Focused Fund reported 32.9 percent returns in 2006 and 74.5 percent returns in 2005. His fund buys large stakes in roughly 50 companies and at any time one stake can represent as much as 30 percent of the total portfolio. It's still a small fund by international standards, with roughly $60 million in assets under management. That's up from $9 million in 2005 and $500,000 in 1999.

Foyil attributes his fund's success in large part to its investment in Ukraine, where he and the majority of his staff of 72 are based. His approach focuses on pressuring or collaborating with Ukrainian companies in an effort to speed their adoption of Western governance and accounting standards. However, the effort has taken an extraordinary amount of time and patience and involved a significant amount of risk—personal and professional.

The fund has about 60 percent of its assets in Ukraine, while the remaining capital is invested mostly in Russia, with smaller allocations in Hungary and Poland. Foyil agrees that the Ukrainian market has liquidity issues that turn off many potential investors. But he points out that what makes the market less attractive can also make investing there more appealing. The lack of liquidity, he says, results in market inefficiencies that can be exploited for strong returns in a way that minimizes risks to investors. To do that effectively requires feet on the ground in Ukraine, he says. It requires researchers that will dig down to truly understand the companies in those markets. Foyil's research team includes nine analysts with varying financial expertise and backgrounds from Ukraine, Azerbaijan, Belarus, Russia, and Scotland.

A background in Western capitalism, of course, is also a necessity. Foyil, a California native, studied accounting and computer science at Temple University in Philadelphia before completing a master's in business administration from the Wharton School of Business at the University of Pennsylvania. Out of school, Foyil took a job at the international investment bank UBS, in corporate finance and international sales. Shortly after that, Foyil moved to London, where he became a securities analyst focusing on continental European telecommunications equipment and service companies. Later, value investing firm, Franklin Templeton Investments, a UBS client, hired Foyil to manage a portfolio known as the Greater European Fund. At the time, this fund invested beyond Western European countries by allocating capital to companies in emerging markets. Foyil was permitted to invest in Hungary and Poland, but whenever he sought approval to allocate funds to other emerging markets such as Russia, Estonia, Czech Republic or Ukraine, Franklin Templeton's board was reluctant to grant that authority. At the time,

Ukraine was just beginning its privatization process and Foyil felt he had to act right away to take advantage of the possibilities there.

So, in November 1996, Foyil launched his own fund in the rough-and-tumble world of Ukrainian finance. His investment vehicle, the Ukrainian Opportunities Fund, was a closed-end fund. Its structure permitted Foyil to invest heavily in illiquid securities. Roughly 75 percent of the fund's assets were invested in Ukraine and results were good early on. The strategy was voucher privatization. In the 1990s, after the fall of communism, Ukraine and many other eastern European countries began giving citizens books of vouchers or coupons representing shares in formerly state-owned companies. Foyil set up a so-called "Skupka team" of 30 or so people he hired to go knock on the doors of pensioners and employees, seeking to buy their vouchers or shares in privatized Ukrainian companies. Every three weeks, Foyil rented an armored truck to physically bring the vouchers to a government office and have them registered. Through this process, Foyil accumulated huge minority stakes in many companies. "We were buying privatization certificates by the boatloads," Foyil says. Foyil points out that at one time in the late 1990s his investment vehicle was the third largest holder of the privatization vouchers in Ukraine.

The investment approach worked exceptionally for less than a year, until the 1998 Russian economic collapse. At that point Foyil's returns tanked and assets declined by 50 percent. Large emerging market hedge funds, such as Renaissance Capital, closed their Ukraine shops. Foreign investor interest dried up, as it did in Russia and other Eastern European markets. But Foyil was there to stay, partly because his fund's structure wouldn't let him leave. Ukrainian Opportunities Fund's bylaws prohibited withdrawal of certain funds. Its remaining investment capital, roughly $50 million, was tied up in illiquid Ukrainian securities. Foyil says he had no choice but to continue investing in Ukraine as everyone else was pulling out. Instead of passively sitting on his stakes, Foyil aggressively began buying up many large blocks of companies that other investors were despondently selling.

By purchasing company shares for "pennies on the dollar," Foyil ended up building large positions in Ukraine's brewery, paper, machinery, and chemicals sectors. In 2003, instead of shutting down the fund, Foyil decided to merge it with what would eventually become his flagship fund: the Eastern Europe and Russia Focused Fund. This time around, Foyil decided he would diversify his investments, focusing a larger chunk of his stakes in Russia and other markets. Even still, Ukraine assets represented the largest part of the investments.

In the process of recovering, which took roughly four and a half years, Foyil found it was necessary to take a proactive role in many of his investments. That's not to say he wasn't actively managing in his previous investments. Foyil met frequently with executives, other investors, and intermediaries working for accounting firms, investment banks, and stock exchanges. In many cases, gaining control of boards or, at the very least, putting independent representation on boards was a necessary tactic to align the incentives of directors and executives with shareholders. To a certain extent, nominating director candidates to boards wasn't particularly difficult. According to Ukrainian regulations, any shareholder with a 10 percent or greater stake in a company could call a special or extraordinary shareholder meeting and control the agenda of that meeting. Foyil employed this tactic frequently to nominate his own director slates for election to company boards.

At the special meetings, Foyil and his team would make a presentation to shareholders outlining a number of factors he believed could improve performance. These points invariably focused on urging the company to produce more frequent financial reports, having those documents meet international accounting standards, and encouraging Ukranian company to hire Western auditors. The strategy was to make Ukrainian companies more attractive to Western investors that otherwise would ignore the opaque Ukraine market. One key initiative was to encourage companies to buy shares in the open market and award the shares to executives. The CEOs of most Ukrainian corporations owned little or no stock and, consequently, had little interest in improving the share value, Foyil says. But executives with shares in the company had a modest incentive to run the business in the best interest of shareholders, Foyil says. In many cases, shares were provided as a form of end-of-the-year bonuses.

OJSC Rogan Brewery, once the second largest brewery in Ukraine, benefited from an effort to grant shares to executives. Foyil accumulated a 25 percent stake in the brewery and urged its managers to auction the business to a Western strategic buyer. To expedite matters, Foyil in 2000 called an extraordinary shareholder meeting, in which he nominated himself to the company's board. At the meeting, Foyil encouraged the brewery to award shares to its managers and make its financial reports compatible with Western accounting standards. Foyil's campaign worked, and he was elected to the board. More importantly, says Foyil, executives received shares in the company. Shortly after that, Rogan Brewery put up a for sale sign. In 2001, it was sold to Belgium brewery, Interbrew NV. Foyil attributes the timely sale to management's newfound stake in the company. Eastern Europe and Russia Focused Fund did well in the auction, posting a 400 percent return on its investment, he says. "By the time they [executives] sold the business, they had made six times the return on their shares," Foyil exclaims.

Foyil launched a more difficult and even dangerous effort at a northwestern Ukraine-based cement company. At this business, Foyil, who owned a 10 percent stake, had little difficulty calling a special meeting to promote his agenda. The problem was actually making sure the extraordinary meeting took place.

Foyil accumulated his 10 percent stake in Volyn Cement Zdolbunivske, a cement company based in Volyn, a province in northwestern Ukraine, through voucher privatization. But by 2001, a Ukrainian financial institution, Grado Bank, had acquired a 54 percent stake in Volyn by appropriating shares, Foyil argues, that they hadn't paid for.

Foyil described the situation like this: Grado bank officials made extraordinarily high bids in Volyn's voucher privatization auctions, but purportedly bribed state officials so they could delay or avoid paying for the coupons. Officials were also probably bribed, he says, to provide information about the bidding process so that Grado bankers could outbid the highest offer. With that information in hand, Foyil says, Grado managers could be assured no one would out bid them.

As new owners of Volyn, Grado Bank stopped paying salaries and suppliers. Equipment and maintenance payments were cut off. Volyn's executives were laid off and replaced. In fact, Grado Bank was attempting to consolidate the Ukrainian cement industry through an investment vehicle called Monolith. Shutting down Volyn's operations was a key part of that strategy. Grado bank allegedly paid off Volyn directors to look the other way while any profit the company produced was siphoned out of the business, as part of their strategy, at the expense of its employees and shareholders, Foyil says. "The idea was to delay payment and make as much money as possible in a minimal period of time."

At one point, 25 percent of Grado's stake was seized by the state property fund. It was then that Foyil realized he had an opportunity to wrest control of the cement company away from Grado. First he pulled two people from his research staff to focus their entire attention on this "special project." Then he proceeded to increase his stake in Volyn Cement to 40 percent. After that, he approached the state property fund to see if officials there would vote the 25 percent stake seized from Grado toward electing director candidates nominated by Foyil in a proxy contest. The state fund appeared supportive, so Foyil launched his proxy contest. Only at this annual meeting Foyil believed he had irritated some pretty hostile opponents. A major effort to make sure the meeting would take place was necessary.

He hired a personal security team complete with two Mercedes minivans, an ex–Ukrainian internal security official and a mini-battalion of 40 soldiers. Foyil says he wasn't worried so much about possible violent retribution from a major block holder of Volyn's stock, as he was that someone might cut the power to the meeting hall prior to the extraordinary meeting. According to Ukrainian laws, no electricity meant the meeting could not go on. Cutting the power prior to the meetings was, at the time, a typical way Ukraine's underbelly of investors could achieve their goals of blocking change. En route to the meeting, Foyil says, his security detail transferred him from a black minivan to a red van as part of its strategy to throw off potential pursuers.

Upon arriving at the location of the meeting, Foyil found that the mini-battalion of soldiers he had hired was completing military exercises around the grounds. At one point the battalion surrounded the building and began marching back and forth. In his effort to make sure the meeting took place as scheduled, with no interferences, Foyil sent word to Kiev-based television media to cover the event. "We did everything to make sure that if there was an incident that would spoil the meeting, there would be a record of it so we could fight it in court if we had to," Foyil says.

The meeting did take place. Foyil voted his 40 percent stake for his own slate of directors. That, combined with the support of the state fund's 25 percent stake and Foyil's slate of directors was installed. Shortly after the meeting, Foyil hired former Volyn executives that were thrown out by Grado Bank and began the process of restructuring the company so that it could eventually be marketed in an auction to foreign buyers.

But during the Grado period, Volyn Cement had deteriorated significantly and was on the verge of bankruptcy. Foyil provided a loan to the company to pay for immediate bills. He cut a deal with the state tax administration to postpone and reschedule late payments. Energy suppliers were also paid. The strategy, he says, was to elevate Volyn to a level where it could buy its own raw materials and return to profitability.

Soon afterward, Volyn organized a sale memorandum. Foyil says he expected at most two foreign strategic buyers to express enough of an interest in Volyn Cement to trek out to Ukraine to complete a due diligence. Surprisingly, seven companies came. Many cement companies from Europe and Japan expressed an interest, including Heidelberg-Cement AG of Germany, Lafarge S.A. of France, and Cemex S.A. de C.V. of Mexico, in addition to others. In the end, Dyckerhoff Zement International Gmbh of Germany won the auction.

Foyil's two-and-a-half year effort at Volyn netted a 115 percent return on his investment. Meanwhile, Grado Bank's investment was diluted and the institution subsequently filed for bankruptcy. One of Grado's key officials, a Ukrainian legislator, was arrested in Germany. He was suspected of being involved in the disappearance of roughly 87 million Deutsche Marks that had been allocated by the German government to pay as reparations to victims of the Holocaust.[14] Grado Bank had won a tender to distribute the funds, Foyil says. "It wasn't that we were trying to change the world, we were just trying to move the company forward," Foyil says.

Looking back at the Volyn effort, Foyil says, he can barely believe the things he did to make sure the company restructured correctly. "Everybody was freaked out in those years," Foyil says. "I look back and think, 'Wow, that was an extreme reaction,' but it was necessary at the time."

More recently, Foyil says, engaging with Ukrainian corporations no longer requires such extreme efforts. Corporate chieftains, he says, are realizing that there is value in talking to shareholders. Managers understand that greater disclosure, Western accounting methods, and a heavily traded stock can make them richer, he says. Instead of pressing companies to make changes in a combative manner, as he might have in the past, Foyil finds that lately, he has been able to collaborate with executives to improve shareholder value.

In 2006, Foyil hosted his second CEO summit, an educational conference bringing in roughly 150 Ukrainian company executives to meet with Western accounting firms, investment banks, and venture capitalists. Key speakers included representatives from the London Stock Exchange and U.K.-based research firms. The event, Foyil says, was set up with the purpose of educating Ukrainian executives in ways they can heighten their profile to international investors. Seminars included lectures on how to take your Ukrainian company public on the London Stock Exchange; how to attract Western analyst firms to cover your company; and why employing an investor relations representative is important to improving communications between company officials and shareholders.

Foyil is also optimistic that Ukraine will soon be added to the MSCI index. Being part of that index will be the catalyst to propel many Ukrainian companies onto the international stage, Foyil says. But even without it, he argues that the Ukrainian market is already more liquid and less risky than international investors perceive it to be. International rating firms, including Moody's Corporation and Standard & Poor's are already rating Ukrainian company bonds. These rating firms are also willing to complete private valuations for Ukrainian companies seeking to sell assets to foreign buyers. To succeed in emerging markets requires a big-picture, long-term perspective, Foyil says. Managers that want to be catalysts for change in Ukraine can't be based in New York or London. Dedicated hedge fund managers must be physically in Ukraine, meeting with executives on a regular basis for their funds to succeed, he says.

Activist investors also need to physically be in these countries not just to meet CEOs but also to establish relationships with political officials, who can use their influence to further their economic interests. Hendin says investors need to know the specifics of local business and political culture to be successful. "Lobbying" can take on entirely different forms in an emerging market than in a developed one. "An investment manager needs to be on the ground in emerging markets to keep the wheels spinning smoothly and make sure solid connections are being made and maintained," Hendin says.

Most of all, Foyil says, activist investors taking their skills to emerging markets need to believe that the backwards, corrupt, fraud-infested markets can turn around. Shareholders who don't want to take the time to understand Ukraine or other eastern European countries won't understand the potential there. Foyil acknowledges that, at times, even he lost his faith in believing that Ukraine could turn around. But he persevered onward. "If you believe that the world will never change, then you are not likely to invest in Ukraine," Foyil says.

But Foyil, Warren Lichtenstein, and other activists have decided that the world will change, or, at the least, they can change it—one company at a time. For many activists, the greater challenges that come with investing in opaque, illiquid, and often volatile countries such as Russia, China, and Ukraine are worth it. Intuitively, these activists understand that their long-term blood, sweat, and tears can and will make a difference in unlocking the value of companies in these regions.

For these activists, being the catalyst is really the only way value can be achieved. There is a major distinction that needs to be made between activists in emerging countries and insurgents in the United States and other Western nations. U.S. activists can expect many of their undervalued investments to improve in value even if their efforts at unleashing a catalyst are unsuccessful. At the same time, activists in emerging countries, which face the most intransient of corporations, know that without their efforts share prices will likely remain low or tank altogether.

Consequently, activists in these emerging countries are employing a wide variety of tools to provoke the corporate changes they deem necessary. Whether it is Hermitage Capital's litigation approach at Surgutneftegas or Foyil's special meetings, proxy contests, and armed escorts at Volyn, activism in emerging markets comes with its own challenges, risks, and price tags. Bribery is a routine cost of doing business in many emerging countries. Just understanding how the system works brings with it a whole other layer of complexities that just aren't there in Western countries with established and transparent regulatory regimes. Obscure accounting procedures, cultural and language differences all lead to complications. In effect, Western activism in emerging countries is a little like walking at night in a forest. Every step leads the investor deeper into the unknown. Only with time and practice can results be obtained.

Chapter 22

Value Investing versus Activism

Which One Is Better?

Mohnish Pabrai, managing partner at Pabrai Investment Funds of Irvine, California, is a true value investor. Fundamental laws of investing have shaped his investment strategy, and those laws do not involve investor-management communications.

The approach has worked for Pabrai. He produced 28.6 percent returns on his investment, year-on-year, after fees since his fund's inception in July 1999. Investing $100,000 with Pabrai in 1999 would have netted roughly $660,000 after all fees and expenses by the end of 2006.

Unlike activist investors, at no point will Pabrai engage or even seek to talk to the executives at the companies he allocates funds. Executives at one company called him one day to see if he had any advice or ideas. Pabrai, an 18 percent investor in the corporation, says the call was a big mistake. "I have never made a phone call to any management of any of the companies I am an investor in," Pabrai says. "The way I see it, if they need my help, there is a problem."

For Pabrai, executives are to be left alone to concentrate their energy on operating businesses. Pabrai's background demonstrates a respect for executives. Born in Mumbai, India, Pabrai moved to the United States where he was employed as an engineer. In 1990, Pabrai launched his own business that Trans-Tech Inc., a systems integration information technology company that employed over 225 people before he sold it in 2000. Around the same time, he created DigitalDistrupters.com, a company that came up with ideas for Internet businesses. DigitalDistrupters.com folded, in part, due to Pabrai's inability to raise sufficient capital. But despite the setback, Pabrai's business operational background left an indelible impression on his mind-set toward executives, investing, and activist investors. "Let CEOs focus on the business," Pabrai says. "My energy is much better spent doing securities analysis than trying to add value to companies."

The strategy of the pure-play value investor runs counter to the fundamental approach that activists take, yet it has produced strong returns for Pabrai and many other value investors. Value investor returns, on average, are comparable to that of activists. According to Morningstar Inc., value-oriented mutual funds had average annual returns of 18 percent in 2006, 5.87 in 2005, and 13.25 percent in 2004. Meanwhile, activist hedge funds averaged 16.72 percent returns in 2006, 16.43 percent in 2005, and 23.16 percent in 2004, according to Hedge Fund Research.

Pabrai questions whether activists, in their drive to raise the value of corporate shares, are actually improving the long-term businesses interests of their target companies. However, he does feel strongly that CEOs and directors should make their own investments in the stock of the companies they oversee, as a means of aligning their interests with shareholders.

Opportunity Partners' Phillip Goldstein takes issue with the idea that activists aren't contributing to the long-term viability of corporations. He says activists must gain the approval of institutional investors, who are typically invested in the business for the long term, for their strategies to come to fruition. Consequently, he adds, activist strategies cannot gain traction if they do not have the approval of a sufficiently large number of long-term investors who are interested in the future outlook for the company. The partial loss and partial victory for Carl Icahn at Time Warner is proof that institutions are looking for long-term results, Goldstein says. At Time Warner, institutions opposed Icahn's proposal for splitting the company up. The media company did hike its stock buyback plan in response to Icahn, demonstrating that the activist did gain some traction with long-term institutions.

Which approach is better? Goldstein says it's unfair to compare the profitability of the two approaches. It depends on a case-by-case, fund-by-fund analysis. Either can be successful or a failure in different instances, and when one strategy is successful, it often may be because it took advantage of the other strategy.

There are some definitive differences and similarities. While value investors, for the most part, quietly sit and wait for their investment to appreciate, activists must be successful at wooing other investors to support their efforts. Traditional value investors are skilled at researching companies and finding ones that will appreciate in value in the next few years. Like value investors, most activists will also buy stakes in companies they consider undervalued. The authors of the 2006 study, "Hedge Fund Activism, Corporate Governance and Firm Performance," discovered that two-thirds of the hundreds of activist 13Ds they sampled between 2004 and 2005 had statements reporting that the dissident shareholder believed the companies they were investing in were undervalued.[1] "Our analysis of the target's financial statements further shows that targets resemble companies typically sought by value investors," the study reports.

But unlike traditional value investors, activists will use their knowledge of the company's legal structure, their ability to file lawsuits, engage and negotiate with management, and launch proxy fights to provoke change and improve value. Insurgents argue that value investors must be careful not to fall in the value trap, that is, invest in a company they expect to appreciate in value within five years and find out five years later that because of management or external factors that company still remains intractably undervalued. Activists argue that they don't fall into the value trap because they agitate to engender changes while passive value investors sit back and wait for share improvements to happen on their own.

But activist hedge fund managers can fall into a similar trap, we'll call it the activist trap. Insurgents expect the time and capital they invest in a particular situation will provoke a catalyst, but if five years later nothing has happened and the company remains in the doldrums, or even worse, bankrupt, the manager has fallen into the activist trap. An argument can be made that falling into the activist trap can be more dangerous than the value trap. The insurgent will have spent such a large amount of time, energy, and capital to provoke value that if no result is produced, the overall result is more likely to hurt the fund than a traditional value investor who has invested less in an unsuccessful value trap allocation.

Zeke Ashton, founder of $50 million Dallas-based value fund Centaur Capital Partners, says a key difference between activists and value investors is temperament. "To be a successful activist investor, in many cases, takes a confrontational personality," Ashton says. "It requires someone that will fight with management to accomplish certain goals."

Goldstein agrees that temperament is important to the approach. A successful activist can't get aggravated or lose sleep when faced with lawsuits or screaming CEOs. He adds that an activist must enjoy being the catalyst. "How much abuse can you take before you say this is not right?" Goldstein asks. "You can't be a shrinking violet and run for cover anytime somebody sues you; otherwise, you're going to get bullied."

Many traditional value managers will become reluctant activists if they become sufficiently aggravated about a particular situation. Even value investor extraordinaire Warren Buffett, arguably the most successful stock picker, has on occasion taken an activist tack. In a 2001 conference call, Buffett expressed his displeasure with real estate company Aegis Realty Inc.'s decision to buy P.O'B. Montgomery & Company, a Dallas-based shopping center developer, for $203 million.[2] He also was involved in several quarrels with management of Berkshire Hathaway before he bought enough shares to take over the company in 1962.[3]

Value investor Christopher H. Browne, managing director of Tweedy, Browne Company LLC, also grudgingly engages in reluctant activist efforts in some situations, when provoked. Tweedy Browne, which at one time attracted value investor Benjamin Graham as a significant investor, manages roughly $10 billion in mutual fund and hedge fund assets following its strategy of seeking out and investing in undervalued companies. Browne's most well-known activist effort took place in 2003 at Hollinger International Inc. After receiving a damning evaluation of Hollinger from a Tweedy analyst, Browne demanded an investigation into what role the media company's board had played in authorizing payments to a private holding company controlled by the corporation's CEO, Conrad Black. The report, which was over 500 pages long, accused Black and others of siphoning over $400 million out of Hollinger's coffers while its stock deteriorated.

Browne later filed a lawsuit seeking roughly $5 million in legal fees for Tweedy Browne lawyers from Hollinger, for their contribution to the efforts that ultimately led to Black's removal.[4] Hollinger agreed to pay Tweedy Browne lawyers $3.5 million in a settlement.[5] But at the end of the costly, drawn-out process, it appears that Browne believes the whole effort may not have been worthwhile, from a shareholder's perspective. In March 2007, the *Globe and Mail* quoted Browne as saying he believes Hollinger shareholders are in a worse position and that if he could turn back time, he would never have engaged Black.[6]

A long, drawn-out litigious process was exactly what reluctant activist Whitney Tilson, cofounder of value shop T2 Partners, did not want at Cutter & Buck, a Seattle-based clothes maker. But after it became apparent that Cutter & Buck had embellished its 2000 revenue figures, Tilson realized he needed to take some action to expedite the recovery of the company.[7] Its stock was slowly tanking. At the time, T2 Partners held roughly a 2 percent stake in Cutter & Buck. That stake represented about 6 percent of the total funds Tilson had under management, a material position for him. He became the lead plaintiff in a class action shareholder lawsuit, with the stated purpose of quickly reaching a settlement so that the company could regain its focus on the business. Tilson says his efforts worked to expedite the whole process. In June 2003, Cutter & Buck settled with Tilson and other investors by agreeing to pay $4 million in cash to shareholders as part of the settlement.[8] "I thought joining the lawsuit was the best way to protect my interests," Tilson says. "A prolonged lawsuit would only slow down the company's recovery."

Roughly a year later, Cutter & Buck's CEO asked Tilson to take a seat on the company's board. Right around the same time, activist investor Pirate Capital bought a large Cutter & Buck stake and threatened to launch a proxy contest. Tilson found himself on the other end of an activist effort. By September 2005, Pirate agreed to drop its contest after Cutter & Buck arranged to remove certain anti-takeover proposals. In April 2007, Cutter & Buck was sold to Swedish apparel maker New Wave Group AB for $156.5 million.[9]

Steven Romick, a partner at value investor First Pacific Advisors in Los Angeles, typically sticks to the shadows. But on a few occasions, he's taken an activist tack at companies. After reviewing Big Lots Inc.'s compensation plan, Romick called up the chairman of the Columbus, Ohio–based retailer's compensation committee and expressed concern about the company's stock option plan. He subsequently wrote the committee a letter, saying he planned to vote against the stock option plan. Later, Romick changed his position and voted for the plan after the company gave him verbal assurances that certain goals would be reached before options were granted. Now Romick is in a wait-and-see position. "It's easy to meet these requirements when the company is doing well, but we'll see if they continue granting options when the company isn't doing so well," Romick says.

The best investors, says Goldstein, are those that can adeptly engage in both value and activist strategies based on changing circumstances. Managers that can quickly transform their strategy from passive to activist when a situation calls for it are likely to be the most successful investors, he adds. Tilson says he believes actively engaging executives behind the scenes is a critical part of making a value investment strategy work. In addition to talking with executives, Romick says he, like most activists, will complete a thorough due diligence. That means talking to suppliers, customers, other investors, and anyone that can help gauge the value of the company. Romick adds that he even, on occasion, hires someone to check up on management. "Buying a stake only according to numbers is not enough," he says.

Tilson says he meets with executives, particularly at smaller companies, that have the time to talk individually to all their shareholders. At larger companies, it becomes difficult to schedule a meeting with the CEO, particularly when the value investor owns only a small stake in the company. But, Tilson says, he can get exposure to these executives through conference calls and their public presentations at conferences. "Some value investors need to meet CEOs, look them in the eye, and get a feel for them before they decide to invest," Tilson says.

Once we acknowledge that many value investors, like activists, engage executives, it becomes apparent that each strategy cannot be looked at in isolation. Goldstein says he gets many of his best investment ideas from value investors that own stakes in undervalued companies. With some investments, value investors realize that the company's stock may never appreciate in value, or at least not in the time frame they would like to see it happen. In a typical circumstance, a management team throws up roadblocks and the company's stock continues to plummet. The value investor has fallen into the value trap, by owning a particular stock for a number of years, expecting that it would have already improved in value through a variety of manners. In some cases, they take actions on their own. In other cases, Goldstein says, many value investors turn to him or other activists for help. "They want to see if I can provoke some change," Goldstein says.

In other situations, successful value investors have so much capital under management that they have no choice but to become activists. Fund of hedge funds manager Michael Van Biema points out that Bill Ackman of the hedge fund Pershing Square Capital was originally a traditional passive value investor who found over time that it was more difficult to continue generating consistently good returns, particularly as more and more investors signed up to his fund. With more capital, Ackman was under increased pressure to find more value investment ideas that not only generated strong returns, but also met the diversification and liquidity demands of his fund, Van Biema says. Ackman decided that to maintain his level of profit he needed to invest in larger companies, such as McDonald's, and begin agitating for change, Van Biema says. "As his asset base got bigger, it became harder for him to wait for returns at the little niche undervalued companies he was invested in," Van Biema says. "He moved into the activist world because he wants to sustain his returns but had a difficult time doing it and at the same time continue to bring in new investors."

In many cases, value investors are already owners of stocks when activists arrive on the scene. Centaur Capital's Ashton points out that he already had a stake in McDonald's before Ackman began to publicly pressure the company to improve its value. Centaur Capital also was a shareholder of Blair Corporation before Goldstein and Santa Monica Partners Lawrence Goldstein began their public pressure campaign there.

(The activists helped convince Blair to sell its receivable division for $176 million in 2005.[10]) But, Ashton adds, value investors are less likely to buy a stock once an activist has started to publicly advocate for change. In many cases, these securities have already risen to the point where it becomes less attractive to buy a stake, Ashton says.

But in some circumstances, value investors will pile in after activists launch public campaigns. In some cases, the stock price continues to rise after an activist 13D is filed, says T2 Partners' Tilson. In those situations, Tilson, like Ashton, is unlikely to make an immediate investment. But in many circumstances, Tilson adds, the stock price of the company the activist is publicly targeting dips back down to a level Tilson is willing to buy. Sometimes, Tilson says, the stock price dips to below what even the activist paid to buy it before taking their insurgency public. In many of those cases, Tilson says, he will buy shares based on the expectation that the activist will ultimately succeed at creating an event that produces significant value. "We're delighted to see activists come into a situation," Tilson says. "Activists focus management and board attention on capital allocation."

Before investing, Tilson says he will consider the activist's track record and reputation. He also takes time to analyze the stock and mull over the likelihood that value creation could take place. Tilson says he also finds investment tips through conversations with activists. "In many situations, the company an activist engages publicly will put out a quarterly report and the stock drops to a more reasonable price," Tilson says. "Then we can pick it up, anticipating the activist will ultimately succeed at unleashing a catalyst."

In addition to keeping an eye on 13Ds, Tilson also monitors 13F filings to find investment ideas. These are the Securities and Exchange Commission (SEC) filings investment managers must periodically file to publicly disclose their investment choices (the same filings Opportunity's Goldstein would like to see axed).

When activists begin to assert themselves at a company, value investors in the stock must start evaluating whether they will be supportive. First Pacific Advisors' Romick says a key part of his decision making in these kinds of situations is based, in part, on his ability to find a new home for any capital the insurgent can extract from the business. "If an activist is pressing a company to sell out or do a leveraged recapitalization,

I am more willing to support their action if I know where to redeploy my capital," Romick says.

Another critical difference between activists and value investors is the size of stakes they are willing to purchase. Ashton says he would need to allocate his entire $50 million fund in a company with a $1 billion stock market capitalization to buy a meaningful enough position for any activist style agitation to have an effect. Most value investors will buy smaller stakes and their lesser size limits the clout they have with executives. A value investor with a 1 percent to 3 percent stake in a company won't take the time and capital to file a lawsuit or launch a proxy contest, simply because any potential reward simply will not cover the cost of their investment. On the other side of that spectrum, only activists with a significant amount of capital can have any meaningful impact at the companies they engage.

Sometimes value investors infuriate activists with their passive approach. Opportunity Partners' Goldstein says he recently approached a value investor who held a substantial position in a company to see if that manager would support a possible proxy fight he was considering. Goldstein was contemplating a proxy contest to oust directors and pressure executives there to sell the business. The support of this particular value investor would go a long way toward putting sufficient pressure on the company's management. But without them, Goldstein says, he didn't believe he had enough leverage to sway the executives.

"I said to them that I believed the company was on a course for declining value and that it needed something to change its direction," Goldstein says. The value investment fund managers responded in a way Goldstein didn't expect. No decision would be made one way or another on a proxy contest until it happened. The manager was unable to tell Goldstein whether he would support his possible endeavor. "Do they even know why they own the stock?" Goldstein asked. "They want to stay aloof, but what they are doing is harming their investors."

In such situations, where value fund managers are unable to make a decision, Goldstein says he wonders whether value investors are fulfilling their fiduciary duty to shareholders by failing to engage management. "If they don't make these kinds of decisions because it's a lot of work for them, they may be breaching their fiduciary duty to their investors," Goldstein says.

Carlo Cannell, who runs Cannell Capital LLC, agrees that at times he needs to take action with obstinate investments; otherwise, he wouldn't be fulfilling his fiduciary duty to investors. Cannell says his firm's investments run the gamut from value investing to long-short or distressed-debt capital allocations. At times, Cannell says, he will engage in activist investing. But he won't take on that strategy full time.

To explain why he doesn't think becoming a dedicated activist is the best strategy for success, Cannell points to his old, beat-up gray file cabinet. The cabinet, which he bought used in 1992, has four sections, with files on hundreds of companies. Some files are thick and hold as many as 200 pages of documents representing all the activist efforts that Cannell has launched at a particular company. These typically include depositions, exhibits, SEC filings, and other papers. Most of the files, though, are thin dossiers with 15 or fewer pages. Comparing profits from investments with the size of each investment's file, Cannell made an interesting discovery: "There is an inverse relationship between the size of the file and the return on the investment," Cannell says. "Large files are our activist efforts, and they require a lot of time, capital and energy."

Cannell says he suspects that professional activist investors have fewer files than he has, though he imagines that all of their files are thick with documents. He also suspects that the amount of work full-time activists need to put in to produce a significant return, in many cases, is significantly greater than the profit obtained. In other words, the costs outweigh the benefits, he says.

But, that said, Cannell will engage in activism reluctantly if a situation emerges that cannot be ignored. A situation fitting that description unfolded at market research firm Opinion Research Corporation. This company eventually became one of Cannell's fatter files, yet the jury is still out on whether the cost of taking an activist approach here was worth all the spent energy and capital.

Originally, Cannell held a passive investment in the market research firm. In 2004, LLR Equity Partners LP, a buyout shop that had two Opinion Research board seats, began questioning the rest of the board's independence. This group of investors was also pressing Opinion Research to auction itself, but the company wasn't listening. In fact, at one point, it appeared that LLR Equity Partners was considering a proxy contest. In response to LLR Equity Partners' pressure, Opinion Research purportedly paid the buyout shop a huge special premium, roughly $20 million for its 19.8 percent stake, so that it would leave the company alone, according to several hedge fund managers following the company. For the group of fund managers watching this transaction unfold, that sale, which met their definition of greenmail, was roughly double what LLR Equity Partners had originally paid for the stake.

At that point, Cannell recognized that Opinion Research's CEO, John Short, was not going to turn the company around. Cannell realized he needed to take action; otherwise, he wouldn't be fulfilling his fiduciary duty to investors. "We wanted them to treat all shareholders equally," Cannell says. "We didn't want any backroom deals."

In December 2004, Cannell filed a lawsuit against Opinion Research's board in Delaware Chancery Court, arguing that the company's directors violated their duty to shareholders by purchasing LLR's stake at an inflated price. Cannell says he was motivated to launch a lawsuit because he suspected that Opinion Research had been rejecting offers by strategic purchasers without consideration and that at the same time the company's chief executive was failing to turn the company around.

In the second quarter of 2006, Opinion Research did retain an investment bank to consider a sale of the company. By August 2006, InfoUSA Inc., another marketing group, acquired Opinion Research for about $12 a share, or about $134 million, including debt.[11] Around the same time, the Delaware court case proceeded to discovery and Cannell realized that many of his suspicions turned out to be true. "There were far more offers presented to the company that they chose to ignore than even we had anticipated," Cannell says.

According to court documents, Opinion Research in 1999 contacted 11 companies and received two serious expressions of interest.[12] But after engaging an investment bank, Opinion Research decided not to accept any offers of less than $14 a share, significantly more than what the company's shares were trading for at the time.[13] Between 2000 and 2003, the company rejected offers of between $14 a share and $16 a share for the entire company. It also rejected offers from several other bidders for one or more divisions. At one point, the company sought to sell its telemarketing division and received two offers, but rejected both.[14] A bid was made in 2003 to buy Opinion Research's management consulting, marketing, and technology unit, ORC Marco. According to the court documents, the sales process lagged and the bidder decided to recall its offer.[15]

To validate their decision to buy LLR's stake at a premium, after rejecting various offers for the company or its divisions, Opinion Research in August 2004 initiated an effort to retain an investment bank to evaluate and justify the LLR purchase. After completing a preliminary review of Opinion Research, a division of the Canadian Imperial Bank of Commerce, or CIBC, reported that it had "concern about ultimately arriving at a favorable analysis and opinion."[16] Another bank, Janney Montgomery Scott LLC, reported that it had completed enough of an analysis to believe it "should be able to arrive at a favorable opinion," according to court documents.[17] Not surprisingly, Opinion Research retained Janney Montgomery Scott.[18] Both banks had worked previously with the company and knew its ins and outs well. "Shareholders could have received more had Opinion Research conducted a full auction," Cannell says.

After the sale to InfoUSA, Cannell cashed out his stake, making a profit. But he hasn't called off the Delaware Chancery Court case. Cannell's attorneys believe they still can obtain a settlement from Opinion Research, based on the argument that company management did not meet their responsibilities to shareholders. In any event, Cannell says, he was reluctant to launch the activist effort at Opinion Research, but after a series of events there, he realized it was the only way he was ever going to realize any value. "If someone steals from investors, we are in breach of our fiduciary duty to our investors if we do nothing about it," he says.

In comparing value investors to activists, we find all sorts of complications, especially if the goal is to decide whether one strategy is better or worse than the other. In the end, it is unclear whether the approach favored by Cannell, Pabrai, or Goldstein makes the most sense. Certainly, as we have seen, it is impossible to consider value investing without looking at the impact of activism on the strategy. The line between what constitutes an activist and what makes up a value investor is often blurred. Most managers do not neatly fit one or the other mold. Sometimes it's hard to see where one strategy begins and the other ends. We have value investors that will become reluctant activists if pressed. There are value investors that partake in activism and a number of other strategies. Devoted activist managers often will split their portfolio between activist investments and passive value-oriented positions. Finally, it seems that most value investors will engage executives, suppliers, and customers privately, in the same way that activists quietly seek out these individuals.

It is important not to look at investment manager results over a short time horizon. Examining long-term results—at the very least a 10-year time frame—is the only convincing way to measure performance. Legendary value investor Martin Whitman's Third Avenue Value Fund had average annual returns of nearly 17 percent a year since the fund's inception in 1990. Also, value investor extraordinaire Walter Schloss's fund averaged 15.7 percent returns a year for 45 years between 1955 and 2000.[19] Whitman and Schloss have produced gains that are pretty hard to beat.[20] The Standard & Poor's (S&P) 500 had averaged annual returns of 11.2 percent during Schloss's investment period.[21]

But is it possible for activists to beat value investors? In many cases, activists have done just that, though usually for shorter periods. Sweden's activist investing duo Lars Förberg and Christer Gardell of Stockholm-based Cevian Capital LP have had average annual returns of roughly 50 percent after fees every year for the past 10 years. Canadian activist hedge fund manager Peter Puccetti reports that his fund, Goodwood Inc., averaged 21.3 percent returns a year since the fund's start in 1996. Insurgent PL Capital's Financial Edge Fund reported a compounded return of 18 percent every year between its launch in 1996 and 2006.

In the end, we find that many value and activist managers are codependent. Value investors introduce activists to investment ideas, typically companies they want to see unlock their true potential faster. Sometimes value investors seek out activists for court cases they feel uneasy about launching on their own. In turn, value investors do well by piggybacking, or investing in companies that already have activists stirring the pot. Many value investors transform into activists as they seek faster and better returns. It appears that value investors, at least lately, can owe some of their performance successes to the activists in their midst. Activist investors can also thank traditional value investors for their support and ideas. The two strategies are joined at the hip.

Conclusion: Saturation or No Saturation?

It would be easy to say that these activist investors are a flash in the pan, that they only have an insignificant amount of capital under management, and that serious long-term institutional investors are not really paying attention to them. That's the perception corporate America would like to have you believe. But most hedge fund managers think differently.

In fact, Hedge Fund Research in Chicago estimates that every year since 2004 more hedge funds state in marketing materials to their investors that activism is their core strategy. Other studies have shown that traditional hedge fund managers believe that there will continue to be more activists with more assets under management in 2008 and beyond.

There are several trends in play behind the perception by many that activist hedge funds are growing in size and numbers. For one thing, there are more new sources of funding for activists than ever before. Fund of hedge fund managers are fueling their investment vehicles with activist funds; they are even setting up devoted activist funds of hedge funds.

Also, institutional investors of all sorts are allocating capital more than ever to activists. Some institutions are becoming new non-traditional activist funds on their own. Previously passive pension funds, such as Toronto-based Ontario Teachers' Pension Plan (OTPP) and the California Public Employees' Retirement System (CalPERS), are getting more involved in activism themselves (in addition to allocating capital to insurgents around the world).

London-based activist Children's Investment Fund has a multimillion-dollar nonprofit division, and its board has officials from United Nations agencies. This fund represents a new kind of activism, especially when considering the types of corporations that are the focus of its efforts. Two months after the hedge fund first pressed Dutch bank ABN Amro Holding NV to sell itself in pieces or as a whole, Barclays Plc agreed to buy it for $91 billion. Lately, Children's Investment Fund has turned its attention to Reuters Group plc, a financial data provider and newswire service, which has agreed to be taken over by Thomson Corp. for $17.2 billion.

A few other trends demonstrate that the growth of activism isn't a short-term phenomenon. Activists have expanded their reach, moving into the distressed arena, for example, where they are vigorously shaking things up at overleveraged, distressed, and bankrupt companies. Others are dabbling in private equity. Driven by larger capital allocations, activists are buying big stakes and prodding a wider variety of companies—of all shapes and sizes—to make changes.

Another indication that activism is on the rise: In a post AOL–Time Warner environment, investors are no longer willing to passively accept mergers they believe destroy corporate value. Instead, they are breaking up deals. They are pressing companies into mergers, breaking those up, and then finding other acquirers to pay more.

They are filing more lawsuits than ever before; they are being hit by more lawsuits than ever as well.

At the same time, activist investors are forming groups and talking to each other in greater numbers. They are communicating with institutional investors, executives, and investor relations officials more than ever, as well. They are also spending more time talking to as many other investors as possible. Online meeting places, physical forums, special shareholder meetings, annual meetings—anywhere they can find each other, activists are talking.

Behind every public-pressure campaign an activist launches, there are dozens of private insurgencies taking place in hush-hush, behind-the-scenes meetings. It's not clear exactly how many private meetings are taking place between investors and corporate execs, but expect there to be a surge in this category of activism, as shareholders become more effective at getting themselves heard.

Some detractors contend that as they grow in size and number, the whole strategy will reach a natural saturation point, leaving activists with fewer undervalued companies to target. Activists have driven many of the going-private transactions that seem to be geting bigger and bigger. As more companies exit the public markets, there are fewer opportunities for activists and private equity companies. Certainly if buyout shops start folding up for lack of good deals, their disappearance will hurt the activists that count on them to come in and buy assets when strategic bidders simply are not there. All this could mean we will see a world with too many activists and not enough opportunities. Legislation under consideration in Congress that, if passed, would hike taxes on hedge fund managers could also discourage activism.

Another factor that some observers argue could stifle activist endeavors is disclosure. If the Securities and Exchange Commission moves to require more timely 13D filings, coupled with additional disclosures, expect some activists to freeze their campaigns for good, at least in the United States. Regulators in the United Kingdom are also taking heed of the growth of activists. Children's Investment Fund's large-scale activism, together with several other insurgent hedge funds, may be responsible for drawing the ire of U.K. regulators who have recently issued guidelines for hedge fund market manipulation. One guideline: Hedge funds that acquire shares of a company to help another activist avoid breaching a disclosure threshold will not be looked at kindly by the U.K.'s Financial Services Authority.

But activists don't appear to be worried about fewer opportunities, potential disclosure requirements or any saturation point, at least not yet. They refer to an interesting fact: Even though each activist typically has files of campaigns that are already under way they also have untouched files filled with numerous potential targets waiting for action. A shortage of capital, energy, time, and manpower means these alternative targets will have to wait on the sidelines or, more likely, no campaign will ever take place there. For now, most activists can't handle more than one or two campaigns at any one time. That means their files, filled with other potential target companies, will, for the short term anyways, remain untouched. Untapped opportunities still exist.

Another key factor is that with more true activists, there is also a greater likelihood one particular insurgent hedge fund will find other dissidents that support its initiative. Activists may have a better chance of provoking a reaction from the companies they are pressing for change as more insurgent-type shareholders pop up, replacing the dusty remains of passive, rubber-stamping, management-endorsing investors. More activists mean better opportunities for every insurgent.

And technology will facilitate everything. Expert insurgents launching proxy contests to employ multimedia campaigns, complete with streaming YouTube videos, blogs, and social networking sites to get their message across electronically. The SEC is leading both companies and shareholders into an electronic proxy, "e-proxy" future. What does it mean? Hedge fund manager, meet retail insurgent, the new activist on the block. Following Eric Jackson's efforts at Yahoo! and Motorola Inc., other retail investors are launching grassroots campaigns seeking to shake up the corporate norm. And watch out, they're looking to get institutional support. But there still are growing pains. The collective performance of activists seems to be diminishing, though they still—as a group—appear to beat out the S&P 500 consistently. Some new entrants are likely having problems employing the strategy. They may not be as adept at making it work, perhaps lacking the aggressive attitude and thick shell insurgencies require. For whatever reason, some activists will disappear by attrition. Or, if they do succeed, they may need time to get the strategy right before they join the ranks of Ralph Whitworth and other successful governance activists.

Corporate responses must also be taken into consideration. Executives and investor relations officials are better prepared and responding more rapidly to insurgent initiatives. The company piggy bank will soon start investing in quick-hit YouTube-like responses to activist campaigns.

At the moment investors prepare to vote they will receive pop-up streaming video of corporate executives explaining their position. Management's growing ability to quickly mobilize an investor base against an activist cannot be ignored.

It may be that, like other strategies, activist investing will come in and out of vogue. Managers, eager to try something new and attractive, may jump into the strategy, not anticipating the extreme time and energy it requires to be successful. Another strategy, convertible arbitrage, which tries to exploit pricing inefficiencies between a convertible bond and the underlying stock, has also come into and gone out of fashion.

But Chapman Capital's Robert Chapman says he doesn't believe the sector can get oversaturated or unfashionable because, at the core, activists invest in fundamentally cheap companies that will appreciate regardless of whether an insurgency campaign is successful. "We focus on risk and reward," he says. Phillip Goldstein says the idea that activism could disappear sounds as crazy as the idea that value investing as a strategy would suddenly vanish. "It's not going to happen," he says.

Institutional Shareholder Service's Christopher Young looks at it another way. While he believes that the increase in activists that buy into small-capitalization corporations may diminish opportunities in companies of that size, other new possibilities abound that just were not available five years ago. The growth in assets under management has opened up large-capitalization companies as a whole new category of advocate investing that didn't exist to most of this class of activists a few years ago. Activists that have traditionally gone after smaller companies because their own asset size made investing in larger companies more difficult are now much larger, managing billions of dollars under management. Their new heft means they can make their presence known at large-capitalization companies, such as The Home Depot, Motorola, Vodafone, DaimlerChrysler, and McDonald's, all of which were untouchable several years ago.

Mid-cap companies represent another new category of opportunities. Breeden Capital Management's public pressure campaign at Applebee's International Inc., which has a $1.9 billion stock market capitalization, demonstrates that activists are finding whole new classes of investments. After the hedge fund's director, ex-SEC Chairman Richard Breeden, agreed to call off his proxy contest, the mid-cap restaurant chain pledged that it would find buyer candidates and put dissident shareholders on its board. By July 2007, Applebee's sold itself to IHOP Inc., and two investors for $2.1 billion.

Clearly, many things have changed over the years. In 1954, Louis Wolfson took on the Montgomery Ward department store chain, based in downtown Chicago. In 2006, Warren Lichtenstein traveled to the other side of the globe to battle his way onto the board of South Korean–based ginseng and tobacco company KT&G Corp. The global expansion of activists to countries that have never previously experienced investor insurgencies represents a whole new world of possibilities that also did not exist just a few years ago. When activists blocked Deutsche Börse's bid to buy the London Stock Exchange, that endeavor brought insurgents to the attention of many Europeans that had never thought about them before. Driven by a desire to make unique and robust returns, activists are taking their tools and setting up shop in Russia, Ukraine, South Korea, China, and Japan, as well as Germany, India, Africa, and Azerbaijan.

Just ask Lars Förberg in Sweden. He believes that the sky is the limit for activism in shareholder-friendly Scandinavia. Guy Wyser-Pratte, once a lonely voice for activism in continental Europe, is now joined by a whole new generation of European activists.

If there is saturation and a weeding out of the weak activists in the North American market, then for sure we will see more activists stepping out and dipping their feet into uncharted waters around the world. Their presence outside of the United States has been met with surprise and confusion. Executives at European or Asian corporations, who once believed they were comfortably at the top of the corporate hierarchy, now must face new and difficult questions about their business strategies from investors that say they are in charge. And insurgents haven't even scratched the surface yet in many markets. The trend of activists taking on targets around the globe is reason enough to believe that the strategy won't be gone tomorrow. Already, regulators, chief executives, and other investors in Russia, South Korea, and Japan are scratching their heads. Who are these activist guys?

Notes

Introduction

1. April Klein, associate professor, Stern School of Business, New York University; Emanuel Zur, doctoral student, Stern School of Business, NYU, "Hedge Fund Activism," September 2006, p. 2.
2. Alon Brav, associate professor of finance, Duke University; Wei Jiang, associate professor of business, Columbia University; Frank Partnoy, law professor at University of San Diego; and Randall Thomas, professor of Law and Business at Vanderbilt University, "Hedge Fund Activism, Corporate Governance and Firm Performance," September 22, 2006, p. 2.
3. Mark Hulbert, "A Good World for Hedge Fund Activism," *New York Times*, February 18, 2007.
4. See note 2.

Chapter 1

1. S. Randy Lampert, Andrew Shiftan, Sasha Soroudi, Amar Kuray, "Management in an Era of Shareholder Activism," Morgan Joseph & Co., July 2006, p. 5.
2. Id.

3. Reinhardt Krause, "MCI Bidding War Calls To Question AT&T Acquisition; SBC Purchase Price Too Low?; Some Analysts Argue AT&T Selling Itself Cheap, in Light of the Verizon, Qwest Saga," April 11, 2005.
4. Lampert et al. p. 6.
5. Anastasia Ustinova, "Prison Firm Going Private: Sale Draws Objections from Some Investors." Houston Chronicle, October 10, 2006.
6. Press release, "Committee on Capital Markets Regulation Recommends Enhancing Shareholder Rights and Curbing Excessive Regulation and Litigation," November 30, 2006.
7. Glenn Hubbard, dean of the Columbia School of Business, and John Thornton, Chairman of the Brookings Institution. The Committee on Capital Markets Regulation is an independent, bipartisan and diverse group of 22 experts from the investor community, business, finance, law, accounting and academia. "Interim Report on U.S. Public Companies Going Private," revised December 5, 2006, www.capmktsreg.org/research.html.
8. Diana B. Henriques, *White Sharks of Wall Street: Thomas Mellon Evans and the Original Corporate Raiders*. New York: Scribner, 2000.
9. Id.
10. Alan J. Wax, "Corporate Raider to Corporate Savior," *Newsday,* October 12, 1986.
11. Id.
12. Ken Auletta, "The Raid; Annals of Communications," *New Yorker*, March 20, 2006.
13. David Smith, "Hedge-Fund Master, Ex-Oilman Pickens to Talk in Little Rock," *Arkansas Democrat Gazette*, November 22, 2006.
14. Mark Tatge, "Irv the Operator," *Forbes*, November 29, 2004.
15. The Associated Press, "Investor Group Increases Stake in Avon," November 28, 1989.
16. Kathleen Pender, "Asher Edelman Says He'd Break Up Lucky," *San Francisco Chronicle*, September 26, 1986.
17. Diana B. Henriques, "Wall Street; Pity These Minority Shareholders," *New York Times*, May 12, 1991.
18. Andrew Dolbeck, "Investors, IPOs, and Shark Repellent," Weekly Corporate Growth Report, June 28, 2004.
19. David Vise, "Fed Proposes Restriction on Financing Takeovers," *The Washington Post*, December 7, 1985.
20. Ralph Whitworth, "United Shareholder Association: Mission Accomplished." Remarks of Ralph Whitworth, Investor Responsibility Research Center, Conference on Shareholder and Management Cooperation, October 27, 1993.

21. Id.
22. Id.
23. Id.
24. Id.
25. Christopher Palmeri, "Meet the Friendly Corporate Raiders; When Relational Investors Buy In, the Board Often Takes Its Advice without a Fight," *BusinessWeek*, September 20, 2004.
26. Barry Rosenstein, "Activism Is Good for All Shareholders,"*Financial Times*, March 10, 2006.

Chapter 2

1. Jonathan Stempel, "Bond Fund Manager Takes Activist Stance/Agitation Is Rare for Listless Investors,"*Houston Chronicle*, March 24, 2002.
2. Brett Cole, "Yankee Candle OKs Buyout by Madison Dearborn LLC,"*Bloomberg*, October 26, 2006.
3. James Politi, "Ripplewood Group to Buy Reader's Digest," *Financial Times*, November 17, 2006.
4. PR Newswire, "Pirate Capital Wins GenCorp Proxy Contest," April 7, 2006.
5. S. Randy Lampert, Andrew Shiftan, Sasha Soroudi, Amar Kuray, "Management in an Era of Shareholder Activism," Morgan Joseph & Co., July 2006, p. 3.
6. April Klein, associate professor Stern School of Business, New York University; Emanuel Zur, doctoral student, Stern School of Business, NYU, "Hedge Fund Activism," September 2006, p. 5.
7. Press release, "Agreement to Include Acquisition of Blair Credit Portfolio," April 27, 2005.
8. Press release, "Ligand Announces Sale of AVINZA, September 7, 2006; press release, Ligand Announces Sale of Oncology Product Lines as Next Step in Shareholder Value Maximization Process; Aggregate Cash Consideration to Ligand from Commercial Products Sales of AVINZA and Oncology Product Lines Exceeds $500 Million Plus AVINZA Royalties," September 7, 2006.
9. Press release, "Ligand Announces Sale of Real Estate," October 26, 2006.
10. Press Release, "Chapman Capital Recommends Reorganization of Cypress Semiconductor Corporation," December 28, 2006.
11. Id.
12. Business Wire, "Six Flags Announces Results of Consent Solicitation," November 29, 2005.
13. Glenn Singer, "Embattled CEO McLain Quites Boca-based Nabi,"*South Florida Sun-Sentinel*, February 16, 2007.

14. Press release, "Carl C. Icahn Appointed Chairman of ImClone Systems," October 25, 2006.
15. Press release, "Multimedia Games and Liberation Investments Resolve Proxy Contest; Special Shareholders' Meeting Will Not Be Held," October 25, 2006.
16. PR Newswire, "Computer Horizons Announces Certified Results of Special Meeting of Shareholders," October 18, 2005.
17. Press release, "Computer Horizons Announces Reorganization of Commercial Division and Corporate Cost Reductions," December 1, 2005.

Chapter 3

1. Alon Brav, associate professor of finance, Duke University; Wei Jiang, associate professor of business, Columbia University; Frank Partnoy, law professor at University of San Diego; and Randall Thomas, professor of Law and Business at Vanderbilt University, "Hedge Fund Activism, Corporate Governance and Firm Performance," September 22, 2006, p. 2.
2. Press release, "Knight Ridder Reports Third Quarter Results," October 14, 2005.
3. Press release, "McClatchy Completes Acquisition of Knight Ridder," June 27, 2006.
4. Brav et al., p. 22.
5. Id., p. 3.
6. Id.
7. Id.
8. Hu, Henry T.C. and Black, Bernard S., "Empty Voting and Hidden (Morphable) Ownership: Taxonomy, Implications, and Reforms." Business Lawyer, Vol. 61, pp. 1011–1070, 2006
9. Id.
10. Press release, "The Brink's Company Closes Sale of BAX Global for $1.1 Billion," January 31, 2006.
11. Press release, "The Brink's Company Announces Self-Tender Offer For up to 10,000,000 Shares of Common Stock," March 8, 2006.
12. Dale Kasler, "GenCorp Replaces Chairman; Amid Pressure over Fiscal Fesults, CEO Position and the Top Board Job Are Split," *Sacramento Bee*, February 17, 2007.
13. Advocate staff report, "Hibernia Stock Deal Triggers Possible Civil Action on Hedge Fund," *Baton Rouge Advocate*, November 2, 2006.
14. "Activist Hedge Fund Pressures Southern Union to Amend Bylaws," *Natural Gas Intelligence*, January 22, 2007.

15. "Gabelli Settlement Underscores Auction Bid Frauds," *Telecom Policy Report*, July 17, 2006.
16. Lisa Gewirtz-Ward, "Outback Walkabout Leads to LBO," *The Deal*, November 7, 2006.
17. Id.
18. Id.
19. Press release, "Bally Total Fitness Announces Closing of Crunch Fitness Sale," January 20, 2006.
20. Press release, "Bally Total Fitness Announces Election Results," February 10, 2006.
21. "Bally Total Fitness Plans to File for Bankruptcy," Reuters, May 31, 2007.

Chapter 4

1. "Liquid Audio to Reimburse Shareholder for Proxy Fight," *Mercury News*, January 18, 2003.
2. PR Newswires, "Delaware Supreme Court Invalidates August 2002 Expansion of Liquid Audio Board of Directors," January 9, 2002.
3. Chuck Bartels, "Wal-Mart Begins Testing Online Music Service," *CMP TechWeb*, December 18, 2003.
4. Tamara Loomis, "Beware Delaware," *New York Law Journal*, May 15, 2003.
5. PR Newswire, "MM Companies, Inc. Responds to Liquid Audio, Inc. Lawsuit," August 22, 2002.
6. "Judge Delays Caremark Shareholder Vote," *AFX Asia*, February 14, 2007.
7. Ben Stein, "Shareholders? What Shareholders?" *New York Times*, January 21, 2007.
8. Lewis Krauskopf and Jessica Wohl, "CVS Boosts Caremark Bid with Sweeter Dividend Plan," *Reuters News*, February 13, 2007.
9. Id.
10. Associated Press, "CVS completes $26.5B Caremark Acquisition, to Buy Back Shares," March 22, 2007.
11. Reuters News, "Carter-Wallace Agrees to Be Split For $1.1 Billion," May 8, 2001.
12. Id.
13. *Cede & Co., Inc. v. MedPointe Healthcare Inc.*, No. Civ. A. 19354-NC, 2004 WL 2093967 (De. Ch. August 16, 2004), p. 2.
14. Geoffrey C. Jarvis, "State Appraisal Statutes: An Underutilized Shareholder Remedy," *Corporate Governance Advisor*, May/June 2005, p. 3.
15. *Cede & Co., Inc. v. MedPointe Healthcare Inc.*, No. Civ. A. 19354-NC, 2004 WL 2093967 (De. Ch. August 16, 2004), p. 31.

16. "Gabelli Gets 40 Pct Premium in Carter-Wallace Deal," *Reuters News*, November 1, 2004.
17. Brett Duval Fromson, "Companies to Watch," *Fortune*, September 28, 1987.
18. Id.
19. Id.
20. Id.
21. "Kahn Brothers' Irving, Alan & Tommy Kahn. We're Dealing in Blemished Fruit. Polished Apples Are Too Damned Expensive." *Outstanding Investor Digest*, Vol. VI, Nos. 8 and 9, November 11, 1991, p. 28.
22. Andrew Bary, "Street Fighter," *Barron's*, March 13, 1995.
23. The proxy rules referred to herein were promulgated by the SEC pursuant to the Securities Exchange Act of 1934.
24. PR Newswire, "Delaware Court Rejects Bally's 'Poison Pill' Motion; Liberation Addresses Bally's Governance Reforms," *Liberation Partners*, January 12, 2006.
25. S. Randy Lampert, Andrew Shiftan, Sasha Soroudi, Amar Kuray, "Management in an Era of Shareholder Activism," Morgan Joseph & Co., July 2006, p. 12.
26. Howard O. Godnick, Partner Litigation, William H. Gussman, Jr., Special Counsel, Litigation, "Beware the Counterattack Against Activist Investors: The Group Trap," Schulte Roth & Zabel, 2006, p. 1.
27. Id.
28. Godnick et al., p. 2.

Chapter 5

1. Jerry Hirsch, "California Farmers Bros. Makes Inquiry into Repurchasing Shares. The Coffee Company Has Held Talks with a Major Investor in Exploring the Possibility of Going Private, Sources Say," *Los Angeles Times*, April 30, 2003.
2. Business Wire, "Farmer Bros. Reports First Quarter Loss of $0.08 per Share," November 8, 2005.
3. Forum for Shareholders of Farmer Brothers, "Request for SEC Action to Require Provision of Information Prior to Voting at Annual Meeting," February 13, 2004, www.shareholderforum.com/farm/Process/20040213_letter.htm.
4. S. Randy Lampert, Andrew Shiftan, Sasha Soroudi, Amar Kuray, "Management in an Era of Shareholder Activism," Morgan Joseph & Co., July 2006, p. 9.
5. Id.
6. Lampert et al., p. 11.
7. Press Release, "Multimedia Games and Liberation Investments Resolve Proxy Contest; Special Shareholders' Meeting Will Not Be Held," October 25, 2006.

8. Lampert et al., p. 8.
9. Sheila McGovern, "Takeover of Cinar Is Completed: Shareholders Accepted Offer of $144 Million U.S.," *Montreal Gazette*, March 16, 2004.
10. Lampert et al., p. 11.
11. Martin Lipton, Eric M. Roth, Marc Wolinsky, Joshua R. Cammaker, Mark Gordon, "Be Prepared for Attacks by Hedge Funds," Wachtell, Lipton, Rosen & Katz, December 21, 2005.
12. Id.
13. Id.
14. PR Newswire, "Golden Gate Capital Completes Acquisition of GEAC Computer Corporation for US$1 Billion, Cash Price of US$11.10 per Share," March 14, 2006.

Chapter 6

1. Press Release, "Glenayre Technologies Proposes Name Change to Entertainment Distribution Company, Clarke Bailey to Serve as Chairman Non-Executive—Jim Caparro Appointed to President, Chief Executive Officer and Elected as Director," November 7, 2006.
2. Institutional Shareholder Services, "Hot Topics for the 2006 Proxy Season and Beyond," 2006, p. 28.
3. Andrew Ward in Atlanta, James Politi in New York, "Home Depot Chief Nardelli Steps Down," *Financial Times*, January 11, 2007.
4. David Cay Johnston and Julie Creswell, "Home Depot Proxy Fight Is Settled," *New York Times*, February 6, 2007.
5. Id.
6. Videsh Kumar, "Yahoo! Holder Building a Dissident Nation," TheStreet.com, January 10, 2007.
7. Jonathan R. Laing, "Insiders, Look Out!" *Barron's*, February 19, 2007.
8. "What's a CEO Worth?" *Globe and Mail*, January 8, 2007.
9. Id.
10. Id.
11. Karen Jacobs, "Home Depot Investors Try to Halt Ex-CEO Exit Pay," *Reuters News*, January 10, 2007.
12. Executive Compensation and Related Person Disclosure, SEC Release Nos. 33–8732A; 34–54302a September 8, 2006.
13. Id.
14. Id.
15. Nicholas Neveling, "SEC Enters Digital Age," *Accountancy Age*, October 5, 2006.

Chapter 7

1. Press release, "Synergy Financial Group, Inc. Announces Annual Meeting Voting Results," April 13, 2006.
2. Id.
3. "New York Community bank buys Synergy for $168 mln," Reuters, May 14, 2007.
4. PR Newswire, "Seidman to Continue to Pursue Board Representation and Improved Financial Performance at Yardville National Bancorp," May 15, 2006.
5. Peter Moreira, "PNC to buy Yardville National Bancorp for $403M," (The Daily Deal, June 7, 2007).
6. Eric Schlelzig, "Massey to Buy Back $500M of Common Shares," Associated Press Newswires, November 15, 2005.
7. "Houston Exploration Rejects Fund's Offer, Will Explore 'Strategic' Options," *Gas Daily*, June 27, 2006.
8. Purva Patel, "ANADARKO'S ACQUISITIONS/Exploration Powers Deals/ Storied Name Likely Getting Local Address/Longtime Oklahoma Drilling Company Already Has 800 Houston Workers," *Houston Chronicle*, June 24, 2006.
9. John Hanna, "Shareholders Re-Elect Three to Payless Board," Associated Press Newswires, May 27, 2004.
10. "US: Cocozza Joins Stride Rite Board," just-style.com, May 30, 2006.
11. PR Newswire, "Steven Madden, Ltd. and the Barington Capital Group Reach Agreement—Company Will Allocate $25 Million to Share Repurchase and/ or Dividends in 2005—Company Will Add an Additional Independent Director to the Board," February 2, 2005.
12. Nancy Dillon, "Nautica Agrees to Dock with VF," *New York Daily News*, July 8, 2003.
13. David Moin and Vicki M. Young, "Investor Group Takes 5.6% Warnaco Stake," *Women's Wear Daily*, August 22, 2006.
14. Elisabeth Butler, "Warnaco's Popularity Just a Flash in the Pan; Surge On Sale Rumors Doesn't Dispel Basic Woes; Chaps Chafes," *Crain's New York Business*, August 21, 2006.
15. April Klein, associate professor Stern School of Business, New York University; Emanuel Zur, doctoral student, Stern School of Business, NYU, "Hedge Fund Activism," September 2006, pp. 10, 11.
16. "Lone Star Says Shareholder Wins Proxy Fight," Reuters, July 12, 2001.
17. "Funds Say to Vote "No" on Lone Star Buyout," Reuters News, November 1, 2006.

18. "GEAC to Be Sold to Golden Gate for $1 Billion," Reuters News, November 7, 2005.
19. Business Wire, "Vector Capital Completes $200 Million Take-Private Buyout of Register.com; Private Equity Firm to Help Register.com Expand Online Services Offered to Small Businesses, November 7, 2005.
20. Kevin Murphy, "Register.com Rejects Rogue Director Buyout Bid," *ComputerWire News*, June 21, 2005.
21. PR Newswires, "Aladdin Finalises US$5 Million Acquisition of Preview System's ESD Business," July 19, 2001.
22. Ross Kerber, "Shareholder's SEC Filing Targets Edgewater's Ties with Customers," *Boston Globe*, January 23, 2001.

Chapter 8

1. "Deals: The Two Sides of Chrysler's War," *Mergers & Restructuring*, July 8, 1996.
2. Ralph Whitworth, "United Shareholders Association: Mission Accomplished." Remarks of Ralph Whitworth, Investor Responsibility Research Center, Conference on Shareholder and Management Cooperation, October 27, 1993.
3. Miriam Hill, Patricia Horn, and Wendy Tanaka, "Disney Strips Eisner of Chairman's Role; He Remains CEO, Aided by Mitchell," *Philadelphia Enquirer*, March 4, 2004.
4. Fran Hawthorne, "What the New SEC Rules Do for Activism," *Institutional Investor*, April 1, 1993.
5. Id.
6. Id.
7. PR Newswire, "JP Shareholder Supports Changes in SEC Proxy Regulations," September 2, 1992.
8. Id.
9. Regulation of Takeovers and Security Holder Communications, SEC File No. S7-28-98; Release No.: 34-42055, October 26, 1999.
10. Disclosure of Proxy Voting Policies and Proxy Voting Records by Registered Management Investment Companies, SEC Release Nos. 34-47304, IC-25922, April 14, 2003.
11. James Paton, "New Rules on Fund Proxies to Help Disclosure," Reuters News, August 25, 2003.
12. Disclosure Regarding Nominating Committee Functions and Communications between Security Holders and Boards of Directors, SEC Release Nos. 33–8340; 34–48825, December 11, 2003.

13. Internet Availability of Proxy Materials, SEC Release No.: IC-27182, File No.: S7-10-05, December 8, 2005.
14. Kaja Whitehouse, "NYSE Postpones Ruling on Broker-Vote Proposal," Dow Jones Newswires, September 22, 2006.
15. Nick Snow, "Institutional Investors Council Offers Its Own Auditor Reform Suggestions," *Petroleum Finance Week*, February 11, 2002.
16. Jennifer E. Bethel, associate professor at Babson College in Wellesley, and Stuart L. Gillan, TIAA CREF Institute, "The Impact of the Institutional and Regulatory Environment on Shareholder Voting," TIAA CREF Institute, 2002, p. 20.
17. Id., p. 2.
18. See note 14.
19. Gretchen Morgenson, "NYSE Postpones Plan on Shareholder Voting," *New York Times*, October 4, 2006.
20. Id.
21. Id.
22. Executive Compensation and Related Person Disclosure, SEC Release Nos. 33–8732A; 34–54302a, September 8, 2006.
23. Security Holder Director Nominations, SEC Release No. 34–48626, October 23, 2003.
24. Id.

Chapter 9

1. Alon Brav, associate professor of finance, Duke University; Wei Jiang, associate professor of business, Columbia University; Frank Partnoy, law professor at University of San Diego; and Randall Thomas, professor of Law and Business at Vanderbilt University, "Hedge Fund Activism, Corporate Governance and Firm Performance," September 22, 2006, p. 4.
2. April Klein, associate professor Stern School of Business, New York University; Emanuel Zur, doctoral student, Stern School of Business, NYU, "Hedge Fund Activism," September 2006, p. 3.
3. Howard Silverblatt, analyst at Standard & Poor's, "Standard & Poor's Investment Services, S&P 500 Industrial (old) cash and Equivalents Levels," 2006.

Chapter 10

1. Julie Jargon, "Big Mac Faces Fund Attack; Agitator's Plan Draws Hedge Funds into McDonald's Stock," *Crain's Chicago Business*, November 21, 2005.

2. "Big Shareholder Says Satisfied with McDonald's Changes," *AFX Asia*, January 26, 2006.
3. Business Wire, "Director Voting Results Certified in Heinz Proxy Contest," September 15, 2006.
4. April Klein, associate professor Stern School of Business, New York University; Emanuel Zur, doctoral student, Stern School of Business, NYU, "Hedge Fund Activism," September 2006, p. 15.
5. Id.
6. David Haarmeyer, "Active Investors Can Go Where Others Fear to Tread," *Financial Times*, August 22, 2006.
7. Business Roundtable, "SEC Response to *AFSCME v. AIG* Decision," September 29, 2006, p. 2.
8. Phineas Lambert, "Icahn Attacks Time Warner Board," *The Deal*, October 12, 2005.
9. David Lieberman, "Icahn Ends Threat to Fight for Time Warner Control," *USA Today*, February 20, 2006.
10. Chris Young, "General Motors—"Know When to Fold 'Em?" *ISS M&A Insight Note*, December 1, 2006.
11. Rachel Beck, "ALL BUSINESS: Motorola's Defeat of Investor Icahn Considered Blueprint for Proxy Fights," (Associated Press, June 5, 2007)
12. Id.
13. Id.
14. "Wagoner Fends off Kerkorian, Ghosn," *Automotive News*, January 1, 2007.
15. "Analysts Divided about Kerkorian's Impact on GM; Buyouts Began after Kerkorian Bought Stock," *Buffalo News*, December 4, 2006.
16. Chris Young, "General Motors, "Darkening Clouds," ISS, October 10, 2006.
17. Id.

Chapter 11

1. David Morrill, "Novartis Raises Chiron Bid," *Oakland Tribune*, April 4, 2006.
2. Michael Liedtke, "Providian Shareholders Approve Sale to Washington Mutual," Associated Press Newswires, August 31, 2005.
3. "BofA to Pay Millions to Retain MBNA Executives after Merger," Associated Press, September 20, 2005.
4. Id.
5. Steven J. Spencer, Special Counsel Business Transactions, Young J. Woo, Associate, Business Transactions, "Considerations for 'Just Vote No' Campaigns," Schulte Roth & Zabel, Fall 2006, p. 1.

6. "MONY Trims Golden Parachute, Boosts Dividend in Bid to Win over Shareholders," *Best's Insurance News*, February 23, 2004.
7. New York University law professor Marcel Kahan and University of Pennsylvania School of Law professor Edward Rock, "Hedge Funds in Corporate Governance and Corporate Control," 2006, p. 38.
8. Id.
9. Id.
10. "Shareholders Kill Steel Merger Plan," *Nikkei Weekly*, February 26, 2007.
11. Andrew Morse and Sebastian Moffett, "A Landmark Vote in Japan: Shareholders Just Say No," *Wall Street Journal*, February 23, 2007.
12. See note 10.
13. Ian Bickerton, "Knight Vinke Backs Down over Consortium's Offer for VNU," *Financial Times*, May 19, 2006.
14. "Mylan Officially Calls Off $4 Billion Merger with Brand Firm King," *Generic Line*, March 9, 2005.

Chapter 12

1. Andrew Countryman, "Shareholders Renewing 'Just Vote No' Campaigns," *Chicago Tribune*, February 11, 2005.
2. Harry R. Weber, "Home Depot to Allow More Questions at Future Annual Meetings," Associated Press, June 1, 2006.
3. Jonathan R. Laing, "Insiders, Look Out!" *Barron's*, February 19, 2007.
4. Jenny Strasburg, "Safeway CEO Burd Survives Vote/Campaign to Strip Him of Chairman Role Falls Short," *San Francisco Chronicle*, May 21, 2004.
5. "Safeway Inc," ISS Proxy Analysis, May 2004, p. 12.
6. Id.
7. Id.
8. Id.
9. Id.
10. James F. Peltz, "Investors Lose Bid to Oust Safeway Chief; Steven Burd retains his board seat, but 17% of votes are withheld in a move led by CalPERS," Times Staff Writer, May 21, 2004.
11. Jim Wasserman, "Activist Blames Ceos, Governor/California Labor Leader Lost Top Job at Pension Fund," *Houston Chronicle*, December 30, 2004.
12. See note 5.
13. Dale Kasler, "Safeway Chairman Beats Back Shareholder Revolt," *Sacramento Bee*, May 21, 2004.

14. PR Newswire, "JANA Partners Announces Material Withhold Votes at Houston Exploration as a Message to the Board," PR Newswires, April 28, 2006.

Chapter 13

1. "Scorecard of Key 2006 Shareholder Proposals Voted On," Institutional Shareholder Services, 2006, www.issproxy.com/proxyseasonreview/2006/index.jsp.
2. Id.
3. "Board Practices/Board Pay—2007 Edition," Institutional Shareholder Services, 2007, p. 12.
4. Id.
5. "2006 Post Season Report, Spotlight on Executive Pay and Board Accountability," www.issproxy.com/pdf/2006PostSeasonReportFINAL.pdf), Institutional Shareholder Services, 2006, p. 3.
6. Id., p. 27.
7. Id., p. 4.
8. Id., p. 27.
9. "US Corporate Governance Core Principles and Guidelines," www.calpers-governance.org/principles/domestic/us/page05.asp#, p. 5.
10. See note 5, p. 22.
11. See note 5, p. 22.
12. Elizabeth Amon, "Majority Rules; Corporate Governance," *Corporate Counsel*, July 1, 2006.
13. Robert Profusek, "Majority Voting for Directors," *Mondaq Business Briefing*, November 1, 2006.
14. Id.
15. See note 5, p. 2.
16. Id.
17. Id.
18. Id.
19. Id.
20. Press Release, "CalPERS to Seek Majority Vote for Corporate Directors – Pension Fund to Use Public Company Accounting Oversight Board Auditor Independence Proposals as Guidelines for Proxy Votes," CalPERS, March 14, 2005.
21. "Corporate Governance Annual Report 2006," www.sbafla.com/pdf/governance/CorpGovReport.pdf), The State Board of Administration of Florida, 2006, pp. 58–59.

22. 2005 Post Season Report, Corporate Governance at a Crossroads,"www.issproxy.com/pdf/2005PostSeasonReportFINAL.pdf, Institutional Shareholder Services, 2005, p. 10.

Chapter 14

1. "CalPERS Approves $275 million investment to Relational Investors LLC," (CalPERS press release, May 19, 1998.
2. Deborah Yao, "Pressured Sovereign Bank Chief Quits," Associated Press, October 12, 2006.
3. Christopher Palmeri, "Meet the Friendly Corporate Raiders; When Relational Investors buys in, the Board Often Takes Its Advice without a Fight,"*BusinessWeek*, September 20, 2004.
4. Id.
5. Id.
6. "California Public Employees' Retirement System Hybrid Investment Monitoring Report," CalPERS, second quarter 2006, p. 41; Relational AUM, "About Us,"www.rillc.com/about.htm.
7. Jonathan R. Laing,"Insiders Look Out!"*Barron's* February 19, 2007, p. 27.
8. Id.
9. Press release, "CalPERS approves $275 Million Investment to Relational Investors LLC," May 19, 1998.
10. Id.
11. Mathew Miller, "The Rise of Ron Burkle; He Built A Fortune Betting on Out-of-Favor Assets—Including U.S. Democrats. Now It's Time to Cash In,"*Forbes*, December 11, 2006.
12. Id.
13. Id.
14. Press release, "New European Venture Gets CalPERS Backing," CalPERS, October 3, 2006.
15. Id.
16. "California Public Employees' Retirement System Hybrid Investment Monitoring Report," CalPERS, second quarter 2006, p. 42.
17. Id., p. 43.
18. Id.
19. Id., p. 45.
20. Id.

21. "California Public Employees' Retirement System Hybrid Investment Monitoring Report," CalPERS, first quarter 2007, p. 80.
22. "California Public Employees' Retirement System Hybrid Investment Monitoring Report," CalPERS, second quarter 2006, p. 50.
23. Lynnley Browning, "From Ethics Overseer to Hedge Fund Boss," *New York Times*, January 19, 2007.

Chapter 15

1. Reuters, "Polymer Group Making Dominion Textile Bid," October 27, 1997.
2. Id.
3. Konrad Yakabuski, "Higher Offer Ends Battle over Domtex Polymer Wants Non-Woven Fabric Business; Other Units Likely to Be Sold," *Globe and Mail*, November 18, 1997.
4. Sheila McGovern, "Hudson's Bay Board Says Yes to Zucker: U.S. Businessman Increases Bid. He'll Pay $15.25 a Share for Canada's Largest Retailer, Oldest Corporation," *Montreal Gazette;Financial Post* contributed to the report, January 27, 2006.

Chapter 16

1. Peter Thallarsen, "Willamette Accepts Rival's Dollars 6bn Bid," *Financial Times*, January 22, 2002.
2. Press Release, "Lone Star Confirms Results from Annual Shareholder's Meeting," July 20, 2001.
3. Jerry Hirsch, "California Timing of Farmer Bros. Meeting 'Bizarre' Some Dissidents Suspect December 26 Shareholders Meeting Is a Move to Defeat Efforts to Elect Independent Directors, Increase Disclosure," December 9, 2002.
4. Mark Harrington, "CA Gets SEC Support," June 27, 2006.
5. Eric Jackson, "Finalized Plan B Sent to Yahoo! Today," *Breakout Performance*, February 23, 2007, http://breakoutperformance.blogspot.com/2007/02/finalized-plan-b-sent-to-yahoo-today.html.

Chapter 17

1. Luisa Beltran, "Newcastle, Steel Chase Fox & Hound," The Deal.com, February 1, 2006.
2. Id.

3. "Shareholders Approve $110 Million Deal to Take Hutchinson Bus Maker Private,"*Kansas City Star*, October 31, 2006.
4. Amos Maki, "ServiceMaster Studies Sale—Company Says Relocation to Memphis Will Proceed," , *Commercial Appeal*, November 29, 2006.
5. Laura Santini, "A Firm Activist Lichtenstein Wins Big in South Korea,"*Wall Street Journal*, August 10, 2006, p. C1.
6. Micheline Maynard, "Kerkorian Offers $4.5 Billion for Chrysler,"*New York Times*, April 6, 2007.
7. "Seitel, Inc. Completes Merger with ValueAct Capital,"*Reuters Significant Developments*, February 14, 2007.
8. "Bulldog Drops Bid for Hector,"*AFX Asia*, June 29, 2006.
9. "Hector Communications Agrees to $147M Buyout,"*St. Paul Pioneer Press*, June 28, 2006.
10. Ian Austen, "Bid for Canada Hotel Firm Surpasses Icahn's,"*New York Times*, February 1, 2006.
11. Id.
12. John D. Stoll, Neal E. Boudette, Gregory Zuckerman, "Icahn Offers $2.75 billion for Lear,"*Wall Street Journal*, February 6, 2007.
13. Riva Atlas, "The Lone Raider Rides Again (corporate takeover specialist Carl Icahn) (includes related article on Icahn's financial advisers," *Institutional Investor,* June 1, 1997.
14. Deepak Gopinath, "Inside Icahn's Empire,"*Bloomberg Markets*, May 2006, p. 34.
15. Id., p. 38.
16. David Shabelman, "Acxiom Awaits ValueAct Offer," TheDeal.com, July 13, 2005.
17. "RC2 to buy First Years, Playing Mantis,"*Reuters News*, June 4, 2004.
18. Ryushiro Kodaira, "Did Steel Partners Really Want Myojo Foods?"*Nikkei Weekly*, November 20, 2006.
19. Id.
20. Edwina Gibbs, "U.S. Fund Fails in Hostile Bid for Japan's Sotoh," Reuters News, February 24, 2004.
21. Claire Poole, "Acxiom Rejects ValueAct Offer," TheDeal.com December 20, 2005.
22. David Shabelman, "ValueAct, Acxiom Find Calm," TheDeal.com, August 7, 2006.
23. Peter Moreira, "ValueAct and Silver Lake take Acxiom Private," *The Daily Deal,* May 17, 2007.
24. Ron Orol, "Truth or Dare," *The Deal*, April 15, 2005.

25. Geraldine Fabrikant, "Big Returns, Minus the Pleasantries," *The New York Times*, February 17, 2002.
26. Id.
27. Susan Chandler, "AutoNation Plan No Lemon for Lampert: Hedge Fund to Reap Millions in Buyback," *Chicago Tribune*, March 8, 2006.

Chapter 18

1. James Altucher, "Lessons from a Few Bruising Battles," *Financial Times*, February 21, 2006.

Chapter 19

1. Jonathan Berke, "Icahn Charts Course for XO," *The Daily Deal*, January 17, 2003.
2. Marie Beaudette, "Vulture' Funds Say They Serve a Purpose: Bankruptcies Prevented," Dow Jones, December 20, 2006.

Chapter 20

1. Ivar Simensen, "FT.com Site: Atticus's D Borse Stake Nears 9%," *Financial Times*, January 4, 2007.
2. Claire Poole, "Blunt Object," *The Deal*, August 4, 2006.
3. Jo Wrighton, "Night, Knight," *Institutional Investor*, February 8, 2007.
4. Associated Press, "Intrawest Stockholders Approve $1.8 Billion Takeover Offer," October 17, 2006.
5. David Lanchner and Guthrie McTigue, "Shareholders Who Scare the #@*% out of Companies," *Global Finance*, February 1, 1998.
6. "Guy Wyser-Pratte Active in France for Ten Years," *Le Figaro*, April 7, 2000.
7. "German IWKA Sells Packing Machines Unit for 255 Mln Euro," *German News Digest*, March 28, 2007.
8. Christiaan Hetzner, "IWKA Chief Executive Quits Amid Power Struggle," Reuters News, June 3, 2005.
9. Christiaan Hetzner, "Germany's IWKA Sees Bleak Outlook Ahead for 2006," Reuters, November 9, 2005.
10. "IWKA Sale of Packaging Seen in 6 Months—Source," Reuters News, October 19, 2006.
11. Les Echos, "Guy Wyser-Pratte Takes Summary Action against Prosodie," November 29, 2006.
12. Alex Armitage, "BT Ends Prosodie Offer after Bernard Accepts Apax Bid," *Bloomberg News*, October 31, 2006.

13. David Ibison, "Funds Call for Volvo Rethink on Cash Pile Activism," *Financial Times*, September 6, 2006.
14. "Interview: Cevian Mulls Activist Tie-ups to Pile Pressure on Scandinavian Firms," *AFX International Focus*, November 10, 2006.
15. "RPT-Update 3-Volvo to buy Ingersoll-Rand Road Unit for $1.3 bln," Reuters News, February 27, 2007.
16. "Analyst: 'Friendly' Shareholder Activists Gaining Influence," *Nikkei Report*, July 25, 2006.
17. Chris Leahy, "Japan's Just-in-Time Corporate Overhaul," *Euromoney*, May 1, 2004.
18. Edwina Gibbs, "U.S. fund fails in hostile bid for Japan's Sotoh," (Reuters News, February 24, 2004)
19. "Nissin Completes Myojo Bid, Raises Stake to 86 Pct," Reuters News, December 14, 2006.
20. Id.
21. Id.
22. "Fallen Murakami Fund to Liquidate," *Nikkei Weekly*, November 13, 2006.
23. Kenji Hall, "High Season for Raiding; Yoshiaki Murakami Is Showing How Japan's Economic Recovery and Deregulation Are Turning Stodgy Companies into Gold Mines," *BusinessWeek*, November 14, 2005.
24. "Murakami Fund Asks Court to Handle Row over Matsuzakaya Share Sale," *Kyodo News*, August 24, 2006.
25. See note 23.
26. Id.
27. Wikepedia, http://en.wikipedia.org/wiki/Chaebol.
28. William Sim, "Icahn Nominees Win Right to Vie for KT&G Board Seats," *Bloomberg*, February 14, 2006.
29. William Sim, "KT&G Says It Will Seek Proxy Votes From Shareholders," February 17, 2006.
30. Christopher Faille, Financial Correspondent, "KT&G Fight: Charges and Alliances Over Weekend," *HedgeWorld News*, March 13, 2006.
31. William Sim, "KT&G Rejects Icahn's Demand to Vie for 3 Board Seats," *Bloomberg*, February 16, 2006.
32. Id.
33. William Sim, "KT&G's Shares Rise on Bid From Icahn, Lichtenstein," *Bloomberg*, February 24, 2006.
34. William Sim and Young-Sam Cho, "Icahn Loses KT&G Ruling, Undermining Asset Sale Purchase," *Bloomberg*, March 14, 2006.

35. Christopher Faille, Financial Correspondent, "KT&G Fight: Charges and Alliances Over Weekend," *HedgeWorld News,* March 13, 2006.
36. Sangim Han, "Franklin Mutual Denies Report It Will Support KT&G (Update1)," *Bloomberg,* February 22, 2006.
37 "KT&G Will Return $2.9 Billion to Shareholders," *Korea Times,* August 10, 2006.
38. William Sin, "KT&G Accepts Icahn's Demand to Sell Stake in Retailer," April, 19, 2006.
39. Wohn Dong-hee, Sohn Hae-yong, "Icahn Turns $111 Million Profit with KT&G Stock Sale," Joins.com December 6, 2006.
40. Laura Santini, "Activism Grows in Asia, Minority Holders Gain Stature at Korea's Gravity," *Wall Street Journal,* January 8, 2007.
41. Id.
42. Id.
43 "S. Korea Gravity says Shareholders Back Management," Reuters News, December 26, 2006.
44. Jon Springer, "Metro to Buy A&P Canada," *Supermarket News,* July 25, 2005.
45. John Partridge, "Dissidents Push for Creo Coup; Canadian and U.S. Shareholders Seek to Force Ouster of Directors and CEO," *Globe and Mail,* October 13, 2004.
46. Craig Wong, "Creo Rebels Welcome Kodak Takeover," February 1, 2005.
47. Wojtek Dabrowski, "Burton Wins Proxy Fight, Takes Helm at Cenveo: Looking to Cut Costs," *Financial Post,* September 12, 2005.
48. "Molson-Coors Merger Approved by Quebec Court," CanWest News Service, February 3, 2005.
49. "Activist Shareholders," *National Post,* July 1, 2006.
50. Mark Evans, "Can Irate MTS Investors Derail Allstream Plan?: Some Say It's a Bad Deal: Analyst Surprised Merger Not Going Before Shareholders," *Financial Post,* March 20, 2004.
51. Oliver Biggadike and Cherian Thomas, "India Gain Looms on Debt Grade; AROUND THE MARKETS BUISNESS ASIA" *Bloomberg News,* February 1, 2007.

Chapter 21

1. "The Boesky Name Lives on in Post-Gordon Gekko Era," *South China Morning Post,* August 28, 2005.
2. Richard Orange, "A Year in Exile, but Still in the Game," *The Spectator,* November 11, 2006.

3. Neil Buckley, Daniel Dombey, and Holly Yeager, "Senators Press Bush over Hedge Fund Chief Russia Ban," *Financial Times,* July 6, 2006.
4. Tom Miles, "Putin says Doesn't Know Why Russia Barred Browder," Reuters News, July 16, 2006.
5. Russia Clears Mystery Winners of Yukos auctions," Reuters News, May 28, 2007.
6. "Oil & Gas Holdings, Government Approves List of Nominees to Gazprom Board," SKRIN Newswire, February 2, 2007.
7. Id.
8. Hermitage Capital Management, "Case Study: Surguteftegas," February 2006, pp. 47, 48.
9. Id., p. 48.
10. Id.
11. Id., p. 52.
12. Id., p. 49.
13. Hermitage Capital Management, "Fund Prices: History for the Period from September 30, 1997 to December 29, 2006," January, 2007.
14. "In Brief—HK Link in Theft of War Victims' Cash," *South China Morning Post,* October 15, 2000.

Chapter 22

1. Alon Brav, associate professor of finance, Duke University; Wei Jiang, associate professor of business, Columbia University; Frank Partnoy, law professor at University of San Diego; and Randall Thomas, professor of Law and Business at Vanderbilt University, "Hedge Fund Activism, Corporate Governance and Firm Performance," September 22, 2006, p. 2.
2. JeAnnine DeFoe, "Buffett Criticizes Aegis Deal," *Bloomberg News*, March 15, 2001.
3. Patrick Hosking, "The Pinball Wizard Who Moved Up to Magic on the Stock Market; The Tao of Warren Buffett," *The Times,* February 26, 2007.
4. "Hollinger International Inc.: $3.5 Million to Settle Suit in Ouster of Black," *Bloomberg News,* May 25, 2006.
5. Id.
6. Joan Crockatt, "Because He Got Under America's Skin; Conrad Black Exudes an Aristocratic Pride That Has Blinded U.S. Prosecutors to Their Prejudice, Says Joan Crockatt—And It's the 'Little Guys' Who Will Pay," *Globe and Mail,* March 17, 2007.

7. Jake Batsell, "Cutter & Buck Settles 2 Shareholder Lawsuits," *Seattle Times*, June 17, 2003.
8. Id.
9. "New Wave Buys Cutter & Buck," *Women's Wear Daily*, April 16, 2007.
10. "Alliance to Buy Private Label Credit Portfolio," Reuters News, April 27, 2005.
11. Associated Press, "InfoUSA to Buy Opinion Research," August 4, 2006.
12. *Cannell Capital LLC and Phillip Goldstein v. Opinion Research Corp., InfoUSA Inc., John F. Short, Frank J. Quirk, Dale J. Florio, John J. Gavin, Brian J. Geiger, Stephen A. Greyser, Steven F. Ladin, Robert D. LeBlanc, Seth J. Lehr, LLR Equity Partners L.P., and LLR Equity Partners Parallel L.P.*, Civil Action No. 895-N, (De. Ch. December 18, 2006), p. 6.
13. Id., p. 7.
14. Id., p. 9.
15. Id., p. 10, 11.
16. Id., p. 16.
17. Id., p. 16.
18. Id., p. 16.
19. Eli Rabinowich, "Going Out on Top: Walter & Edwin Schloss," *The Bottom Line*, April 17, 2003.
20. Id.
21. Id.

About the Author

Ronald D. Orol is a financial reporter in Washington for Dow Jones MarketWatch, where he reports on securities, hedge funds and banking regulation, as well as other topics including Capitol Hill. Prior to MarketWatch, Orol spent seven years as a senior writer for *The Deal* magazine and *The Daily Deal* newspaper, financial publications focused on the mergers-and-acquisitions economy. At *The Deal*, Orol covered the hedge fund industry, with a focus on the interplay among activist investors, corporations, and Washington regulators. Orol is a commentator on BBC World television, CNBC, CTV and National Public Radio. In addition, Orol, a well-known hedge fund journalist, regularly organizes and moderates panels on hedge funds and Washington regulators.

Prior to joining *The Deal*, Orol covered activist hedge funds and mergers and acquisitions for the Washington Dow Jones Newswires office. He also has followed the hedge fund industry and the financial issues for Forbes.com in New York and as a Washington correspondent for the *Providence Journal* and other newspapers. In 2000, Orol interned with acclaimed financial journalist Jeffrey Birnbaum at *Fortune* magazine in Washington.

Before moving to Washington, Orol spent three years as a business and technology reporter covering emerging markets for the *Prague Post* in the Czech Republic. While in Prague, Orol also reported on Eastern European privatization and the political transformation of the region for The Southam News Wire Services, the *Montreal Gazette*, the *Toronto Star*, and the *Ottawa Citizen*.

There he developed an expertise in post-Soviet eastern European financial systems that facilitated his knowledge of how insurgent-style investors are taking their skills to previously untapped global locations. Over the years, Orol has interviewed hundreds of hedge fund managers in dozens of countries. Orol has taken advantage of his global network of hedge fund contacts by traveling to dozens of cities in the United States and around the world, including Moscow, London, Toronto, and other locals, to meet with managers on the front lines of activist investing. He's interviewed a long list of high-profile hedge fund managers including Carl Icahn, Ralph Whitworth, and Guy Wyser-Pratte.

Orol holds a master's degree in business and economics journalism from Boston University, where he graduated with distinction. He received his undergraduate degree in journalism with honors from Carleton University in Ottawa. He is married and lives in Washington, D.C.

Index

13F rule, 82, 326

A

ABN Amro Holding NV, 334
Ackman, William, 163–165, 171–172, 215, 325
  Pershing Square Capital, 163, 165, 325
Acxiom Corporation, 240
Adams, Guy, 128, 222
Ajdler, Arnaud, Crescendo Partners, 51, 148, 290
Altman, Jeffrey, 70
Amazon.com Inc., 221
Ambartsumov, Sergei, xiv
American Federation of Labor-Congress of Industrial Organizations (AFL-CIO), 205
American Federation of State, County, and Municipal Employees (AFSCME), 149, 215–216
American Industrial Partners, 232
American International Group, 10, 149
American Real Estate Partners LP, 238
American Stock Exchange, 166
Anadarko Petroleum Corporation, 124
Antoszyk, Peter, Proskauer Rose LLP, 266, 268
Apax Partners, Inc., 275–276
Applebee's International Inc., 337
Ashton, Zeke, founder Centaur Capital Partners, 322, 325–327
Atticus Capital LLC, 272
AutoNation Inc., 245
AutoZone Inc., 245
Azerbaijan, xxviii, 338

B

Barris, Jay, Cramer, Levin Naftalis & Frankel LLP, 244
Bartoli, Christopher, partner at Baker & McKenzie in Chicago, 111–112
Bailey, Clarke, Glenayre Technologies Inc.'s CEO, 104, 115
Bally Total Fitness Holding Corporation, 69–70, 72
Bankruptcy, xxiii, 28–29, 70, 127, 212, 244, 263–264, 266–268, 304, 316
Batchelder, David, Relational Investors, co-founder, 19, 109, 202
BAX Global, 65, 66
Bear, Stearns & Company, 69

Bebchuk, Lucian, professor Harvard Law School, xiii, 105–107, 116
Beijing Foreign Affairs College, 300
Berkshire Hathaway, 322
Bernard, Alain, 275–276
BKF Capital Group Inc., 70–72, 253
  CEO John Levin, 70–72, 254
Black, Bernard, 62,176
Blair Corporation, 34, 72, 325–326
Bloomberg Television, 81, 287
Boesky, Aaron, 299–301
  Marco Polo Pure China Fund, 299–300
Boesky, Ivan, 300
Bornstein, Ben, 131–132
  Prospero Capital Management LLC, 132
Brav, Alon, xxviii, xix, 62
Breeden, Richard, xv, 135, 207, 216, 337
  Breeden Capital Management LLC, 207, 216, 337
  SEC chairman (1989–1993), 207
Brinks Company, 65, 66
Broker non-votes (broker discretionary votes), 144–147, 153
Browne, Christopher H., 322
  Tweedy, Browne Company LLC, 322
Buffet, Warren, 28, 257, 322
Bulldog Investors, *see* Opportunity Partners
Burnham and Company, 16, 31
Burton Jr., Robert G., 294–296
  Burton Capital Management LLC, 294
Bush, George, W., President, 140, 273, 303
Business Roundtable, 167–168
Buyout shops, 272–273, 275, 281, 294

C

California Public Employees' Retirement System (CalPERS), 19, 139, 150, 166, 167, 184, 186, 195, 199, 201–203, 205–207, 210, 215–216, 280, 334
Callon, Scott, Ichigo Asset Management Ltd., 177, 178
Canada, xxi, xxix, 49, 209–210, 212, 213, 258, 271, 277, 290, 295–296
Canadian Coalition for Good Governance, 291
Cannell, J. Carlo, 70, 328–330
  Cannell Capital LLC, 70, 328
Caparro, James, the CEO of Glenayre's Entertainment Distribution Company LLC 104, 115
Caremark RX Inc., 78–79
Carreker Corporation, 60, 61, 72
  Carreker, John, CEO, 38, 60, 61, 72, 115, 116
CBS Corporation, 5
Cerberus Capital Management LP, 10, 235
Cevian Capital LP, 276–279, 295, 331
Chaebol, 283–284, 290
Change-of-control, 104, 107, 111, 113
Chapman, Robert, Chapman Capital, xiii, xvii, xxi–xiv 21, 38, 60, 94, 130, 228, 337
  Social lever, xxii, 39, 51, 54
Chavern, David, U.S. Chamber of Commerce, 22, 91, 105, 114, 160
CheckFree Corporation, 60
Check Solutions Company, 60
Children's Investment Fund, 272, 334–335
China, xxviii, 207, 255, 297, 299–302, 307, 318, 338
Chrysler Corporation, 10, 110, 111, 137, 337
Cinar Corporation, xxi–xxii, 40, 94
  Animated children's television series *Arthur* and *Caillou*, xxii
  CEO, Després Robert, xxi
  Columbia Business School, xiii, 256
CNBC, 81
Cnet Networks Inc., 5
Cocozza, Mark, 125
Columbia Business School, 256–257
Commodities, xxiii
Compaq Computer Corporation, 141
Compensation Discussion and Analysis, 112, 147
Computer Horizons Corporation, 50, 51, 91
Conglomerates, 93, 283
Corporate Raiders, xxvi, 3, 5, 12–22, 28, 37, 88, 136, 237
Council of Institutional Investors, 144, 199
Cox, Christopher, SEC Chairman, 149, 227
Crescendo Partners II LP, 36, 50, 51, 91, 101, 128, 129, 148, 290, 293–295
Cronin, Barry, 250–256, 259–260
CSX Corporation, 5
CtW Investment Group, 145, 198–199
Currencies, xxiii
Cutter & Buck, 323–324
CVS Corporation, 78–79
Czech Republic, xiii, 311

D

Delaware Chancery Court, 76, 78–79, 329, 330
Delaware Supreme Court, 76–78, 80
Denmark, xxix, 276

Derivatives, xxiii, 176
Deutsche Börse, 272, 338
Disney, Roy, 139, 143, 146, 182, 204, 206
Distressed debt, 235, 244, 265–267
Distressed investing, xxvi, 265, 268, 270
Dividend, 9, 22, 41, 42, 79, 90–93, 126, 160, 175, 239, 240, 278–282, 284, 278, 293
Dodd, David, 257
Dominion Textile Inc., 211–212
Donaldson, William, 148–149
Dow Jones Newswires, xi
Drexel Burnham Lambert, 16, 31

E

Eastern Europe, 307–314, 318
Eisner, Michael, Walt Disney Company CEO, 139, 182, 204
Elson, Charles, University of Delaware, 20, 97, 114, 160, 171
Emerging markets, xxiii, 297, 301–302, 307–311, 317–318
Endean, John, American Business Conference, 145
Enron, x, 5, 10–11, 77, 93, 96, 112, 180, 265, 269, 297
"E-proxy" proposal, 142–144, 226, 336
Express Scripts Inc., 78–79

F

Farmer Brothers Company, 89, 90, 93, 220, 222–223
Fatheree, James, 282
Faulk, Anne, Swingvote LLC, 227
Ferlauto, Richard, AFSCME, 149, 167–168, 183–184
Fidelity Investments, 30, 40, 158, 178, 188
Financial Services Authority of the U.K., 335
Finland, xxix, 276
First Years Inc., 32–34, 40, 179, 239
Flaschen, Evan D., Bracewell & Giuliani LLP, 266–268
Förberg, Lars, Cevian Capital LP, 276–279, 295, 297, 331, 338
Fortress Investment Group, 273
Foyil, Dorian, president of Foyil Asset Management, 254, 310–318
France, xxix, 272–274, 296
Frank, Barney, (D-Mass) House Financial Services Committee Chairman, 108, 273
Franklin Mutual Advisers LLC, 169, 223, 286
Franklin Templeton Investments, 311
Frist, Bill, (R-Tenn) former Senate Majority Leader, 303
Funds of funds, 254, 256, 260–261
Funds of hedge funds, 6, 131, 235, 311, 331

G

Gabelli, Mario, 66, 68, 70, 79–81, 83, 257
  Appraisal action, 79–81
  Carter-Wallace Inc., 79–81
  Gabelli Asset Management, 66, 79, 257
Gardell, Christer, 276–278, 331
Garland, Michael, 199
Gazprom, 303–305, 310
GDX Automotive, 66
GenCorp, 66–69, 72
Gendell, Jeffrey, Tontine Management LLC, 123, 132, 133
General Motors Corporation, 10, 137, 170, 215, 235
Generally Accepted Accounting Principles (GAAP), 221, 305
Germany, xxix, 272–273, 296, 316, 338
Gibson, Brian, 210–213
Globe and Mail, xxi
Gold, Stanley, Shamrock Holdings, 90, 139, 143, 182
Golden Gate Capital, 128
Golden parachute, 107–108
Goldman Sachs & Company, 59, 273
Goldstein, Lawrence, 31, 34, 40, 179, 196, 236
Goldstein, Phillip, Opportunity Partners, Bulldog, xiii, 27, 65, 81–82, 141–142, 235, 252, 256, 320, 337
Governance for Owners' European Focus Fund, 205, 216
Graham, Benjamin, 257, 322
Gravity Company Ltd., 288
  Gravity Committee for Fair Treatment of Minority Shareholders, 288
  Ryu, Il Young, Gravity's CEO, 288–289
Great Atlantic & Pacific Tea Company, 292
  A&P Ontario, 292
Greenmail, xxvi, 13, 21–22, 329
Greenwich, Connecticut, 29, 123, 161, 294

H

Haft, Herbert, 83
Harris Associates LP, 58

Harvard Law School, xiii, 105, 116
Headrick, Roger, director of CVS/Caremark Corporation, 199
Hector Communications Inc., 237, 256
Hedge Fund Research Inc., 3, 4, 6, 320
Hedge Fund Solutions, 4, 11
Heilligendamm, Germany, G8 summit, 273
Hendin, Ross, Hendin Consultants, 303–304, 307, 317
Hermes Pension Management Ltd., 205, 206–207, 209, 214, 216, 275
Hermitage Capital Management Ltd., 302–308, 310, 318
  Browder, William, founder, 303
Hewlett Packard Company, 141, 150
High-net-worth investors, 7, 23, 235
H. J. Heinz & Co., 5, 164–165, 167–168, 215
Hollinger International Inc., 323
Holocaust, 316
Holtzman, Seymour, 75–78, 83
Home Depot, The, xiii, 17, 61, 109–110, 113, 116, 164, 171, 183–184, 188, 202–204, 215, 220, 229, 337
Howard, Steven, 39, 40
Hu, Henry, University of Texas Law School professor, 62,176
Hubco Inc., 122
Hyman, James, xiv, CEO Cornell Companies, 95, 98, 115

I

Icahn, Carl, 14–16, 28, 48, 56, 124, 214, 143, 166–167, 169–172, 215, 224, 235, 238, 245, 266–267, 277, 284–288, 321
InBev SA, xi
Industrial Bank of Korea, 286
InfoUSA Inc., 239, 329, 330
Inmet Mining Corporation, 212
Institut de Participations de l'Ouest, 273
Institutional Shareholder Services (ISS), 21, 27, 35, 44, 107, 123, 137, 165, 168, 171, 177, 184, 186, 192–198, 226
Intrawest Corporation, 273
Investment bankers, xii, 274
Investor relations, xii, 57, 98, 221, 279, 317, 334, 336
IWKA AG, 275
  Wiedemann, Gerhard, 275
  Fahr, Hans, 275
  Hein, Wolfgang- Dietrich, 275

J

Jackson, Eric, 224–226, 229,
Jana Partners LLC, 5, 15, 21, 124, 166, 169, 187
Japan, xi, xxviii, 206, 239–240, 272–273, 280–283, 286, 289, 290, 295, 297
Japan Liberty Square Asset Management LP, 280
Japanese Ministry of International Trade and Industry, 282
Jarvis, Geoffrey C., Grant & Eisenhofer PA, 79–81
Jin Jiang International hotels, 299–300
Jones, Charles, GEAC Computer Corporation's CEO, 101, 161
J. P. Morgan Chase & Company, 69
Junk bonds, 16, 31
Just vote no, 138, 143–146,197, 199, 215, 227, 229

K

Kahn, Alan, 82–83, 258
Kaplan, Steven, professor, University of Chicago, 108
Keiretsu, 280, 283
Kennesaw, Georgia, 106
Kentucky Fried Chicken, 299
Kerkorian, Kirk, 137, 170–172, 215, 235, 245
Kerr-McGee Corporation, 124
King Pharmaceuticals Inc., 176, 178
Klein, April, Stern School of Business at New York University, xxvii, xix, 34, 42, 55–56, 127–28, 159, 166
Kleiner, Vadim, Hermitage Asset Management, 307
Kmart, 137, 244, 245, 265, 268
Knight Ridder Inc., 58–59
Knight Vinke Asset Management LLC, 178, 205, 216, 273
Kohlberg Kravis Roberts & Company (KKR), 184, 236, 294
Korea Securities Depository, 286
Kornstein, Don, 69
KPMG LP, 118
KT&G Corp., 14, 284–288, 295, 338
  KT&G Growth Committee, 286
Kyoon, Kwak Young, KT&G CEO, 284–286

L

Lamont, Ned, Connecticut Democrat Senatorial candidate, 224–225
Lampert, Randy, 9, 20–22, 64, 93, 126–127, 237

Lapides, Paul, Kennesaw State University's Corporate Governance Center, 106
Lashley, Richard, PL Capital LLC, 117–120, 133
PL Capital LLC, 117–121
Lear Corporation, 238
Lehman Brothers Holdings Inc., 10, 23
Levitt, Arthur, 138, 140
Liberation Investment Group, 15, 50, 60, 85
Lichtenstein, Warren, 14, 29–30, 66, 70, 71, 100, 232, 273, 296, 318, 338
Steel Partners II LP, xi, 29, 65–68, 70,100, 231, 232, 233, 240
Steel Partners' Japan Strategic Fund LP, 280
Lieberman, Joe, Senator, (D-Conn), 225
Ligand Pharmaceuticals, 36
LinkedIn, 225
Lipton, Martin, Wachtell, Lipton, Rosen & Katz, 97
Liquid Audio, 75–77, 78, 220
Loblaw Companies Inc., 292
Loeb, Daniel, Third Point LLC, 36, 47, 48, 53, 54,126
London, xiv, 272, 296, 334, 338
London School of Economics, 303
London Stock Exchange, 272, 338
Lone Star Steakhouse & Saloon, 128, 222
Longs Drug Stores Corporation, 5
Lorber, David, 66
Louisiana Municipal Police Employees' Retirement System, 78
Lukoil, 305
Lutin, Gary, 42, 72, 90, 219–224, 228

M

MacDonald, J. Cameron, Goodwood Inc., 291, 293–294
Mackenzie, William, 291
Maeil Business Newspaper, 286–287
Majority vote, 193–194, 196–199
Management Discussion and Analysis, 112
Maple Leaf Foods Inc., 213
Massachusetts Secretary of the Commonwealth William Galvin, 82
Matsuzakaya Hanshin Electric Railway Company, 282
Maxwell Shoe Company, 124, 125
McClatchy Company, 59
McDonald's, 5, 128, 163–165, 171, 215, 337
McGurn, Pat, 17–18, 138, 149, 171, 184, 226
Mergers-and-acquisitions (M&A), x
Merkel, Angela, German Chancellor, 273
Metro Inc., Montreal, 292
Microsoft Corparation, xi
Milken, Michael, 16, 31
Minow, Nell, editor of The Corporate Library, 11, 115, 173, 187, 192, 199
Mitarotonda, James, Barington Capital Group LP, 75–78, 83
MM Companies, 76
MMI Investments LP, 65, 66
Monarch Community Bancorp Inc., 123
Monks, Robert, 136
Montgomery Ward, 13, 338
Moon Capital Management LP., 288
Morgan Joseph & Co., 8, 9, 11, 20–21, 27, 34, 39, 90, 91, 95, 126, 127, 237
Morgan Stanley's Capital International Inc. (MSCI) Emerging Markets index, 307
Moscow, xiv, 303, 306
Motorola Inc., 170, 172, 226, 336–337
MSC Software Corporation, 240–241
Municipal bonds, xxiii, 244,
Murakami Fund, 281
Murakami, Yoshiaki, 281–282
Mutual funds, xxiii, 73, 141, 142, 151, 157–159, 168–169, 174, 178, 201, 212, 226, 248, 264, 320, 322
Mylan Laboratories Inc., 176, 178
Myojo Foods Company, 239, 281

N

Nabi Biopharmaceuticals, 47, 48
Nardelli, Robert, xiii, 17, 109–111, 113, 164, 172, 183, 204, 215, 229
NASDAQ, 10, 96, 112, 166
Natbony, William, Katten Muchin Rosenman LLP, xxv, 118–119, 243, 246, 290, 301, 309–310
New York City Employees' Retirement System, (NYCERS), 184, 204, 216
Musuraca, Mike, 204–205
New York Society of Securities Analysts, 220
New York Stock Exchange, 96, 112, 144, 156
Nichter, Mitchell E., 236, 239, 241, 243–244, 260
Nissan Motor Company, 170–171
Nissin Food Products Company, 239, 281
Norway, xxix, 276

O

OAO Gazprom, *see* Gazprom
OAO Lukoil, *see* Lukoil

Olson, John, partner at Gibson Dunn & Crutcher LLP in Washington, 105, 107, 111
O'Malley, Terrance, partner at Fried Frank Harris Shriver & Jacobson LLP, 88, 106
Online forums, xxvi, 220, 224, 227
Ontario Municipal Employees Retirement System, 203
Ontario Teachers' Pension Plan (OTPP) 209–216, 334
Opportunity Partners, 27, 36, 38, 49, 51, 57, 58, 64, 65, 70, 71, 82, 87, 141, 237, 235, 239
Osaka Securities Exchange, 282
OSI Restaurant Partners, 68
  Owner of Outback Steakhouse, 68, 128
Owl Creek Asset Management, 70
Oxley, Michael, (R-Ohio), 10

P

Pabrai, Mohnish, 319–320, 330
  Pabrai Investment Funds, 319
  Mumbai, India, 320
  Trans-Tech Inc., 320
  DigitalDistrupters.com, 320
Pardus Capital Management LP, 69–70
Park, Damien, Hedge Fund Solutions, president, 4, 11
Pasquale, David, The Ruth Group in New York, 57, 98–101
Pathmark Stores Inc., 292–293
Paulson, Henry, U.S. Treasury Secretary, 272
Payless ShoeSource Inc., 124–126
Pearlman, Emanuel, Liberation Investment Group, 15, 19, 31, 43, 45, 46, 50, 69, 70, 92
Pegasystems, 60
Peltz, Nelson, 137, 172, 215, 224
People's Republic of China, 299
Perquisites, 104, 107
Pickens Jr., Thomas Boone, 14–17, 19, 94
Pirate Capital LLC, 66–69, 93, 98, 32
Poison pen letters, xii
Poison pill, 9, 16, 18, 27, 62, 193–196, 200, 209, 215, 245
Polaroid, 33
Prague Post, The, xxi
Prescott Capital Management LLC, 60–61
  President Jeffrey Watkins, 60–61
Private Capital Management, CEO, Bruce Sherman, 58–59
Private equity, 5, 8, 20, 24, 29, 30, 94, 99, 178, 207, 211, 232, 233, 235–237, 241–243, 245, 246
Pro-forma financial statements, 221
Prosodie SA, 275
Puccetti, Peter, 256, 291–295
  CEO, Goodwood Inc., 256, 291–295
Putin, Vladimir, Russian President, 303

Q

Quants, xxiii
Quinn, Tom, vice president, FactSet Research Systems, New York, 100

R

Railroad freight car leasing industry, 31, 96
Ramius Capital Group, 288–290, 297
Rancho Cordova, California, 66
Real estate, 21, 41, 66, 67, 93, 102, 127, 132, 238, 281, 284, 287, 322
Red Zone LLC, 44
Reliant Energy Inc., 37, 150
Renault SA, 170–171
Reuters Group plc, 334
Riley, Bryant R., B. Riley & Company, 60, 61
Romick, Steven, partner, First Pacific Advisors, 324, 326–327
Rosenfeld, Eric, 101, 128–129, 294–295
Rosenstein, Barry, Jana Partners LLC, 15, 21, 124, 166, 169, 187, 272
Ross, Wilber, 206
Royal Philips Electronics, N.V, 83
Royce, Chuck, 257
Russia, xxviii, 242–243, 254, 297, 301–308, 310–314, 338

S

Safeway Inc., 184–186, 188
Sandell Asset Management Corporation, 66–68
Santa Monica Partners LP, 31–33, 40, 96, 179, 196, 239
Sarbanes-Oxley Act (SOX), 10, 12
Sarbanes, Paul, (D-MD), 10
Schedule 13D, xii, 54, 85, 88, 105, 120, 123, 125, 174, 214, 221,
Schloss, Walter, 257, 331
Schwarz, Mark, president, Newcastle Capital Group LLC, xiii, 16, 231–234, 237, 243, 245,
Schwarzman, Stephen, Blackstone Group LP's chief executive, xiv
Schwarzenegger, Arnold, California governor, 186
Securities and Exchange Commission, xi, xxii, 37, 54, 81, 89, 135, 168, 174, 207, 221

Seidman, Lawrence, Seidman & Associates LLC, xiii, 121
Selby, Tim, Alston & Bird LLP, 254, 301–302, 308–309
Semel, Terry, 225–226
Shapiro, Mark, 44
Shareholder access, 149–153, 168–169
Short-slate, 135–139, 148, 150, 151, 153
Siberia, xxviii, 304–307
Sidman, Marshall, 32–33, 40
Smith, Dave, CEO of Coast Asset Management, 252
Sobeys Inc., 292
South Korea, 284–290, 296
Southeastern Asset Management Inc., 58
Sovereign Bank, 137, 202–203
Sovereign Global Investment fund, Dubai, 288
SPARX Value Creation Fund, 206, 280
Stamps.com, 131
Standard and Poor's (S&P), x, 3, 27, 90, 145, 160, 166, 193, 203
Star Gas Partners LP, 53
  CEO, Sevin, Irik, 53
State of Wisconsin Investment Board, The, 210
Steel Partners, *see* Lichtenstein, Warren
Steel Partners' Japan Strategic Fund LP, *see* Lichtenstein, Warren
Steve Madden, 124
Stock buyback, 29, 42, 53, 90–92, 105, 126, 160–161, 164, 169, 205, 239–240, 266, 278–280, 321
Stride Rite Corporation, 124–126
Stubbe, Sebastian, Landmark Investors LLC, 64, 246–247, 249–256, 258–259, 261
Sun-Times Media Group Inc., 5
Surgutneftegas, Surgut, Tyumen, Russia, 305–308, 318
Sweden, xxix, 272–273, 290, 295, 298, 338
Sword of Damocles, 271
Synergy Financial Group Inc., 120, 121
  CEO John Fiore, 121
  Chief operating officer Kevin McCloskey, 121
  Chief financial officer Rich Abrahamian, 121

T

T2 Partners LLC, 169, 322, 326
Taiyo Fund, 206
Taiyo Pacific Partners LP, 206, 280
Tannenbaum, Michael, Tannenbaum Helpern Syracuse & Hirschtritt LLP, 301, 309
TeliaSonera, 278
Templeton Global Advisors Ltd., 178
Third Point LLC, 36, 47, 94, 126
Thornton, John, 12
Thrifts, xxvi, 117–124
Tilson, Whitney, 169, 323–324, 326
Time Warner Inc., 5, 18, 169–171, 179, 215, 321, 334
Tokyo Broadcasting Systems Inc., 282
Tokyo Kohtetsu Company, 177–178
Topps Company Inc., 36
Toronto, xiv, 290–291, 293, 295
Toronto Dominion Bank, xxii, 94

U

Ubben, Jeffrey, ValueAct, 14, 30, 158, 243
Ukraine, xxviii, 310, 311–318, 338
UnitedHealth Group, 150
United Shareholders Association, 17, 136, 139
U.S. Chamber of Commerce, 91, 105, 114, 160
U.S. Department of Justice, 68
U.S.-Japan Business Council Inc., 282
U.S. Treasury Department, xi
U.S. New Mountain Vantage, 207

V

Value investors, 26–28, 31, 33, 124, 127, 158, 222, 246
ValueAct Capital Partners LP, 14, 30, 158, 174, 235, 239, 240, 241, 243
Van Biema, Michael, Van Biema Value Partners, 256–258
Venture capital, 129, 273
Verizon Communications Inc., 7
Volvo, 276, 278–279
Volyn Cement Zdolbunivske, 314–316
Vulture investors (also, vulture funds), xxiv, 265–265, 268

W

Wagoner, Rick, General Motors Inc., 170–171
Wal-Mart Stores Inc., 76, 292
Walter Industries Inc., 68
Warnaco Group Inc., 126–127
Warwick Valley Telephone Company, 27, 38
Washington D.C., 10, 12, 18, 22, 44–45, 83, 105, 111, 136, 138, 171, 252, 282
Waste Management, 137, 203
Weiner, Perrie, partner, DLA Piper Rudnick Gray Cary US LLP, 59, 119

Weingarten, Marc, partner, Schulte Roth & Zabel LLP, 166
Wendy's International Inc., 5, 18, 128
Wharton School of Business, University of Pennsylvania, 311
Whitman, Martin, Third Avenue Management LLC, 265, 269, 331
Whitworth, Ralph, 17–29, 35, 109–110, 116, 136–139, 164, 183, 184, 202, 216
  Relational Investors, xiii, 17–18, 35, 109, 164, 183, 202, 204, 210, 216, 336
  United Shareholders Association (USA), 136, 139
Whole Foods Market Inc., 5
Wilcox, John, 176–177
Wirz, Matt, Debtwire, 265–266, 270
Wolf packs (or activist packs), xxv, 59, 268
Woori Financial Group, 285
Written consent solicitations, 43–51, 150, 195
Wyser-Pratte, Guy, xiii, xiv, 271–276, 279, 296–297

X

XO Communications, 239, 267

Y

Yahoo! Inc., 221, 224, 225
Yardville National Bancorp, 123
York, Jerome B., 137, 170–171
Young, Christopher L., ISS, 21, 27, 165, 175
YouTube, xxvi, 224–229, 336
Yushiro Chemical Industries Company Ltd., 240, 281

Z

Zaibatsu, 280
Zale Corporation, xv
Zucker, Jerry, 212
Zur, Emanuel, doctoral student, Stern School of Business, NYU, 55–56

Printed in the United States
By Bookmasters